GOOD CITIES, BETTER LIVES
How Europe Discovered the Lost Art of Urbanism

This book has one central theme: how, in the United Kingdom, can we create better cities and towns in which to live and work and play? And, in doing so, can we provide lessons for other countries facing similar dilemmas?

Urban Britain is not functioning as it should. Social inequalities and regional disparities show little sign of going away. Efforts to generate growth, and spread it to the poorer areas of cities, have failed dismally. Much new urban development and redevelopment is not up to standard. Yet there are cities in mainland Europe, which have set new standards of high-quality sustainable urban development. This book looks at the best-practice examples – in Scandinavia, Germany, the Netherlands, and France – and suggests ways in which the UK and elsewhere could do the same.

The book is in three parts. Part 1 analyses the main issues for urban planning and development – in economic development and job generation, sustainable development, housing policy, transport and development mechanisms – and probes how practice in the UK has fallen short.

Part Two embarks on a tour of best-practice cities in Europe, starting in Germany with the country's boosting of its cities' economies, moving to the spectacularly successful new housing developments in the Netherlands, from there to France's integrated city transport, and then to Scandinavia's pursuit of sustainability for its cities, and finally back to Germany, to Freiburg – the city that 'did it all'.

Part Three sums up the lessons of Part Two and sets out the key steps we need to make to launch a new wave of urban development and regeneration on a radically different basis.

Sir Peter Hall is Bartlett Professor of Planning and Regeneration at University College London, and President of both the Town and Country Planning Association and Regional Studies Association. He has produced over fifty books in his career and is internationally renowned for his studies on all aspects of cities and regions.

Planning, History and Environment Series

Selection of published titles

GOOD CITIES, BETTER LIVES
How Europe Discovered the Lost Art of Urbanism

Peter Hall

with contributions from Nicholas Falk

Routledge
Taylor & Francis Group
LONDON AND NEW YORK

First published in paperback 2014

First Published 2013
by Routledge
2 Park Square, Milton Park, Abingdon, Oxon OX14 4RN

and by Routledge
711 Third Avenue, New York, NY 10017

Routledge is an imprint of the Taylor & Francis Group, an informa business

British Library Cataloguing in Publication Data
A catalogue record for this book is available from the British Library

Library of Congress Cataloging-in-Publication Data
Routledge international handbook of food studies / edited by Ken Albala. – 1st ed.
    p. cm.
  Includes bibliographical references and index.
  1. Nutritional anthropology. 2. Food–Research. I. Albala, Ken, 1964-
GN407.R88 2012
394.1'2–dc23
        2012003797

ISBN: 978-0-415-78264-7 (hbk)
ISBN: 978-1-138-01949-2 (pbk)
ISBN: 978-0-203-81922-7 (ebk)

Typeset in Bembo by
Taylor & Francis Books

Printed and bound in the United States of America by Publishers Graphics, LLC on sustainably sourced paper.

Contents

A Note on the Illustrations

We are grateful to all those who have given permission to reproduce photographs and diagrams. With the exception of the illustrations on the Part title pages and opening each chapter (which are listed below), sources are included in the captions; those photographs without attribution were taken by Peter Hall.

Introduction: 'The New Jerusalem' from the fourteenth-century Tapestry of the Apocalypse, Chateau d'Agners. (*Photo*: CC Kimon Berlin)

Part One: Brick Lane, Sunday, 17 February 2013. (*Photo*: Yasser Elsheshtawy)

Chapter 1: Old two-pan scales. (*Photo*: CC Nikodem Nijaki)

Chapter 2: Beddington Zero Energy Developmaent (BedZED) eco-village, Hacker-bridge, London. (*Photo*: CC Tom Chance)

Chapter 3: Blackpool tram. (*Photo*: CC Mark S. Jobling)

Chapter 4: Wind turbine ignored by cows in Wesselburener Deichhausen Schleswig-Holstein Wesselburener. (*Photo*: CC Dirk Ingo Franke)

Chapter 5: Repairing a tractor, 1966. By courtesy of the Bundesarchiv (Bild 183-E0208-0005-001/CC-BY-SA).

Part Two: Plan of the Model Town from James S. Buckingham, *National Evils and Practical Remedies with a Plan of a Model Town*, 1849.

Chapter 6: 1920s motorized charabanc from Harold F.B. Wheeler, *The Book of Knowledge*, 1924.

Chapter 7: The Millionth VW 'Beetle'.

Chapter 8: Geestmolen (The Spirit Mill, built in 1565), Alkmaar. (*Photo*: CC Guido Kieven)

Chapter 9: Old postcard showing a tram on line H tramway, Porte de Tournai, Lille before 1906. (Scanned by Claude Villetaneuse)

Chapter 10: Copenhagen city bikes. (*Photo*: CC Ehedaya)

Chapter 11: Meister N.J.W. Freiburg im Breisgau, *c.* 1580. (*Photo*: CC Andreas Praefcke)

Part Three: Old main entrance to the main building of the Karlsruhe Polytechnicum, (now the Technical University), designed by Heinrich Hübsch and built 1833–1836.

Chapter 12: A medieval class and teacher.

PREFACE

This book came out of a conversation with Nicholas Falk, founder Director of URBED, one of many over four decades. For some years, we had been leading study tours for British planners – he for URBED, I for the Town and Country Planning Association – to the places in mainland Europe that had become celebrated as examples of 'best practice': these were the best places in Europe to live in and to work in. They had created good jobs, built superb housing in fine natural settings, and generated rich urban lives. But not only that: simultaneously, these cities had become models of sustainable urban life, minimizing energy needs, recycling wastes, and reducing emissions. They seemed, in their different ways and to varying degrees, to do best at almost everything. Why not, then, share our experience of them with a wider professional and student audience?

That was the concept. We would start with an introductory section, spelling out what we saw as the main things that have gone wrong in British cities and with British urban life. Then, in the central section of the book, we would lead readers on a twenty-first-century Grand Tour, from Germany through the Netherlands and France to Scandinavia, and back to Germany detailing the cities we had come to admire. Finally, we would seek to distil the lessons they had to offer and would seek to apply them in a series of concrete positive recommendations to policy-makers and professionals – not only in the United Kingdom, but in countries across the world where people were seeking the secrets of urban success.

I hope that this, the resulting book, has succeeded in this aim – though not quite in the way we intended. For reasons that neither of us could have foreseen, I perforce took on the job of developing the text through successive drafts, drawing on material that we had brought to the work, and aided by conversations between the two of us about the conclusions at the end of each chapter. I also benefited hugely from extended conversations with professional and academic friends, who are acknowledged separately. Thus the resulting book, 'authored by Peter with contributions from Nicholas', reflects the original joint concept.

Immeasurable thanks are owing to the many people and institutions who offered suggestions, provided material and made critical comments on successive drafts. Foremost among these are the TCPA staff who organized the study tours to Scandinavia, Freiburg and the Netherlands: Chloe Theobald, Alex House, Stephanie Dickins, Fiona Mannion, and Diane Smith – and also to Graeme Bell for leading the Netherlands trip. Thanks are also due to the many collaborators, too many to mention individually, for their role in presenting their developments and leading the study tours through them, in fair weather and (sometimes) foul. But one individual must be named: Wulf Daseking, the legendary city planner of Freiburg for 27 years until his retirement in 2012, now Professor in the University of Freiburg and Visiting Professor at UCL. This book is dedicated to him in recognition of his achievement.

Second, I owe a debt to UCL colleagues on the EU projects, SINTROPHER and SYNAPTIC: Colin Osborne, Charles King, Iqbal Hamiduddin, Robin Hickman, Peter Jones, Veronique Shipley and Lenore Scott – and to our many European project partners – in Blackpool, Valenciennes, West Flanders, Nijmegen and Kassel.

In three places, as will be only too evident from the extended citations, the account relies very much on primary research by others, notably my UCL colleague Claire Colomb, on Berlin and Lille/Roubaix, and Anne Power and Jörg Plöger for their book *Phoenix Cities*, on Leipzig.

For excellent constructive criticism on parts of the manuscript, thanks are due to Frieder Hartung on Germany; Karl (Friedhelm) Fischer on Kassel; Klaus Kunzmann on Dortmund; Han Lorzing who advised the URBED group's visit to the Netherlands, Neil Corteen and Rainer Nagel on Berlin, and Ulrich Pfeiffer for our earlier work together on Leipzig.

Small parts of Chapters 8 and 10 had an earlier incarnation in articles for *Town and Country Planning*. Since I think my verdicts there were right, they seemed worth recycling.

Basak Demires Ozkul used extraordinary computer-cartographic skills to produce the scaled maps and figure ground plans. Thanks to the Balzan Foundation and UCL's Bartlett School of Planning for their financial support in this enterprise.

Richard Burton expertly typeset the manuscript and elegantly inserted the illustrations. Combining this role with that of a postman working just out of earshot of the busy A34, one interchange away from the business park where Routledge publish to the world, his is a remarkable tale of flexible specialization in today's knowledge economy.

And as ever over our long thirty-year association, Ann Rudkin has been an editor beyond compare. She has gone far beyond all normal requirements for the job, in researching sources and checking often obscure references. In this, its final manifestation, I feel that the book is almost as much hers as mine.

Finally, thanks to Magda, without whom – as ever – nothing would have been possible.

Peter Hall
London
June 2013

Building the New Jerusalem:
Five Challenges for Cities

Rouse up O Young Men of the New Age! Set your foreheads against the
ignorant Hirelings! Sculptors! Architects! Suffer not the fashionable Fools to
depress your powers … if we are but just & true to our own Imaginations…

I will not cease from Mental Fight,
Nor shall my Sword sleep in my hand:
Till we have built Jerusalem,
In England's green & pleasant Land.

William Blake (1804) *Preface to Milton: A Poem*

Blake's *Jerusalem* has become an alternative national anthem. Its origin was,
for Blake, characteristically strange: a myth that Jesus Christ had once visited
Glastonbury (a place for visions, however induced, long before the first festival)
and that we should seek to create an earthly paradise in his memory. And its
musical manifestation was equally incongruous: first sung to Sir Hubert Parry's
score in 1916 as a desperate device to inspire resilience among war-weary soldiers
in the trenches, and shorn of its mystical religious foundations, it has provided
an inspiration for millions to create a better world.

Significantly, it was first sung at a Labour conference in 1945, just as the party
swept to power on Clement Attlee's promise to build a new Jerusalem, there to
create not only the National Health Service but – an equally enduring monument

– the first wave of British new towns. Places like Harlow and Stevenage and East Kilbride, followed a generation later by Washington and Telford and Milton Keynes, paralleled by the post-war reconstruction of London's East End, were the outcome. But they represented the culmination of a long and distinguished British tradition of creating great urban places, which goes back centuries to the gracious streets and squares of London, Bath, Edinburgh and Dublin, and many smaller gems tucked away in almost every town and city. And of course this tradition drew more directly, not only on the early garden cities at Letchworth and Welwyn, but before that on the visionary industrial villages created by philanthropic industrialists, from Blake's contemporary Robert Owen at New Lanark, through William Hesketh Lever's Port Sunlight to Joseph Rowntree's New Earswick. These places are the subjects of reverential visits, appreciative books and countless pamphlets and television programmes.

The Splintering of Urban Britain

Yet, in recent decades, we seem to have faltered and lost our way. Too many of our attempts at urban regeneration have been tawdry and superficial. Our cities and towns bear witness to our failure to create balanced urban economies which respond to the challenges of a globalized world. Our urban society sometimes seems more polarized than ever, as during the riots of August 2011. Riots and anti-social behaviour are of course signs of a deeper malaise. They are not so much about poverty, though the majority of the perpetrators lived in the most disadvantaged areas, but rather reflect a sense of alienation from the wider society, whatever the policy of the government of the day (Glazer, 1988). Hence we need to understand why our efforts to generate growth, and spread it to the poorer areas of our cities, failed dismally.

The Great Urban Exodus

Meanwhile, people have voted with their feet – or with their wheels. Millions continue to flee the cities and towns for the small towns and villages, testifying to the fact that they no longer find urban life attractive or appealing. And there they succumb to a pattern of life in which everything – work, school, social life, leisure – is completely car-dependent, separated from the cities by vast areas devoid of effective public transport.

True, the 2011 Census shows that over the previous decade not only London but other large cities increased their populations: in London, by no less than 0.9 million. But this was a remarkable net outcome, produced by a movement into London from abroad and a slightly larger compensating out-movement of people from London to the rest of the country, coupled with a high birth rate associated with London's relatively young population. And this had an additional component: in London, the share of the white British population fell dramatically, from 59.8 per cent in 2001 to 44.9 per cent in 2011: 'the historic white British majority in the city is now a minority' (Goodhart, 2013, p. 31). This is due not only to high levels of immigration – both white and non-white – but also to an exodus of white Londoners: their number fell by 600,000 in the decade, three times the loss in the previous 1991–2001 decade. In two-thirds of London's boroughs, twenty-three out of thirty-three, white Britons are now a minority.

For whatever reason, large and increasing numbers of us have effectively turned our backs on urban life. Britain, which a century and a half ago became the first urban nation, has now become the first to lead an anti-urbanization counter-revolution. Evidently, we have seen the cities and we do not like what we see. Of course, this trend is not unique to Britain. Virtually all our European neighbours, and also other advanced nations like the United States, Canada and Australia, are following the same universal trend: decentralization from cities to suburbs, and from suburbs to smaller towns. In the process, cities become the cores of wider city regions and then, with further growth, incorporate smaller towns and cities into even wider mega-city regions. We can see this process in the Pearl River and Yangtze River deltas of China, in Randstad Holland and the Rhine-Main region of Germany, and above all in the Greater South East England. Some may regret this, hoping like Canute to stop the tide and return to medieval-style high-density urban living. Some, like the followers of Ebenezer Howard, may actually welcome it – but with the critical proviso that it has to be handled well, by creating new urban places that are as good as the old. We do not propose to re-enter this controversy here, because we think it is fruitless and ignores the real, central issue.

The overwhelming evidence is that we need both to provide for existing cities to renew themselves, especially to rebuild the parts that are no longer fit for purpose, and to extend themselves, while providing for new growth within the ever-widening mega-city regions that represent the emerging urban form of the twenty-first century. The critical question and the critical distinction is how well we handle these different tasks. Elsewhere, cities are rebuilding abandoned docklands and shipyards and steel works close to their city centres, which meet the most exacting international environmental standards. Elsewhere, cities are growing gracefully and sustainably through well-designed urban extensions connected by excellent public transport to their centres and to concentrations of employment. Elsewhere, the movement out into smaller towns is being creatively handled through regional frameworks which relate the parts to the whole through integrated transport networks. The individual city or town is no longer an adequate framework to understand or plan for the future; these different parts have to be related to an entire city region, even a mega-city region. It is from their examples, above all, that we need to learn.

The Central Theme: Creating Better Cities

This book therefore has one central theme: how, in the United Kingdom, can we create better cities and towns in which to live and work and play? And, in doing so, can we provide lessons for other countries facing similar dilemmas? And, in particular, how can we learn from the best places now being created in our near European neighbours? Some of these countries, and some of the cities in them, seem to be responding faster and more imaginatively to the challenges that face us all. Their economies are generating new and worthwhile jobs in new industries, both in the manufacturing and service sectors. Their old inner-city industrial areas are being reshaped into exciting new urban neighbourhoods that meet the highest standards of environmental excellence. Their new urban areas, both at the edges of the cities and in satellite communities within their wider spheres of influence, demonstrate exemplary achievements in urban design and environmental standards. And all these different places, old and new, are linked into seamless webs of public transport – regional trains, trams, buses – that make the private car a second-best choice for many journeys.

In Part One of this book we will first explore the roots of the malaise that has gripped our cities and towns, touching on – but not at this stage exploring in depth – possible solutions to them. Then, in Part Two we will embark on a tour – the twenty-first-century equivalent of the Grand Tour which eighteenth-century aristocrats took to acquaint themselves with the best of the culture of European antiquity – but this time seeking the places, across Europe, that offer lessons for the future: places that are leading the rest of the world in creating different and better patterns of urban work and life. And finally, in a concluding chapter we will reflect on this experience to suggest how UK cities and towns can do as well, and better.

The Five Basic Challenges

First, then, let us set the scene. What are the things that are going wrong, and what do we need to do in order to challenge them? I want to argue that there are five basic challenges that call for new approaches, new powers and new investment mechanisms:

♦ *Rebalancing our urban economies* so as to create the potential for good jobs and new sources of work for everyone.

♦ *Building new homes* in enough quantity, to meet demand, in the right places and to good standards.

♦ *Linking people and places* through integrated land-use and transport planning.

♦ *Living with finite resources* and the impacts of climate change.

◆ *Fixing the broken machinery so as to* bring public and private agencies together in the process of development and redevelopment.

These are the five key areas where other countries – especially but not exclusively our European neighbours – seem to be responding more creatively and more effectively than we are. But, before we turn to the answers they suggest, we need to probe each of these challenges more closely. That is the objective of the five chapters that follow.

Part One:
Facing the Challenges

1 The First Challenge: Rebalancing Our Urban Economies

The first challenge is one first posed by Ebenezer Howard in his famous diagram of the *Three Magnets*, in 1898: *The People: Where will They Go?* It has lost none of its potency in the intervening century. Indeed, it is more urgent and more relevant than ever. For the underlying question is: *The People: Where will They Work?* It has become ever more evident, ever since the 1930s, that the British economy is suffering from a chronic problem of regional imbalance. It is often, but inadequately, labelled the North–South Divide. During the immediate post-war period, from 1950 to 1970, this problem was temporarily obscured by a burst of economic growth that appeared to be lifting the industrial areas of the North and Midlands out of the deep structural depression that had afflicted them in the 1930s. But then, rather like a malignant cancer that aggressively reasserts itself, the disease reappeared, now affecting regions, like the West Midlands, that had been hitherto thought immune. Deepening through the 1990s and 2000s, appearing in stark form in the global economic crisis of 2007–2008, it is now effectively dividing the United Kingdom into two starkly contrasted nations: a small urban island plus a few privileged subsidiaries, and a vast urban territory that has lost the capacity to earn its living. Understanding its nature and its causes is the basic key to any solution.

The deep trends that are affecting the British economy, and its constituent towns and regions, are well-enough known:

◆   the shift from a residual manufacturing sector to advanced producer services (not just financial ones) as the economic driver;

◆   skill shortages in high-level science and engineering and in middle-range technology, and a surplus of under-qualified workers, requiring a major drive to educate and retrain the workforce.

The North–South Divide; and the Great Cities versus the Rest

In consequence there is a new geography of England: the old North–South divide remains, but is overlaid by a distinction between the major cities and the rest. London and South East England are successfully making the transition to the knowledge economy, but there are big differences even there, between the successful towns and the sleepier rural hinterlands. In the North, the Core Cities[1] are increasingly polarized internally, with successful centres and university quarters contrasted with deprived middle-city rings and outer-ring estates; outside them, many former one-industry towns (including towns whose single industry was seaside holidays) are proving much less successful in forging the transition into the knowledge economy; farther out in wide-ranging attractive rural areas, small country towns are flourishing as commuters and retirees bring their incomes with them from the cities.

The Centre for Research on Socio-Cultural Change at the University

Figure 1.1. The North–South divide. (*Source:* http://sasi.group. shef.ac.uk/maps/nsdivide/ns_line_ detail.html)

of Manchester (CRESC) show that in the 2007–2010 period of recession, some 712,500 jobs were lost nationally, but more than 85 per cent of these, a total of 621,200, were lost in the ex-industrial regions of the West and North, notably in the West Midlands, Wales and Scotland (figure 1.2). CRESC argue that London has in effect become a new version of the medieval city-state like Florence, essentially autonomous and pursuing its own ends which may be at variance with those of the rest of the country – a view increasingly echoed in many media commentaries: 'There is a case now, financial, social and ethnic, for treating London as a separate island within England rather than as a part of it. There is no dimension of life in which London is typical of the nation of which it is the capital city and centrifugal force' (Collins, 2013, p. 29). This is illustrated by longer-term changes in regional Gross Value Added (GVA) per head, where every region – even the South East – has declined in relation to London (figure 1.3) (Ertürk *et al.*, 2011; cf. Heseltine, 2012, chart 1.11, p. 26).

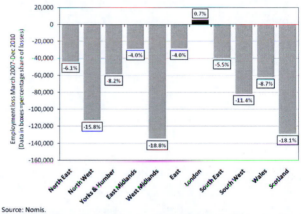

Figure 1.2. Regional share of total UK job losses, 2007–2010. (*Source*: Ertürk *et al.*, 2011, p. 4)

Source: Nomis.
Notes: Data relates to employees. Excludes self-employed and N.Ireland. Total jobs losses from March 2007 and December 2010 was 712,500.

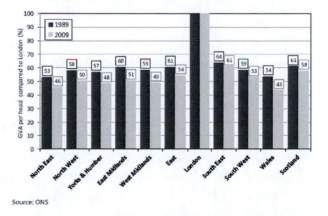

Figure 1.3. Regional GVA per head compared to London, 1989 and 2009 (as a percentage of London). (*Source*: Ertürk *et al.*, 2011, p. 10)

Source: ONS

A further critically-important piece of this story is that these peripheral regions have become increasingly dependent on state employment plus what CRESC calls the para-state sector – that is, publicly-funded but privately-employed workers, the numbers of which CRESC has been able to estimate for

Table 1.1. Regional employment change in the state and para-state sectors, 1998–2008.

Total (net new jobs) No.	of which Private sector %	State & para-state %	Female Total (net new jobs) No.	of which Private sector %	State & para-state %	Male Total (net new jobs) No.	of which Private sector %	State & para-state %
North East 85,372	26.9	73.1	38,876	−5.4	105.4	46,496	53.9	46.1
North West 215,535	38.4	61.6	120,642	15.2	84.8	94,893	68.0	32.0
Yorks & Humber 182,627	33.2	66.8	111,534	6.5	93.5	71,093	75.0	25.0
East Midlands 138,857	40.0	60.0	50,394	−29.1	129.1	88,463	79.3	20.7
West Midlands 64,609	−79.0	179.0	42,559	−103.0	203.0	22,050	−32.6	132.6
East 204,884	45.9	54.1	98,644	21.8	78.2	106,240	68.2	31.8
London 404,438	67.2	32.8	196,405	56.0	44.0	208,033	77.8	22.2
South East 332,643	56.4	43.6	133,581	25.1	74.9	199,062	77.4	22.6
South West 289,744	54.7	45.3	141,769	32.4	67.6	147.975	75.9	24.1
Wales 144,955	45.6	54.4	73,615	21.4	78.6	71,340	70.6	29.4
Scotland 258,542	40.7	59.3	148,085	13.4	85.7	109,457	76.6	23.4
Total 2,322,296	45.4	54.6	1,157,104	18.4	81.6	1,165,102	72.2	27.8

Note: The table is a measure of employees not jobs (where an employee can have more than one job).
Source: Ertürk *et al.*, 2011, p. 11 and Nomis (www.nomisweb.co.uk).

the first time (Buchanan *et al.*, 2009). Figure 1.3 shows that while in London these two classes of worker accounted for only 32.8 per cent of job growth between 1998 and 2008, in the North West the proportion rose to 61.6 per cent, in Yorks and Humber to 66.8 per cent and in the North East to 73.1 per cent. In the West Midlands, the extreme case, they provided the sole growth since private employment declined.

CRESC argue that from the 1980s – when deindustrialization had already destroyed much of the traditional employment base of the midland and northern regions – Thatcherite and subsequently New Labour governments effectively made a kind of Faustian bargain, allowing the finance-driven London economy freedom to expand, while providing massive subsidy to the other regions either by way of social services universally available in all regions, or by state or quasi-state new jobs (many of which provide the services), or by generously subsidizing the long-term unemployed through incapacity benefits: what the CRESC researchers call 'a new Speenhamland which offered full maintenance for a wholly unemployed industrial population' (Ertürk *et al.*, 2011, p. 29).[2] As the CRESC report puts it, 'in the absence of any other signs of economic life in the deindustrialising regions, these universal provisions became a de facto regional policy' (*Ibid.*, p. 30). But, in the crisis that began in 2007, this has come to a sudden halt as both are suffering from public expenditure cuts.

HALL, PETER, 1932-

GOOD CITIES, BETTER LIVES: HOW EUROPE DISCOVERED
THE LOST ART OF URBANISM.

Paper   346 P.

LONDON: ROUTLEDGE, 2014
SER: PLANNING, HISTORY AND ENVIRONMENT SERIES.

AUTH: UNIVERSITY COLLEGE LONDON. EXAMINES
BEST-PRACTICE CITIES IN EUROPE.
LCCN 2013-10517
   ISBN 0415840228   **Library PO#** GENERAL APPROVAL

		List	55.95	USD
5461 UNIV OF TEXAS/SAN ANTONIO	**Disc**	10.0%		
App. Date 3/12/14 URB.APR 6108-11	**Net**	50.36	USD	

SUBJ: 1. URBAN POLICY--GT. BRIT. 2. URBAN POLICY--
EUROPE.

CLASS HT133   DEWEY# 307.76094   LEVEL ADV-AC

YBP Library Services

HALL, PETER, 1932-

GOOD CITIES, BETTER LIVES: HOW EUROPE DISCOVERED
THE LOST ART OF URBANISM.

Paper   346 P.

LONDON: ROUTLEDGE, 2014
SER: PLANNING, HISTORY AND ENVIRONMENT SERIES.

AUTH: UNIVERSITY COLLEGE LONDON. EXAMINES
BEST-PRACTICE CITIES IN EUROPE.
LCCN 2013-10517
   ISBN 0415840228   **Library PO#** GENERAL APPROVAL

		List	55.95	USD
5461 UNIV OF TEXAS/SAN ANTONIO	**Disc**	10.0%		
App. Date 3/12/14 URB.APR 6108-11	**Net**	50.36	USD	

SUBJ: 1. URBAN POLICY--GT. BRIT. 2. URBAN POLICY--
EUROPE.

CLASS HT133   DEWEY# 307.76094   LEVEL ADV-AC

True, prosperous southern cities like Oxford and Cambridge show the highest dependence of all – but much of this is in sophisticated R&D, well supported by national and international funds. In contrast public sector employment in Hastings (42.2 per cent), Belfast (40.7 per cent), Swansea (38.5 per cent), Dundee (37.3 per cent) and Liverpool (36.0 per cent) is much more vulnerable to public expenditure cuts – and, apart from Hastings, these places are heavily clustered in the north of England and the Celtic peripheries (Larkin, 2009).

This in turn is related to another key indicator: the UK labour force generally is underskilled, and this deficit is worse in the northern cities. Unsurprisingly, therefore, these cities still have major concentrations of deprived households. The consolation is that between 2004 and 2007 they improved. But other, smaller, northern places deteriorated. In fact, if there is one striking contrast between northern and southern England, it is found in the medium-sized towns: in the south, these places – typically county market towns with a strong service component like Reading, Maidstone, Oxford and Cambridge – have gone from strength to strength, while their northern equivalents – typically one-industry towns that have lost their former economic base – have steadily sunk.

Beyond the North–South Divide: A New Geography of Britain

To characterize this emerging post-industrial geography simply as a north–south divide is too crude, though that divide – first recognized in the great depression of the early 1930s – is an important element in it. Rather, at the risk of some simplification, it can be described in terms of a four-fold taxonomy:

1. *The South East Mega-City Region*: a vast complex comprising London and its commuter catchment area, plus fifty separate cities and towns, all medium-sized or small, and their catchment areas, stretching as far as 180 kilometres from central London, and in course of permanent enlargement.

2. *The Rural Periphery of Southern England*: a vast penumbra to the first region, stretching out through extensive rural areas as far as the North Sea on one hand, the Atlantic Ocean on the other, and embracing much of Wales.

3. *The Archipelago Economy of Midland and Northern England*, characterized by a relatively few Core Cities that have suffered from major deindustrialization but are now in course of slow transition to the service-based knowledge economy, surrounded by wide rings of ex-industrial towns that are having much greater difficulty in achieving this transition.

4. *The Rural North*: the wide intervening areas of northern England, separating the Core Cities and their surrounding regions, and stretching far out across

thinly populated scenic areas, much of which are protected National Parks, as far as the west and east coasts.

Over the half-century or so since 1960, these four regions have experienced very different trajectories in terms of economic change, migration and consequent demographic evolution, and social change. But they are in course of constant dynamic evolution, and some individual sub-regions of the country can be said to be transiting from one to another. So their fortunes may change from decade to decade, sometimes at bewildering speed.

The South East Mega-City Region

South East England is an example of a new spatial scale: the *Mega-City Region* (MCR) (Hall and Pain, 2006). Originating in the 1990s in Eastern Asia, where it was applied to areas like the Pearl River Delta and Yangtze River Delta regions of China (Lin and Ma, 1994; McGee, 1995; Sit and Yang, 1997; Hall, 1999; Scott, 2001; Wo-Lap, 2002, quoted in UN–Habitat, 2004, p. 63), it is essentially a new form: in the South East England example, some fifty Functional Urban Regions (FURs), around a major central city, physically separate but functionally networked, and drawing economic strength from a new functional division of labour. These places exist both as separate entities, in which most residents work locally and most workers are local residents, and also as parts of a wider functional urban region connected by dense flows of people and information along motorways, high-speed rail lines and telecommunications cables. It is no exaggeration to say that this was the emerging urban form at the start of the twenty-first century.

A recent study of eight such MCRs in North West Europe[3] (Hall and Pain, 2006) found that South East England is the largest of these regions in terms of population, with 18,560,000 people in an area of 27,332 km²: one-fifth of the land area of England with nearly two-fifths of its population. It is also the most complex, with no less than fifty-one constituent FURs including London itself (figure 1.4). It consists of London and its immediate commuter catchment, stretching approximately 40 km from central London, together with fifty other cities and towns and their individual catchments, ranging in population from 600,000 down to 80,000, and extending as far as 180 km from London. Planning controls, imposed since the 1947 Planning Act, have successfully maintained physical separation between these units, producing a pattern on the ground, and still more strikingly as seen from the air, of 'towns against a background of open countryside', the traditional British planning ideal first enunciated in the 1920s by Raymond Unwin. But, especially west of London, they are functionally interrelated through daily commuter exchanges and still more by exchanges of information in the course of daily business. Thus, illustrating that the region is polycentric not only in a physical but also in a functional sense (*Ibid.*).

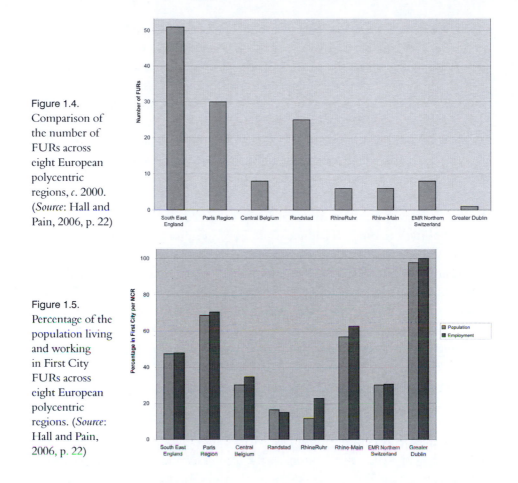

Figure 1.4. Comparison of the number of FURs across eight European polycentric regions, *c*. 2000. (*Source*: Hall and Pain, 2006, p. 22)

Figure 1.5. Percentage of the population living and working in First City FURs across eight European polycentric regions. (*Source*: Hall and Pain, 2006, p. 22)

Another notable feature is the degree of self-containment, measured by the percentage of the resident workforce that lives and works in the same relatively small FUR (figure 1.5). Generally, close to London this percentage is low (often less than 50 per cent), indicating commuter linkages to London and, to a lesser degree, neighbouring towns. But beyond a critical point about 70 km from central London, self-containment rises rapidly: towards the edge of this vast region, beyond 100 km from London, it reaches 75 or even 80 per cent. This conclusion has been fortified by other work covering a slightly larger region, which suggests an even greater degree of self-containment farther away from London (de Goei *et al.*, 2008). There is an important policy implication here: to reduce daily travel, it is better to encourage decentralization out of London to more distant places than to nearer ones.

These functional relationships help to explain the evolution of this huge and extraordinarily successful region. The dynamics of its growth have not so far been fully analysed, but it is reasonably clear that a central role was played by the expansion of London's commuter field after 1950, which – distorted by the establishment of the London Green Belt – essentially leapfrogged over it and then, because planning controls contained urban growth, reconcentrated in distant towns. Then, as these commuter towns developed their own local service base and many attracted inward investment in offices which housed jobs decentralized from London, they too became important independent centres in their own right: a process observable in Bournemouth, Reading, Woking, Southend and Milton Keynes. The designation of no less than eleven new towns between 1946 and 1968, together with major planned expansions of towns like Basingstoke and Swindon, further assisted the process. These were planned to be as far as possible self-contained, and had from the start a strong economic base both in manufacturing and service industries.

The key question is how far this vast polycentric region actually functions, in terms of flows of information within an advanced service economy. And the most important findings (Hall and Pain, 2006, chapter 15) were that London, like other major European cities, constitutes the key centre for global advanced producer services (APS) – but that secondary centres like Reading or Milton Keynes are also important. True, the communication flows occurring within a major city like London, and articulated through it, are of a far superior intensity and value to those occurring within firms across the wider region. Despite this, the Greater South East appears to have a significant degree of real functional polycentricity.

The Rural Periphery of Southern England

The boundary between the South East Mega-City Region and its rural periphery is ambivalent and constantly shifting as the former extends ever farther outwards in the zone approximately 130–180 km from London. Cities like Bristol, Coventry and Leicester, and smaller towns like Nuneaton, Lichfield, Kettering, Corby, Melton Mowbray and Grantham, are not currently enveloped but could undergo this fate in the future. Improvements in rail services, including the upgrade of the West Coast Main Line from London to the North West and the impending electrification of the Great Western Main Line from London to Bristol, will powerfully assist this process. The experience of towns in London's commuter belt, as described above, may well be replicated in other locations more distant from London.

It is in places like this that we can see some of the most buoyant growth in all England. A report from the Halifax (2010) shows that over the half-century 1959–2009 house prices rose by 279 per cent, whereas real earnings only rose 169 per cent. Thus the people who invested in buying houses won out, with a major switch in living patterns: there was a huge fall in private renting, from 33 per cent to 14 per cent, and also in living as part of a larger household, and a parallel growth in owner-occupation, from 43 per cent to 68 per cent. Over this period 13 million homes were built, fully half the current stock of 26.6 million, with a great increase in the numbers of detached homes far distant from the centres of cities. It is these new neighbourhoods where the most skilled are to be found, and their preferred mode of travel is the car, of which they now typically own two or more. Here are the homes of Motorway Man and his family, the archetypal middle-middle-class voter, who – it is always asserted – determine the result of successive British elections.

Beyond the towns, rural locations in high-quality countryside and within easy reach of train stations, particularly those lines accessible to London Heathrow airport, have proved attractive to Londoners seeking second homes and also to a wide range of small businesses such as advanced consulting and high-technology R&D; indeed these two processes may be synergistic. There is thus an observable thickening of the settlement pattern, coupled with upward pressure on the housing market which may have the effect of pricing out lower-income local buyers – a politically contentious point.

The Archipelago Economy of Midland and Northern England

Beyond some critical limit from London, difficult to state and constantly liable to shift, the economic geography of England takes a different form best described in the term coined by Pierre Veltz: the archipelago economy (Veltz, 1996; Dorling and Thomas, 2005): the major Core Cities (Birmingham, Manchester, Liverpool, Leeds, Sheffield, Newcastle) form islands of economic growth, separated by wide seas of economic stagnation or decline. This spatial structure arises from a very unequal process of transition, over the period 1960–2000, from the nineteenth-century manufacturing economy to the twenty-first-century service-based knowledge economy. But in fact, the spatial pattern is more complex and subtle than just described.

Two major studies – the *State of the English Cities*, from the UK Office of the Deputy Prime Minister, in 2006 (Parkinson, Champion *et al.*, 2006), and the *State of the European Cities Report: Adding Value to the European Urban Audit*, from the European Union DG Regio, in 2007 (ECOTEC *et al.*, 2007) – show convincingly that British cities have not performed as well as their surrounding regions, in complete contrast to the rest of Europe, where the major cities have generally been in the lead.

The *State of the English Cities* report uses a comparison of GDP per capita for sixty-one top cities in Europe based on figures from Barclays Bank in 2002, which found that outside London, even the best British performers, such as Bristol and Leeds, come far down the European performance league. The star performers – such as Karlsruhe and Munich, both of which, significantly, are many miles away from the old industrial areas of the Ruhr – produce some three times the output per head of cities like Birmingham and Manchester (or cities such as Bordeaux and Lille, Gothenburg and Turin, which still have substantial industrial legacies). An interesting chart reveals that the best-performing German cities also have the highest numbers working in high-tech manufacturing sectors. The suggestion is that the places that do best manage to combine both the capacity to innovate with the functions of a well-connected regional capital (for all the leading centres are highly accessible by air and rail). The physical expressions of economic success, such as galleries and stadia, follow on from economic dynamism, and are no substitute (though they can play a crucial role in changing a city's image and self-confidence, as examples like Bilbao illustrate).

More recent research, from Tony Champion and Alan Townsend, concludes that Core Cities have overall performed worse than the remainders of the regions save in one short period, 1998–2002, when they were fortified by a massive injection of public service jobs (Champion and Townsend, 2011).

The 2007 EU report confirms the 2006 UK study: many European cities – particularly in the UK – still underperform, lagging behind their national average figures. This is a problem, because differences in income levels within cities are greatest where overall unemployment is highest. It goes on to develop a comparison of European city types and arrays them in terms of their performance on four separate indices: employment creation, qualified workers, multimodal connectivity (on the vertical scale), and population size (on the horizontal scale). The really successful cities are those that are making the most rapid transition to the knowledge economy, while conversely those on the bottom left are the old industrial cities that are to some extent failing to make the transition. The most successful cities of all are the so-called *international hubs*, the big cities that top the league of growth; they include established capital cities such as London, Paris and Madrid, which are comfortably off but are showing local unemployment. In the same highly successful league are the so-called *research centres*: smaller cities with a very high gross domestic product per head, such as Grenoble in the French Alps or Cambridge in England. In sharp contrast, at the other end

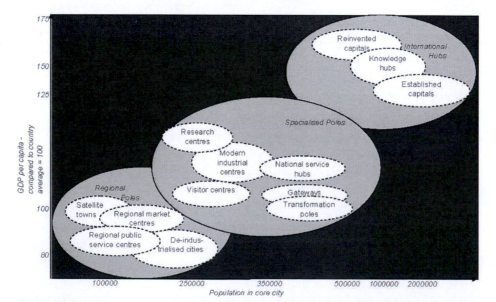

Figure 1.6. City types positioned. (*Source*: ECOTEC Research and Consulting Ltd *et al.* (2007), figure S.3, p. x)

of the scale, are the so-called *deindustrialized cities*: they include many major UK cities – Sheffield is an example – and many smaller towns in Northern England and Scotland and Wales. Figure 1.6 shows essentially that there are specialized places in the top right corner, outstanding in making the transition to the new knowledge economy, contrasted with the much less successful cities at bottom left, generally smaller older industrial cities including a number in Eastern Europe, and in between a more mixed group of cities with moderately good economic performance, but some problems.

The real issue emerging from these comparative studies is that some generally smaller cities are finding it easy to make the transition to the new economy, partly because, for instance, they have universities and strong research centres; while at the other extreme, some cities are finding it extremely difficult to make that transition because they have a heritage of old industries that have more or less disappeared, and their former workforces are insufficiently educated or insufficiently skilled to provide a support for the new service economy. Yet some larger cities, in particular the very biggest capital cities, are making the transition quite successfully in terms of knowledge-based service industries, such as financial services and the media, but are leaving some problems behind in the form of populations in some parts of those cities that are not equally making a transition to the New Economy.

Thus one of the most interesting questions for public policy today is how far these synergistic relationships in the very biggest European capital cities – like London, Paris, Madrid and Berlin – can spread downwards and outwards into the next level of cities and then the next level down from that, into the smaller cities – including those ex-industrial cities that often have the very biggest problems. The final point, however, is that much of this activity is face-to-face: you have to be there to be part of it. That is equally true whether you come as a tourist or you work as a trader in a London bank or in a headquarters office of a major corporation – you have to meet face-to-face. We can export some of these activities from the big cities to smaller cities, we can create museums and galleries, and we can foster tourism in smaller cities outside the major capitals. To some extent we can move other media activities – in 2011 the BBC moved an important part of its whole activity out of London to Salford in Greater Manchester. The paradox is that just as we do that, so more and more other activities in the big cities grow to take their place. This constitutes a process of constant refreshment, which means that the other cities can perhaps grow in these areas, but the really big cities tend to keep powering ahead too.

But this downward-and-outward shift, so pronounced in the South East Mega-City Region, has simply failed to trickle through from the North's Core Cities into the wider spatial economy. Historic weaknesses in the UK economy, apparent as far back as the Great Exhibition in 1851, have persisted over the decades despite endless inquiries and attempts to change the educational and incentive systems. While in the UK manufacturing employment has given way to services, other countries – Germany, France and Italy – have successfully adapted their manufacturing economies to compete in a globalized economy through switching to advanced manufacturing of products like railway or optical equipment, made on a major scale on the edges of historic cities such as Stuttgart, Valenciennes and Turin.

In contrast, while some UK Core Cities have succeeded in regenerating old industrial areas on the fringe of their centres, as in Birmingham's Jewellery Quarter, the weaker industrial towns around them, including coastal towns, have borne the brunt of decline without finding viable new roles. As the more-highly-motivated or better-qualified young people leave, the remaining population – the grandsons of the former industrial workforce, the sons of the immigrants who took their place before the mills shut down, the drifting benefit-seekers who colonize seaside B&Bs – are increasingly characterized by multiple social problems. Over time a new population emerges, subsisting on a combination of temporary jobs and benefits, and constituting what is sometimes called the 'black economy' or even the 'non-working class'. Thus, in these northern places, clustering – that process extolled by management gurus like Michael Porter – may ironically have negative effects. The black economy can damage whole neighbourhoods, for example through drug-fuelled crime and prostitution, and the resulting image may put off the very knowledge workers and investors on which growth depends. Activities such as social services or security might correctly then be counted as deductions from the local GVA.

These changes cumulatively result in huge and increasing geographical disparities. First, the Core Cities are themselves unequal cities (Centre for Cities, 2008, p. 9). As noted above, within cities differences in income are greatest where overall unemployment is highest, and Danny Dorling (2011) has shown that income disparities in major cities are bigger than they have been for many years – on one comparison since the end of World War One, 1918, and on another comparison even since the 1850s at the height of the Industrial Revolution. This is alarming evidence of a paradox, found in other cities, presented by the evident contrast between the very high-earning, highly-educated, highly-skilled, highly-specialized individuals working in the knowledge economy, especially in industries like financial services or the media, and very poorly paid recent immigrants to the cities doing basic service jobs. Perhaps this is a sort of intermediate position which eventually will resolve itself as the children of the immigrants pass through the educational system and then qualify to do the new jobs in the New Economy. But we should not automatically assume that this will happen – at least for a long time – because we are seeing quite strong educational differences, also highlighted in Danny Dorling's study, between the children of the workers in the knowledge economy, who can get into the best schools, and the other children who are often pushed into the worst-performing schools and as a result have the worst academic performance.

This inequality is reflected in a new geography of the Core Cities. Their central business districts are the chief locations for the growth of the knowledge economy, together with their university campuses and – in a few cases – the perimeters of their airports. Sometimes city centre growth washes out into regenerated inner-ring locations, such as Salford Quays in Greater Manchester or Merry Hill in the West Midlands, producing what are effectively supplementary or alternative CBDs. But large areas of the middle and outer rings of these cities have failed to make the adaptation, leaving many of their inhabitants unemployed and deeply deprived. The process has particularly impacted on young white males growing up in isolated communities, such as peripheral public housing estates, who have failed mentally to adapt to the expectations and constraints of the New Economy (McDowell, 2003). These cities therefore present a paradox, with new jobs attracting young in-migrants (particularly those who have graduated from the city universities) and commuters who may choose to live in the surrounding countryside, but with high rates of localized long-term unemployment and low expectations, which may extend from one generation to the next. This is why, despite their prosperity, these cities still record extraordinarily high levels of deprivation.

This process is even more clearly seen in the rings around them, comprising former industrial towns which grew in the nineteenth century, but have demonstrably failed to make the critical transition out of the manufacturing economy. In *The State of the English Cities* (Parkinson, M., Champion, T. *et al.*, 2006) they show lower rates of GVA per head, lower rates of GVA growth, higher unemployment and significantly higher proportions of lower-income households. Successive editions of the Index of Multiple Deprivation, published in 2004, 2007 and 2010 (DCLG, 2004, 2007, 2010), show a clear pattern: the Core Cities are still the most deprived places in England, but have shown steady improvement, while the one-industry towns around them have stagnated or fallen back. But there are significant differences here. Some towns, perhaps because they are well located on main national transport corridors, have done significantly better than average: Warrington in the North West, located on the M6 motorway and West Coast Main Line, is an example. Others, particularly those located at greater distances from the Core Cities, seem to be deteriorating. In the so-called Central Lancashire City Region, embracing five separate medium-sized urban areas (Blackpool, Preston, Blackburn, Accrington and Burnley-Nelson-Colne), all showed sharp increases in multiple deprivation between 2004 and 2010.

The 2010 update of the Index of Multiple Deprivation, based mainly on figures from 2008 – just as the economy crashed – highlights this picture of the increasingly uneven geography of England. It shows broadly the same picture as on the last occasion, in 2007: the big northern cities, plus a few East London boroughs, are the country's most deprived places. Liverpool, Middlesbrough, Manchester, Knowsley, Hull, Hackney, Tower Hamlets and Birmingham have the highest proportions of very deprived Lower Layer Structural Output Areas

(LSOAs) in England. But in the next positions come Blackpool, Hartlepool, Blackburn with Darwen, and Burnley: a seaside resort and three medium-sized one-industry (more accurately, ex-one-industry) towns, three of the four in the Central Lancashire corridor. Further, since 2007 the big cities have improved their position, while the other places have slipped down. In Liverpool the number of very deprived neighbourhoods fell by 9 per cent, in Manchester by 13 per cent. And in London the improvement was even more spectacular: Hackney down 25 per cent, Tower Hamlets 28 per cent. Contrast Blackpool, up 17 per cent, or Burnley, up a spectacular 43 per cent. This strongly suggests that the cities are successfully making the transition from the industrial economy to the knowledge economy, and that this benefits even their most deprived citizens. The one-industry towns – including Blackpool, whose industry is tourism – are failing to make that transition. Of the ten most deprived neighbourhoods in the entire country, three are in Blackpool – two within a mile of the town centre, the third in a post-war housing estate on the edge of town. The most deprived people in the country, it appears, are moving to the seaside. And the Coalition government's proposed changes to housing benefit will be certain to accelerate this trend.

The Rural North

One striking feature of the recent geography of England is the contrast between the state of these ex-industrial towns and the rural areas, including those immediately next to them. This is captured by two key indices. First, while the towns feature in the top thirty or forty of the most deprived local authorities in the Index of Multiple Deprivation, the adjacent rural areas typically are found at the opposite end of the scale. Second, house prices are typically 50–100 per cent higher – in extreme cases, as between Burnley and Ribble Valley, as much as three times higher (Hall, 2006). This contrast is visible in the prosperous state of the villages and small towns, which appear almost indistinguishable from their equivalents in southern England. It has arisen from a long process of out-migration of the middle class who populate the service economies of the cities and towns, but prefer a rural lifestyle, and it has been assisted by a system of motorways which, especially in North West England, facilitate long-distance commuting and have generated very wide commuter catchments around the cities for professional and managerial workers (Harding and Robson, 2006).

This prosperous rural North, which extends far out into remote upland areas such as the northern Pennines and the Lake District and North Yorkshire National Parks, is characterized by small market towns, typically with populations of 20,000–40,000 people: Macclesfield, Knutsford, Clitheroe, Ripon, Northallerton, Barnard Castle, Kendal, Keswick. It also includes a relatively few larger county towns with populations as high as 100,000–150,000: Chester, York, Lancaster, Darlington. (Preston, an interesting case, appears to belong to this

Table 1.2 North v. North: deprived towns, affluent countryside.

Urban District	IMD2004 Rank	Rural District	IMD2004 Rank	Difference
Burnley	37	Ribble Valley	288	251
Blackburn with Darwen	34	Chorley	172	138
Preston	59	Wyre	161	102
Blackpool	24	Fylde	240	216
Wigan	53	West Lancashire	127	74
Leeds	68	Harrogate	277	209
Bradford	30	Craven	262	232
Sheffield	60	High Peak	211	151
Hull	9	East Riding Yorks	208	199

Source: Hall, 2006; figures from DCLG.

Table 1.3 North v. North: the rural property premium, first half 2006.

Urban District	Average Price £	Rural District	Average Price £	'Premium' %
Burnley	72,189	Ribble Valley	198,979	+175.6
Blackburn with Darwen	98,662	Chorley	151,465	+53.5
Preston	130,815	Wyre	155,956	+10.2
Blackpool	120,176	Fylde	197,997	+64.8
Wigan	119,515	West Lancashire	169,933	+42.2
Leeds	157,153	Harrogate	235,437	+49.8
Bradford	126,354	Craven	195,501	+54.7
Sheffield	140,144	High Peak	153,282	+9.4
Hull	82,521	East Riding Yorks	154,805	+87.6

Source: Hall, 2006; figures from Land Registry.

group but shares some characteristics with the ex-industrial towns). Many are just at the rural edges of the city regions. They are typically located on major motorway and rail arteries which give them fast links to the Core Cities but also to London. They have strong economies based on public services (county administration, public health, higher education) and are attractive retail centres with wide catchments, having many of the characteristics of their southern English equivalents. And, like their southern English equivalents, they have seen rapid growth of new housing estates, often less constrained by rigid planning controls than in the South. So here too, close to interchanges on the M6, M61 and M62, are the new homes of the archetypal Motorway Man and his family.

Conclusion

This increasing discrepancy of fortunes between different parts of the English and British economy – not merely north versus south, but also big city versus small town and urban-rural – is clearly deep and apparently deepening, as the *State of the English Cities* report demonstrates with a wealth of figures. Are there any ways in which public policy could address it? We will return to this issue in the final chapter. But one preliminary word of warning is in order. The present imbalance in the economic geography of the UK is the cumulative outcome of decades of change. Any attempt to develop counter-compensating processes is likely to be equally slow and also arduous (Hall, 2006). We should not expect instant remedies, and we should distrust anyone purporting to offer them.

Notes

1.　The Core Cities are the economically most important cities outside of London in England. See http://www.corecities.com/about-us/core-cities.

2.　The Speenhamland system, introduced in 1795 by magistrates in Speenhamland (Berkshire) to mitigate agricultural distress, in effect paid unemployed workers to live at home. In 1834 it was replaced by the New Poor Law, in which most relief was available only in workhouses.

3.　South East England; Central Belgium; Randstad Holland; RhineRuhr; Rhine-Main; Northern Switzerland; Paris Region; and Greater Dublin.

2 | The Second Challenge: Building New Homes

The United Kingdom, but particularly England, is simultaneously suffering from four huge housing challenges. First, we are not building nearly enough new homes. Second, we are not building enough of the right kinds to meet expected demographic change. Third, and associated, we are not building them in the right places. Fourth, we are not yet building them to the right standards of best design, especially to meet future environmental standards (see Chapter 4).

Not Enough New Homes

One of the most extraordinary facts about UK national housing performance, noted by commentator after commentator, is that for many years there has been a failure to build enough new homes to meet the predicted growth in population and households. Indeed, even more remarkably, the deficit has progressively got worse. And, though party political points can and will doubtless be struck, this has happened both under Labour and Coalition governments.

The number of annual dwelling completions in the UK since the Second World War reached a peak of 425,830 in 1968, but then went on a steep downward trend until the early 1980s before entering into an uneven plateau of around 200,000 a year (Goodier and Pan 2010) (see figure 2.1). Over the 10 years to 2002, output of new homes was 12.5 per cent lower than for the previous 10 years (Goodier and Pan, 2010, quoting Barker, 2003). In 2001 the construction of new houses fell to its lowest level (173,770) since the Second World War. Despite a gradual increase from 2001 to 2007, the number of housing completions dropped dramatically after the autumn 2007 fiscal crash, with the annual completions in 2009 estimated below 150,000 (Goodier and Pan, 2010): fewer homes than in any year since 1946 – indeed, if the table extended farther backwards, any peacetime year since 1923. And this is a long-term trend. The recent fall has been as steep as anything recorded over the entire 65-year period. Since early 2010 completions have averaged 112,000 per year, and house building is currently at approximately 65 per cent of pre-downturn levels (DCLG, 2012).

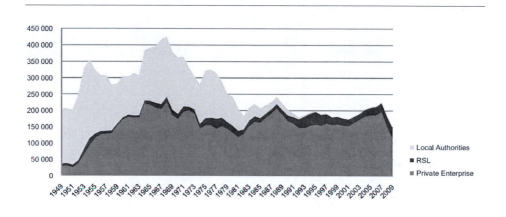

Figure 2.1. Permanent dwellings completed, by tenure, UK. (*Source:* Goodier and Pan, 2010, p. 9), from CLG Live tables 211 and 241)

Figure 2.2 demonstrates that this trend is unusual among European Union nations. Some like Spain and Ireland have of course experienced frenetic housing booms, fuelled by artificially cheap and easy mortgage finance, leading in both countries to a huge surplus of unoccupied – and even unfinished – housing and a catastrophic outcome for the public finances. But the UK's performance has fallen not only behind these, but behind every comparable country on the chart. Figure 2.1 amplifies this by demonstrating the major source: the drastic fall in public housing completions during the 1980s, which Registered Social Landlords (Housing Associations) failed to compensate for, and more recently the drastic fall in completions by the private sector.

One clear symptom was that over the previous 30 years UK house prices have risen in real terms by around 2.5 per cent per year compared with a European average of only 1.1 per cent per annum. In other countries, such as France, Sweden and Germany, real house prices have remained broadly constant or even declined. The only comparable cases of price inflation were Ireland and Spain. One key reason is that in the UK, housing supply responds weakly to changes in demand, so that higher demand generates higher house prices rather than increased output of houses (Barker, 2003, para. 3, p. 5; para. 5, p. 6).

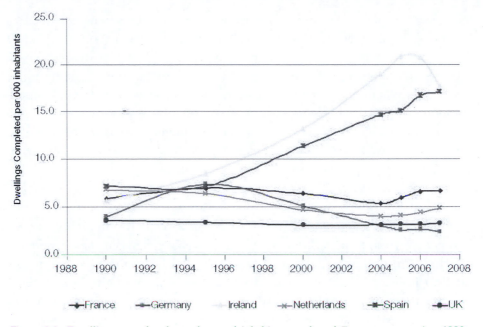

Figure 2.2. Dwellings completed per thousand inhabitants, selected European countries, 1990–2007. (*Source*: Oxley *et al.*, 2009, p. 62)

Demand side factors alone cannot explain the high rate of house price growth seen in the UK, nor are they independent of supply, Barker concluded. The UK has had a long-term weak housing supply, having invested a low proportion of GDP in housing compared to other EU countries since 1960 and having completed relatively few new homes in relation to the existing housing stock. At current rates of replacement a new house built today would need to last around 1,200 years (*Ibid.*, para. 10, p. 8). International comparisons show that the supply of housing in the UK is less price responsive than in other major economies. It is only half as responsive as the French housing market, a third as responsive as the US market, and only a quarter as responsive as the German housing market. Further, it has become less responsive over time. Before World War Two, it was up to four times as responsive, as it was through most of the post-war period. And it declined further in the 1990s, falling almost to zero, implying no change in housing output at all in response to the increases in price. Increasing demand has therefore fed directly into higher house prices (*Ibid.*, para. 11, p. 8).

House building rates became such an embarrassment to the Labour government that they launched several reviews into the causes. In 2004 Kate Barker's *Review of Housing Supply* noted: 'By 2002 only 37 per cent of new households could afford to buy a new property compared to 46 per cent in the 1980s' (Barker, 2004, p. 3, quoted by Gallent *et al.*, 2011, p. 3). The Review concluded that in 2003 there was a shortfall of 39,000 homes in England per annum, of which 8,000 were private sector and 31,000 were affordable homes. In addition there was a backlog of around 450,000 households without self-contained dwellings. Putting it another way, to keep houses as affordable as they were in the 1980s would imply a shortfall of between 93,000 and 146,000 homes per annum in England, of which, 20,000 to 45,000 are owner-occupied private-sector homes and 73,000 to 101,000 are affordable. Put yet another way, to reduce the long-term trend in house prices to zero real growth would imply an additional 240,000 homes per annum across the UK; to lower real trend price to 1.1 per cent, 145,000 more houses per annum might be needed, about double the current private-sector housing output of 150,000 units (Barker, 2003, para. 14, p. 9).

Barker's report identified land supply as the critical issue, despite persistent efforts by government over the previous quarter-century to maintain supply. One reason was a sharp rise in small (one- and two-person households) over the period. And, as Nick Gallent and his colleagues argue in their report for the Royal Institution of Chartered Surveyors, the Urban Task Force's report in 1999 had not helped, by recommending that new housing be concentrated on urban or brownfield sites as a means to stimulate urban renewal and protect the countryside (Urban Task Force, 1999) – a recommendation accepted by government in its 2001 Urban White Paper (DETR, 2000). In fact, Kate Barker found, some brownfield sites were not easy to develop, or were in the wrong places to meet demand (Gallent et al., 2011). She found that the root cause was a planning system that was both slow and parochial. She recommended that planning should instead become a proactive tool, adapting to the rapidly changing dynamics of the market. Government responded through a new Planning Policy Statement, PPS3 (DCLG, 2006) and a Green Paper (DCLG, 2007), setting ambitious targets for future housing delivery, both operating in the context of 15 to 20 year (legally-binding) housing targets set out in the Regional Spatial Strategies (RSS) interlocking with the Local Development Framework (LDF) system (Gallent et al., 2011). But all this has been swept away by the Coalition's abolition of Regional Spatial Strategies.

Both Kate Barker (2004) and then John Callcutt (2007) put the blame on the failure to build enough homes to match demand. The volume house builders, five of whom accounted for over half private house-building in the early twenty-first century, built around the same numbers each year up to the collapse of the market in 2008, and so did not fill the gap left by the decline in building social housing. As an economist Kate Barker was well qualified to look at both supply and demand. She saw how the growing number of households, a natural product of living longer and couples breaking up, were competing for a limited supply of homes. Housebuilders struggled with planning systems designed to protect the interests of those who were already on the housing ladder, and had little incentive to take risks in building family housing on expensive brownfield sites. Government made the process ever more complicated, for example requiring builders to provide for a mix of tenures and to help fund infrastructure.

And all this is before we start to take into account future demand. Alan

Holmans and Christine Whitehead (2011) have used the official DCLG 2008-based projections to forecast that demographic changes alone will result in the need for 234,000 additional dwellings per annum if households are to be able to live separately. And they drill deeper, to calculate the need from different sizes and kinds of household. We need to follow them there.

The Wrong Kinds of Housing

Holmans and Whitehead (2011) also show that the new evidence on numbers of children suggests an increasing need for dwellings large enough for three or more children – although the rate of growth of these larger households is much slower than for childless households. The rate of growth in the number of lone-parent households is projected to be twice that for the overall total. If this position were to be fulfilled, it would almost certainly imply a large increase in the need for affordable housing. The increase of 1.2 million couple households with no other members implies a large increase in under-occupation of the housing stock.

The biggest changes in the new projections are in relation to household types. This is partly because of the far greater detail about household structures included in the new projections. However, they also suggest some large differences from earlier projections which are not just the result of greater detail. Table 2.1 provides a summary of projections for the main household types used in earlier projections. They suggest a very large increase in the number of lone-

Table 2.1. Summary of household types – comparison between the 2008-based projections and previous projections.

	2001	2006	2011	2016	2021	2026
			thousands			
2008-based						
Couple households	11,441	11,394	11,504	11,727	11,949	12,060
Lone-parent households	1,438	1,607	1,811	2,035	2,292	2,495
Other multi-person households	1,341	1,318	1,301	1,287	1,264	1,268
One-person households	6,304	7,024	7,773	8,558	9,340	10,194
All households	*20,523*	*21,344*	*22,389*	*23,608*	*24,843*	*26,016*
2006-based						
Couple households	11,497	11,583	11,841	12,146	12,446	12,703
Lone-parent households	1,477	1,663	1,767	1,852	1,919	1,976
Other multi-person households	1,386	1,446	1,550	1,648	1,735	1,816
One-person households	6,163	6,822	7,590	8,460	9,339	10,178
All households	*20,522*	*21,515*	*22,748*	*24,107*	*25,439*	*26,674*
2004-based						
Couple households	11,497	11,596	11,787	11,994	12,182	12,322
Lone-parent households	1,476	1,655	1,760	1,830	1,882	1,928
Other multi-person households	1,387	1,452	1,538	1,629	1,708	1,775
One-person households	6,163	6,816	7,562	8,384	9,200	9,951
All households	*20,523*	*21,519*	*22,646*	*23,837*	*24,973*	*25,975*

Source: Holmans with Whitehead, 2011, p. 4.

parent households compared with earlier projections. One-person households are also expected to increase more quickly, while slower growth is projected among couples and other multi-adult households. The 2008-based projections show an increase of 600,000 in the number of couple households between 2001 and 2026, made up of an increase of 1 million households without dependent children and a fall of 400,000 in households with one or more dependent children. Over the same period there is a projected increase of 1.05 million in the number of lone-parent households.

As important from the point of view of housing requirements is that the overall number of households with children is expected to grow by 660,000. Two-thirds of these households will have only one dependent child, but there is a 73 per cent increase in lone-parent families with three or more children.

In summary:

♦   The 2008-based projections suggest that demographic changes alone will result in the need for 234,000 additional dwellings per annum if households are to be able to live separately.

♦   The new evidence on numbers of children suggests an increasing need for dwellings large enough for three or more children – although the rate of growth is much slower than for childless households.

♦   The rate of growth in the number of lone-parent households is projected to be twice that for the overall total. If this position were to be fulfilled, it would almost certainly imply a large increase in the need for affordable housing.

♦   The increase of 1.2 million couple households with no other members implies a large increase in under-occupation of the housing stock.

Housing in the Wrong Places

Housing in the Wrong Regions?

Holmans and Whitehead (2011) go on to the look at the regional distribution of future demand. Their conclusions are set out in table 2.2. They find that the new projections suggest somewhat lower growth in the Midlands and parts of the North, and more in the South and East. This is a partial reversion towards the earlier pattern before the surge in house prices in the South and East relative to the rest of the country in the later 1990s and early 2000s, which led to less migration to – and more outmigration from – the South. But, as house price rises slowed in the South and accelerated in the Midlands and North, there was less outmigration from the South, and this is reflected in the new estimates. In a sense, this is a simple reciprocal model: as the South East economy heats up, house prices there rise and force more people out over longer distances beyond the fringe of the region, especially into the adjacent East Midlands region, which acts as a kind of escape valve. Then, as the economy cools, the pressure on the escape valve lessens again. However, particularly notable about the new projections is the renewed and very rapid rise in the figure for London. This could reflect the very high rate of migration into the capital from overseas in the mid- and late-2000s, including large numbers of young migrants who naturally move into rented property in the inner city. If they remain and start to build families, the outward pressure could rise again, particularly if the mortgage famine of 2008–2012 eventually eases.

Table 2.2. Distribution between regions of the projected increase in households.

	2004-based (2006–2026)	2006-based (2006–2026) percentage	2008-based (2006–2026)
North East	2.7	3.3	3.7
North West	11.5	11.0	9.3
Yorkshire and Humber	10.5	11.8	11.5
East Midlands	9.9	10.9	9.4
East of England	8.3	8.4	7.9
London	13.4	13.4	14.0
South East	14.8	13.4	15.5
South West	16.1	15.5	17.0
England (total increases in thousands)	4,457	5,159	4,672

Source: Holmans with Whitehead, 2011, p. 4.

Some observers, however, believe that the demand for owner-occupied property has peaked, and that new households will increasingly look to rent long after the age at which previous generations sought to buy their own homes. And this is fortified by the evidence on household composition, particularly the large increases in lone-parent households who will be seeking affordable housing. Many of these, needless to say, will be concentrated in London – and also in other large cities, not separately distinguished in these projections.

Brownfield or Greenfield?

There is another key question that has exercised policy-makers for decades, without resolution: how many of the new homes could and should be built on previously-developed brownfield land, and how much on previously-undeveloped greenfield? The starting point must be to establish the exact extent of urban development in the country, and the most recent serious attempt to do this was made by Nick Gallent for a major investigation of Land Use Futures by the Government Office for Science in 2009 (Gallent, 2009). He found that in

2005 the total land take for housing in England was 150,770 ha, or 452,310 ha including domestic gardens but excluding access roads, car parking, incidental open spaces and children's play areas (DCLG, 2007). This represented 3.4 per cent of all land use. If all non-domestic buildings, roads, railways and paths are added, then total 'urban' land use was 1,129,417 ha, or 8.53 per cent of all classified land. This excludes areas of land within built-up areas that is considered 'open' (e.g. areas of water or green space), so the developed area is likely to be somewhat higher. However, Gallent suggests, it is a useful baseline, which can be related to the 22 million homes existing at roughly the same time. He then draws on a previous study by Holmans and Whitehead (2008) suggesting a need for an additional 9 million homes by 2056, bringing a total of 31 million. These would use another 292,500 ha of land for the homes themselves, plus gardens and directly associated uses. The total land take for development, including the infrastructure and economic development needed for a bigger population, could increase by 41 per cent, to a total developed area of 1,592,578 ha, 12 per cent of the total.

We earlier saw that this Holmans and Whitehead paper, on which Gallent relied, suggested a relative shift of this development to the North, now contradicted by the latest evidence. However, both projections suggested a big absolute weight of development in London, the South East and South, as table 2.1 has demonstrated. Further, Gallent argues, it seems likely that the existing trend of residential deconcentration from big cities to small towns and rural areas will continue. The implication is that gains in the North, as in the South, will be concentrated in lower-tier settlements and will not guarantee any renaissance of northern cities.

The Urban Task Force proposed that the percentage of development on brownfield land, then 56 per cent, should rise to 60 per cent, and in 2000 a government White Paper accepted this (DETR, 2000). But meanwhile the actual percentage had inexorably and dramatically begun to rise, to reach 80 per cent in 2008. In this spate of urban development, much consisted of apartments on former industrial sites. But how far did the tide extend? In 2000 Urbed and UCL were asked to review the state of urban renaissance in the South East. Their report *Living Places* (Carmona *et al.*, 2000) found plenty of well-designed schemes in cities like Brighton and Reading, but little underway in the suburbs where most people lived. Councillors were generally not convinced that any more housing could be squeezed into their areas. A subsequent report on the state of twenty-four towns and cities in the run-up to England's first ever Urban Summit, *Partners in Urban Renaissance* (Urbed, 2002), found a major renaissance underway in the hearts of major cities such as Birmingham and Leeds, but the benefits were not spreading far. Older industrial towns like Blackburn were not attracting anything like the investment they needed, and there was a surprising level of dissatisfaction in the new estates that had sprung up around Swindon.

The World in 2013

Over a decade later, despite a mountain of reports, and some landmark buildings and regeneration schemes, including the government's ambitious *Sustainable Communities Plan* (ODPM, 2003), progress has ground to a halt. House prices have far outpaced income levels, partly because (as shown above) house building has lagged behind demand (and European levels), as the first Barker Report brought out. Social disparities have widened as the rungs on the ladder have become ever further apart. Though there has been a shift towards building on brownfield sites and at higher densities, with a swing towards flats, the quality has been widely criticized as lamentable. The cramped city centre flats have largely been bought by investors for letting to young professionals, and this market collapsed like a pack of cards following the credit crunch and banking collapse brought on by over lending. Those on higher incomes still prefer to live in older houses in established neighbourhoods. Hence there are major doubts over whether new developments in government Growth Areas, such as in the Thames Gateway or the housing renewal areas, will ever work out as planned.

At the same time as house prices rocketed in the South, the phenomenon of '*housing market failure*' was identified in northern industrial cities. Attempts to repeat the Comprehensive Redevelopment Areas of 30 years ago, often in places where the white working class have voted with their cars, and moved out, were resisted. As the '*urban exodus*' continues, rising congestion and travel times to work, increasing social polarization, and ethnic pockets are a formula for stress and conflict. Welcome measures to promote liveability, and deal with social disorder in the worst places through a massive Neighbourhood Renewal programme, failed to stem the loss of social capital that condemns so many areas to gradual decline. Small wonder then that some of the worst problems are in suburban estates like Benchill in Manchester where young people complain of nothing to do, and where some streets are unwalkable at night. Seductive concepts like the night-time economy and café culture end up as binge drinking on Friday and Saturday nights, a world apart from the Continental model that the Urban Task Force wanted to promote.

So radical new mechanisms are needed both to upgrade existing neighbourhoods, and to build new sustainable urban neighbourhoods where people will really want to live. This means attracting investment into the economic base and social capital as well as the physical infrastructure. For despite Britain's success in creating new jobs, unemployment levels among ethnic groups, particularly young people, remain unacceptably high, as are the levels for unqualified white working-class youth. Most young people cannot afford to get on the housing ladder. With low levels of productivity and innovation, and large budgetary and balance of payments deficits, financing better neighbourhoods has become very difficult.

In June 2010, soon after taking office, the Minister for Decentralisation and Cities, Greg Clark, announced a dramatic change to halt the process of increasingly-dense development on urban brownfield land: power would be granted to councils and communities to prevent garden grubbing and to decide what types of homes would be suitable for their area. To this end, the previous minimum density figures in PPG3 – 30 dwellings per hectare – would be scrapped: local councils would have the power to determine what level of density was appropriate (Speech to RTPI, Annual Conference, 29 June 2010). A few days earlier, his colleague Grant Shapps had argued that:

> The current system with its push for high density has resulted in developers building one or two bedroom executive flats, when the greatest need is often for affordable family homes. That's why from today communities will be allowed to make their own decisions about what homes are needed in their area, and no longer be victims of a system designed to maximise profits and minimise choice.[1]

Gallent found that in fact evidence on housing densities is mixed. Recent residential densities in England have been low but are increasing. Forecasts of future land use assume average densities of 40 dwellings per hectare on brownfield land and 20–30 on greenfield sites. Resurgent concern for space standards – coupled with the objective of using land effectively and efficiently – would keep densities on an upward trajectory although investment-driven super-densities in inner urban areas are likely to fall as homebuyers question the long-term utility of 'micro flats' (Gallent 2009, p. 102).

Poorly Insulated, Poorly Designed Housing

The government's standards for new housing, to be considered in greater detail in chapter 4, are designed to ensure a rapid and radical improvement in energy conservation by 2016 when, under government policies laid down in 2008, all new housing must be Zero Carbon with net carbon dioxide emissions, taking account of emissions associated with all energy use in the home, equal to zero or negative across the year. These homes will be cheaper to run because of high energy efficiency requirements, and occupants will be less vulnerable to rising gas and electricity prices. As exemplars, in 2008 the then government announced the construction of four pioneer locations for English eco-towns: Whitehill-Bordon, St Austell (China Clay Country), Rackheath (Norwich) and North West Bicester, which would set the highest possible standards for green living, supported by special government funding. They include zero carbon status across all the town's buildings, including commercial and public buildings as well as homes – a significantly tougher threshold than any existing or agreed targets. Forty per cent of the area within the town would be green space, at least half of which should be open to the public as parks or recreation areas. A minimum of one job per house should be reached by walking, cycling or public transport to reduce dependence on the car. All homes would be located within 10 minutes walk of frequent public transport and everyday neighbourhood services. Homes would take their energy from the sun, wind and earth.

These are fine intentions, and not the least impressive feature is that after the 2010 election, the new Coalition government undertook to maintain them. There is however an overwhelming problem: the new measures will apply only to new housing built after 2016. And, due to the very slow turnover of stock, England's existing housing stock is relatively old, with around 38 per cent of dwellings (or 8 million homes) built before 1945, of which almost 5 million were built before 1919. Historically, the UK housing stock has been built without much regard for elementary design qualities or for basic standards of insulation against the external environment. As Chris Huhne, when Secretary of State for Energy, put it:

> Britain has some of the oldest building stock in Europe. Our draughty homes are poorly insulated, leaking heat and using up energy. As consumers, we pay a high price for inefficient housing – and so does the planet. A quarter of the UK's carbon emissions comes from the energy we use to heat our homes, and a similar amount comes from our businesses, industry and workplaces. (DECC, 2012, p. 2)

There have been some improvements in recent years:

♦   Improved energy efficiency has increased the average energy performance (SAP, Standard Assessment Procedure) of homes from 41 in 1996 to 54.5 by 2010, on a scale of 100 – better, but still a long way to go.

♦   The social housing sector achieved the highest rating (of over 60) by 2010. This higher rating reflects the younger age profile of the social housing sector (e.g. only a fifth of homes owned by local authorities were built before 1945 compared to over half of the private rented market), and local authority actions to improve energy efficiency for its tenants.

♦   However, given that the social housing sector (which also comprises housing association stock) only accounts for around 17 per cent of all residential housing, and that SAP ratings are well below the average for new homes of around 80, there still remains significant scope to reduce emissions from the existing housing stock.

The main opportunities for reducing emissions in the existing stock of homes are insulation, boiler replacement, and more efficient appliances:

♦   *Insulation*. Simple cost-effective measures include loft and cavity wall insulation, giving a 6 per cent cut in emissions across the housing stock as a whole. Solid wall insulation is more expensive and disruptive but could offer an additional 5 per cent reduction.

◆   *Boiler replacement*. Building regulations require that when a boiler is replaced, it must be with an energy efficient condensing type. Between 2012 and 2020, 8 million boilers could be replaced, resulting in emissions reductions of around 6 per cent.

◆   *More efficient appliances*. Buying more efficient domestic appliances (refrigerators, washing machines) and using them efficiently could reduce indirect (electricity-related) residential emissions by around 14 per cent in 2020.

In total these measures would reduce direct residential emissions by 23 per cent and indirect emissions by 36 per cent by 2020 – and pay for themselves, so that typical household energy bills in 2020 remained at around current levels. They could also generate local jobs; in Kirklees on Merseyside, a programme to insulate 51,000 homes is estimated to have created almost 250 jobs (Committee on Climate Change, 2012, pp. 32–33).

Three-quarters of the energy we use in our homes is for heating our rooms and water, most of which comes from gas-fired boilers. Together this accounts for 13 per cent of the UK's CO_2 emissions while our workplaces are responsible for 20 per cent. To help meet the carbon budgets we need by 2022 (compared with 2008) to cut emissions in our homes and communities by 29 per cent and by 13 per cent in our workplaces. To do this we need to make our homes, communities and workplaces more energy efficient, and heat and power them from low carbon sources. The scale of the challenge is dramatically illustrated in figure 2.3 (DECC, 2012, p. 7).

Clearly, with the vast majority of the UK housing stock built in previous decades and centuries when no such standards applied, retrofitting is an important priority but one that has received far less attention. But the London

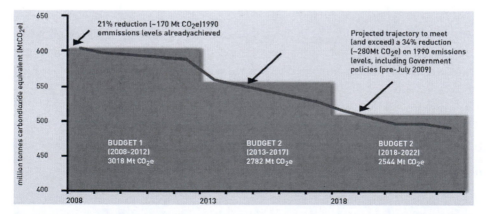

Figure 2.3. Carbon budgets: the challenge to reduce UK emissions. (*Source*: DECC, 2012, p. 7)

Borough of Sutton, which has established an enviable reputation among local authorities as a trend-setter in environmental policy-making, has commissioned a report that analyses it in detail (Parity Projects, 2008). Like any typical outer London borough, compared with national averages Sutton's housing stock is heavily concentrated in the middle-age range; 61 per cent of its private housing (as against 13 per cent nationally) was built in the period 1939–1959, when insulation standards were poor. The poorest houses in this respect are the oldest and the biggest. Nonetheless, the report concludes that over time very great improvements – of 92 per cent in CO_2 emissions and 89 per cent in energy requirements – can be obtained. But this can be achieved only at a considerable cost, and with varying rates of return over time.

The government's Green Deal programme, announced in 2010, specifically addresses these challenges nationally. It claims to remove many of the barriers faced by householders and businesses wishing to install energy efficiency measures. By making investments possible at no upfront cost (repaid through energy bills), it increases the incentive for owner-occupiers, tenants and landlords to take action (DECC, 2010). The critical question is how quickly, and on what scale, people and institutions are inspired to seize the initiative.

But at the same time, the government have rowed back on the previous timetable set by its Labour predecessor in 2006: to make all housing products zero-carbon by 2016, with interim targets of 25 per cent reduction in emissions in 2010 and 44 per cent in 2013. George Osborne changed the definition of zero-carbon in the March 2011 Budget so housebuilders would no longer have to provide zero-carbon energy for domestic appliances, just heating, fixed lighting and hot water. Then there were cuts in feed-in tariff rates for renewable technologies. Most seriously, the 2013 Part L consultation proposes to slash the 25 per cent cut in carbon emissions 2010, to just an 8 per cent cut. This will mean that housebuilders face a much bigger jump in 2016 to keep the zero-carbon deadline on track – perhaps too big for the industry to handle. The reason of course is cost. According to official figures, a three-bedroom semi-detached house on a brownfield site would cost 4 per cent extra if carbon emissions were cut by 25 per cent over 2010 Part L but only 15 per cent extra to meet the new definition of zero-carbon. Meeting the target set to the original definition of zero carbon would cost an extra 29 per cent. But some builders and designers have already shown that they can deliver lower-cost solutions. What the industry needs, above all, is clear targets that do not get changed every year (Lane, 2013).

Priorities for Housing

The priorities, then, are clear. They are:

◆   To deliver much more new housing, without abrupt fluctuations, in order to meet projected demand.

♦   To deliver the right kinds of housing to meet the projected growth of different household sizes and compositions.

♦   To deliver it in the right places to meet the growth of population.

♦   To deliver it at the highest possible environmental and design standards.

Evidently, at present, the system is not delivering these priorities. To understand better why this is so, in Chapter 5 we look more deeply at the underlying mechanisms.

Note

1. See   http://www.planningresource.co.uk/news/1009439/Housing-density-target-abandoned-coalition/.

3 | The Third Challenge: Linking People and Places

In 1957, the economist Colin Clark published a paper, which was rightly destined to become a classic in the urban literature: it was called 'Transport: Maker and Breaker of Cities'. He argued that – at least since the first industrial revolution, two hundred years ago – the growth of cities had been shaped by the development of their transport facilities. But these in turn were dependent on the evolution of transport technologies. For each successive development of the technology, there was a corresponding kind of city. However, the relationship was more complex than that: it was a *mutual* one, in which the transport system shaped the growth of the city, but on the other hand the previous growth of the city shaped and in particular constrained the transport alternatives that were available. So the pattern of activities and land uses in the city, and the transport system, existed in some kind of symbiotic relationship. But these, Clark argued, could get out of step. In fact, over the past 150 years cities worldwide have experienced four successive crises of transport technology and urban form, of which the fourth is still in progress.

It was a very profound vision of the ways in which cities grow and change, and the years have done nothing to shake it; if anything, they have shown just how profound it was. For in that time, all cities in the advanced world have seen a pattern of decentralization of people and jobs, associated with a shift of balance from public transport to the private car, which now is seen to present huge challenges from the viewpoint of sustainability.

Down to about 1850, most cities – even the biggest ones – did virtually without what we would today regard as a transport system. Within this *pre-public transport city*, personal travel was on foot. Such cities were extraordinarily small and dense. The result, as Clark showed in another classic paper (Clark, 1951), was an extraordinarily steep density gradient: within the city densities were very high, but they soon descended to rural levels. About 1850, such cities experienced a crisis: they could not grow much further as long as the jobs remained in or near the centre, and as long as there was no personal transport. The answer was horse trams and steam-hauled commuter railways: steel wheels on steel rails reduced the frictional resistance of travel and made it possible to shift not merely bulk goods, but also bulk loads of people, over land; from around 1870, 'streetcar suburbs' developed around North American and European cities. Cities that developed on this pattern, characterized by London, Manchester, Paris, Berlin or New York around 1890, can be described as *early public transport cities*.

This second crisis started in London in the 1850s; even then a city of two million people, it was grievously overcrowded as more and more people crammed into a tiny area, set by the average speed of walking to work, a radius of about 5 kilometres or an hour's walk. Charles Pearson, the Solicitor to the City of London Corporation, argued for cheap trains to disperse 'the superior order of the mechanical poor' (quoted in Sheppard, 1971, p. 136), 100,000 of whom came into the City each day from the suburbs; his ideas culminated in the Metropolitan Railway of 1863 and the Inner Circle (today's Circle Line) of 1884. As the system extended into the suburbs, villa developments followed, though not always (not even usually) for the mechanical poor; the main beneficiaries were the Victorian middle class.

But, because the technologies were relatively unsophisticated, a second crisis was in the making. This early public transport city – dominated by steam trains and horse buses and trams – could manage to operate adequately until around 1900. The bigger cities, which had reached populations of over one million by 1890 (and London had reached over four million), could not grow much further on the basis of the existing bundle of technologies; there was a social housing crisis. At this point, around 1890–1900 there was a new phase: electricity was applied to propelling trams and commuter trains; underground electric railways were constructed in the biggest cities, and soon they were extended above ground to serve new suburban rings, earlier and more aggressively in London and New York than in Paris or Berlin. The result, by the 1920s and 1930s, was a new kind of city, the *late public transport city*.

In London between the two world wars, 1918 to 1939, this shaped the underground system which provided a model for the rest of the world. Trains ran in tunnels under the central and inner areas, emerging above ground and running for some 20 kilometres into what was then open country; stations, spaced roughly every 2–3 kilometres, were served by feeder bus services, thus allowing an almost uniform pattern of medium-density development (typically

30 houses per hectare) as far as this radius. In the many smaller cities and towns of provincial England, typically between 100,000 and 1 million in size, electric trams and later motor buses performed the same role in serving suburban development, typically stretching out only about 5 kilometres in the smaller places, but up to 10 kilometres in bigger cities like Birmingham, Leeds or Manchester. The houses built in these years were a mixture of great municipal public housing estates like Wythenshawe in Manchester, Speke in Liverpool or Middleton in Leeds, and speculatively-built homes for owner-occupation – the latter made possible by a combination of cheap manual labour, cheap materials (prices of primary products were depressed in the 1920s and 1930s), middle-class affluence and the availability of mortgage finance.

London: From Classic Public Transport Metropolis to Mega-City Region

London's Underground system was largely unified by 1912 and totally so in 1933. A management team – Albert Stanley (Lord Ashfield), who had earlier experience in running American urban transit,[1] and his commercial manager Frank Pick – rapidly extended the system above ground into open fields, linking with a bus company under the same management to provide feeder services, and allowing mushroom suburban expansion. South of the river, the newly unified Southern Railway electrified its suburban services with similar consequences. By the outbreak of World War Two in 1939, medium-density suburbs extended almost uniformly to distances about 12–14 miles (19–23 km) from the centre, making London the classic example of the public transport city in its heyday.

But, as Pick reminded academic audiences at the end of the 1930s, the system was neither fast nor comfortable enough to extend far beyond these limits. At that point Pick himself joined the chorus of voices calling for limits to London's growth, which finally found expression in the report of a Royal Commission published early in 1940, after World War Two had broken out. Following on from this, a regional Greater London Plan produced by the leading planner of the day, Professor Patrick Abercrombie, called for London's further growth to be curbed by a surrounding green belt, with surplus population from London's overcrowded slums decanted to new and expanded towns beyond it. Rather remarkably, perhaps, this was done. The green belt firmly stopped further planned Tube extensions; the earthworks can sometimes still be seen in the fields. Beyond it, eight new towns, started in 1946–1950 and completed some 20 years later, lay 20–35 miles (35–55 km) from London; three successors, started in the 1960s, were located 50–80 miles (80–130 km) distant. Over a score of town expansions were located among and beyond them. And, to judge by subsequent research, this increasing distance contributed to a higher degree of self-containment in these planned developments than in other places of similar size and at similar distances from London.

But the comfortable assumptions of the planners were thwarted by an unexpected event: a rising birth rate, combined with a failure to stem migration from the less economically successful peripheral regions of Britain. The result was widespread suburban growth around towns on the other side of the belt, over 25 miles (40 km) from London, served by faster commuter main line railways, most of which were progressively electrified in the 1950s and 1960s. London thus evolved from a classic public transport metropolis into a new urban form, the *polycentric mega-city region*. By the year 2000, as already seen in Chapter 1, this South East England Mega-City Region had come to occupy a huge area, more than one-fifth of England, containing nearly two-fifths (38.6 per cent) of its population. Stretching northwards for some 80 miles (130 km) from London and south-westwards as far as 110 miles (180 km) from the capital, it was dominated by the huge built-up mass – about 15 miles (25 km) in radius – of Greater London, bounded by the green belt and the M25 orbital motorway, also part of the Abercrombie plan but completed only in 1986. Together this built-up area and its immediately-surrounding commuter belt – its Functional Urban Region (FUR) – dominated the entire wider region with over 9 million people, just under half its total population. But outside this were no less than fifty other FURs, ranging in population from 80,000 to 600,000, which had shown consistent and strong growth in the previous half century (Hall and Pain 2006). And the overwhelming trend, for both people and jobs, was outward.

The resulting pattern of daily commuting was understandably dominated by strong radial flows into and out of London, some of them long-distance, and especially evident along strong transport corridors representing parallel motorways and rail main lines. But notably, many centres along these corridors, located between 40 and 100 miles (65–160 km) from London, also showed complex and increasingly important cross-links with other centres. This was particularly noticeable in a wide crescent north-west, west and south-west of London, from Northampton and Milton Keynes round to Bournemouth-Poole, Southampton, Portsmouth, Brighton-Hove and Eastbourne, which almost seemed to be developing as a networked sub-mega-city region within the larger MCR, confirming a pattern of much stronger independent economic growth on that side of London.

None of this had been foreseen by the planners of the 1940s, who had fondly imagined that the whole process of movement to the new and expanded towns would be a once-and-for-all process. And this was accompanied by an explosion of car ownership, which rose three times between 1961 and 2008. The result, inevitably, was increasing congestion on Europe's most intensively used road network. There was one crumb of comfort: despite this high degree of interconnectivity, within the entire region in 2001 no less than 70 per cent of all workers lived and worked within the same FUR, representing a high degree of self-containment, rising as high as 75–85 per cent for some FURs near the edges of the MCR.

Los Angeles: First Full-Motorization City

In the United States, they showed an altogether finer appreciation of the commercial potential of subway construction. New York's first line, opened in 1904, connected the City Hall in the heart of the downtown financial district with still undeveloped districts in the Bronx; they did not remain undeveloped for long. During its first year of operation the subway carried 106 million passengers. It was overcrowded from the start, because of the new traffic it generated: the five-cent flat fare subsidized longer trips and thus new development. Population in the Bronx grew by 126 per cent between 1890 and 1900 and by 1910 it would reach 400,000. In the decade that followed, lines were run under the East River and through Brooklyn, all focusing on the downtown commercial core.

But the most spectacular case of all, and the most unusual, was that of Los Angeles. The Pacific Electric Railway Company, created between 1901 and 1911 out of no less than seventy-two separate light rail systems, was the largest electric inter-urban system in the United States, serving fifty-six communities within a 160-km radius of Los Angeles; at its peak, in the mid-1920s, it stretched for 1,164 miles (1,873 km) of standard-gauge track, and its 800 'Big Red Cars' ran 6,000 scheduled trips daily; together with it went the Los Angeles Pacific Company, running streetcars over 326 miles (525 km) of narrow-gauge track in Los Angeles itself.

It was the creation of the tycoon Henry E. Huntington, a figure little known, even to the thousands who visit the galleries or library that bear his name. But his network was merely the basis of his real operation, which was land speculation. As the Los Angeles historian Robert Fogelson explains, Huntington's system had to be financed quite differently from those in eastern cities like New York: there, the subway generally followed growth, and profits were more or less guaranteed; here, the rails came before the houses, and the lines seemed so risky that the stock market would not respond (Fogelson, 1993). So Los Angeles entrepreneurs like Huntington actively sought to share in the rising land values that would result, and land development, not fare revenues, became the object of the entire exercise. Huntington brought this to a fine art, simultaneously organizing the Pacific Electric Railway, Huntington Land and Improvement, and San Gabriel Valley Water companies. It lost money, but the land company made millions.

Amazingly, it did not last long. For, even before 1920, the overwhelming fact in Los Angeles was that it was the first place in the world to experience mass car ownership, decades before any other city on earth. In 1915, Los Angeles already had one car for every eight residents, compared with a national average of one per forty-three people; by 1920, one to 3.6 against one to 13.1; by 1930, one to 1.5 against one to 5.3. By 1938 the average resident of Los Angeles owned a car, and car ownership was not limited to any particular area of the city. What this meant, simply, was that in 1920 Los Angeles began to experience effects of mass car ownership that were unknown in other American cities until after World War Two, and in Western European cities until the 1980s. As Rayner Banham (1971) put it, the people who were coming here were turning their backs on the old kind of city: they wanted 'the dream of a good life outside the squalors of the European type city'. They came from small towns where driving was taken for granted.

As a result, the Los Angeles light rail system went into free fall. Even from 1912, passenger traffic dropped; between 1923 and 1931 there was a 24 per cent decline in traffic into downtown, with big losses in off-peak and weekend service, and during the Depression, things got even worse: traffic fell by one-third between 1929 and 1934; with petrol prices at 11 to 14 cents a gallon, many families found it cheaper to drive than to ride. In 1930 the company had fifty interurban routes and thirty local streetcar lines; 10 years later it was left with less than thirty interurban lines and about twenty local service routes. So, almost from its inception in 1911, the newly-combined system went over the equivalent of a financial Niagara Falls. Even during the prosperous 1920s the losses averaged well over $1 million almost every year; during the 1930s, they mounted to more than $2 million a year. Overall, between 1912 and 1940, the system made a profit only three times. In the late 1930s, significant cutbacks had to be made: all rail service ended in 1961.

The fact was that no one much cared. In the mid-1920s, when the system was plunging into crisis, there was a great local debate on the future of the city. The majority view was put by Clarence Dykstra, Efficiency Director of the City's Department of Water and Power, in a brief article published in 1926, 'Congestion Deluxe – Do We Want It?', arguing that cities no longer need develop on the basis of a dense, congested Central Business District on the London or New York model. Everywhere, he noted, businesses – banks, factories, theatres, stores – were decentralizing. He commended an alternative vision, that 'the city of the future ought to be an harmoniously developed community of local centers and garden cities in which the need for rapid transportation over long distances will be reduced to a minimum'. Los Angeles could become the first such dispersed city in the world, dependent on the private car for personal travel, the truck to move goods, and universal electric power. 'Under such conditions', Dykstra argued, 'city life will be not only tolerable but delightful…' (Hall, 1998a, p. 822).

Perhaps it was, at least after the first of the freeways opened in 1940. Meanwhile Los Angeles was acting as a kind of laboratory experiment in alternative urban lifestyles, an experiment that was to be followed by many other cities in the second half of the twentieth century.

Three Kinds of City

This then was and is a third crisis, which Los Angeles experienced in the 1920s and other cities only in the 1960s: the clash between the old urban morphology and the car. The Los Angeles answer, even if politically incorrect in our latter-day eyes, was astonishingly innovative: it was to let the public transport system decline, and to become an auto-oriented city. A few other cities, all of them in the American west – Phoenix, Salt Lake City, Dallas – effectively adopted full motorization with low-density dispersal of homes and jobs. But the problem is that other, older, cities kept strong central business districts, and in the great redevelopment booms of the 1960s and the 1990s they often became stronger still. They could not adopt full motorization on the Angelino model. The biggest, like New York, Paris, Tokyo and London, are 'strong centre cities', as Michael Thomson called them in his book of 1977; they have one million and more downtown office workers crowded into an area typically 10 square miles (26 km²) or less, and it is this feature that makes them rail-dependent: they depend very largely on their early twentieth-century rail systems to get people to work, because only rail systems can handle those kinds of flows along corridors: up to 40,000 people per hour on one lane or track.

The next rung of cities, which includes most of the great regional centres of Europe and the United States, and many smaller European capitals – Birmingham and Manchester, Brussels and Copenhagen and not least Stockholm, Frankfurt and Milan, Atlanta and San Francisco – are what Thomson calls 'weak centre' cities: they typically have between a quarter million and a half million workers in their downtown office cores, and they bring them in by a mixture of buses, trams and light rail, with a minority using commuter rail.

But there is a crucial further point, which is that both strong and weak centre cities are hybrids: outside their dense cores they are as car-dependent as the Los Angeles type of city. Everywhere, even in the strong centre cities, only a minority of the total metropolitan area workforce works downtown, and very commonly that workforce is shrinking. There are suburban clusters of offices and shops, and these are growing, resulting in the phenomenon of what the American journalist, Joel Garreau, has called Edge City (Garreau, 1991). These clusters are highly car-dependent, and often have weakly developed public transport systems, though that varies greatly from one city to another, and – as the studies in Part Two will show – European cities in particular have better suburban public transport. Further, the people who live in these suburbs use the car almost exclusively in their nonwork journeys: for shopping, entertainment, recreation and weekend social life. So, in effect, such urban areas have two transport systems: one used by a minority of commuters and a small group of carless people, and one used by virtually everyone else and indeed by the commuters outside commute hours.

Inefficiencies and Contradictions

The result is a set of contradictions, which constitute a fourth crisis in the organization of urban transportation. As Clark stressed in 1957, transport and the city could get out of step, and indeed very often did so. That was particularly the case because cities change more slowly than the available technologies change. Because of this, old cities have trouble in accommodating modern traffic; this is why many of them – in Europe especially – have excluded the car from their downtown areas, returning by choice to the pedestrian world of the Middle Ages.

The first such contradiction, which is fairly well-known, is the private and social cost and benefit: there is a massive social cost which all car drivers impose on all other users at congested times. A second, which is really a special case of the first, is the energy-consumption and environmental-impact implications of our increasing dependence on the car as the only available means of moving around. Well-known work from Peter Newman and Jeffrey Kenworthy (1989, 1999) indicates that average petrol consumption in American cities was nearly twice as high as in Australian cities, four times higher than in European cities and ten times higher than in Asian cities. Even within the United States, per capita petrol consumption was as much as 40 per cent higher in 'full motorization' cities like Houston than in 'strong centre' cities like New York or even 'weak centre' cities like Boston. Differences in gasoline prices, income and vehicle efficiency explained only about half of these variations. What was significant was the urban structure: cities with strong concentrations of central jobs, and accordingly a better-developed public transport system, had much lower energy use than cities where the jobs were scattered; denser cities performed better than less dense ones.

Overall, there is a strong relationship between energy use and the use of public transport, especially rail, and provision for the car. In European cities, 25 per cent of all passenger travel is by transit and only 44 per cent use a car for the journey to work. The importance of walking or biking in these more compact cities is highlighted by the fact that 21 per cent use these modes for their work trip. In Amsterdam the proportion rises to 28 per cent and in Copenhagen to 32 per cent. Asian cities show even higher proportions. Newman and Kenworthy (1999) show that a rail-based transit system can compete with the automobile and that in Europe and Asia train speeds are generally faster than the average traffic speed. Central area pedestrianization, which is so extensive and so popular as a means of revitalizing central areas of European cities, is made possible by strong transit operations.

But there is yet a further problem: as already noted, in many large urban areas the central workforce, on which was based the whole traditional radial pattern of public transport, is no longer growing. It is at best static and at worst declining, as both homes and jobs decentralize to ever more far-flung suburbia. In any case, employment is everywhere decentralizing in a relative sense, because the growth of jobs in the suburbs is far faster than that in the central business district. This is true not only of American cities, but in Europe also. In large city-regions like the mega-city around London, the many smaller towns show far higher car use than central and inner London, though the outer suburbs of Greater London, developed in the interwar years, are also car-dependent. Far from America adopting energy-conserving European patterns, it appears that Europe is going down the profligate American road.

The fact is that even where strong central concentrations of jobs remain, the growth of new jobs is occurring mainly in the suburbs, including smaller towns that are becoming connected into the ever-expanding mega-city regions. That is one reason why public transport systems are showing poor financial results: they are still serving patterns of travel, predominantly radial, that are declining. In the United States during the 1980s, one of the most remarkable geographical changes has been the appearance of new so-called back office complexes, as along the I-680 corridor in the San Francisco Bay Area, or the Zip Strip around Princeton in New Jersey. There are exactly similar campus office complexes at the periphery of major metropolitan areas elsewhere in the United States and in Europe: Stamford in Connecticut, 43 miles (69 km) from downtown New York City, Reading, 40 miles (64 km) west of London, and Parisian new towns such as St Quentin-en-Yvelines. However, all these three are different from the earlier examples in having good access to public transport, including both feeder buses and commuter rail.

Coordinating Transport and Land-Use Planning

Overall, in the future as in the past, there is likely to be a close connection between transportation technology and land use. Whatever system evolves to take the place of the conventional single-occupant, driver-controlled car, it is likely to stimulate certain types of land-use response. Work in the UK and the USA is highly relevant here.

Susan Owens (1984) suggests that a sustainable urban form would have the following features. First, at a regional scale, it would contain many relatively small settlements; but some of these would cluster, to form larger settlements of 200,000 and more people. Second, at a sub-regional scale, it would feature compact settlements, probably linear or rectangular in form, and with employment and commercial opportunities dispersed to give a 'heterogeneous', i.e. mixed, land-use pattern. Third, at the local scale, it would consist of sub-units developed at pedestrian/bicycle scale; at a medium to high residential density, possibly with high linear density, and with local employment, commercial and service opportunities clustered to permit multi-purpose trips. Her work strongly suggests that a cluster of small settlements may be more energy-efficient than one large one; the optimum upper limit would be 150,000–250,000; that linear or at least rectangular forms will be the most efficient; and that though densities should be moderately high, they need not be very high to be energy-efficient. Thus, a density of 25 dwellings per hectare, which in terms of future composition might translate into about 40 people per hectare, would allow facilities with a catchment area of 8,000 people to be within 600 metres of all homes, and a pedestrian scale cluster of 20–30,000 people would provide a sufficient threshold for many facilities without resort to high densities, which actually might be energy-inefficient. These arrangements rather closely accord with what Markelius and Sidenbladh were achieving around the Stockholm *Tunnelbana* stations in the 1950s (Hall 1987, 1998). Owens also points out that district heating systems are viable at moderate densities of 30–37 dwellings per hectare; on a greenfield site this break-even density would be even lower, particularly if land uses can be made heterogeneous.

The Netherlands have taken a worldwide lead in trying to integrate land-use and transport planning, within an environmental strategy, at a national level. The fourth report (EXTRA) on Physical Planning in the Netherlands (Netherlands, 1991) identified a policy that aims to cope with growth pressures and to improve the quality of urban life and reduce car traffic in cities and urban regions, through an integrated approach encompassing traffic and transport policy, environmental policy and physical planning policy. The key is to concentrate residences, work areas and amenities so as to produce the shortest possible trip distances, most being possible by bicycle and public transport. So housing sites are being sought first in the inner cities, next on the urban periphery and only as a third option at more distant locations; wherever the sites are found, availability of public transport will be a key factor. Businesses and amenities are planned by relating their user requirements to location features. Those activities involving a large number of workers or visitors per hectare, such as offices oriented to the general public, theatres and museums, are rated A-profile, that is they should be located close to city-centre stations. B-locations are those with both good station access and good access to motorways, making them suitable for access by both car and public transport; activities suitable for location here include hospitals, research and development, and white collar industry. C-locations, close to motorways, are suitable only for activities with relatively few workers and visitors per hectare and with a need for high accessibility by car or truck. Associated with this, the Report calls for integrated transport/land-use planning so as to enhance the role of public transport, including restrictions on long-term parking places, associated with the provision of good public transport.

Michael Breheny and Ralph Rookwood have given some theoretical illustrations of how sustainability would be developed at different scales and in different geographical contexts (Breheny and Rookwood, 1993). All of them feature settlements of different sizes, strung like beads on a string along public transport corridors, which range from bus routes up to heavy rail systems (figure 3.1). Again, there is a very strong similarity to what Danish and Swedish planners were attempting in the 1950s and 1960s.

More recent work, financed by the Economic and Social Research Council, is more empirical. Peter Headicar and Carey Curtis at Oxford Brookes University looked at a crucial question: whether, in terms of car dependence, it matters where you put new suburban development (Headicar and Curtis, 1998). They

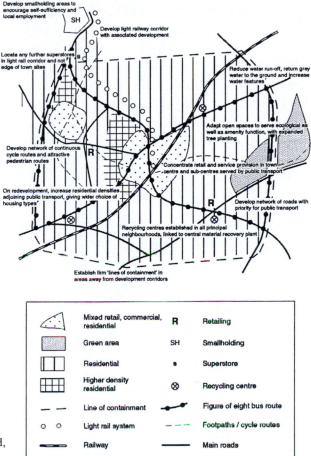

Develop smallholding areas to encourage self-sufficiency and local employment

Develop light railway corridor with associated development

Locate any further superstores in light rail corridor and not at edge of town sites

Reduce water run-off, return grey water to the ground and increase water features

Adapt open spaces to serve ecological as well as amenity function, with expanded tree planting

Develop network of continuous cycle routes and attractive pedestrian routes

Concentrate retail and service provision in town centre and sub-centres served by public transport

On redevelopment, increase residential densities adjoining public transport, giving wider choice of housing types

Develop network of roads with priority for public transport

Recycling centres established in all principal neighbourhoods, linked to central material recovery plant

Establish firm 'lines of containment' in areas away from development corridors

Mixed retail, commercial, residential	**R**	Retailing
Green area	SH	Smallholding
Residential	s	Superstore
Higher density residential	⊗	Recycling centre
— — Line of containment	—•—	Figure of eight bus route
o o Light rail system	— – –	Footpaths / cycle routes
▬▬▬ Railway	▬▬▬	Main roads

Figure 3.1. How sustainability might be developed for small towns and new communities. (*Source*: Breheny and Rockwood, 1993, figure 9.7)

conclude that it very much does. If you put new suburbs close to big towns and on corridors with good public transport, like Botley and Kidlington outside Oxford, even then most people moving out of the city to these places commuted by car before the move and even more did so afterwards; but fewer did so before, and do so after the move, than people who moved into smaller country towns like Bicester and Witney, farther away from Oxford. And at Didcot, located on a good rail line, more people used the train – though even there, four in five commuted by car. In terms of total car usage, miles per week, the near-in suburbs of Kidlington and Botley generated the least travel, the more distant towns of Bicester and Witney generated two to three times as much; of the three country towns Didcot generated the least car travel, close to the Botley total, and the biggest amount of rail travel. These differences, the researchers concluded, are linked not just with size and density, but with location within a broader sub-region. The policy implication seems to be this: it is best to locate developments on strong public transport corridors, close to medium-sized towns that will continue to provide the main sources of employment, and rail corridors offer particularly good prospects.

From America we have some interesting ideas from Peter Calthorpe, a Californian English émigré architect-planner (figure 3.2). He proposes walking-scale suburban developments around public transport stops, clustering some job and service opportunities at the nodes, and with high-density single-family housing built in traditional terraces with street parking. His concept, which he calls Transit-Oriented Development (TOD) (Calthorpe, 1993) bears an astonishing physical resemblance to the ideas of Breheny and Rookwood, developed independently and published in the same year. Californians seem to like it; he has developed whole neighbourhoods in San Jose, the capital city of Silicon Valley, and his ideas have now been made a mandatory part of the General Plan for the state capital of Sacramento.

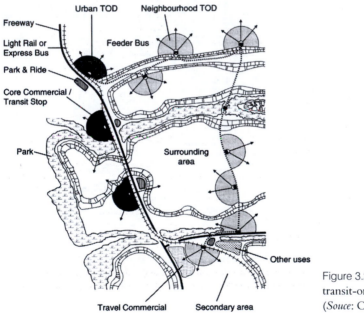

Figure 3.2. Peter Calthorpe's transit-oriented development. (*Souce*: Calthorpe, 1993)

The definitive review of research on the relationship between transport and urban form comes from David Banister (Banister, 2005). He concludes:

> Underlying much of this debate and the empirical evidence is a lack of detailed analysis. Much of the thinking has been constrained by convention with protagonists being seen as favouring intervention through planning and other controls, or favouring technological fixes, or allowing much greater freedom for the market to operate. As usual, reality is more complex and requires a combination of approaches, not just one. Also, the approaches used may not be compatible and lead to counter intuitive results. (Banister, 2005, p. 124)

Many of the studies have been severely limited by the amount and the quality of available data. The results are not necessarily precise but indicative, and this has made comparison of results difficult. And the results very often appear contradictory (table 3.1). Nevertheless, Banister finds that six reasonably robust conclusions emerge from this mass of research.

Table 3.1 Summary of differences in research findings.

Resident Population Size: dispute as to whether population size impacts on modal choice, travel distance and energy consumption.
♦ No correlation between urban population size and modal choice in the US (Gordon *et al.*, 1989).
♦ The largest settlements (>250,000 population) display lower travel distances and less by car (ECOTEC, 1993).
♦ The most energy efficient settlement in terms of transport is one with a resident population size of 25,000–100,000 or 250,000 plus (Banister, 1997).

Resident Population Density: dispute as to whether increasing densities impact on modal choice, travel distance and energy consumption. Various conclusions as to the optimum urban form in reducing car travel; ranging from compact cities to 'decentralized concentration' and even low density suburban spread.
♦ Increasing densities reduces energy consumption by transport (Newman and Kenworthy, 1989).
♦ There is no clear relationship between the proportion of car trips and population density in the US (Gordon *et al*, 1989).
♦ As densities increase, modal split moves towards greater use of rail and bus (Banister *et al.*, 1997).
♦ Compact cities may not necessarily be the answer to reducing energy consumption, due to effects of congestion, also decentralization may reduce trip length (Breheny, 1997, 2001; Gordon and Richardson, 1997).
♦ 'Decentralized concentration' is the most efficient urban form in reducing car travel (Jenks *et al.*, 1996).
♦ Density is the most important physical variable in determining transport energy consumption (Banister *et al.*, 1997).
♦ Higher densities may provide a necessary, but not sufficient condition for less travel (Owens, 1986).
♦ As people move from big dense cities to small less dense towns they travel more by car, but the distances may be shorter (Hall, 1998*b*).

Provision and Mix of Services: dispute as to whether local provision of services and facilities impacts on modal choice, travel distance and energy consumption.
♦ Local provision does not determine modal choice. Personal and household characteristics are the main determinants (Farthing *et al.*, 1997).
♦ Diversity of services and facilities in close proximity reduces distance travelled, alters modal split and people are prepared to travel further for higher order services and facilities (Banister, 1996).

Location: dispute as to impact of location – in terms of distance from urban centre, strategic transport network and influence of green belt – on modal choice, travel distance and energy consumption.
♦ Location of new housing development outside existing urban areas, or close to strategic transport network, or as free-standing development increases travel and influences mode split (Headicar and Curtis, 1998).
♦ Location is an important determinant of energy consumption and car dependency (Banister *et al.*, 1997).
♦ Development close to existing urban areas reduces self-containment and access to non-car owners (Headicar, 1996).
♦ Urban design quality: some anecdotal evidence in the US showing the differential impact of the new urbanist versus cul-de-sac route networks on travel behaviour. Some initial evidence in the UK from Marshall (2001).

Socio-Economic Characteristics: dispute as to impact of personal and household characteristics on modal choice, travel distance and energy consumption. Also as to whether personal and household characteristics are more important determinants of travel than land-use characteristics.
♦ Trip frequency increases with household size, income and car ownership (Hanson, 1982).
♦ Travel distance, proportion of car journeys and transport energy consumption increases with car ownership (Naess and Sandberg, 1996; Naess *et al.*, 1995).
♦ Dual-income households: assessment of how the choice of new housing location is influenced by the location of two workplaces, extent of 'excess travel' and reasons behind it, role of travel factor in choice of location of new home. No research known.
♦ Surrounding mobility levels: impact of the surrounding level of mobility on travel behaviour in terms of mode choice, journey to work length and energy consumption. Some anecdotal evidence in the US. No known assessment in the UK.
♦ Attitude: some research in California as to the impact on travel behaviour. No known assessment in the UK.

Source: Banister, 2005, pp. 125–126, based on Hickman and Banister, 2002.

First, new development, particularly housing, should be of a substantial size and located near to or within existing settlements with a total population of at least 25,000 and probably nearer to 50,000. Local facilities and services should be phased to encourage local travel patterns.

Secondly, journey lengths by car are relatively constant (12 km) at densities over 15 persons per hectare, but at lower densities car journey lengths increase by up to 35 per cent. Similarly, as density increases, the number of trips by car decreases from 72 per cent of all journeys to 51 per cent. Car use in high-density locations is half that in the lowest-density locations.

Thirdly, the larger the settlement size, the shorter the trips and the greater the proportion of trips by public transport. Diseconomies of size appear for the largest conurbations, as trip lengths increase to accommodate the complex structures of these cities.

Fourthly, linked with the reasons above, mixed-use developments should reduce trip lengths and car dependence. Although research here is limited and concentrates on work journeys, there is considerable potential for enhancing the proximity of housing to all types of facilities and services.

Fifthly, development should be located near public transport interchanges and corridors so that high levels of accessibility for all can be provided. But this may also encourage long distance commuting.

Finally, availability of parking is a key determinant of whether a car is used or not. Overall, the availability of the car and other socio-economic variables are the two most important factors in determining travel demand and mode choice, explaining about 70–80 per cent of the variation. Land-use factors explain the remaining 20–30 per cent of the variation and provide the main ways whereby policy interventions can influence sustainable development, particularly when combined with actions in the transport sector (Banister, 2005, pp. 124–125).

Soon after the Banister review, a major research project, conducted in five UK universities and funded by the EPSRC (Engineering and Physical Sciences Research Council), reported a remarkable, even a sensational, conclusion. SOLUTIONS (the Sustainability of Land Use and Transport In Outer Neighbourhoods) reported that spatial strategies by themselves could make little difference to the level of greenhouse gas emissions over the next 20 years (Echenique *et al.*, 2009, 2010). Even when land-use and transport measures were combined with road pricing, the impacts were still overwhelmed by long-term social and economic trends, which make people more prone to want more spacious homes and more travel. The implication was that planning policies aimed at mitigating climate change – such as the compact city strategy – were misguided and indeed in some ways counterproductive.

The SOLUTIONS researchers looked at two regions: the wider South East around London, and Tyne and Wear. In both, they looked at three alternative scenarios: compact city, Richard Rogers-style; market-led dispersal, American-fashion; and planned expansion on the garden city model. They found that in the South East, a compact city would cut energy use and CO_2 emissions by just 1 per cent – but overall, costs would rise because of housing shortages in the outer areas where demand is greatest, and there would be more crowding and exposure to traffic noise. American-style sprawl would raise energy and CO_2 emissions by 2 per cent, but there would be gains in lower house prices and congestion, plus less crowding. A garden city solution would have effects somewhere in between, and might represent the best compromise – but again, in percentage terms the effects are minuscule.

But in 2011, key members of the research team caused a parallel sensation when they wrote an article strongly criticizing these conclusions (Barton *et al.*, 2011). They had been based on only one element of the research, a broad-based land-use-transport model, which ignored the findings of parallel research (which they had conducted) into local, neighbourhood patterns of behaviour; and the mainstream modelling work incorporated debatable assumptions.

The other part of the work, the local studies, was based on a household survey questionnaire in twelve contrasting localities across four cities, including suburbs, recent urban extensions and commuter settlements around London, Newcastle upon Tyne, Bristol and Cambridge. The results showed a surprisingly wide range of behaviour across different neighbourhoods: the level of car dependence varied from four in five trips in Broxbourne (82 per cent) to just over a third in Cherry Hinton (35 per cent). In parallel, the proportion of walking/cycling trips ranged from 18 per cent to 62 per cent. This behavioural variety within suburbs is not widely recognized, and LUTI (land-use/transport interaction) studies do not allow for it.

The explanations, the authors argued, are far from straightforward. In general, a powerful explanatory factor appeared to be the spatial characteristics of the neighbourhood, including the location and viability of available facilities. However, there was no simple spatial variable accounting for differences. The most frequently cited variable – residential density – had, in fact, a very poor correlation with modal choice. The more influential variables were location, neighbourhood coherence, degree of integration with the city, and permeable route networks. In relation to location, for example, the newer peripheral estates were more car-dependent than both the older suburbs and the more mixed-age urban fringe areas. This does not bode well for new urban extensions. The behavioural differences between places are strongly related to their spatial characteristics in terms of location within the city-region, the size of local facilities like shops, and local urban form.

A second component of the local research was a design-led exploration of alternative neighbourhood forms in eight of the twelve localities. This showed that alternative neighbourhood designs can profoundly affect the pattern of accessibility and therefore both social inclusion and the likelihood of active travel, with its health benefits. So, the researchers argued, 'while the modellers may claim to predict the limited significance of land use/transport planning (for carbon emissions) if nothing changes, over a relatively short timescale and at a strategic scale, they cannot thereby conclude that land use/transport planning has limited significance overall' (Barton *et al.*, 2011, p. 344).

On the contrary, other studies show that integrated land-use and transport planning is an essential part of a sustainability strategy which also includes fiscal and technological innovation. One of the weaknesses of the case made in the SOLUTIONS final report, they argued, is just this lack of comparator and contextual studies – which had been the essence of the Banister review.

In 2012 the Committee on Climate Change presented further evidence, suggesting that large and densely populated cities with more frequent bus services and homes in close proximity to bus stops and other amenities are associated with lower levels of car travel. This is apparent in transport emissions data for major English cities, which show variation in transport emissions per capita. They recommended that planning and transport policy should aim to focus new developments within existing cities and large towns, and/or those that are well served by public transport which could result in significant emissions reductions (Committee on Climate Change, 2012, p. 46). The Committee's evidence (figure 3.3) is clear that the best-performing places in this respect are

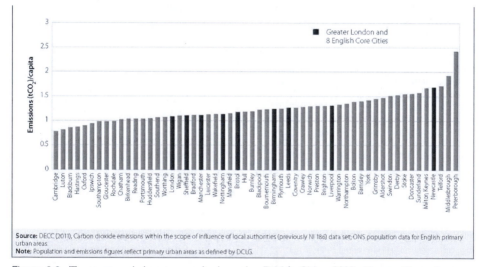

Figure 3.3. Transport emissions per capita in major British Cities, 2009. (*Source*: Committee on Climate Change, 2012, p. 47)

not only the larger cities and some northern English places with low car owner-ship (Blackburn, Rochdale, Birkenhead), but also a large number of relatively prosperous medium-sized places in southern England – Cambridge, Luton, Oxford, Ipswich, Southampton, Gloucester, Chatham and Reading outstanding among them. These surely provide models for what could be done more widely. The Committee notes that the opportunity to limit transport emissions through siting of new development is recognized in the 2012 National Planning

Policy Framework (NPPF), which recommends that new developments which generate significant movement should be located where the need to travel will be minimized (e.g. avoiding out-of-town retail developments) and where the use of sustainable transport modes can be maximized. (*Ibid.*, p. 47).

Resolving the Dilemma: Learning from Best-Practice Places

A few places around the world, especially but not exclusively in Europe, are finding imaginative and innovative ways of meeting these challenges, providing innovative examples of sustainable urban transport for the twenty-first-century mega-city region. To an extraordinary degree, the most interesting examples are concentrated in a few relatively small 'learning regions' of Europe, and in a few other places across the world, where cities and regions seem to be engaged in a mutual process of innovation, imitation and improvement. In Europe, three of the most notable are the two great Scandinavian city-regions of Stockholm and Copenhagen-Malmö; the tri-national urban region that embraces the province of Baden in southwest Germany, Alsace across the Rhine in eastern France, and Basel in Switzerland; the remarkable polycentric urban region of Randstad Holland, which incorporates the four leading Dutch cities of Amsterdam, Utrecht, Rotterdam and the Hague, together with the smaller cities of Delft, Leiden and Haarlem as well as Almere, the fast-growing satellite city east of Amsterdam; and, a more scattered but coherent example, the major French cities like Strasbourg, Grenoble, Montpellier and Lille, which are developing new models of combined transport/land-use planning that integrate new tramway networks with regional rail systems. These regions and their cities are innovative in multiple ways – but nowhere more so than in urban transport. In Part Two, we travel to each of them to discover how they achieved it.

Note

1.   Hence the Americanism, to this day: 'pass down the *cars*, please'.

4 | The Fourth Challenge: Living with Finite Resources

Less than half a century ago, planners did not worry about natural resources. The word sustainability had not entered the popular vocabulary. Climate change was unheard of. The world's resources appeared almost infinitely capable of supporting economic growth and increasingly affluent lifestyles. That began to change in 1972 when the Club of Rome, a self-appointed group, published *Limits to Growth*, setting out hitherto-unthinkable forecasts about the world's future; exponential population growth and consumption, the Report argued, had already outstripped the world's carrying capacity (Meadows *et al.*, 1972). Thirty-two years after that some of the same authors suggested that with the world's population set to rise from 4 billion to 7 billion, the limits had already been overshot and the planet faced catastrophe (Meadows *et al.*, 2004). In the four decades since *Limits to Growth* was published, ideas such as a city's ecological footprint, the effects of carbon emissions on global warming, and the impact of climate change have entered popular discourse and have changed radically our thinking about development (Wacknernagel and Rees, 1996).

This chapter analyses the present record and future prospects for sustainable development in the United Kingdom, particularly in comparison with other member states of the European Union, whose environmental standards and targets are binding on all. It relies heavily on official sources, some governmental, some from independent scientific bodies, summarizing the achievement so far, the future targets and the obstacles in reaching them, and the governmental actions designed to achieve a stable environmental future over the decades to 2030 and beyond.

The starting point is a progress report from the Adaptation Sub-Committee of the UK government's independent Committee on Climate Change, published in 2011. It found that the UK is coping with the current climate, but that even now some sectors – such as water supply – are near their limits. Vulnerability to climate change is potentially increasing as a result of patterns of development in some areas and demographic trends such as the ageing population. There are minor low-regret actions that could be taken now to reduce that vulnerability – for example measures to improve water efficiency, reduce damage to buildings from flooding, and protect buildings from overheating in summer. These measures would save householders money today. However, the Sub-Committee found little evidence that people were adopting such measures, particularly in existing homes. They also found that climate risks were not being fully incorporated into major strategic decisions, such as land-use planning and investment in water infrastructure. Embedding climate change more fully into decision-making could reduce future costs, such as building new flood defences and maintaining existing defences, and also ensure that climate risks are appropriately balanced against other risks and benefits (Committee on Climate Change, 2011a, p. 8).

The First Sustainability Challenge: Energy

The UK is fully committed to an EU Directive on Renewable Energy (2009/28/EC), implemented in December 2010, which sets ambitious short-term targets for all Member States: they must ensure that, by 2020, 20 per cent of all energy will come from renewable sources and that 10 per cent of energy in the transport sector will come from renewable sources. British electricity suppliers are now required by law to provide a proportion of their sales from renewable sources such as wind power or pay a penalty fee.

But the UK performs far from impressively in comparison with its neighbours: its targets are modest and it has not succeeded in reaching them (table 4.1). One commentator has written that 'The UK is tiptoeing towards an energy cliff. The country's ageing nuclear and coal-fired power stations are nearing the end of their lives and will have to be decommissioned in the next two decades. A plan on how to fill the potential black hole is becoming increasingly urgent' (Cook, 2013, p. 17).

The UK cannot offer the excuse that it lacks potential: it has the best wind, wave and tidal resources in Europe. And recently, it has dramatically begun to exploit them. At the beginning of 2013, its installed wind power capacity was 8,445 MW, with 362 operational wind farms and 4,158 wind turbines; it ranks as the world's eighth largest producer of wind power. Wind power is the second largest source of renewable energy after biomass. 1.8 GW of new wind power

Table 4.1. Share of renewable energy (in % of gross final energy consumption).

Country	2006	2007	2008	2009	2010	2020 target
EU27*	9.0	9.9	10.5	11.7	12.4	20.0
Austria	26.6	28.9	29.2	31.0	30.1	34.0
Belgium	2.7	3.0	3.3	4.6	–	13.0
Bulgaria	9.6	9.3	9.8	11.9	13.8	16.0
Czech Republic	6.5	7.4	7.6	8.5	9.2	13.0
Denmark	16.5	18.0	18.8	20.2	22.2	30.0
Germany	6.9	9.0	9.1	9.5	11.0	18.0
Estonia	16.1	17.1	18.9	23.0	24.3	25.0
Ireland	2.9	3.3	3.9	5.1	5.5	16.0
Greece	7.0	8.1	8.0	8.1	9.2	18.0
Spain	9.0	9.5	10.6	12.8	13.8	20.0
France**	9.6	10.2	11.1	11.9	–	23.0
Italy	5.8	5.7	7.1	8.9	10.1	17.0
Cyprus	2.5	3.1	4.1	4.6	4.8	13.0
Latvia	31.1	29.6	29.8	34.3	32.6	40.0
Lithuania	16.9	16.6	17.9	20.0	19.7	23.0
Luxembourg	1.4	2.7	2.8	2.8	2.8	11.0
Hungary	5.1	5.9	6.6	8.1	–	13.0
Malta	0.2	0.2	0.2	0.2	0.4	10.0
Netherlands	2.7	3.1	3.4	4.1	3.8	14.0
Poland	7.0	7.0	7.9	8.9	9.4	15.0
Portugal	20.8	22.0	23.0	24.6	24.6	31.0
Romania	17.1	18.3	20.3	22.4	23.4	24.0
Slovenia	15.5	15.6	15.1	18.9	19.8	25.0
Slovakia	6.6	8.2	8.4	10.4	9.8	14.0
Finland	29.9	29.5	31.1	31.1	32.2	38.0
Sweden	42.7	44.2	45.2	48.1	47.9	49.0
United Kingdom	1.5	1.8	2.3	2.9	3.2	15.0

Source: Eurostat, 2011.
Notes: * EU27 aggregate contains estimates of missing data.
** France métropolitaine, excluding the four overseas departments (French Guyana, Guadeloupe, Martinique and Réunion).
– Data not available.

capacity was brought online during 2012, a 30 per cent increase in the total UK installed capacity, including four large offshore wind farms with over 1.1 GW of generating capability. By 2020, the United Kingdom is expected to have more than 28,000 MW of wind capacity.

The government's *UK Renewable Energy Roadmap*, covering the short term to 2020, showed that together, onshore and offshore wind provide enough power for more than two and a half million homes. And renewable energy already employs more than a quarter of a million people; by 2020, this could rise to over half a million (DECC, 2011*b*, pp. 4–5). But the government accepts that much more could be done. Though the UK is starting from a low level, it can still meet the target to deliver 20 per cent of energy consumption from renewable sources by 2020. Renewable electricity is well established, and can deliver 29

GW of operational capacity. Renewable heat is less well developed, but following the introduction of the world's first incentive scheme it could deliver 124,000 renewable heat installations. Road transport biofuels represent over 3 per cent by volume of road transport fuels and are proposed to increase to 5 per cent by 2014, with planned increase after that. The challenge is to bring costs down and deployment up. (*Ibid.*, pp. 5–6).

The government's policy focuses on eight technologies that could deliver more than 90 per cent of the renewable energy target for 2020 in a cost-effective and sustainable way, or offer great potential in following decades (*Ibid.*). For each, there are key actions:

◆ *Onshore wind:* Provide long-term certainty for investors through electricity market reform. Co-fund technical solutions to overcome wind farm interference with aviation radar.

◆ *Offshore wind:* Establish a Task Force to reduce the costs of offshore wind to £100/MWh by 2020. Provide up to £30m of direct government support over the next 4 years. Ensure timely development of the grid.

◆ *Marine energy:* Provide up to £20m over the next 4 years to support innovation in wave and tidal devices.

◆ *Biomass electricity:* Publish a UK Bioenergy Strategy, and apply a year ahead of the original timetable. Focus on measures to support long-term waste fuel supplies.

◆ *Biomass heat:* Increase the attractiveness of biomass heat and biomethane injection into the grid through introduction of a Renewable Heat Incentive (RHI) and the Renewable Heat Premium Payment (RHPP).

◆ *Ground source and air source heat pumps:* Introduce incentives for both domestic and non-domestic heat pumps.

◆ *Transport:* Support plug-in vehicles by making up to £30m available for investment in recharging infrastructure and providing a grant of up to 25 per cent of the purchase price (capped at £5,000) for eligible electric, plug-in hybrid or hydrogen fuel cell cars.

The medium- to long-term strategy is to enable all these technologies to compete on a level playing field, without additional support, against other low-carbon technologies (such as solar power) (*Ibid.*, p. 7).

The *Roadmap* accompanied a major government White Paper for the development of energy supplies over the longer term down to 2030 (DECC,

2011*a*, para. 2, p. 5). This admits that over the next two decades the UK faces an unprecedented set of challenges:

◆   By 2020 around a quarter (around 20 GW) of existing electricity generation capacity will be lost, as old or more polluting plant closes, critically reducing capacity and increasing the risk of blackouts. Future electricity generation will include more intermittent generation (such as wind) and inflexible generation (such as nuclear), introducing additional challenges to meeting demand at all times – for example, when the wind does not blow.

◆   Action must be taken now to transform the UK permanently into a low-carbon economy and meet a 20 per cent renewable energy target by 2020 and an 80 per cent carbon reduction target by 2050. To achieve the latter, power sector emissions need to be largely decarbonized by the 2030s; otherwise, in 2030 the electricity sector will generate over three times the emissions advised by the Climate Change Committee.

◆   Despite improvements in household and non-domestic energy efficiency, overall demand for electricity may double by 2050, due to the electrification of the transport, heating and other carbon-intensive sectors.

◆   Increases in wholesale costs, the carbon price and environmental policies are likely to lead to higher bills, even without factoring in the huge investment needed in new infrastructure. This makes it critical to reform the system (*Ibid.*, para. 3, pp. 5–6). Current market arrangements, the White Paper says, will not meet these challenges. Up to £110 billion of investment in electricity generation and transmission is likely to be required by 2020, more than double the current rate.

In addition, current arrangements do not meet the challenges of decarbonization and security of supply:

◆   The current market price for electricity is driven by fossil plant, with much lower fixed costs – relative to their operational costs – compared with nuclear or offshore wind.

◆   New low-carbon generators often have to overcome high barriers to market entry, in the form of construction costs and market illiquidity. Small and independent producers are particularly affected by the risk of not being able to find long-term buyers for their electricity.

◆   The social cost of carbon is not fully reflected in the market price, which does not take into account all of the damage caused by climate change.

◆ The capacity and appetite of existing market participants to finance the unprecedented necessary investment is uncertain (*Ibid.*, para. 4, pp. 5–6).

In September 2012, the Committee on Climate Change – chaired by the former Conservative minister John Gummer – took the unprecedented step of sending an open letter to ministers criticising the 'apparently ambivalent position of the Government' about whether to commit to new zero-carbon electricity generation or to build new gas power stations as replacements for Britain's ageing coal-burning power stations. The committee added that the mixed signals from the government risked putting off investment in renewables. The Chancellor of the Exchequer, George Osborne, is well known to oppose spending on renewables or nuclear power generation, preferring a 'dash for gas'. But he faces fierce private opposition from the Liberal Democrats who have warned that any dilution of current proposals to subsidize renewable generation to make production economically viable will result in Britain breaching its legally binding carbon reduction commitments. They are pushing for the government to adopt a new legally binding commitment, specifying how much carbon can be produced through electricity generation by 2030, as a way of spurring investment in renewables. But this is being blocked by the Treasury (Wright and Cooper, 2012).

The outcome was a strange contradiction. The Energy Bill, introduced into Parliament in November 2012, is designed to meet the White Paper targets, by providing incentives to replace large old coal-fired plants and old nuclear power

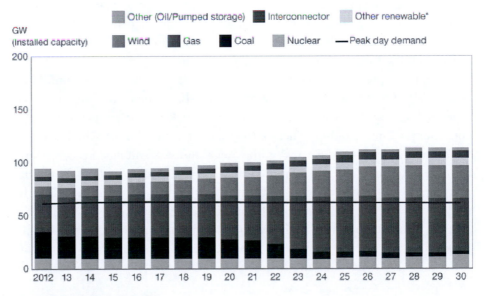

*Marine/Hydro/Biomass/Solar PV
Source: National Grid

Figure 4.1. This scenario shows how the mix of electricity sources changes where developments in renewable and low carbon energy are slow and targets are missed. Gas fills the gap left by coal. Demand is expected to fall as economic growth is slow. (*Source*: http://www.bbc.co.uk/news/business-20458326)

plants by wind and nuclear power, as well as other forms of clean energy such as biomass – and to make the UK more self-sufficient in energy (figure 4.1). It proposes to offer investors in low-carbon energy projects – renewables, carbon capture and storage, and nuclear – long-term deals, known as 'Contracts for Difference' (CFD), under which they would be paid compensation if the market price of electricity falls below a price set by the government. CFDs are intended to provide long-term price stability for developers of – and investors in – these projects (Cook, 2013, p. 17). But this could create a highly volatile situation, especially over a period of about eighteen months while the new regime is being set up (*Ibid.*, p. 19).

There is disagreement on exactly what this will cost the consumer. The government has told energy companies that by 2020, they can add a total of £7.6bn to household bills to help pay for all the new capacity – roughly about the same as the UK currently spends on importing gas. The government says that bills to help pay for clean energy projects will rise from £20 extra per year in 2012, to £95 in 2020. The Committee on Climate Change says they will rise by £110, although this figure includes £10 for energy efficiency measures. The government says that, overall, the new policies will reduce bills by £94 a year on average by 2020, through energy efficiency and less reliance on expensive gas. (Rising gas prices added about £100 to the average bill between March 2011 and March 2012, according to Ofgem. And the International Energy Agency has forecast natural gas prices to rise by 40 per cent by 2020, even with an influx of cheap shale gas.) The Committee on Climate Change agrees that bills would be higher without significant investment in clean energy. It is possible, therefore, that the Energy Bill, together with other measures to reduce carbon emissions, will actually save consumers money in the long run.

The major problem is the length of time needed to build new wind farms and nuclear power stations. For example, the UK's largest onshore wind farm – Scout Moor in the North West of England – took 8 years simply to get from concept to commissioning. There is also the vital question of whether power companies are prepared to invest the huge sums of money needed. Some commentators have already suggested the Energy Bill does not go far enough and does not provide the long-term certainty that is a pre-requisite for heavy investment. Ultimately, of course, the government is not going to let the lights go out. If investment falls short and not enough clean energy capacity is built, it will have to resort to short-term measures, such as building new gas plants, that can be constructed relatively quickly, or simply import more energy from overseas (BBC, 2012).

So the Bill is supplemented by a Gas Strategy, published in December, which 're-emphasizes' conventional energy generation, notably gas and nuclear (Cook, 2013, pp. 17). New gas-fired power stations will be needed to supply 26GW of energy, equivalent to 29 per cent of the UK's entire power plant capacity, in part to replace older coal, oil and nuclear plants (*Ibid.*). This of course was exactly what the letter from the Committee on Climate Change was seeking to stop. And, at the time of writing, the outcome is extremely uncertain.

Meanwhile, Alistair Buchanan, the outgoing chief executive of regulator Ofgem, has calculated that delays in the nuclear rebuild and the offshore wind programme will mean that the share of gas in power generation will not fall from 40 to 20–30 per cent as originally intended, but actually increase to no less than 60 per cent by 2020. Shale gas, where prospects look promising, will not come significantly on stream until some time after that. So the share of gas will rise just as supplies across Europe will be tightening, inevitably increasing bills to the consumer. Richard Lambert, a former editor of the *Financial Times* and an energy expert, blames this on dithering by a series of government ministers (Lambert, 2013).

And this uncertainty has had a negative effect on investment in green technologies, according to the EEF manufacturers' association. They show that manufacturing's share of low-carbon goods and services shrank marginally in 2011–2012, while China, India, South Korea and the USA showed double-digit industrial growth. 'We are currently failing to take advantage of this opportunity to be a world leader in low-carbon goods and services', they argue (Groom, 2013*a*).

The Role of Local Actions

Clearly, these actions will be driven by government in close interaction with private-sector producers, and will generate impacts nationally across the country. But the Committee on Climate Change has responded to a ministerial request to consider how local government could generate impacts at a local level.

The key messages in their report are:

◆ Local authorities have scope to influence emissions in buildings, surface transport, and waste, together accounting for 40 per cent of UK greenhouse gas emissions, reducing emissions by 20 per cent in 2020 from 2010 levels. The biggest opportunity is in residential buildings, but opportunities also exist in non-residential buildings, sustainable transport and waste management (Committee on Climate Change, 2012, p. 8).

◆ Local authorities can support power sector decarbonization through planning approval for onshore wind projects and supporting investment in electric vehicle charging infrastructure.

◆ Local authorities should draw up low-carbon plans to achieve a 20 per cent reduction across buildings, surface transport and waste by 2020 relative to 2010 levels, focusing on elements over which they have influence (e.g. number of homes insulated, car miles travelled).

♦   The government should seriously consider additional funding (e.g. for local authorities to be Green Deal providers/partners, and to roll out sustainable travel programmes) and/or introducing a statutory duty for local authorities to develop and implement low-carbon plans (*Ibid.*, p. 9).

In particular, the Committee stresses, local authorities have key levers in their planning powers. It is particularly important that they use these levers to enforce energy efficiency standards in new buildings and extensions; reduce transport emissions by concentrating new developments in existing cities and large towns and/or ensuring they are well served by public transport; work with developers to make renewable energy projects acceptable to local communities; plan for infrastructure such as low-carbon district heating networks, green infrastructure and sustainable drainage systems; and locate new development in areas of lowest flood risk.

Local authorities can also play a unique role in developing and making district heating schemes commercially viable. In the UK, although district heating has been used since the 1950s, it currently only provides a very small proportion (approximately 2 per cent) of total heat demand, with many schemes abandoned in favour of individual heating systems. Where it has succeeded, it has brought benefits of lower heating costs – reflecting the relatively high efficiency of CHP plants – and carbon savings, in particular where district heating has been supplied by low-carbon fuels or where it replaced electric heating. Cities in Scandinavia and Germany (see table 4.2) have performed sensationally better

Table 4.2. District heating in Scandinavian and German cities.

♦   *Malmö:* The 550 km district heating network – originally owned by the municipality and now by E.ON – supplies 95 per cent of buildings in district heating areas. The fuel mix supporting the system has changed substantially since the 1950s, from oil and coal to energy-from-waste, surplus heat from industry, natural gas CHP and large biomass boilers. Approximately 65 per cent of district heating is supplied from renewable sources.

♦   *Gothenburg:* The district heating network, owned by energy company Göteborg Energi, extends over a length of 700 km, and provides heating for more than 90 per cent of all blocks of flats and commercial premises, and 20 per cent of all houses. In 2008, the energy used for district heating output was 81 per cent waste heat (including from refuse incineration, refineries and other industries), 15 per cent renewables and 4 per cent fossil fuel. Current plans include a major effort to produce biogas through the gasification of forestry waste.

♦   *Copenhagen:* The municipally-owned district heating system now covers more than 98 per cent of heating demand in Copenhagen through a 1,500 km network supplied mainly by CHP plants and waste incineration. In 2008 the fuel mix in the heat production was 41 per cent gas, 19 per cent coal, 33 per cent biomass and waste incineration, 7 per cent oil. Current plans include replacing coal with renewable energy.

♦   *Munich:* Owned by the local authority, Munich's 800 km district heating network supplies heat from gas-fired CHP (70 per cent), coal-fired CHP and energy from waste. The network is being expanded by a further 100 km and by 2040 aims to operate on 100 per cent renewable sources (primarily geothermal heat, with some biogas).

♦   *Flensburg:* This German town on the border of Denmark has the highest connection rate to district heating anywhere, with 98 per cent of buildings supplied with heat from the 80 per cent efficient central CHP plant. Until 2007, the plant was exclusively coal-fired but is now co-firing with up to 25 per cent waste-derived fuel and wood chips. The municipally owned energy company has committed to switch the heat network to 100 per cent renewable energy by 2050 (Committee on Climate Change, 2012, p. 41).

Source: Committee on Climate Change, 2012, p. 40.

in this regard (*Ibid.*, p. 41). In future, however, district heat based on gas-fired CHP will be incompatible with meeting long-term emissions reduction targets. Therefore, the focus should be on low-carbon sources of heat, from bioenergy or waste heat from low-carbon power generation – especially the latter. But there are difficulties. New low-carbon power stations would need to be located within reasonable connection distances to thermal heat demand to avoid prohibitively long connections, and this may evoke public opposition. Investors may be reluctant to raise the high capital cost unless they see a degree of certainty that demand will be there. And there would need to be transmission pipelines – a challenge in terms of the distances and the number of connections, requiring the digging up of many roads. Further assessment, the Committee concludes, will be required. Meanwhile, local authorities should focus on using heat from local sources of bioenergy (especially waste) (*Ibid.*, p. 42).

The Second Sustainability Challenge: Housing

More than a quarter of Britain's total energy consumption goes into homes – a larger fraction than is used by business, and about the same as road transport. Despite widespread uptake of central heating and increased ownership and use of appliances, energy use per household has fallen by 16 per cent since 1970. But this efficiency improvement has been more than offset by a growth in the number of households (some 7 million more), so overall energy use in homes has increased by 17 per cent. The fuel mix for generating electricity in Britain has changed radically since 1970 – with coal-fired power displaced by electricity from natural gas and an increasing contribution from renewable electricity (Palmer and Cooper, 2011, p. 53).

The forecast is that energy use will continue to rise. More homes mean more energy use and more CO_2 emissions, unless offset by energy efficiency improvements to existing homes – as already discussed in Chapter 2. And although smaller homes for smaller households tend to use less energy, there seems to be a minimum 'base load', unrelated to household size or floor area. Finally, the growth in detached homes with proportionately larger areas of external walls increases heat loss in winter compared to terraced houses or flats (*Ibid.*).

Energy bills for households have fallen overall in real terms since 1970, although they rose from 2003 to 2008. Energy spending also fell in relation to total household spending – on average from 6 per cent of weekly expenditure in 1970 to just 4 per cent today. As some households become richer over time, they spend a smaller fraction of their incomes on energy than poorer ones. This will affect the way people respond to incentives (*Ibid.*, p. 54).

But homes with central heating tend to use much more energy – often twice as much – because households heat the whole of their home, instead of just one or two rooms. This increase would have been even greater but for improved insulation and boiler efficiency in most existing homes. And in recent years there has been a significant reduction in energy used for heating: down by 10 per cent since 2004. This does not seem to be due to milder winters; it is probably due to recent increases in fuel prices plus better energy efficiency. But for better insulation and more efficient heating systems in homes, twice as much energy might now be used in housing (*Ibid.*, pp. 54–56; see also Chapter 2, pp. 25).

Average CO_2 emissions per household have nearly halved since 1970, because of changes in the fuel mix used to generate grid electricity, as well as greatly increased use of natural gas as a heating fuel in homes instead of (high-carbon) solid fuels and oil. One factor that has grown in recent years is renewable electricity supplied to the grid, which expanded dramatically from 2003 to 2009. To date there are only limited data about changes in the direct use of renewables in homes, whether heat from solar panels or electricity from photovoltaic panels. So far, this direct use of renewable technologies in housing is mostly to provide hot water (*Ibid.*, p. 56).

Against this background, the UK's policy for environmental sustainability in housebuilding focuses on the Code for Sustainable Homes (CfSH), launched by CLG in December 2006. Based on the EcoHomes version of the BREEAM (Building Research Establishment Environmental Assessment Method) methodology, adapted to relate closely to building regulations and government policy, it sets mandatory minimum standards for energy, water, construction, household waste and use of materials (Goodier and Pan, 2010).

It has six potential star ratings, 6 being the highest. Achieving Level 1 for energy and water entails a 10 per cent improvement over 2006 Building Regulations; Level 3 demands a 25 per cent improvement, until zero carbon is reached at Level 6 (*Ibid.*, para. 6.4, p. 28). In 2007 the government accepted a target that 100 per cent of all new homes should be zero carbon by 2016 (DCLG, 2007) – an approach confirmed in 2009 (*Ibid.*, quoting DCLG, 2009). (Oddly, Code Level 6 precludes any use of community or off-site based energy systems like the highly successful examples on mainland Europe.) Builders are cautiously optimistic that they can achieve these targets, but fear that Code Level 6 homes will be significantly more expensive to build. Although they hope that component prices will fall as volumes rise, they do not believe that Code Level 6 homes can be built profitably by 2016, especially on difficult sites (*Ibid.*, quoting Davis and Harvey, 2008). Customers are not prepared to pay a price premium for homes at a higher 'Code Level', and may not accept some of the resulting lifestyle constraints (*Ibid.*, para. 6.5, p. 29). Current take-up of the CfSH is low, with overall 17,401 CfSH certificates issued at design stage and 4,883 issued at post-construction stage, during the period from April 2008 to March 2010 – a very small proportion of the new build homes. The vast majority of the certificates (90 per cent) were for Code Level 3, a half-way house to zero carbon and thus a long way from the mandatory 2016 standard (*Ibid.*, para. 5.5, p. 18, figure 6).

The Third Sustainability Challenge: Waste Management

In 2009, for the first time, the UK's municipal dry waste recycling rate moved ahead of the European Union average, figures published by the European Union statistical body Eurostat showed. But the UK continued to lag behind the average percentage of municipal waste composted across the EU's twenty-seven member states, and it had an above-average reliance on landfill.

The data show an average dry recycling rate across the EU27 of 24 per cent, a composting rate of 18 per cent, an incineration rate of 20 per cent and an average of 38 per cent of waste sent to landfill. In comparison to this, the UK sent 26 per cent of its waste for dry recycling, 14 per cent for composting, only 11 per cent for incineration and 48 per cent to landfill. This was a continued improvement on the UK's performance in 2008.[1] And the amount of municipal waste generated per person continues to sit above the EU-wide average – although the gap between the 529 kg per person generated in the UK and the 513 kg for the European Union as a whole is much less than that recorded for 2008.

In comparative terms, Germany maintained its status as the country with the best dry recycling rate (48 per cent), ahead of Sweden and Belgium, which both reached 36 per cent and Ireland and the Netherlands (both 32 per cent). At the other end of the table, Bulgaria recorded no dry recycling rate, with 100 per cent of its municipal waste being landfilled, while just 1 per cent of Romania's municipal waste was sent for dry recycling and only 2 per cent of the Czech Republic's (see table 4.3). The UK's total dry recycling and composting rate 40 per cent in 2009 sat below the European average of 42 per cent, and significantly below the 70 per cent total recorded in Austria, 66 per cent for Germany, 61

Table 4.3. Municipal waste treatment, EU Member States, 2009.

	Municipal waste generated (kg per person)	Landfilled (%)	Incinerated (%)	Recycled (%)	Composted (%)
EU27	513	38	20	24	18
Belgium	491	5	35	36	24
Bulgaria	468	100	–	–	–
Czech Republic	316	83	12	2	2
Denmark	833	4	48	34	14
Germany	587	0	34	48	18
Estonia	346	75	0	14	11
Ireland	742	62	3	32	4
Greece	478	82	–	17	2
Spain	547	52	9	15	24
France	536	32	34	18	16
Italy	541	45	12	11	32
Cyprus	778	86	–	14	–
Latvia	333	92	0	7	0
Lithuania	360	95	–	3	1
Luxembourg	707	17	36	27	20
Hungary	430	75	10	13	2
Malta	647	96	–	4	–

continued on page 68

continued from page 67

	Municipal waste generated (kg per person)	Landfilled (%)	Incinerated (%)	Recycled (%)	Composted (%)
Netherlands	616	1	39	32	28
Austria	591	1	29	30	40
Poland	316	78	1	14	7
Portugal	488	62	19	8	12
Romania	396	99	–	1	0
Slovenia	449	62	1	34	2
Slovakia	339	82	10	2	6
Finland	481	46	18	24	12
Sweden	485	1	49	36	14
United Kingdom	*529*	*48*	*11*	*26*	*14*
Iceland	554	73	11	14	2
Norway	473	14	42	48	16
Switzerland	706	–	49	34	17

Source: Eurostat, 2011; see epp.eurostat.ec.europa.eu/cache/ITY.../8.../8-08032011-AP-EN.PDF.
Note: '0' equals less than 0.5%, '–' indicates a real zero.

per cent for the Netherlands, and 50 per cent in Sweden.[2] This would appear to add weight to arguments advanced by incineration advocates such as the Energy from Waste UK group, that a high recycling rate can be achieved alongside relatively high incineration rates.

Figure 4.2 shows that the waste deposited onto or into land fell between 2004 and 2008, while the quantity of waste recovered in the UK (excluding energy recovery) increased by 50 per cent. Total household waste in England in 2009 fell by 2.7 per cent, following annual decreases seen since 2006/2007. Recycling showed a rise to 39.7 per cent, having risen from only 10 per cent over a decade, with evidence suggesting that higher rates (up to 70 per cent) may be possible.[3]

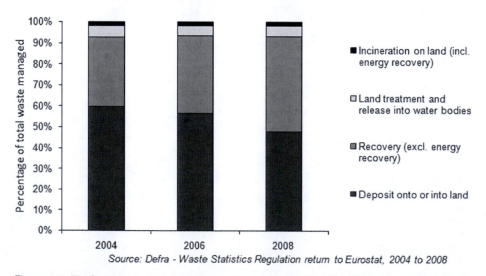

Source: Defra - Waste Statistics Regulation return to Eurostat, 2004 to 2008

Figure 4.2. Total waste disposal by management method, UK, 2004–2008. (*Source*: http://www.defra.gov.uk/statistics/environment/waste/wrfg01-annsector/)

Reducing Emissions from Waste

Waste emissions, mostly methane (CH_4), have fallen by around 70 per cent since 1990, mainly due to a reduction in biodegradable waste going to landfill in response to the landfill tax, which was introduced in 1996 to meet EU Landfill Directive targets; diversion of waste from landfill accounts for around 95 per cent of the waste emissions reduction between 1990 and 2010. The landfill tax is imposed on landfill site operators, but is passed on to local authorities and ultimately to residents through council taxes, creating powerful incentives for local authorities to divert waste away from landfill and towards recycling (e.g. of paper and card), composting and anaerobic digestion (e.g. of food waste), and incineration with or without energy recovery. In line with targets under the EU Landfill Directive, the government projects that waste emissions will be reduced by a further 20 per cent by 2020 relative to 2010.

The Fourth Sustainability Challenge:
Water – Too Little, Too Much

In 2012 the Committee on Climate Change's Adaptation Sub-Committee devoted a major report to water supply (Committee on Climate Change Adaptation Sub-Committee, 2012). Incongruously, it found, the UK suffers simultaneously from too little water, and too much.

Too Little

The UK Environment Agency had already reported that climate change and population growth will increase the pressure on water availability. Current medium projections suggest that by the 2050s, summer temperatures may increase and summer rainfall may decrease. Short droughts (12–18 months) could become more frequent, so that droughts like 1976 could be more common. And the population is forecast to increase – by no less than 9.6 million people, some 15 per cent, by the 2030s in England and Wales. And the sharpest increases – over 40 per cent – are likely to happen in the areas already experiencing water stress: Thames and South East England.

The Agency concluded that by the 2050s there could be less water available for people, businesses, agriculture and the environment than today. And these pressures will not be limited to the south and east of England; under many of the scenarios Wales, south-west and northern England are likely to be affected. Though demand management will have an important role, significant new resources will need to be developed. What is clear, its report emphasized, is that simply continuing with the current approach to water resource management will compromise the environment, the economy, or society – singly or in combination (Environment Agency, 2011, pp. 7–8).

Over recent decades England has experienced a drought on average every 7 years. The water companies have invested to ensure that we rarely suffer major interruptions such as the use of standpipes, but restrictions – hosepipe bans, constraining abstraction – are more common. They estimate that without action by the 2020s nearly half of all water resource zones could be at risk of deficit during a drought, averaging 7 per cent of existing supply.

Indicators show that household use of water per person has declined since 2000 but remains one of the highest in north-western Europe: 145 litres per day per person. Current trends suggest that use could fall to 130 litres per day per person by 2035, saving around 700 million litres of water per day – around half the deficit in the 2020s. By way of comparison, water company plans deliver savings of 440 million litres of water per day by 2035 from reductions in water use. An even faster rate of reduction could be achieved through water efficiency measures and information campaigns – above all by extension of metering, currently at 40 per cent of households in England and Wales, and on current trends rising to 85 per cent by 2035. But this may need a stronger policy framework.

There will also be a demand for parallel changes in water supply. The government's Water White Paper, *Water for Life*, published by DEFRA (the Department for the Environment and Rural Affairs) in December 2011 is a highly technical document, so much so that even the broadsheet press largely ignored it. Its key proposal is to reform abstraction licensing to establish a stronger market framework ensuring efficient allocation of water between all users, including power stations, heavy industry and agriculture. This will only be fully implemented in the mid to late 2020s. Meanwhile, DEFRA will use its existing powers to reduce environmental damage from abstraction, including a power in the Water Act 2003 to remove or vary licences causing serious damage to rivers, lakes and groundwater without compensation. At the same time, it will work to develop a market in which abstraction licences can be traded, allowing businesses to access the water they need (DEFRA, 2011, Executive Summary, paras 1–52, pp. 4–9).

Meanwhile, the Committee on Climate Change stresses, there is a risk that policy decisions that are sensitive to water availability (such as in energy and agriculture) fail to take full account of future water availability or the underlying requirement to support the natural environment (Committee on Climate Change Sub-Committee, 2012, pp. 12–14).

Too Much

On the other hand, the Sub-Committee's report stresses, there is a real and rising threat of flood risk. This currently affects around one in seven properties: 3.6 million homes and businesses. Around 10 per cent of critical infrastructure (power stations, water treatment works) and emergency services (fire, police and ambulance stations) are currently located in the floodplain. Climate change could increase the number of properties in England with a significant chance of flooding from rivers or the sea: from 330,000 now to between 630,000 and 1.2 million by the 2080s. The annual expected costs of flooding could increase from £1 billion now to between £1.8 billion and £5.6 billion (in present day prices) over that time.

Worse, development in the floodplain in England increased by 12 per cent over the 10 years to 2012, compared with a 7 per cent increase outside the floodplain. Around 21,000 new homes and business premises (13 per cent of all new development) have been built in the floodplain every year over this time period. The majority of these followed Environment Agency advice, by incorporating features such as raised ground and floor levels or safe evacuation routes. But one in five were in areas of significant flood risk even today. Reviewing forty-two of the most up-to-date local development plans, the committee could not be sure whether local authorities were properly assessing the potential for accommodating growth elsewhere before deciding to allocate land for development in the floodplain; or accounting for the long-term costs of flooding with climate change, both in terms of the increasing costs of flood damage and any additional costs of flood protection.

The prospect is an increasing risk of flooding from climate change. The Environment Agency estimates that to keep risk levels constant in the face of climate change and deterioration of flood defence assets, investment needs to increase by £20 million above inflation every year. By 2035, the combined effect of increased investment in flood defences (£20 million per year on top of inflation) and faster uptake of property-level measures could reduce the number of properties at significant risk by half from current levels, even accounting for climate change (Committee on Climate Change Sub-Committee, 2012, pp. 9–12).

The Fifth Sustainability Challenge: Food Supply

Agriculture has created Britain's cherished rural landscape. In many areas it sustains habitats that are crucial to wildlife. UK farming employs over half a million people, and in 2007 it contributed £5.3 billion to the economy. A flexible, skilled and market-orientated domestic agriculture sector is showing it can thrive and compete in an international market. This in turn makes an important contribution to global food supply and to the diversity and resilience of domestic food supply.

Food imports have been a crucial element of Britain's food supply since the industrial revolution. They were severely disrupted during the two world wars. Maintaining food supply then involved securing the flow of imports, as well as boosting home production. The post-war drive for greater self-sufficiency across Europe was a response to wartime and post-war shortages. In the 1970s the

Table 4.4. Approximate British self-sufficiency over different periods.

Date	Self-sufficiency
Pre-1750	around 100% (in temperate produce)
1750–1830s	around 90–100% except for poor harvests
1870s	around 60%
1914	around 40%
1930s	30–40%
1950s	40–50%
1980s	60–70%
2000s	60%

Source: DEFRA, 2006.

incentives provided by the EU Common Agricultural Policy or CAP boosted the UK's self-sufficiency. Since the 1980s the return of globalization and other economic trends have weakened self-sufficiency arguments, especially at national level, while self-sufficiency has also declined. Nevertheless table 4.4 shows that current levels of UK self-sufficiency are in fact pretty normal by historical standards (RuSource, 2006, pp. 1–2; DEFRA, 2006).

The recent decline in self-sufficiency reflects a lack of export growth after 1994 and a tailing off and reduction in agricultural output. Short-term factors included a BSE-inflicted ban on UK beef exports, Foot and Mouth Disease in 2001, an appreciating Pound Sterling between 1995 and 2000, and CAP reforms of 1993 and 1999 which ended the expansionist trend of the 1970s and 1980s. Long-term factors driving these trends include changing tastes towards more exotic and varied produce, fewer trade restrictions, cheaper transport and communications and wider sourcing by supermarkets. Taken together, these factors do not suggest that underlying food security has materially worsened. They relate more to UK agriculture's ability to meet consumer demands, i.e. its 'market share', both at home and abroad.

The UK is about 60 per cent self-sufficient in food overall, and about 74 per cent self-sufficient in the types of food that can be grown in the country. But there are wide variations between commodities, and in addition home-produced foods may depend on imported inputs such as energy or animal feedstuffs. Self-sufficiency levels have declined since the 1980s, but are not unusual: the UK has depended on food imports for over a century. And though the UK is more dependent on food imports than some comparable EU countries, 68 per cent of its food imports come from other EU states (Barling *et al.*, 2008, p. 2). Currently no single country accounts for more than 13 per cent of UK food and drink food imports. Maintaining a range of supply sources means that any risk to total food supply is spread, lowering the impacts of unforeseen disruptions involving any particular trading partner or from within our domestic agriculture sector (RuSource, 2006, pp. 1–2; DEFRA, 2006).

The big debate is about the 'resilience' of the food supply: its ability to withstand serious shocks. David Barling and his colleagues at City University conclude that contingency planning is inadequate to meet challenges – the 'new fundamentals' –including climate change; water; biodiversity and eco-systems support; energy and non-renewable fossil fuels; population growth; land use; soil; labour; and dietary change and public health. They conclude that there is compelling evidence for government to rethink national food security policy, but that this must be built into and on a sustainability framework (Barling *et al.*, 2008, p. 2).

Facing the Five Sustainability Challenges: Can the UK Manage?

Taken together, these five challenges constitute a formidable agenda for any UK government. In comparison with near EU neighbours, with a few notable exceptions, the UK record to date has been below average. And, although successive UK governments of different political complexions have shown a commendable resolve to tackle the issues, the obstacles in achieving the targets are considerable. Not least this is because they depend on exceedingly complex and delicate relationships between a government, attempting to impose a regulatory regime, and a great variety of private-sector players whose first concern, logically enough, must be with their profit-and-loss accounts. Further, these private-sector players embrace a huge span, from global suppliers of electricity and water, to small builders and individual generators of do-it-yourself electricity. The potential for organized lobbying and regulatory capture – not only nationally, but also at a European level – is immense. What does need underlining is that other EU member states fully share the same commercial and regulatory regimes, and that some at least seem to have managed to handle the challenges more successfully than the UK. We shall need to return to this central question both in Chapter 5, and at the end of the book.

Notes

1. See http://www.letsrecycle.com/news/latest-news/waste-management/uk-achieves-average-eu-municipal-recycling-rate.

2. See http://www.letsrecycle.com/news/latest-news/waste-management/uk-moves-above-eu-average-municipal-recycling-rate.

3. See http://www.guardian.co.uk/news/datablog/2011/jan/07/household-waste-recycling-by-area#data.

5 | The Fifth Challenge: Fixing Broken Machinery

Behind the long discussion of issues in the previous four chapters – and, if discussion could have resolved them, they would have been resolved long ago – a deeper issue is lurking, just visible beneath the surface. It is: how do we go about building and changing our cities? What mechanisms could we use to improve the ways in which we influence the distribution of economic activity and employment, build homes in adequate numbers and of adequate quality, in the right places to meet demand, meet the challenge of climate change, and provide sustainable connections between the places where people work, study, live and play? For it has become increasingly evident, over the last four chapters, that the existing mechanisms are not working well, or in some cases are hardly working at all.

In Part Two of this book, we will go on tour, visiting countries and cities in mainland Europe that seem to have used different mechanisms to produce better outcomes. But before we pack our bags, it is worthwhile to stand back and look more specifically at the UK model, asking why it self-evidently has not worked. Specifically, this means trying to understand how property, financial and land markets work in the UK, and why planning as generally practised has not been able to turn visions into reality, except in some isolated instances.

Rather as in a good detective story, there are a number of obvious suspects, but the truth emerges as something much more complex.

Suspect No. 1: The Homeowners

For nearly a century, since the end of World War One, the UK has become steadily and increasingly a nation of owner-occupiers. The process has been interrupted only twice: first, during and for a few years after World War Two, when first house building simply stopped save for isolated defence-based sites, and then resumed under strict state controls; and second, since the financial crisis of 2007–2008, which has seen the first significant fall in six decades. It would be an obvious conclusion to assume that the UK's addiction to home ownership has been at the root of the problems – and indeed, the proposition deserves examination. But one major difficulty is that the trend has been general throughout affluent countries, including nearly all our neighbouring European countries.

In 2010, just over seven out of ten (70.8 per cent) of the EU-27 population lived in an owner-occupied house, of whom over a quarter (27.9 per cent) lived in a home for which there was an outstanding loan or mortgage, while more than two-fifths (42.9 per cent) lived in a mortgage-free home. Of the remaining EU population, 17.8 per cent lived in dwellings with a market price rent, and 11.4 per cent in reduced-rent or free accommodation. In every EU Member State in 2010 more than half of the population lived in owner-occupied dwellings; the share ranged from 53.2 per cent in Germany to 97.5 per cent in Romania. In the Netherlands (59.5 per cent), Sweden (68.0 per cent) and Denmark (52.7 per cent) more than half the population lived in owner-occupied dwellings with an outstanding loan or mortgage.

These figures are significant because European countries which have produced notably high-quality urban developments to be considered in Part Two of this book, such as Sweden, Denmark and the Netherlands, have done so on the basis of a model of ownership very similar to that of the UK. True, Germany has a remarkable and much-quoted higher proportion of households who rent: around three-quarters, a figure comparable to the UK in the 1920s. It therefore suffered much less from the crisis in real estate that followed the 2008 crash in many other EU countries. But the German pattern reflects a different pattern of taxation that favours renting – or, more specifically, does not favour owner-occupiership – which is not followed elsewhere in Europe, and is not likely to be followed. In any case, the critical point is that it does not explain why the quality of development is so much higher both in Germany and in countries that share with the UK a high-level of owner-occupiership, like the Netherlands. The explanation must be sought elsewhere.

Suspect No. 2: The Bankers

Since the 2007–2008 crash was particularly associated with massive structural failure in the banking system, and much of this – especially in Spain, Ireland

and the United States – was in large part a consequence of bad mortgage loans, the next obvious suspects are the banks. But it turns out to be not quite so simple. Professor Michael Ball's comprehensive Europe-wide study for the Royal Institution of Chartered Surveyors shows that though after the 2007 crash house prices declined in many countries, most seriously in the UK, Sweden and Switzerland have recently recorded increases. Construction showed even greater variation. Spain, Ireland, Greece and Portugal recorded catastrophic declines, the UK together with Denmark and the Netherlands demonstrated serious contraction, while in Germany construction barely fell and in Switzerland it actually expanded. And mortgage loans, again, showed a different pattern: in 2010–2011, most Eurozone countries recorded significant upswings, while in the UK there was still extreme constraint. However, throughout the Eurozone mortgage loans rebounded after the 2007 crisis but were again contracting sharply at the end of 2011 (Ball, 2012, pp. 11–14).

The conclusion appears to be that there is no simple relationship between the amounts of money that banks lend out as mortgages, the consequent rate of construction and the oscillations in house prices. The extreme observations suggest an obvious common-sense truth; countries where banks lent a lot in mortgages (Spain, Ireland) had real estate crashes, while countries where banks did not (Germany, Switzerland) did not. But the UK, as ever, remains the odd man out. With a few minor exceptions – like Northern Rock, the building society-turned-bank that crashed and had to be rescued – British banks did not engage in risky mortgage lending, as evidenced by a relatively very low rate of repossessions of mortgaged properties: in 2011 the number, 36,200, represented a 4-year low. British banks were extremely cautious lenders before the crash, and became even more so after it. So they can be blamed in part for the UK's chronically poor housing delivery performance over the long term, but not for what has happened subsequently. Indeed, the example of Ireland – which during the 2000–2007 boom annually delivered over twenty times the housing completion rate of England, in relation to its population – is a salutary lesson: if our banks had behaved like Irish banks, we could have done very much worse.[1]

Suspect No. 3: The Landowners

Over the longer term, however, there has been one distinct feature of the UK model, already discussed in Chapter 2: sharply rising house prices. Research by Hilber and Vermeulen (2010) shows that in the long housing boom of the 1990s and early 2000s, while Germany and Finland kept prices fairly constant, the UK, along with Spain and Ireland, demonstrated the most spectacular escalation in prices. The oddity was that, in comparison with these two cases, in these years the UK built far fewer homes: we had a housing bust without the preceding boom. Not only were average UK house prices four times higher in

2010 than in 1990, doubling in 20 years after allowing for inflation (Diacon *et al.*, 2011), prices in London rose much faster than in the north of England, so that by late 2011, prices for equivalent properties in the South were twice those in the North (Rightmove, 2011). But – as already seen in Chapter 4 – this did not trigger an increase in supply, as should have occurred in a textbook free market: instead the UK experienced a classic instance of what economists call 'market failure', where a rise in prices does not lead to an equivalent increase in supply due to barriers to entry or oligopolistic behaviour on the part of developers. It is this distinct failure that demands closer attention. And it has been exacerbated since the great fiscal crisis of 2007, with the proportion of mortgages going to first-time buyers falling from the usual 40 per cent to only 20 per cent in Summer 2011.

The explanation appears to lie in a failure in land supply: house price escalation filters through immediately to land values, with supply lagging behind. This in turn encourages builders to build as many small units as possible on brownfield sites which are inherently more difficult than building on green fields on the edge of towns and cities, and can be blamed in part for poor urban design.

Suspect No. 4: The Builders

Underlying this is a distinct feature of the UK development industry: the role of the volume builders. Private housebuilders have dominated the market since the collapse of local authority building in the 1980s, with almost a 90 per cent market share of new homes built in the country (Goodier and Pan 2010, figure 1). Of the National House Building Council Register of around 18,000 builders, just under 200 firms produce more than fifty homes per year (*Ibid.*, quoting Barker, 2003) and less than fifty housebuilders built more than 500 dwellings annually during the past 20 years (*Ibid.*, quoting Callcutt, 2007). According to statistics in the *Private Housebuilding Annual* (*Ibid.*, quoting Wellings, 2006), the top 100 housebuilders contribute around two-thirds to the housing unit completions by the industry as a whole. And in 2002 the top ten housebuilders completed 70,205 homes: 38.5 per cent of the total (Barker 2003, table 1). But that of course meant that on average, these big builders each contributed less than 4 per cent to the total. This was not, and is not, a monopoly or even an oligopoly.

These builders are on the whole extremely risk-averse. The Callcutt Review (*Ibid.*, quoting Callcutt, 2007, pp. 180–181) identified their concerns:

♦ *Running out of land.* A developer will ideally require around 18 months to 2 years before land on new sites can be brought into production, but this is seldom achieved. Failure will force a builder either to buy 'oven ready' sites at very high prices or to try and increase volumes from existing outlets which will necessitate price discounting.

◆ *Cost overruns.* The increasing complexity of construction and development has made building cost control more difficult.

◆ *Failure to assess market demand correctly.* Putting the wrong product on a development site will significantly affect sales proceeds and may require significant discounting to achieve sales.

◆ *Failure to assess the future market.* The housing market is very difficult to assess and many economic forecasters have made incorrect predictions.

◆ *Generic product failure.* A single component failure, design fault or poor quality workmanship can and often does affect more than one dwelling, meaning potentially expensive rectification works.

These risks help to explain why the housebuilding industry is reluctant to make long-term fixed commitments. The Callcutt Review (*Ibid.*, quoting Callcutt 2007, p. 181), suggested that 'after more than 15 years' steady growth in house prices, conservative risk-averse attitudes still prevail and are probably justified. The City still regards housing as relatively high risk because of its inherent unpredictability and requires a high premium on its use of capital' (*Ibid.*, para. 4.3, p. 12).

This might suggest an industry that is averse to competition. Kate Barker found no compelling evidence of anti-competitive behaviour associated with build-out rates for large sites, but she considered it desirable to ensure that sites are built out at a rate that is socially optimal as well as privately optimal for housebuilders, through an incentive to develop land more quickly. This could be a land value tax, but with the tax levied after the granting of planning permission. For example, developers could be charged for every uncompleted house on a site (Barker, 2004, para. 6.22, p. 109).

In fact the UK house building industry does not appear notably inefficient compared with its European competitors. But evidently it is relatively smaller. Construction in the UK accounts for about 5 per cent of UK Gross Value Added (GVA) – similar to the share in its main competitors – France, Germany and the US. But compared with them, the share of residential building in Britain is low at 26 per cent – compared with over a third in France, Germany and the US. Britain has a high share of non-residential output: 56 per cent of construction output, compared to one-third in the US, France and Germany. The overall evidence suggests that construction in the UK is no less productive than in Germany but there is a large productivity gap with the US. The relative position of France is inconclusive with some estimates suggesting that UK construction productivity is on a par with France whilst alternative measures suggest that the UK is considerably less productive, and productivity in France is on a par with the US (Blake *et al.*, 2004).

Suspect No. 5: The Planners

Does then the problem lie with the planning system? Kate Barker's Review concluded that 'The underlying constraint on housing is the supply of land' (Barker, 2003, para. 10, p. 10). But she listed more than one suspect:

◆ the housebuilding industry, its response to risk and the speculative nature of land leading to a reluctance to build out large sites quickly;

◆ the increasingly complex nature of sites (especially brownfield), where significant remediation might be required;

◆ land ownership and the incentives to bring land forward for development along with the difficulties of site assembly, where ownership is fragmented;

◆ the planning system and its influence over the amount of land which is made available and whether development is viable through the delivery of necessary infrastructure; and

◆ the fact that land use is also politically contentious (*Ibid.*, para. 10, pp. 10–11).

Barker concluded that there might also be 'a more fundamental interaction between the existence of a housing shortage and the performance of the housebuilding industry': with limited land supply, competition tends to be focused on land acquisition rather than on satisfying consumers. Housebuilders' profitability depends on obtaining valuable land rather than building products efficiently. This, she suggested,

> might indicate a degree of regulatory complacency which has allowed the industry to settle into a low output equilibrium. Low output in the short run appears to suit many players – local authorities, homeowners and arguably the industry. The only people it does not suit is the homeless, first time buyers and those inadequately housed. (*Ibid.*, para. 31, pp. 13–14)

The Callcutt Review in 2007 likewise found it difficult to identify the culprit:

> There is much public debate about the supply of land. The development industry and its advocates complain that the planning system releases too little land, and that its release is slow and unpredictable. The industry's critics assert that developers do not take full advantage of the available land, preferring to profit from land value inflation with the minimum of effort given to actually building houses. (Callcutt, 2007, p. 32)

The Killian Pretty Review (Goodier and Pan, 2010, quoting Killian and Pretty, 2008), drawing on research into sixty-four individual case studies of major developments, revealed that over half encountered substantial problems such as significant blockages and delays during the processing of their planning applications. NAO (*Ibid.*, quoting NAO, 2008) reviewed the case history of 100 major residential applications (i.e. developments of more than ten homes) approved in 2006–2007 by eleven authorities. The percentage of major residential planning applications decided within the targeted 13 weeks improved from 37 per cent in 2002–2003 to 67 per cent in 2007–2008. The time taken to approve however was, on average, over 25 weeks. The average time taken for the whole process, from pre-application discussion to the start of construction, was almost 98 weeks on average.

In her 2004 report Barker logically proposed that planning at regional and local levels needed to respond by allocating more land for development. This does not mean removing all restraints on land use; on the contrary, more attention should be given to ensuring the most valuable land is preserved. But housebuilders should have greater choice as to which sites to develop, increasing competition. And more land would also allow a quicker and more flexible response to a rising market (Barker, 2004, para. 22, p. 6).

A more effective planning system, she suggested, would be characterized by:

◆ a system that responds to market signals;

◆ decision-making procedures that take full account of the wider costs and benefits of housing development, including environmental and amenity costs;

◆ appropriate incentives for development at the local level;

◆ clear and timely mechanisms to provide the necessary infrastructure and services to support development and deliver sustainable communities; and

◆ sufficient resources to enable effective decision making (*Ibid.*, para. 2.4, p. 32).

When she was again asked to look at the planning system in 2006, Barker concluded that 'further action needs to be taken to deliver an *efficient* planning system, by reducing delays, addressing unnecessary complexity and increasing certainty' and 'progress is needed in terms of delivering an *effective* planning framework'. Among the structural issues underlying these concerns was the absence of any clear financial incentive for local authorities to promote growth. 'The failure of planning to respond sufficiently to market and price signals, including the impact on land prices of restricted supply, needs to be addressed, particularly in the context of the likely contribution of land supply constraint to high occupation costs', she wrote (Barker, 2006, para. 2, p. 4). Her key recommendations included:

◆ Streamlining policy and processes through reducing policy guidance, unifying consent regimes and reforming plan-making at the local level so that future development plan documents can be delivered in 18–24 months rather than 3 or more years.

◆ Updating national policy on planning for economic development (PPS4), to ensure that the benefits of development are fully taken into account in plan-making and decision-taking, with a more explicit role for market and price signals.

◆ Introducing a new system for dealing with major infrastructure projects, based around national Statements of Strategic Objectives and an independent Planning Commission to determine applications.

◆ Promoting a positive planning culture within the plan-led system so that when the plan is indeterminate, applications should be approved unless there is good reason to believe that the environmental, social and economic costs will exceed the respective benefits.

◆ Ensuring that new development beyond towns and cities occurs in the most sustainable way, by encouraging planning bodies to review their green belt boundaries and take a more positive approach to applications that will enhance the quality of their green belts.

◆ Supporting the 'town-centre first' policy, but removing the requirement to demonstrate the need for development.

◆ In the context of the findings of the Lyons Inquiry into Local Government, to consider how fiscal incentives can be better aligned so that local authorities are in a position to share the benefits of local economic growth (*Ibid.*, Key Recommendations, p. 6).

Ironically, despite their fundamental ideological differences, the Labour government in 2006–2007 and the Coalition government in 2011–2012 did succeed in responding to most of these proposals. Labour established an Infrastructure Planning Commission to handle major development proposals; the Coalition demoted it to an arm of the Planning Inspectorate and made it responsible to ministers, but did retain it. The Coalition's revised National Planning Policy Framework (NPPF) has reduced the volume of policy guidance, embodies the principle of a presumption in favour of development where the plan is indeterminate, and adopts a definition of sustainable development that embodies economic as well as environmental considerations. The major difference, of course, is that the Coalition has scrapped the Regional Planning Strategies with their binding targets for new house construction. It substitutes a local market-led approach to planning for a strategic top-down approach.

Will it work? Time will tell soon enough. Certainly the intention is to achieve what successive governments, of varying political persuasions, have failed to achieve over the six decades since the passage of the historic 1947 Town and Country Planning Act: to devise a system that allows the planning system and the market system to work coherently in partnership rather than in permanent opposition. The clue must be to release sufficient development land to ensure that developers can develop, rather than landowners (including developers) finding it more attractive to hoard it as a mechanism for speculative gain. And it must work everywhere, including the most pressured parts of the country where the system has so demonstrably fallen behind its capacity to deliver.

Even if it succeeds in this, however, there is another issue. The system has become ineffective in influencing the quality of development. With the bulk of finance for development coming from the private sector, planners have had little control over the process other than to issue advice and targets. Despite a flood of advice on better design from bodies such as the erstwhile CABE (the Commission on Architecture Building and the Environment), the general result – with rare exceptions such as Upton in Northampton, where a public landowner insisted on higher standards – the general result has been dismal design, lack of neighbourhood amenities, and overstretched infrastructure. And this paradoxically created a vicious circle, as criticisms of the design fuelled resistance to new building (Rudlin and Falk, 2009).

One possible answer was noted in Kate Barker's 2004 Review: most European countries have legally binding local land-use plans. In the Netherlands such a plan is known as a *Bestemmingsplan* and covers all or part of a municipality. Public statutory consultation over land allocated in the plan is carried out before the plan is adopted. Then, it is legally binding on all parties. Developers submit applications for land allocated within the plan and these are given a building permit as long as they comply with the plan; there are no material considerations. Building permits are administered by a technical officer (Burgomaster) rather than an elected politician. If a developer submits an application for development on land that is not allocated or covered by the plan, the plan may have to be revised – which can take around 3 years.

The big advantage with such binding local plans, Barker found, is that once the plan is adopted the principle of development is established, and so achieving planning permission is quicker and more certain. But plans take much longer to adopt in the first place, because of the level of consultation required, and are relatively inflexible to changes in the market or other events. The *Bestemmingsplan* is often very prescriptive, setting out the size, design and tenure of houses to be built on certain sites – an attribute that many in the UK would commend (Barker, 2004, Box 2.2, p. 45). But, she concluded, it is not necessarily any more responsive; indeed the responsiveness of housing supply in the Netherlands appeared to be lower even than in the UK. So she recommended against it, preferring a clear presumption in favour of granting planning permission for development that conforms to the local plan – a key element in the 2012 NPPF (*Ibid.*, para. 2.46, p. 45).

Conclusion: The Need for a New Model

So there is general agreement, even among opposed politicians, on the need for change. The UK model has failed to achieve development in the right quantity and of the right quality, and has performed demonstrably worse in these key respects than the systems in comparable EU countries. These other countries, not far from the UK in mainland Europe, have successfully developed other approaches to land supply, land-use planning, the financing of infrastructure, and the design and management of new settlements. If we are to develop new and innovative policies to replace the tired and outdated models of the past, a study visit to these countries is a vital first step.

Note

1. See http://www.guardian.co.uk/money/2012/feb/09/uk-home-repossessions-fall-four-year-low.

Part Two:

Learning from Model Cities: A Twenty-First-Century Grand Tour

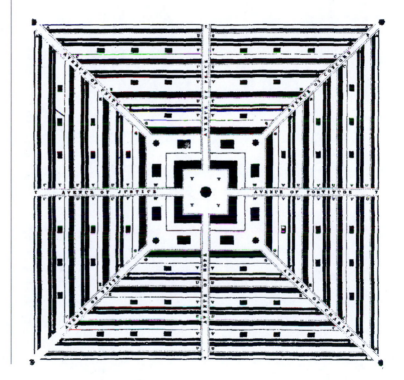

6 The Sixth Challenge: Going on Tour

Planning an itinerary for the twenty-first-century Grand Tour does not prove easy, because there are so many admirable examples of urban good practice that almost demand to be seen, and because they are scattered across the length and breadth of Europe – from Umeå to Barcelona, from Bilbao to Helsinki. Compelled to choose, we elected to organize the tour, as any tour organizer would logically do, by country and by theme. And associating countries and topics proved to be both easy and useful: no country has a monopoly of good practice under any one heading, but some do offer remarkably good examples in selected areas. Further, these examples often score highly outside those special fields, and so offer interesting lessons in how successful cities manage multi-dimensional policies.

It was only logical to take up the key themes that have emerged for the United Kingdom in Part One of this book, and this made the process of selection even easier.

Economic Growth: Germany

For creating the conditions for successful economic growth, especially for re-starting it when traditional sources of growth have stumbled and fallen, German cities provide the outstanding example. First, in recent years Germany has become the outstanding case of economic growth in Europe, far outdistancing most of its rivals – and, remarkably, unlike other advanced economies it has succeeded in maintaining and expanding its manufacturing base. Second, it has done so even though it has long suffered from a problem of regional imbalance: between an old northern heavy-industrial region that has seen decline and even closure of its traditional industrial base, the Ruhrgebiet, and the south-western states of Bavaria and Baden-Württemberg, characterized by buoyant growth of advanced engineering firms that exploit the latest advantages in technology. And third, over the decades since 1990 it has faced an even starker contrast, between the old West Germany and the so-called eastern New *Länder*, formerly communist, where reunification in 1990 was followed by sudden and stark economic collapse. In Chapter 7 this story is told by visiting places, both in the old West and the old East, that faced economic challenge and found new ways to meet it: *Hamburg*, the *Ruhrgebiet* and *Kassel* in the west, *Berlin* and *Leipzig* in the east.

Housing and New Communities: The Netherlands

Again, European cities offer many fine examples of model housing developments. But the Netherlands fall into a class of their own, with the huge decade-long national VINEX programme to build nearly half a million new homes in new planned settlements in and adjacent to the country's major cities. The tour in Chapter 8 will start with an urban example, *IJburg* in the Amsterdam docklands, and will continue via an extension to *Almere*, a 1970s new town in a reclaimed polder that has become the fastest-growing city in the country, via *Vathorst*, a new satellite town next to the city of *Amersfoort*, concluding in *Ypenburg*, another large satellite town in the heart of the Randstad outside The Hague.

Sustainable Transport: France

Examples of superb public transport are found all over Europe, in Germany and in Sweden, in Italy and in Spain. But France has taken a particular lead, in the last two decades, in the scale of development of its urban tramway systems, now in every major city and rapidly extending also to many smaller places. Financed by exceptionally generous dedicated taxation, the investment goes far beyond the mere improvement of accessibility between city centres and suburbs, but also uses high-quality urban public transport as an agent of urban regeneration through the creation of high-quality urban space and its use in city image-building and city marketing. The visit in Chapter 9 will range from *Montpellier*, France's fastest-growing major city in the far south of the country, through *Lille*, a regenerating old industrial city at the northern extremity, to *Strasbourg* on the German border in the east. And from there it will take an excursion across the Rhine to look at a remarkable transport innovation from Germany: the tram-train in *Karlsruhe*, now being copied and developed in cities across Europe.

Environmental Conservation: Scandinavia

Likewise, though Europe offers many good examples of successful urban sustainability, Sweden and Demark are outstanding. In Chapter 10 we start in *Stockholm*, where the inner-city regeneration project of *Hammarby Sjöstad* has become a place of pilgrimage for planners studying its extraordinary total approach, the 'Hammarby Model', to recycling and conservation of liquid and solid waste – but it is also one of Europe's outstanding cases of integrated land-use planning, notably in the way it combines housing, work spaces, shops, open space and transport on the linear site of an old factory complex. At the far southern end of Sweden, abutting Denmark, the Öresund region – on either side of the dramatic new bridge linking *Malmö* with *Copenhagen* – offers another brilliant example in Malmö's *Västra Hamnen* (Western Harbour), an urban regeneration scheme on an old industrial site next to the city centre. And Copenhagen across the bridge has combined city-centre waterside regeneration with construction of a new town in-town, on a linear site served by a new Metro line, and with some of Europe's most radical strategies to create a cycling capital.

The City That Did It All: Freiburg

Logically, *Freiburg* should appear in each of the preceding four chapters: as an example of outstanding economic development, Germany's 'solar city', taking a lead in new environmentally-sustainable industries; as an internationally-recognized case of environmental sustainability in practice throughout its planning and urban development processes; as an exemplary instance of urban development integrated with high-quality public transport, and finally as a demonstration of different kinds of housing – market, cooperative, social – integrated in a total concept of high-quality development. Precisely because it proves impossible to place squarely under any one of these heads, because it qualifies outstandingly on all of them, it deserves a chapter of its own as the city that achieved rare excellence in every aspect of good-practice development: the quintessence of the good city that creates the basis for better lives. And this is Chapter 11.

We now pack our bags. First we will wend an indirect way across Germany, from Hamburg to Berlin, down to Leipzig and back to the Ruhr before a final visit to Kassel. From Kassel we travel north-west to the Netherlands to take a short tour around housing developments in and around the cities of Randstad Holland. Next we take a long journey to the southern end of France, to Montpellier, before taking the TGV northward to Lille and eastward to Strasbourg, from where we take a final short excursion to Karlsruhe. Then we will travel to the northernmost point of our journey to start our Scandinavian tour in Stockholm, continuing south to Malmö and its twin city Copenhagen, before another long journey to Freiburg in the extreme south-west of Germany. This will be a long tour – but a highly instructive one.

7 | Boosting Economic Growth in Germany

Germany, it can be argued, is a nation of cities. For the cities came long before the nation, and in an important sense the nation is an aggregation of its cities and of the historic region-states of which they became mini-capitals (Harrison Church *et al.*, 1967). As trade – never quite expunged in the Dark Ages, as historians once believed – revived in Europe from the tenth century onwards, cities naturally arose at the great crossing-points between the rivers, which flowed from south to north from the great Alpine mountain barrier to the North Sea, and east–west routes: the great water route of the North Sea and Baltic with Hanseatic port cities like Bremen, Hamburg, Lübeck, Rostock and Danzig (Gdańsk); the equally great land route that led along the fertile belt of light soils at the border of the northern plain and the central uplands, with major cities like Cologne, Essen, Dortmund, Hannover, Braunschweig and Magdeburg; and other routes etched by west-flowing tributaries of the River Rhine into the higher lands of south Germany, along which emerged cities like Frankfurt, Mannheim, Heidelberg, Stuttgart and Nürnberg. And, in the extreme south, another great river – the east-flowing Danube and its tributaries – formed other lines of easy access and provided the basis for city formation: Augsburg, Ulm and Munich.

And these were literally free cities, given trade privileges which excepted them from the feudal rule of the surrounding countryside. Freiburg, founded in the year 1120 by Konrad and Duke Bertold III of Zähringen, encapsulates it: the name literally means 'free fortified town', for *burg* in German simultaneously translates as 'fortress' and 'borough'. Hundreds of such places were founded across Germany in the late Middle Ages, though they did not always keep their autonomy in the war-wracked years that followed the Reformation. And they became important centres of cultural and intellectual life: Freiburg's Albert-Ludwigs-Universität, one of Germany's oldest, was established in 1457 by the local Regent of Further Austria. When the German geographer Walter Christaller published his famous study of Central Places in South Germany in 1933, his maps recorded them: they ranged in a seven-level hierarchy from the *Landstadt* with a population of 500,000 and a catchment population of 3.5 million, represented by centres such as Munich, Nürnberg, Stuttgart and Frankfurt, and immediately below this the *Provinzstadt* with 100,000 and a regional population of 1 million, represented by places like Augsburg, Ulm, Würzburg and Regensburg, all the way down to the tiny *Marktorte* with a typical population of 1,000 and a catchment area of 3,000 people. Eighty years later these smallest places have been demoted to villages as increasing mobility has extended the catchments of the places above them, but they are testimony to the extraordinarily diffused nature of the German urban system and of the power structure of small principalities and dukedoms that rested upon it.

What temporarily and profoundly disturbed this structure, starting at the end of the seventeenth century and culminating at the end of the nineteenth, was the rise of Prussia and its achievement in 1871 of effective hegemony over a unified Germany, finally subordinating even the proud kingdom of Bavaria. It was followed by the dizzy 40-year rise of Berlin, long derided as merely a 'garrison city' for the Prussian army, into one of the great cities of Europe, with four million people at its apogee at the end of the 1930s. By 1914 Berlin was effectively a compact new city of uniform five-storey apartment blocks, alike in middle-class districts like Wilmersdorf and Kreuzberg or in working-class quarters like Wedding or Prenzlauer Berg. It had also become Europe's greatest economic powerhouse; *Elektropolis*, dominated by the huge modern factories of the electrical giants Siemens and AEG. But Berlin was always something of an anomaly: owing its rise to the Prussian territories to its east, even then – when, as the proud verses of the old national anthem proclaimed, Germany stretched from the River Maas to the River Memel, now part of Russia – it was peripherally located in relation to the main urban centres to its west. Today, with Germany's former eastern territories lost to Poland, Lithuania and Russia, that eccentricity is extreme: one can board a suburban stopping train in the city's new *Hauptbahnhof* and arrive at the Polish border in just over an hour.

After World War Two and the long division both of Germany and of Berlin into western and eastern zones, effectively West Germany reverted to an older historic pattern of local states around medium-sized provincial capital cities. The new *Länder* were based on traditional kingdoms and principalities; the ancient Hanseatic cities of Hamburg and Bremen became separate city states, with the proud title *Hanse-und-Freistadt* (Hanseatic and Free City). The Federal government was run from the small Rhineland city of Bonn, which the Germans fondly referred to as the *Bundesdorf*, Federal Village. Major functions like the media established themselves in different provincial capitals: Germany's three major broadsheets comprise *Die Welt* edited in Hamburg, *Frankfurter Allgemeine Zeitung* in Frankfurt and the *Süddeutsche Zeitung* in Munich. Local capital cities competed vigorously to build or extend art galleries and opera houses, producing an unequalled level of cultural life across the country. After reunification in 1990 and the transfer of the capital (but not all of government) back to Berlin, many of these functions stayed where they were. True, Berlin remained uniquely endowed – partly because, in the long years of division, both sides had competed to run two of everything. But fundamentally Germany appeared to have returned to an historic pattern: a land of strong provincial cities with the capital being just one among many.

Most of these cities share another key characteristic: very early on, they established strong craft guilds in which traditions of high-quality craftsmanship were taught and passed on and developed, and when the industrial revolution came to Germany in the nineteenth century – later than in Britain – this was fortified by a strong system of technical education which extended through the schools – with a vocational educational system that equips young people with useful skills – up to the *Technische Hochschule*, Technical Universities, which owed their origins to the Prussian educational reforms of the early nineteenth century and have no real equivalent in the United Kingdom, where an attempt in the 1960s to create a Polytechnic stream parallel to the universities failed as they all-too-soon diversified into humanities and social sciences. In *Technische Hochschule*, scientific advances were soon converted into industrial innovations, in practice as well as theory. And, in recent decades, this has been massively supplemented by the development of two great groups of scientific institutes: one, belonging to the Max-Planck Gesellschaft, devoted to high-level basic scientific research; the other, belonging to the Fraunhofer Society, with the mission of applying that research. The research institutes of the Max Planck Society, nearly eighty in number, with their budget of some €1.4 billion, and the sixty Fraunhofer Institutes, with a budget of some €1.65 billion and a payroll of 18,000 scientists and engineers, go a long way to explaining Germany's continued predominance and economic success in applied manufacturing.

The geography of this German manufacturing activity is quite distinctive – at least in comparison to the UK. With one great exception – the Ruhr area, which was opened up after 1850 and became the greatest single centre of heavy industry in mainland Europe – industry did not develop in clusters on the coalfields, as in the UK. The highly technical industries that characterized the German economy, ranging from automobiles to electrical products to manufacturing chemicals, did not need coalfield locations. They thus grew up in the established cities where the medieval crafts had been. So it proved much easier to pursue a path of continued technical progress, whether this came from industrial giants like Mercedes-Benz (whose origins go back to their founders' simultaneous invention of the modern automobile in 1886 in Mannheim and Stuttgart), or from the tens of thousands of medium-sized family firms, the famous *Mittelstand*, on which German economic strength is built to this day.

Just as a century ago this spirit of innovation expressed itself in new industries like cars and electrical goods and pharmaceuticals, now it is manifesting itself in a twenty-first-century new industrial revolution: in green energy. Germany has created new industries such as solar power and waste management, turning the idea of sustainable development into business opportunities, and in the process opening up new export markets such as China. Germany was only able to take the radical step of closing down its nuclear power stations because it had established a commanding lead in renewable energy, using a series of International Building Exhibitions (IBA) to implement pilot projects. It is this ability of German industry to keep reinventing itself, and open up new export markets, that makes it a model for all other long-industrialized economies. The German economy of the 2010s seems uncannily to have been repeating the famous economic miracle of the 1950s, the *Wirtschaftswunder*, when German factories rebuilt themselves from the wartime ruins and overtook their British – and other – competitors. And the major economic motor has again been the advanced engineering giants of southern Germany like Mercedes-Benz, BMW, Audi, Bosch, Miele and Siemens – not to mention specialized firms like Herrenknecht, founded in 1975, that now has 6,000 employees busily making many of the world's tunnel-boring machines, including the monsters working on London's Crossrail.

At the same time, German cities have demonstrated remarkable success in upgrading public transport and offering attractive alternatives to the ubiquitous – but too often gridlocked – private car. They led the rest of Europe in pedestrian-izing their town centres. Germany has been ahead of the UK in environmental protection, with lower car usage per head despite higher levels of car ownership. There is a very active 'green movement', particularly in protecting wildlife.

Germany achieved this, despite the fact that in the decade after 1990 it found itself faced with the colossal task of reintegrating the former communist German Democratic Republic (GDR), containing 30 per cent of the area and 20 per cent of the population of the reunited Federal Republic, back into the economic and social fabric of an advanced capitalist economy. The five new *Länder*, plus the eastern part of Berlin that was folded back into the old West Berlin, had suffered over four decades from catastrophic lack of investment and the loss of major industrial firms like Siemens, AEG and Zeiss to the West at the end of World War Two. The factories left behind by these companies, sheltered as they were from the global economy by the Iron Curtain, steadily lost all competitiveness. By the late 1980s, even a casual visitor could see that they were virtual industrial ruins, in the same dismal state as the antique railways and motorways that connected them. Productivity was less than half the level in West Germany. When the

Berlin Wall came down, within an astonishingly short time they went out of business. Over half the four million industrial jobs were lost between 1990 and 1993. Rebuilding the economy from the ruins proved to be a task almost equal to the West German achievement in the years immediately after 1945.

This raises a question, central to this chapter. At least since that first *Wirtschaftswunder*, for nearly half a century the Germans have worried about their own north–south divide, except that their word for it is slope: the *Nord-Süd Gefälle*. And the root cause was precisely the same: the old coal and steel and heavy engineering companies of the Ruhr industrial area, their precise equivalent of England's great northern industrial belt, began to lose work and eventually to shut down, while the southern states of Bavaria and Baden-Württemberg boomed on the basis of the new advanced engineering industries. The vast Meiderich steel plant in Duisburg lay rusting until someone had the brilliant idea to turn it into a tourist attraction that acts as a backdrop for rock and operatic concerts. That was part of a vast regeneration programme that ran from the 1980s into the 1990s, the Emscher Park, to be described below – but even that did not succeed in replacing all the lost jobs.

Meanwhile, for 40 years the real gap in Germany was not between north and south, but between west and east: a gap consisting of barbed wire and minefields, the Iron Curtain. When in 1990 it came down and Germany was reunified, the impacts on the economies of the cities of the old GDR were drastic. In Leipzig and in Chemnitz, in Erfurt and in Jena, the Saxony-Thüringen industrial region that had once been a European centre of advanced manufacturing simply imploded: neglected and under-invested for half a century, firms simply shut down. The same happened to the great electrical factories of East Berlin, where a nationalized AEG found itself suddenly exposed to the realities of the competitive capitalist world. It was as if all the long agonizing industrial decline of northern England happened in one catastrophic event over a couple of years.

Slowly, painfully, balance is at last being restored. There are new and highly competitive Volkswagen and BMW factories in Saxony. Jena has recovered its legendary reputation for optical goods. But there is a long way to go. At the start of 2012 the German weekly economic magazine *Wirtschaftswoche* published its eagerly-awaited annual verdict on its survey of the economic performance of the top fifty German cities, conducted for it by a consultancy, *Institut der deutschen Wirtschaft Köln* (IW, 2011). Its 2011 survey showed that all of the top ten cities are in the old West. And six are in the south. None is in the Ruhr, though one – Leverkusen, a city whose economy is based on advanced chemistry – is close. Of the bottom ten, five – including Berlin, the capital – are in the old East; the other five are in the Ruhr.

As here in the UK, one might conclude that this is yet another example of long deep trends perpetuating themselves. But some German observers were excited, because on another measure – urban dynamism – the results were quite different, even opposite. Of the ten cities showing the most improvement in their economies, seven – including Berlin – are in the old East. Of the three in the old West, one, Kassel, is an old industrial city that has had a history of difficult adaptation but is fighting back with new high-tech industries.

The consultants themselves urge caution in over-interpreting these results. Their dynamism index, they say, is volatile: it depends a lot on where one starts from. Just like a patient in intensive care, if one is in a near-terminal condition, then any improvement can seem sensational. But at least, German cities like Leipzig and Erfurt and Halle and Rostock are travelling in the right direction.

The central question for this chapter, therefore, is: how, for decades, has the German economy outstripped Britain's in productivity and growth rates, and in the contribution of manufacturing to the economy? How have German cities significantly outperformed their UK counterparts in terms of economic output, despite (and perhaps because of) having to rebuild most of their housing stock and infrastructure after 1945, and then repeating the exercise for eastern Germany after 1990? (Parkinson *et al.*, 2004). How have old industrial areas, like the Ruhrgebiet in the old West and Saxony in the old East, managed to reinvent their economies? There are relatively few studies of the underlying causes, and this chapter cannot comprehensively fill the gap. Instead, this first stage of our European journey will travel across Germany's west–east divide and up its north–south slope, visiting a selection of urban success stories in order to seek out the causes of German economic strength. They are chosen not from Germany's great industrial powerhouse, the southern states of Bavaria and Baden-Württemberg, but from the more problematic northern and eastern regions which have had to reconstitute their economies after unprecedented physical destruction and deindustrialization.

The itinerary starts from the great North Sea port of Hamburg, which is carrying through a massive urban regeneration of its old inner docklands as a tool of economic change, then going east to Berlin, now again the capital city, but engaged in a massive exercise to discover its precise economic role in the new Germany. A trip south to Leipzig, a major erstwhile East German city that suffered catastrophic deindustrialization after reunification in 1990 but has fought back successfully, provides an illuminating contrast with the next visit: to the Ruhr industrial area embracing cities like Duisburg, Essen and Dortmund and in particular to its remarkable Emscher Park, a massive exercise in physical regeneration on a regional scale, with the aim of economic transformation and environmental restoration. We then finally travel south to visit Kassel, a medium-sized industrial city that suffered from its marginal position close to the Iron Curtain but that has emerged as Germany's most dynamic place in IW's 2011 survey.

There is one last German city on our itinerary: the university city of Freiburg-im-Breisgau, in far south-west Germany near the borders of Switzerland and France, which has become a global icon for sustainable development – so much so, that it deserves a chapter of its own at the end of Part Two.

Hamburg's HafenCity:
Turning a Great Port into a Vibrant Knowledge-Economy City

If comparisons are in order – they always are, but they never quite work – Hamburg is the German Liverpool: a city with roots that go back to the Middle Ages, that owes its present-day significance to the massive growth of the Atlantic economy in the nineteenth century, but that faced huge challenges of economic change in the twentieth. There however the comparison begins to break down: Hamburg has successfully fought back, adapting to the service-based knowledge economy in one of Europe's biggest and most ambitious urban regeneration projects. In the 2011 IW survey, Hamburg rates top in prosperity, and is ninth overall. Its biggest activity in employment terms is life sciences (104,000) and it is one of the largest media locations in Germany with 63,000 employees; *Der Spiegel* and fifteen of the top twenty magazines are published there. It supplies engineering services for the civil aviation industry; some 20 per cent of all employment is in manufacturing industry, similar to the proportion for Germany as a whole.

The contrast goes back deeper into history. Germany's second largest city has an ancient history as a trading port 100 kilometres above the point where the River Elbe enters the North Sea. Growing around two lakes, the inner and outer Alster, where a local river was dammed to provide waterpower, the medieval city prospered as a powerful member of the Hanseatic League. But Hamburg's real rise came after the unification of Germany in 1871, when it became gateway to the vast basin of the Elbe and its tributaries, stretching as far as Berlin and deep into the great industrial state of Saxony. Thus Hamburg in 1900 was already far more significant a port than Liverpool. Then, as Liverpool lost its liner traffic first to Southampton and later to air travel, and as its northern English industrial hinterland stagnated in the 1920s and 1930s, Hamburg continued to grow in pace with the wider German economy.

The medieval port was soon bordered by vast enclosed docks on the north side of the river and then by even more extensive port development on the opposite south side (figure 7.1).

After World War Two its historic status made it one of only three city states (together with Berlin and its fellow-Hanseatic city of Bremen) that have the status of independent *Länder* within the Federal Republic of Germany, which gives it a particularly high degree of independence in evolving its own development policies.

But, for four decades after the end of the war, Hamburg suffered from its location only 60 kilometres from the Iron Curtain to the east, which blocked inland trade on the Elbe. It lost significant trade to its better-located rivals Rotterdam and Antwerp, but became a city with a notably relaxed atmosphere, which attracted a cosmopolitan artistic community: the Beatles first entered the scene there even before they were recognized in their native Liverpool. Then, after reunification in 1990, which brought the basin of the River Elbe back into its natural catchment, it began to recapture its position within the hugely buoyant German economy. The third biggest port in Europe (after Rotterdam and Antwerp) and the second biggest container port, it has strong connections

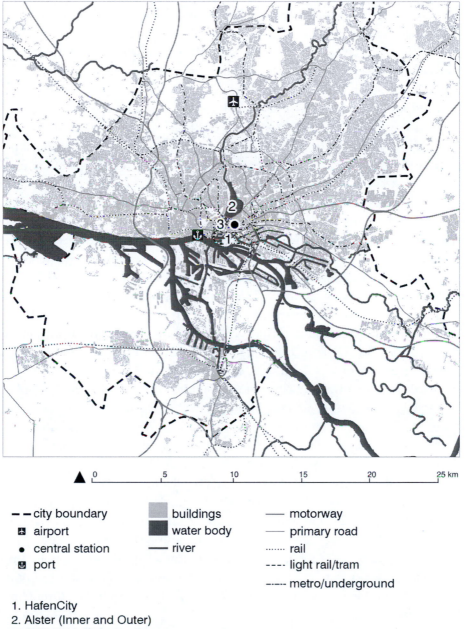

| | 0 | | 5 | | 10 | | 15 | | 20 | | 25 km |

- – – city boundary
- ✈ airport
- ● central station
- ⚓ port

- ▨ buildings
- ▮ water body
- — river

- — motorway
- — primary road
- ······· rail
- - - - light rail/tram
- - · - · - metro/underground

1. HafenCity
2. Alster (Inner and Outer)
3. CBD (Old City)

Figure 7.1. *Hamburg map.* The medieval city grew up around two lakes formed by damming the small river Alster just before its entry into the broad River Elbe. A Hanseatic port grew up around this confluence, but was largely displaced to the opposite south bank in the modern era, especially after containerization, leaving vacant a waterside site next to the city centre.

with all of the rest of Europe as well as other parts of Germany. The ubiquitous high-speed ICE trains connect it with the country's other great cities, in effect creating a polycentric city region on a national scale. In 1990, after a 30-year decline, the city's population started to rise again; in 2010 it was 1.77 million and growing, including 15 per cent who are resident aliens. There is a wider catchment area of 4.3 million people for whom the city provides a shopping and cultural centre.

The historic centre was largely flattened through wartime bombing. Almost miraculously the great nineteenth-century warehouses in the innermost docks, immediately south of the centre, largely escaped wartime destruction (thanks, it is said, to the inhabitants putting small burning boats on the lakes that form the centre of the city, thus diverting most of the bombs away from the real port). Then, in the 1970s and 1980s, as the port moved out to huge container-ship basins on the other southern bank of the river Elbe, these small innermost dock basins became redundant in the same way, and for the same reasons, as their equivalents in other cities like Rotterdam and London. But, because they were so close to the rebuilt city centre and to underground stations, the elaborate warehouses were already being used for temporary purposes as diverse as carpet trading and model railways. They became a natural focus for creative people to carve out loft space.

The central business district had lost virtually all its population: from a peak in the second half of the nineteenth century of about 170,000, to a mere 14,000 permanent residents. The docklands, less than a mile away, could provide the answer. *HafenCity* (Harbour City), the redevelopment of the old docklands area, extends over an area of 157 hectares, of which one third is water. The plan that emerged was to enlarge the city centre by no less than 40 per cent, providing high-quality space for internationally-oriented companies, while attracting people back to live in the centre. This involves constructing a new quarter of some 5,500 dwellings for 12,000 residents, plus offices, retail and cultural facilities projected to employ some 40,000 people by 2025. The HafenCity vision is superficially similar to urban regeneration schemes in comparable derelict dockland areas in a score of European cities, but on deeper analysis is ambitiously different: a vibrant, 24-hour inner-city district with numerous attractions (cruise terminal, philharmonic orchestra, several museums, shopping and eating) as well as temporary events: a base for a modern knowledge-based economy that is also a 'social city', or attractive place for all to live. And, in contrast to other examples – notably London and Liverpool – it was closely controlled throughout by the city council.

The story started in 1991 when the then-mayor, Henning Voscherau, unofficially commissioned a confidential study to look into the transformation of the inner-city port fringes. The city already owned more than half the area (88 hectares) and it purchased another 30 hectares from DB (*Deutsche Bahn*), the German national railways. Quietly, it began to buy the derelict buildings on it, through a 100 per cent city-owned company, now *HHLA Hafen und Logistik AG*, and a 100 per cent city-owned subsidiary, now *HafenCity Hamburg GmbH*. It confidentially commissioned a well-known Hamburg architect, Professor Volkwin Marg. Presented in December 1996, his report laid out many of the development principles that would govern the area's redevelopment.

Finally, in May 1997, the mayor unveiled his 'Vision HafenCity' to the public: an area of around 157 hectares was to be developed into an upmarket inner-city district with mixed residential, work, cultural and leisure uses. The key was to be a special fund under public law to hold 'city and port' assets and simultaneously to develop a new, state-of-the-art container terminal at Altenwerder, which would effectively be financed out of the redevelopment of HafenCity.

Thence, events unfolded rapidly. A competition for a draft master plan was launched in April 1999; in October, an international jury announced the winner to be Hamburgplan, a Dutch-German team, and its plan was approved by the Hamburg Senate on 29 February 2000. This fixed the key elements which would subsequently govern the development process: intensive interaction between existing and new buildings and the water, the elevation of buildings as flood protection, the public character of many ground-floor uses, with 10.5 km of new waterfront and around 26 hectares of public parks, squares and promenades, and a fine-grained mix of uses – homes, service businesses, culture, leisure, tourism and commerce (figure 7.2). The entire scheme, as Hamburg's city

Figure 7.2. *Hamburg HafenCity*. An aerial view of the project under development, with the medieval city centre and the two Alster lakes behind it. (*Photo*: Fotofrizz, by courtesy of HafenCity GmbH)

planning director Jörn Walter puts it, is a deliberate rejection of most twentieth-century urban planning as 'a disaster' in its addiction to single-use planning, its separation of home and work and shop (Turner, 2011).

The Master plan also establishes an eighteen-stage plan for the development over a 25-year time frame, until 2025. It specifies that the area will be progressively developed from west to east and from north to south. Within this framework, development can take place more rapidly than in the UK because the procedures are simpler. *HafenCity Hamburg GmbH* provides not only planning briefs but also the basic infrastructure, including a gas-fired district heating system with each building producing its own hot water, as well as a superb public realm. The master plan stipulates six-storey blocks, which may be for either residential or commercial use, giving great flexibility to adapt to changing circumstances. The blocks look out to the river, and there is continuous access for pedestrians on the waterside; car parking is relegated to underground garages at the back, off the main perimeter road. HafenCity is built at three different levels. To guard against future floods and potential sea-level rise, much of the area is on a street level 5 metres above the level of the old dock; the original dock level is preserved as 10.5 kilometres of quayside promenades; and additional open space is provided on floating pontoons, adding to the total of public space (Turner, 2011).

Within this fixed template, the company then lays down a strict procedure for the development of each individual section of the project. Any prospective developer must compete not only with respect to cost but also to the quality and creativity of the proposal. It must articulate its brief, conduct an architectural competition and, together with the selected architect, submit a scheme to the company, down to the level which would traditionally be needed to gain local planning approval. *HafenCity Hamburg GmbH* then judges the scheme relative to its own set of sustainability standards which includes energy performance, benefit to public amenity, health and comfort, mix of use, and ease and efficiency of building maintenance over time. Housing sites are advertised with a fixed bid price. Non-housing sites are sold to companies that want to occupy at least 50 per cent of the space, and the process of agreeing a contract takes about 18 months to ensure adequate quality and avoid speculation.

The master plan promotes different uses for a range of income groups, and specifies overall densities, land use, and performance requirements. But beyond that, it encourages variety. Even within a single urban block, the mix – of developers and of functions – is deliberately far from uniform. One block combines an office for the main German headquarters of Greenpeace, private apartments and a design studio. Another block combines an elementary school with an apartment building and the developer is responsible for school maintenance for the first 25 years. HafenCity is also witness to a new developer type; the joint building venture. This involves a cooperative of future residents who purchase land and procure the design and construction of their own building whilst HafenCity facilitates the process. Often joint building ventures are able to realize high-quality living space at prices that are well below market rates.

The residential apartments are extremely spacious and remarkably economic to rent: the Hamburg average is 30 m² of living space per person, and apartments cost roughly half the price of a similar place in London Docklands. Prices for new apartments in the Dalmannkai neighbourhood, with approximately 45 per cent rented, range from subsidized units with rents between €5.80/m² and €8.00/m², through housing cooperative rental units at €9.50–13.5/m², to open rental market units at €12–18/m². This difference represents the scale of the savings to be made by taking some of the risks (or profit margin) out of development.

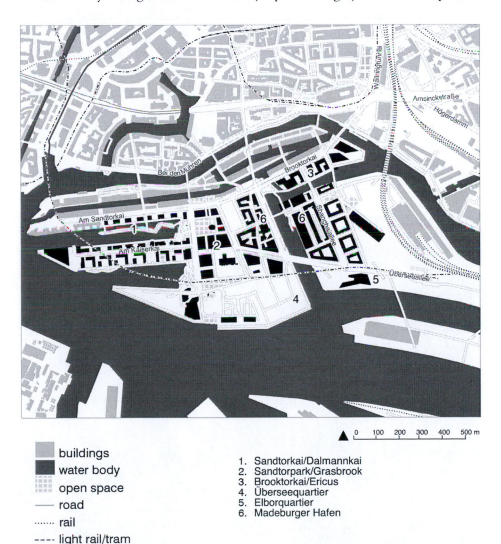

buildings	1. Sandtorkai/Dalmannkai
water body	2. Sandtorpark/Grasbrook
open space	3. Brooktorkai/Ericus
road	4. Überseequartier
rail	5. Elborquartier
light rail/tram	6. Madeburger Hafen
underground/metro	

Figure 7.3. *Hamburg HafenCity plan*. Figure ground plan showing the state of development in 2011, about one-fifth completed.

Privately-owned apartments sell from approximately €2,850/m² for units in so-called joint building ventures, through €3,500–4,500/m² for developer-managed units, to €6,000–8,000/m² for luxury units; isolated cases, e.g. penthouses, may sell for over €10,000/m². These prices have hardly been affected by the great crash of 2007 and its aftermath.

By 2011, one-fifth of the area had already been redeveloped (figure 7.3). The completed western neighbourhoods – Am Sandtorkai/Dalmannkai, Sandtorpark/ Grasbrook and Brooktorkai/ Ericus – already housed 1,700 residents and 8,400 workers in over 300 businesses (figures 7.4 and 7.5). Forty-seven projects were completed and another thirty-five were under construction or in the planning stage. Two major specialized quarters were also taking shape: Überseequartier, the commercial heart covering 13.7 hectares with a new subway station, opened at the end of November 2012, and Elbtorquartier, the future 'knowledge quarter', including International Maritime Museum Hamburg in an historic warehouse, open since 2008, and the new HafenCity University (HCU, the University of the Built Environment and Metropolitan Development), due to open in summer 2013. Here, around Magdeburger Hafen, an ensemble of promenades and squares is already linking HafenCity to the historic city centre only 900 metres distant (figure 7.6). By 2015, fully half of the scheme will be completed.

One element of the project has been quite openly controversial. *HafenCity Gmbh* adopted a deliberate policy of attracting wealthier residents and international investors, which could be easily be criticized as regeneration

Figure 7.4. *Hamburg HafenCity Dalmannkai.* View of a completed section of the HafenCity project, with medium-rise mixed use developments carefully massed along the waterfront. (*Photo*: ELBE&FLUT, by courtesy of HafenCity GmbH)

Figure 7.5. *Hamburg HafenCity Brooktorkai*. Another representative view of an early-stage completed part of the project, demonstrating the imaginative use of the waterfront. (*Photo*: Thomas Hampel/ ELBE&FLUT, by courtesy of HafenCity GmbH)

Figure 7.6. *Hamburg HafenCity Magdeburger Hafen*. Development along an arm of a canal, skilfully incorporating older warehouse buildings next to the city centre, rehabilitated for new uses. (*Photo*: HafenCity GmbH)

through gentrification, but which the company justified on the grounds that poorer people were already well housed elsewhere in the city, and that the policy made the financing of development much easier. So too did the German system whereby many of the blocks are privately or cooperatively owned, and are then rented out, drawing finance from local or state banks.

A study of the new residents found they were of all ages, and include career-centred couples and singles, families who moved even before schools had opened, empty nesters aged over 50, and retired people. They were drawn by the waterfront location and a stimulating environment close to the heart of the city (Menzl, 2010). The population mix, coupled with the extensive use of cooperatives and private housing for rent, has helped to generate a sense of community in a remarkably short time.

Closely associated with the new residential mix, parts of the development are deliberately aimed at digital or media companies, including all sizes of enterprise to ensure the development is less vulnerable to downturns. There have been major debates over the role that creative people and activities should play, as artists protested at being squeezed out by higher rents once an area took off. After one sit-in, the city decided not to sell a group of historic buildings to a foreign investor. But in fact, while the master plan favours temporary cultural or artistic uses, the new offices are now too expensive for creative businesses.

The main positive lesson from HafenCity is how the public and private sectors can work together if the municipality takes the lead. Because the development agency is entirely owned by the municipality, it is not bound to offer sites up to competition or to secure the best price. Instead it may either nominate a developer it believes is appropriate, or ask for proposals, choosing primarily on quality rather than price.

The main question mark is whether the area might become a 'rich man's ghetto', full of wealthy pensioners. To avoid that, according to Jürgen Bruns-Berentelg, the executive chairman of *HafenCity Hamburg GmbH*, the key is to mix in cultural and social institutions – art galleries, museums, the university – alongside commercial structures and residential buildings. Penthouses for the wealthy will sit next door to apartments for lower-income neighbours. Schools are opening; so is a retirement home. And this is combined with a communication strategy to attract the right mixture of people to live in the development. The company has employed a sociologist, Marcus Menzl, to liaise with the residents. Early on, in 2008, he found that the 600 inhabitants included forty children, a surprisingly high number given the lack of a kindergarten and playground. A playground was high on the parents' wish list. So the company built a temporary one that could be moved later. It also agreed to co-finance an indoor recreation area; the parents financed the other half (Schaer, 2010).

Early research has shown that residents already identify strongly with their neighbourhood. 'That sort of emotional connection usually only comes with time', Menzl commented. 'But they seem to have identified with HafenCity very quickly and they want to support the philosophy. You cannot build a neighbourly feeling... But I think that architecture can help certain processes and hinder others' (*Ibid.*). So early auguries are good – but a definitive verdict on HafenCity, clearly, will take years. The central issues are first whether the redevelopment will succeed in its objectives, and second whether its very success will prove problematic in threatening the balanced social mix that lies at its heart. To appreciate how these issues may play out on a larger urban canvas, we need next to visit Berlin.

Berlin: Planning Regeneration Carefully and Creatively

Comparisons, again, can never be exact. In Berlin immediately after 1989, as its historian Claire Colomb puts it, almost everything that could happen to a city happened almost at once, in 'a sudden acceleration of history' (Colomb, 2012, p. 72): 'the transition to a united city after a history of conflict and division; the transition to a capital city in a nation defining its national identity; the transition from a socialist to a capitalist city; and the transition from an industrial to a post-industrial or post-Fordist metropolis' (*Ibid.*, p. 7). Processes that had happened elsewhere over decades – globalization, European integration, structural economic change, the shift to a service- and knowledge-economy, rising unemployment and welfare expenditure, pressures for the transformation of the local state and cuts in public expenditure – all hit the city simultaneously (*Ibid.*, p. 72). But, despite its exceptional history over half a century after World War Two, Berlin today faces many of the same problems as former industrial conurbations in the United Kingdom, like Greater Manchester, that have to support rising demands for urban services with income from a static population.

After its dramatic rise from remote Prussian garrison city to capital city of Europe's most powerful nation and industrial powerhouse, in 1945 Berlin suffered sudden political and economic meltdown. After 363 air raids over five years, the city was in ruins. One-fifth of all its 250,000 buildings and nearly a quarter of all industrial capacity had been destroyed. The population had shrunk from 4.3 to 2.8 million (*Ibid.*, p. 51). Then, both Germany and Berlin were divided up between the four victorious powers (the USA, the USSR, UK and France), the capital shifted to Bonn, and West Berlin was left as an isolated island within Soviet Eastern Germany. Big companies like AEG and Siemens left for Frankfurt and Munich; the remaining firms suffered from low levels of technological innovation and private investment. A physically isolated island in the middle of the communist GDR, West Berlin was supported by massive subsidies from the West German federal budget which directly funded half the city's budget (*Ibid.*, p. 52).

The masonry shells of the city's distinctive five-storey nineteenth-century apartment blocks survived the bombing and were rebuilt so that Berlin retained the monumental character of a planned nineteenth-century city, with ornate

grand buildings, wide boulevards and huge public spaces. The Wall, which
stood from 1961 to 1989, not only divided the city but created a no-man's land
running right through the centre. It led to the creation of two parallel cities, with

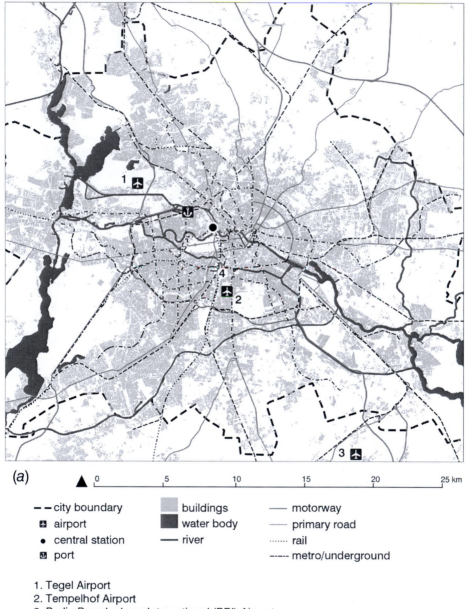

(a)

| | 0 | 5 | 10 | 15 | 20 | 25 km |

- − − city boundary   ▨ buildings   ⎯ motorway
- ✈ airport   ▨ water body   ⎯ primary road
- ● central station   ⎯ river   ⋯⋯ rail
- ⚓ port   − − − metro/underground

1. Tegel Airport
2. Tempelhof Airport
3. Berlin Brandenburg International (BBI) Airport
4. Bergmannstrasse/Bergmann Kiez

Figure 7.7. (a) and (b). *Berlin maps*. The German capital, which has lost one quarter of its peak
1939 population, remains a remarkably compact nineteenth-century tenement city. The West
Berlin airport at Tegel and its East Berlin replacement at Schönefeld, BBI (Berlin Brandenburg
International, due to open after delays in 2014) are both only a short drive from the city centre. Since
the city's reunification in 1989–1990, most of the important scenes of regeneration – illustrated in
following figures – have been in or close to the historic city centre, Berlin-Mitte – see figure 7.7(b).

two centres – Kurfürstendamm for West Berlin, Alexanderplatz for East Berlin – and a duplication of museums and other public buildings. All this represented an important legacy for the future.

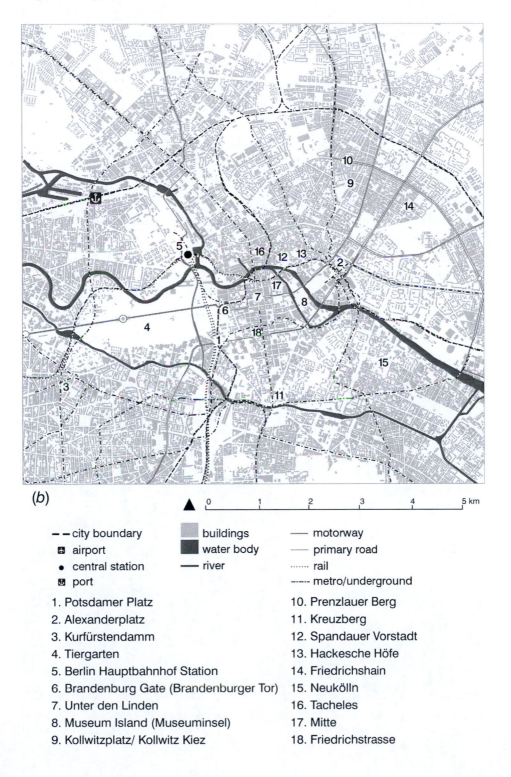

(b)

0   1   2   3   4   5 km

– – city boundary   ▨ buildings   —— motorway
⬛ airport   ▨ water body   -------- primary road
● central station   —— river   ········ rail
⬓ port   ----- metro/underground

1. Potsdamer Platz
2. Alexanderplatz
3. Kurfürstendamm
4. Tiergarten
5. Berlin Hauptbahnhof Station
6. Brandenburg Gate (Brandenburger Tor)
7. Unter den Linden
8. Museum Island (Museuminsel)
9. Kollwitzplatz/ Kollwitz Kiez

10. Prenzlauer Berg
11. Kreuzberg
12. Spandauer Vorstadt
13. Hackesche Höfe
14. Friedrichshain
15. Neukölln
16. Tacheles
17. Mitte
18. Friedrichstrasse

When the Wall came down in 1989 and Germany was reunited (in German *die Wende*, the turnaround), Berlin was re-designated the capital of a united Germany. The first priority for the Berlin Mayor and Senate was physically to reunite the two halves of the city, including the separate transport systems and the huge swathe of vacant land through the centre left by the demolition of the wall (figure 7.7). Aided by a *Fördergebietgetetz* (Assisted Area Law) which offered tax breaks – up to 50 per cent until 1997 – in the eastern *Länder* which did not find tenants, 'Berlin became a haven for Western consultants, developers and investors' (*Ibid.*, p. 91). Nearly 7 million square metres of office space were built in Berlin between 1990 and 2000 – one million for Federal government functions. Between the old West and the old East Berlin, a whole new city centre was built on the abandoned 'neutral' area of Potsdamer Platz, to complement the existing centres that had developed in the divided city (figure 7.8). Larger even than London's Canary Wharf, it rapidly became the symbol of the new Berlin: 'the greatest architectural marketing plan of the contemporary era' (*Ibid.*, p. 150, quoting Watson, 2006, p. 100).

Initiated by the private investors – Daimler, Sony and others – at the very start of the project, but then taken over by *Partner für Berlin – Gesellschaft für Haupstadtmarketing GmbH*, created by the city in 1994 to carry out 'capital city marketing' with the aid of the private sector, Potsdamer Platz was used as an

Figure 7.8. *Berlin Potsdamer Platz*. This megaproject, completed a decade after the reunification of the city, was designed to re-establish the historic heart of pre-1939 Berlin, but proved to be based on over-optimistic projections of the return of commercial functions to the capital.

emblem of the new Berlin in its official marketing campaigns (*Ibid.*, pp. 105, 118–119, 150). It served two purposes: first, to establish both a temporal and geographical continuity with the Berlin of the past; secondly, to serve re-image Berlin as a global – or at least European – metropolis. The place marketers depicted the target groups they regarded as desirable customers: young and middle-aged professionals in suits, tourists and 'creative urbanites' in trendy clothes. Many Berliners regarded the development as a sell-out to corporate interests, which confirmed their suspicion by showing little loyalty to it: in 2007 Daimler sold its interest to a Frankfurt-based management group and in 2008 Sony sold its centre to Morgan Stanley (*Ibid.*, pp. 150, 158, 166–167).

A little further north across the Tiergarten – Berlin's equivalent of London's Royal Parks – the grand plan proposed creating a totally new central railway station on a site close to the seat of government, duly completed in 2006 with fast train links to Leipzig and Dresden, to serve as 'the City's calling card' as a basis for major development alongside. A new €5 billion international airport, Berlin Brandenburg International (BBI), plagued by faults and delayed in opening, at last should put Berlin in its proper place in the air traffic map of Europe.

But great architecture is not enough to create a successful new heart for a major city. Though half the government moved with about 12,000 jobs, the other half remained in Bonn. Staff in private companies resisted having to move (and there is a saying that 'it is better to be unemployed in Freiburg than to have a job in Berlin!'). Many auxiliary services, embassies and media-based companies did move to the city, but many of the anticipated larger company headquarters stayed away. With a population of only 3.5 million within a Germany of 82 million, it could not exert the same influence over the country that it once did. Dreams of becoming a 'global city' soon faded.

Meanwhile, in West Berlin deindustrialization had already begun in the 1970s and 1980s. Between 1989 and 1998 manufacturing jobs in the reunified city shrank from 400,000 to 130,000 (*Ibid.*, p. 83, quoting Krätke, 2000, p. 7). The share of the working population in production (excluding the building trade) fell from 20.6 to 15.1 per cent between 1991 and 2009, while the share of service employment grew from 71.2 to 80.5 per cent. Thus the growth in service jobs did not compensate for the loss in manufacturing, and unemployment rates grew steadily throughout the 1990s and early 2000s. Berlin lagged behind other *Länder* in growth rates and suffered from higher unemployment, achieving the unenviable title of the only capital city in the EU with a GDP per head below the national average. Far from growing to five million as originally predicted, population declined in the second half of the 1990s (*Ibid.*, pp. 83, 113).

All too soon, alarming evidence emerged of a surplus of retail and office space. A sharp initial rise in office rents reversed as early as 1993; by 1995 rents were back to 1990 levels (*Ibid.*, pp. 91, 115). By 1998 vacant office space was estimated at 1.5 million square metres (*Ibid.*, p. 115, quoting Krätke and Borst, 2000). Though the Potsdamer Platz was completed, other schemes – the

Figure 7.9. *Berlin Alexanderplatz*. The historic core of the east side of Berlin, and of the communist post-World War Two city, rebuilt in the 1960s in a monumental monumentalist style dominated by the celebrated Funkturm (TV Tower) designed to dominate the view from West Berlin. Its redevelopment, planned in the 1990s, was put on hold when early bright expectations failed to materialize. (*Photo*: Taxiarchos228, 2012)

redevelopment of Alexanderplatz (figure 7.9), new large-scale settlements on the outskirts of the city – were put on hold (*Ibid.*, p. 115).

In 1994 all subsidies to Berlin stopped, meaning a one-third reduction in the *Land* budget and a financial crisis in the second half of the 1990s (*Ibid.*, p. 84). The loss of special subsidy, and the incorporation of Berlin into the general system of financial redistribution within the Federal Republic, led to a sudden loss of income of 30 per cent between 1993 and 1995. Exacerbated by declining GDP and a rising welfare burden, plus tax write-offs to investors, the city's debt rose from €10 billion in 1991 to €40 billion in 2001 and to €55 billion in 2004 (*Ibid.*, p. 223). 'The loss of the status of economic exception, the intensity of economic restructuring, the new symbolic role as the capital of a united Germany and the search for a new collective identity in a previously divided city called for new types of imaging and place marketing activities...' (*Ibid.*, p. 73). In 2002 the new mayor, Klaus Wowereit, announced massive spending cuts: public expenditure per head in 2005 was only 89 per cent of its 1995 level, and employees in public administration fell from 207,000 in 1991 to 145,000 in 2001 and to 114,000 in 2006 (*Ibid.*, p. 205, quoting SenFin, 2007). By 2010 the debt stood at €60 billion, and 12 per cent of the city's €20 billion budget was being used to pay the interest (*Ibid.*, p. 226).

The mismatch between the official marketing imagery of the 1990s and the economic reality helps to explain the continuous search for a new 'Berlin brand' on the part of the Wowereit administration. In 2005 an important report to the Berlin Senate concluded that priorities should shift to promoting tourism and the cultural industries. Berlin thus followed the lead that so many other cities were adopting, seeking an answer in what Richard Florida calls 'the creative class'. It decided to make the most of being 'poor, but sexy' (*Arm, aber sexy*), Wowereit's brilliant phrase first used in an interview in 2003 and then frequently repeated (*Ibid.*, p. 259). 'Be Berlin', the new strategy launched by Wowereit in 2009 (*Ibid.*), sought to bring Berliners back into the marketing process, directly appealing to them. PR at last celebrated the ethnic diversity of the city (*Ibid.*, pp. 260, 262).

In pursuing the new strategy, Berlin had two major advantages. First, convenient public transport running 24 hours a day, plus abundant cultural offers, ample open space and scope for creativity, give the city a distinctive quality of life. Thirty per cent of the city is covered by parks, and the vast central Tiergarten helps to make the city a pleasant place for families, with its open-air café, zoo, and waterside walks. On the east side of the Brandenburg Gate, the magnificent Unter den Linden and adjacent Museumsinsel (Museum Island) (a UNESCO World Heritage Site since 1999) form an outstanding ensemble of cultural buildings, largely left untouched by wartime destruction. Within a reunited city this stretch of the Berlin's east–west axis received huge public and private investments for its unequalled concentration of museums and cultural facilities on Museumsinsel.

Second, given the huge amount of new housing that had to be built in a hurry after 1945, Berlin provides many excellent examples of liveable places. Many of the apartment blocks are built around courtyards, with play facilities as focal points. Berliners value their '*Kieze*', tightly-knit districts that offer everything they need within walking distance. These 'urban villages' are often located near larger squares or lively streets such as the Kollwitz Kiez near Kollwitzplatz in Prenzlauer Berg, or Bergmann Kiez around Bergmannstrasse in Kreuzberg or the Spandauer Vorstadt, a central district of Mitte nestled between Alexanderplatz and Friedrichstraße. Gradual sympathetic and often modern infill development, together with the restoration of some key buildings such as the Hackesche Höfe and the creation of high-quality public space, have resulted in a bustling and upmarket district that is extremely popular with tourists and locals.

To exploit this quality, the city planners embraced 'critical reconstruction', a concept developed by the architect Josef Paul Kleihues as part of an International Building Exhibition in Berlin as far back as 1984–1987, which 'involves the preservation or active restoration of the features of the 'historical' urban layout and fabric of the city as a guiding principle for contemporary inner-city redevelopment' (*Ibid.*, p. 210). In Berlin it meant the built form developed between the late nineteenth century and the end of the Weimar Republic, characterized by small-scale plot structure, clearly defined mixed-use urban blocks, legible street paths, moderate heights and homogenous building materials (*Ibid.*). It too easily became a tool of developer-led gentrification, but it has not evoked much opposition (*Ibid.*, p. 215).

This may well have been because of demographic change. During the 1990s, about half of Berlin's 1989 population left the city, replaced by roughly the same number of newcomers, mainly young people; 1.7 million new residents have moved to the city since 1989. They, and the tourists who flooded into the city, were drawn less by official place marketing than by alternative, informal communication (*Ibid.*, p. 309). 'It has been facilitated by the availability of affordable working and living spaces, by a tolerant and liberal culture inherited from the 1970s and 1980s, and fed by pre-existing concentrations of cultural producers, artists and networks of alternative culture (e.g. the techno music scene)' (*Ibid.*, p. 232).

Tourism, heavily promoted by Mayor Wowereit, grew from 3 to 9 million annual visitors between 1993 and 2010 and from 7 million to just under 21 million overnight stays over the same period excluding day visitors, who totalled 130 million in 2010. 'In all, this means that just under half a million tourists or daily visitors were, on an average day, present in Berlin at the end of the 2000s', making the city the third most visited in Europe after Paris and London (*Ibid.*, p. 234). Tourism generated a net turnover of €9 billion in 2009, with 230,000 jobs (*Ibid.*). The rising number of exchange students, plus flexible working practices, has led to a blurring of boundaries between tourists and residents: 'temporary city users' (*Ibid.*, p. 246). This development occurred especially in new local clusters on the inner east side of the city, including the Spree banks with the relocation of the European HQ of Universal Music in 2001 and of MTV Europe in 2004; fashion designers in Prenzlauer Berg, art galleries in Mitte, product design in Friedrichshain and music labels in Kreuzberg (*Ibid.*, pp. 236, 240). These areas, particularly Prenzlauer Berg (figure 7.10), have also appeared on the

Figure 7.10. *Eberswalder Strasse U-Bahn station, Prenzlauer Berg.* Heart of this inner-city tenement district, left to languish during the years of communist rule, but now a preferred residential location for new urban professionals. (*Photo*: CC by Abaris at the German language Wikipedia)

tourist map, in a new form of 'new urban tourism', 'post tourism', 'alternative tourism' or 'tourism off the beaten track' (*Ibid.*, p. 246, quoting Maitland, 2007 and Maitland and Newman, 2009), aided by low-cost air travel: a journalist calculated that there are 10,000 'Easyjetsetters' in Berlin every weekend (*Ibid.*, p. 246).

These 'funky neighbourhoods', with much lower property costs than in London or in Scandinavian cities, became a key factor in the take-off of Berlin's 'creative economy', which by 2007 accounted for 20 per cent of jobs with 1,200 businesses in the centre and 4,500 in the inner city. The internet boom of the early 2000s, so abruptly ended, soon regained momentum around the trendier places with hundreds of internationally mixed start-up companies flourishing in 'Silicon Alley' (as labelled by the *New York Times*). National and international start-up investors and catalysers pinned their hopes on the next 'big thing' being made in Berlin. *Time* magazine, on 16 November 2010, headlined *Hip Berlin, Europe's Capital of Cool* (*Ibid.*, p. 239).

Berlin thus established itself as an 'alpha media world city' on a level with Los Angeles, New York, Paris, London, Munich and Amsterdam (*Ibid.*, p. 232, quoting Krätke, 2003; Krätke and Taylor, 2004). There is a noteworthy discrepancy between Berlin's position in the global system of 'strategic economic centres' and what Krätke calls the 'global system of media cities' (*Ibid.*, p. 232). 'Berlin has been a hotbed of cultural innovation in spite of, or rather because of, its rather weak economic performance in the conventional sense' (*Ibid.*, p. 232, quoting Bader and Scharenberg, 2010).

The strategy appears to have worked. Berlin seems to have turned a corner: though in 2011 it still only ranked forty-seventh out of fifty on the IW ranking of comparative urban performance (IW, 2011), it moved up to ninth place on dynamics, while its GDP grew by 17 per cent between 2005 and 2009. Unemployment has sunk to 12 per cent, the lowest level in 15 years, though it is still double the national average. The growth of the creative economy, helped by low property prices, has boosted the city's image and created a major urban tourist industry.

But all this was not enough to achieve the city's ambitions. Large development schemes around transport nodes are only just beginning to pay off in attracting major companies. There are still key issues in achieving social cohesion and overcoming polarization and an East-West mentality. Most of the new housing is aimed at the upper end of the market. 'It is perhaps slightly ironic that the intensification of tourism marketing and the extension of place marketing to new symbolic frontiers were carried out by a nominally Left wing government' (Colomb, 2012, p. 265). But the irony is that the growing knowledge-intensive and creative sectors, the focus of economic development in the 2000s, are the very same ones threatened by cuts in public expenditure (*Ibid.*, pp. 265–266).

The city's radical image and low costs attract young people from other parts of Germany, who come as students and trainees but stay to become the new elite (*Ibid.*, p. 284; *Ibid.*, p. 191, quoting Hesselmann, 2011). They look especially to the inner neighbourhoods within the S-Bahn ring – especially the eastern districts of Prenzlauer Berg and Mitte, and parts of Kreuzberg and Friedrichshain. But the resulting pressures of redevelopment, rising rents and renewal have brought problems for small businesses and low-income residents, triggering a counter-reaction. In the late 2000s the streets of Friedrichshain, Kreuzberg and Neukölln were affected by radical car-burning protests against brutal evictions of former squats ordered by the nominally leftwing coalition (*Ibid.*, p. 291).

> A recent meeting at SO36 discussed non-violent ways to keep out 'unwanted' residents. Erwin Riedmann, a sociologist, proposed an 'uglification strategy' – to 'go around wearing a ripped vest and hang food in Lidl bags from the balcony so that it looks like you don't have a fridge'. The suggestion drew laughs, but is a strategy being adopted. An 'anti-schiki micki' website, esregnetkaviar.de (it's raining caviar), offers the following tips to make a neighbourhood unattractive to newcomers: Don't repair broken windows; put foreign names on the doorbell, and install satellite dishes (*Ibid.*, p. 292, qoting Connolly 2010, n.p.).

Rising rents continue to threaten the city's creative base – as highlighted by the huge battle, early in 2012, to occupy and redevelop the derelict Tacheles factory, squatted since the 1990s by a huge artistic colony who refuse to leave (figure 7.11). In early 2012 the media began to report a new phenomenon: a threat to the

Figure 7.11. *Tacheles building:* this former department store, in a key location at the northern end of the Friedrichstrasse, was squatted in 1990 by artists and became a celebrated home of alternative culture, but was reoccupied in 2011–2012 by the owners for redevelopment, symbolising the end of Berlin's 'Poor but Sexy' era. (*Photo:* CC by Nicor, 2006)

city's many clubs that occupy old low-rent spaces. The German language added a new noun to its vocabulary: *Clubsterben*, death of the clubs.

Berlin has thus struggled successfully to create a new image, but paradoxically that very success is generating new problems. They are however problems that many cities in the former East Germany would be glad to experience – as the example of Leipzig shows.

Leipzig: Economic Growth in a Shrinking City

Leipzig, 190 kilometres south-west of Berlin with 523,000 people (in 2010) is the second largest city in eastern Germany. First documented in 1015, a city since 1165, located at the crossroads of major European trade routes, it soon became a hub of commerce with the oldest trade fair in Europe. With Germany's second oldest university, founded in 1409 (Power *et al.*, 2010, p. 107), it also became a major centre of European culture, home of Bach and Goethe. Logically, it developed a major publishing industry dating back to 1481, only 30 years after Gutenberg's invention of the movable-type printing press; by the late eighteenth century, concentrated in the city's famous *Graphisches Viertel*, it had grown into developing into a 'true' Marshallian industrial district with a large number of competitive, as well as complementary, trades, well-connected with interregional and international markets. In 1938, it housed over 300 book publishers and 500 allied firms, as well as the German equivalent of the US Library of Congress, the Deutsche Bücherei (Bathelt and Boggs, 2003, p. 281).

Between German unification in 1871 and World War One, Leipzig became a major manufacturing city specializing in textiles and metal working as well as publishing. Between 1870 and 1900, its population more than quadrupled, from 107,000 in 1871 to 456,000 in 1900 (Power *et al.*, 2010, p. 108). Between the world wars (1918–1939), with new electrical, chemical, mining and energy industries, Leipzig continued to grow, reaching its population peak in the 1930s with almost 750,000 inhabitants in 1939 – the fourth largest German city.

Leipzig was less damaged during World War Two than other major German cities; its urban structure, dominated by compact tenement buildings, remained almost intact. But the division of Germany into two states in 1949 brought significant political, social and economic rupture. Industrial life revived with large socialist conglomerates (*Kombinate*) based on the traditional industrial sectors. But the socialist GDR concentrated most functions in East Berlin, and Leipzig experienced a gradual decline in significance. The Iron Curtain disrupted Leipzig's traditional commercial ties; only the annual international trade fair, which functioned as the showpiece of the Eastern Bloc's industrial production, continued to offer tenuous links with the West. Although the publishing quarter was rebuilt, it was integrated into the international socialist division of labour and interacted little with the West, which was taken over by publishers in Munich, West Berlin, Hamburg, Stuttgart, Frankfurt, and Cologne.

Key Leipzig institutions – the *Börsenverein* (Book Exchange), the *Buchmesse* (Book Fair), the *Deutsche Bibliothek* (German National Library) – were all replicated in Frankfurt. The Leipzig workforce knew little of Western business practices and operated with aged equipment. Thus the industry was poorly equipped for integration into the larger West German economy. The city's population fell by nearly a third, to 530,000 in 1989, when the population took the lead in peaceful demonstrations that led to the fall of the Iron Curtain and the Socialist regime (*Ibid.*, pp. 108–110).

Immediately after reunification, there was a euphoric belief that East Germany would quickly catch up with West Germany. To assist, massive transfer payments were made: as late as 2003, subsidies represented one-third of the gross economic product of the new *Länder*. Leipzig like Berlin became a 'boom town', with a wave of construction. A new trade fair complex was built on the northern outskirts; there were plans for the city to become a leading regional centre for banking and finance (Heinker, 2004, quoting Power *et al.*, 2010, pp. 115, 120). Major investments revitalized the city centre, with refurbishment of historic buildings including the new and old town halls, churches, merchant

Table 7.1.

Location	Project	Sector	Period	Investment € × 10⁶
City	Technical infrastructure (gas, electricity, water)	technical infrastructure	1993–1994	1,000
	Main train station (modernization, shopping mall)	transport infrastructure, retail	1996–1998	280
	Fine arts museum	museum, arts	2000–2004	73
	City tunnel	transport infrastructure	2003–2010	572
	University campus (modernization)	higher education	2004–2009	150
Urban fringe	New Leipzig Fair	trade fairs, commerce	1993–1995	2,060
	Leipzig Airport (modernization and expansion)	transport infrastructure	1993–2000	660
	Leipzig-Hall Cargo Handling Centre (GVZ)	transport infrastructure, logistics	1993–1994	50
	Medical scientific centre	health services	1992–1996	1,500
	(Re)development of enterprise zones	business/industrial park	1993–1996	1,200
	Various media-related projects (Media City, printing quarter, etc)	media, publishing	1993–2003	1,150

Note: Although mainly financed with public funding, many of these projects also received funding from the private sector.

Source: Power *et al.*, 2010, based on Stadt Leipzig (2006*a*) and Nuissl and Rink (2003).

houses and Leipzig's typical historic shopping arcades. By the late 1990s, the city centre had regained mass and confidence, as reflected in a series of retail and, to a lesser degree, office developments, with modernization of the main train station – Germany's biggest – including a shopping mall, the first such project in Germany (figure 7.12) (Power *et al.*, 2010, p. 120).

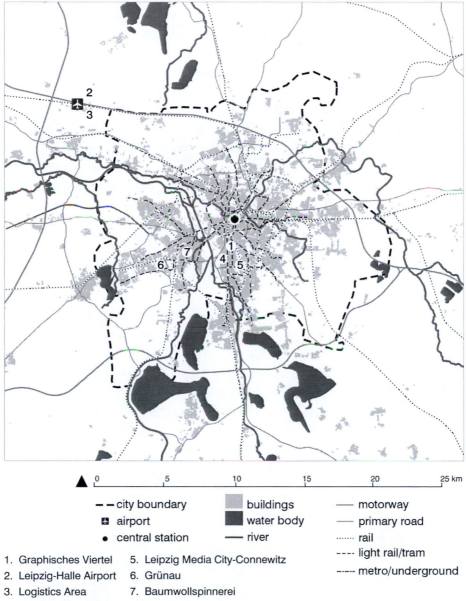

0   5   10   15   20   25 km

- – city boundary   buildings   —— motorway
- ✈ airport   water body   —— primary road
- • central station   —— river   ······· rail
                                              ---- light rail/tram
1. Graphisches Viertel   5. Leipzig Media City-Connewitz   ----- metro/underground
2. Leipzig-Halle Airport   6. Grünau
3. Logistics Area   7. Baumwollspinnerei
4. Südliche Vorstadt

Figure 7.12. *Leipzig map*. This great medieval trading city became the home of the German publishing industry and a major cultural centre, but withered under 40 years of communist rule. The inner south side of the city has quickly been restored to its former elegance, aided by the establishment of a Media Centre, but much of the east side continued to languish as new development took place outside the city limits.

But it all too soon emerged that the 'blossoming landscapes', which Chancellor Kohl had promised East Germany in 1990, would not quickly materialize. Deindustrialization in Leipzig was particularly severe: 800 companies changed hands, 300 immediately closed. In only 7 years – from 1989 to 1996 – 90,000 manufacturing jobs disappeared, a decline of 90 per cent: manufacturing fell from 27 per cent of the workforce in 1991 to only 11 per cent by 2004. The service sector expanded, but could not compensate. Though many workers were given generous social packages and early-retirement schemes, unemployment increased steadily, reaching almost 20 per cent by the late 1990s – substantially higher than for Germany as a whole and, in 2005, even higher than East Germany. In the decade following reunification, Leipzig lost almost 100,000 inhabitants or 20 per cent of its population, reaching an historic low of 437,000 in 1998 (Power et al, 2010, pp. 111–113).

During this time, Leipzig suffered from a strange combination of shrinkage and growth. With a dilapidated housing stock of decayed inner-city apartment blocks and a ring of depressingly uniform industrialized housing estates in the outer area, coupled with a pent-up demand for home ownership, the predictable result was a construction boom that produced 50,000 homes in new suburban estates, countless commercial parks and large shopping centres. They were built in municipalities outside the city limits which lacked adequate planning controls – a process described by two German observers as 'Wild East Suburbanization' (Power *et al.*, 2010, p. 113, quoting Nuissl and Rink, 2003). Within the city, in contrast, speculation and confusion over property rights delayed investment in the existing building fabric, while the declining population drastically lowered demand for living space and stressed the urban infrastructure. By 2000 62,500 housing units, 20 per cent of the stock, were vacant. An estimated three-quarters of the 258,000 housing units required renovation in 1990 (Power *et al.*, 2010, p. 114 quoting Stadt Leipzig, 2005). The problems were concentrated in the pre-1918 housing stock which housed almost 60 per cent of the population, and, from the mid-1990s, in the large outer-city socialist estates (Stadt Leipzig, 2007) which housed slightly over 30 per cent, half of them (75,000) in Grünau (figure 7.13), East Germany's second largest *Plattenbau* (slab block) estate.

With remarkable speed, the city and private investors acted. By the end of the 1990s, three-quarters of the remaining pre-1918 housing had already been refurbished. Older apartment blocks on the south side of the city – the traditional prestigious bourgeois area – were already renovated to meet the needs of a new wave of arrivals from western Germany, who were coming to fill jobs in a revived media industry (figure 7.14). But identical blocks in the old industrial area east of the centre remained dilapidated.

Leipzig thus became a microcosm of the one million vacant homes in East Germany as a whole, facing an acute case of the problem of 'shrinking cities'. The core of this problem was an oversized (and obsolete) public infrastructure (tram lines, sewers), which had to be maintained even if used by fewer people.

Figure 7.13. *Leipzig Grünau*. The huge Communist-era *Plattenbau* (system-built) apartment complex, in course of selective demolition and restoration. (*Photo*: CC by Martin Geisler at the German language Wikepedia, 2008)

Figure 7.14. *Leipzig urban regeneration*. Old tenement blocks in the inner city, in course of restoration to their former glory. (*Photo*: By courtesy of Marco Bontje)

But in parallel, the local tax base shrank because of falling population and closure of companies. Increasing numbers of welfare-dependent households put further pressure on strained urban budgets. Because of these fiscal pressures, the city had only limited flexibility to confront its problems and design long-term regeneration policies (Power *et al.*, 2010, p. 115).

Growing the Economy: The Cluster Strategy

Wolfgang Tiefensee, the city's Mayor from 1998 to 2005, who went on to become the Federal minister for transport, building and urban development, coined the term the 'bipolar city'. Recognizing that subsidies and other public funding could not last, he shifted the city's economic development strategy to one based on a cluster approach, developed by university academics and then adopted by the city's economic development department and a lobby group of large regional companies called 'Economic Initiative Central Germany' (*Wirtschaftsinitiative Mitteldeutschland*). They identified five key clusters: car manufacturing and components; media, IT and communication technology; health, biotechnology and medical technology; energy and environmental technology; and a cross-cluster group including the trade fair, financial services and logistics. A sustained effort was made to attract major German and global companies (*Ibid.*, pp. 121–122), with considerable success.

Table 7.2.

Location	Company	Economic Sector (and Project)	Construction Period	Investment € × 10⁶	New Jobs
Urban fringe	Quelle	logistics, mail order, storage	1992–1995	500	2,500 peak
	Porsche	car manufacturing	2000–2002/09	130 (+ 120)	400
	BMW	car manufacturing	2002–2005	1,400	currently: 3,000 planned: 5,500
	DHL	logistics, mail services, transport	2005–2008	300	currently: 3,000 planned: 7,000
	Amazon	logistics, mail-order, storage	2006–2008	90	300
	Belantis	leisure and entertainment (theme park)	2001–2008	580	40
City centre	Deutsche Telekom	communications (office building, technical equipment)	1992–1995	580	
	Karstadt	retail (department store)		−100	
	Different property developers	offices, retail (refurbishment of Messe tower)	2003–2005	−60	

Note: Although mainly financed by the private sector, many of these projects also received public sector funding.

Source: Power *et al.*, 2010, based on Stadt Leipzig (2006) and Nuissl and Rink (2003).

Cars: Both BMW and Porsche decided to build new plants to produce new models in Leipzig. Including suppliers, this sector has created some 6,000 new jobs in the region. Leipzig's success in winning the bid to attract BMW against the competition of 250 other national and foreign cities is considered as particularly important. Benefitting from an investment incentives package including cash incentives, loans at reduced interest rates, and public guarantees at state and national levels, it employs 5,000 people and produces 650 cars a day out of thousands of parts. Designed by the renowned Iraqi-British architect Zaha Hadid, the new BMW building also helped promote the city's new creative image among the design world.

Logistics: The first major company that invested in Leipzig was the mail-order company Quelle. More recently, DHL and Amazon followed. Both decided to locate their European distribution centres in or – as in the case of DHL – nearby Leipzig. About 5,000 predominantly low-skilled jobs had been created in this sector even before 2010, when DHL added around 4,000 more. The expansion of the logistics sector may be related to Leipzig's history as a trade hub. With the expansion of the EU, Leipzig is now centrally located in Europe's transport networks. Still, the success is even more closely related to the heavy subsidies into transport infrastructure, especially the airport, which operates without flight restrictions during the night for freight traffic. The development of a cargo handling centre near the airport with public-sector funding in the mid-1990s is another strategic investment in this direction (*Ibid.*, pp. 120–121).

Culture: Two outstanding initiatives helped to restore Leipzig's lost position as a leading German city of culture: the new Media City in the southern inner city, and the redevelopment of the *Leipziger Baumwollspinnerei* (Cotton Spinning Mill) in the inner-western district of Plögwitz. But the two stories could not have been more different.

The New Media Cluster: MediaCity in Leipzig-Connewitz, the southern end of the inner city (*Südliche Vorstadt*), was an artificial political implantation, effectively owing nothing to the city's historic book publishing industry. After reunification, local politicians, city officials, and some book publishers saw an opportunity to recapture the city's former importance as a publishing centre. But they monumentally failed: the central institutions stayed in Frankfurt and the publishers remained where they were. The anaemic *Graphisches Viertel*, recipient of substantial redevelopment funds, sheltered only a small number of book publishers in the late 1990s. But by then Leipzig-Connewitz, 4 kilometres distant on the inner city's southern edge, next to the old Fairground, housed a growing new media industry based on television/film production and new digital media centred around the regional public broadcasting service MDR (*Mitteldeutschen Rundfunks*). This new cluster – which already had about 8,000 permanent employees in several hundred firms in 1998, not including thousands of freelance consultants, and now has some 33,000 – is thus embedded neither in book publishing's traditional industrial structures and institutional settings, nor is it located in its former industrial district.

Nor did it have any base in electronic media, where Leipzig had never played an important role. The GDR television and film sector was concentrated in East Berlin and nearby Potsdam, with some regional activities in Dresden and only a small studio in Leipzig. The decision to establish the MDR in Leipzig was partly due to Leipzig's physical location in the centre of south-eastern Germany ('Middle Germany'). An interview in 2000 with the Saxon media representative, Michael Sagurna, revealed that the decision was a political compromise between the three *Länder* involved: Saxony, Saxony-Anhalt, and Thuringia (Bathelt and Boggs, 2003, pp. 283–284).

There are some tenuous connections with the old publishing industry: universities and technical schools, such as the *Hochschule für Graphik und Buchkunst* (College for Graphic Arts and Book Design), originally affiliated with book publishing, have added programmes to train workers for the new media industries and create specialized skills (*Ibid.*, p. 284). But the new cluster does not represent a renewal of pre-existing industries; it is not embedded in historical structures and traditional social relations.

Instead, Leipzig's new media industry has grown primarily out of local start-ups and branch facilities established to serve the MDR. This did not result from any grand plan, but from an MDR strategy to spin off functions into separate subsidiaries and subcontract other functions to local suppliers and services, so as to establish a local supply and support sector for television and film production, and to reduce costs. These firms benefit from localized capabilities, such as the development of particular institutional structures, a regional customer base, local labour market relations, and a distinct local identity. Further, the cluster has grown to include a number of creative activities, such as graphics, design, internet services, marketing, public relations, theatre and music, none of which is closely related to the MDR.

The new firms were overwhelmingly founded within the Leipzig region by people born in Leipzig or who had studied or worked in the city for many years, and who felt an attachment to Leipzig that went beyond the purely economic (*Ibid.*, p. 285). Employees from the former GDR television and film industry were sceptical about working for people from West Germany; they preferred to establish their own businesses with those they already knew through work. They were joined by West German television and film firms which established branches in Leipzig or relocated part of their activities to acquire contracts from and offer services to the MDR. In some cases, MDR deliberately asked professional film teams, technicians, cutters, reporters, news agencies, and other media specialists from other regions to establish branches in Leipzig and offered them future contracts. These 'transplants' played an important role, bringing professional expertise and specialized experience into the region.

The Baumwollspinnerei, founded in 1884, was the largest cotton mill in continental Europe, with a workforce of 4,000 in an entire industrial town with over twenty factories, workers' housing, kindergartens and a recreational area. But in 2000, the last production line closed down and the Cologne-based owner, who had bought it in 1993, began seeking a buyer for an industrial complex, with twenty buildings on a site measuring approximately 10 hectares and with 90,000 m² of usable space, only about 6,000 m² of which was rented to sixty tenants – thirty by artists, the others by craftspeople, engineers, a custom-built bicycle workshop and an art gallery. A group of three idealistic entrepreneurs – one from Munich, one from Berlin and one from Leipzig – took the challenge and bought it in July 2001, believing in its tremendous potential. The banks refused to finance them; they were left on their own. Because of the outstanding quality of construction, it took little investment to make the space rentable at low rents to creative individuals, and running costs were quite low.

With the aid of a foundation, the Federkiel Foundation, they turned Hall 14, the largest of the buildings, into a non-profit centre for contemporary art, allowing them to concentrate on the other halls. They attracted a specialist computer dealer 'Zur 48'. The reputation of the 'New Leipzig School' grew: the first WERK-SCHAU, a collective exhibition of work by all the Spinnerei artists, was held in summer 2004, the 120th anniversary of the factory. Rapidly, the team attracted a whole series of art galleries; in May 2005, when they officially opened, Leipzig was on the global art tourism map. In February 2007, the Spinnerei was flatteringly described by *The Guardian* as 'The hottest place on Earth' (figure 7.15).

Aided by funding from the City of Leipzig, the Free State of Saxony and the Federal Republic, the team deliberately developed the complex both as a

Figure 7.15. *Leipzig Baumwollspinnerei*. This vast nineteenth-century factory complex, once the greatest spinning mill in Europe, is being progressively transformed by imaginative social entrepreneurs into a major artistic centre and tourist attraction. (*Photo*: SPINNEREI, 2006)

workspace and a venue with a great appeal to the public. Under the slogan *From Cotton to Culture*, more than half the available space has been rented out to ten galleries, a communal arts centre, and around 100 artists, restaurants, fashion designers, architects, printers, a goldsmith, a pottery, a film club, a porcelain manufacturer, and an arts supply store.[1]

Outcome of the Cluster Strategy

The cluster approach has produced mixed results. Three of the clusters – car manufacturing, logistics, and the media-IT-communication technology cluster (with 33,000 employees) – have shown impressive growth. The first two have benefited from major improvements to the transportation infrastructure. The third mostly depends on the broadcasting station MDR. But the other clusters have shown relatively little development (Power *et al.*, 2010, p. 126). Employment in manufacturing consolidated in the mid-1990s and has increased slightly since then. But only 11 per cent of the workforce is now employed in manufacturing, considerably below other German cities. Employment grew by 16 per cent between 2005 and 2010, mainly thanks to new companies. Unemployment continued to rise in Leipzig until 2004, when it reached almost 25 per cent. With general economic growth in Germany, since then it has fallen to about 11 per cent, typical of other German cities. But many of the new jobs were taken by job seekers from surrounding municipalities; there has been a growth in less-secure, temporary and lower-paid employment, resulting in the emergence of a class of 'working poor'; and the proportion of long-term unemployed remains high (*Ibid.*, p. 128).

The Role of the University: One further element did not appear specifically in the cluster strategy, but has undoubtedly played a significant role in Leipzig's economic revival. The University of Leipzig, whose former students include Angela Merkel, is particularly successful in the fields of area studies, biomedicine and smart materials. Its new city-centre campus, opened to celebrate its 600th anniversary in 2009, contributes to the on-going revitalization of the centre. Numerous high-profile research centres, such as Helmholtz Centre for Environmental Research, Institutes of the Max Planck and Fraunhofer Society support the transition to a knowledge-based economy. Student numbers at the university (now totalling nearly 30,000), which is strengthening its position as a leading regional higher education institution and attracting many of the relatively large late-1980s generation, have been boosted by a change in taxation which has increased the number of students living in Leipzig (*Ibid.*, pp. 124–125).

Housing: Selective Shrinkage

In parallel to the economic strategy, Mayor Tiefensee's administration took a bold decision on housing. The Strategic Development Plan 2000 established two priorities: to demolish 7 per cent of the units in the worst peripheral system-built housing estates by 2010, and to upgrade the inner-city areas in a 'fight against suburbia'. The numbers living in pre-1918 housing rose from 260,000 in 1998 to 300,000 in 2005, while the vacancy rate dropped from 20 per cent (62,500 housing units) in 2000 to 14 per cent (45,000 units). The policy certainly attracted criticism from those who argued that it focused too much on reinstating a functioning property market and continued relentlessly with unnecessary demolition, especially through the *Stadtumbau Ost* (Urban Redevelopment East) programme (*Ibid.*, p 127).

West Leipzig soon recovered quite strongly, driven by an overflow of demand from the already-gentrified Südvorstadt. But East Leipzig still shows high levels of deprivation: welfare dependency and unemployment, low incomes, low educational levels, many one-parent households, all reflected in high levels of political frustration. It also has high vacancy rates (32 per cent) and a less attractive public sphere. On the other hand, the influx of immigrants to this area may partly compensate for ongoing population losses. The main problem now is in the outer estates: Grünau alone lost 37 per cent of its population in only 10 years, from 76,000 in 1996 to 48,000 in 2005, threatening its sustainability as a neighbourhood (*Ibid.*).

From a low point in 1998, when it counted only 437,000 inhabitants, Leipzig has now grown again to 533,000 people (in 2012). Part of this was a statistical illusion, since in 1999 the city incorporated surrounding suburban municipalities (Power *et al.*, 2010, O. Weigel, interview). But more fundamentally, in contrast to most other Western European metropolitan areas, the Leipzig region began to show a reverse trend of population decline in the suburban municipalities and growth in the central city. Leipzig has successfully attracted younger households. The biggest single group moving to the city is aged 18 to 30 (Power *et al.*, 2010, pp. 124–125, quoting Stadt Leipzig, 2007). This partly reflects successful urban renewal, which has created attractive and inexpensive inner-city housing options, with monthly rents (excluding heating) that average around £4/m², and that rarely top £6/m², even in prime locations.

The 'Leipzig model', based on 'consensual decision-making and cross-cutting political leadership', is showing results. The city showed the fastest rise in population of any of the post-industrial towns studied by Anne Power and her colleagues in their book *Phoenix Cities* (Power *et al.*, 2010), demonstrating that secondary cities can stage a come-back when actions are combined on a number of fronts. But pure serendipity allied to imaginative entrepreneurial risk-taking can play a crucial role, as the case of the *Baumwollspinnerei* shows.

Duisburg to Dortmund:
Using Landscape to Upgrade Post-Industrial Cities

Germany's astonishing industrial rise between 1871 and 1914 was rooted in the coal and steel and heavy engineering industries concentrated in the *Ruhrgebiet*, an 80-kilometre wide belt of cities and towns that stretches eastwards from the River Rhine in north-west Germany within the country's most populous *Land*, North Rhine-Westphalia. Together this vast polycentric urban agglomeration contains some 5.4 million people, with fifty-three independent local governments including eleven cities and four counties – but lacking any single regional capital or regional administration (Kunzmann, 2010, p. 2). And all this in turn is part of an even larger Rhine-Ruhr region embracing major cities like Düsseldorf and Cologne, with some 12 million people living in an area of over 7,000 plus square kilometres: the greatest single industrial-urban area in Europe.

Already in the Middle Ages this was an important east–west trade route, the *Hellweg*, following the light and fertile soils of the narrow belt between the central uplands of Germany and the great north European plain, giving rise to the medieval market towns of Duisburg, Mülheim, Essen, Bochum and Dortmund. That medieval route is today's B1/A40. Then, coal began to be mined along the narrow Ruhr valley in the hills to the south of these cities, which gave the region its name. But that has become a misnomer: in the late nineteenth century, as the mines advanced deeper into the rich coal measures, industrialization and urbanization advanced northwards to the wider River Emscher on the northern plain, producing a new wave of cities that were in effect aggregations of mining and industrial villages: Oberhausen, Bottrop, Gelsenkirchen, Herne, Castrop-Rauxel. As industrialization receded, the Ruhr valley slowly turned into a desirable residential area with beautiful landscapes and pleasant neighbourhoods, while the densely populated northern part increasingly suffered from degraded landscapes, huge brownfield areas and generally low urban quality. The river Emscher and many of its small feeders were systematically transformed into an open waste system (Seltmann, 2007, p. 2).

After 1960 the area suffered a sudden and sharp reversal in fortune. Coal mining in 1956 had 141 pits with 470,000 miners; by 2006 there were just six pits with 28,000. The share of industrial jobs fell from 58 per cent in 1970 to 28 per cent in 2006, while service jobs soared from 40 per cent to 70 per cent, but failed to compensate for the losses in manufacturing. And the area's population, which rose from 5.1 million in 1950 to 6.2 million in 1960, then fell to 5.3 million in 2006 (*Ibid.*, p. 1). Meanwhile, after 1990, national priorities shifted to reconstruction of the new *Länder*, and the area's structural problems received less attention.

Nonetheless, the *Ruhrgebiet* remains a very powerful economic region. Thirteen of the fifty largest German companies are based in the region. Steel production, chemical industry and large-scale power generation are now supplemented by light metal manufacturing, car production, electronic industries and health industries. Research institutions and companies are growing; student numbers in the area's universities rose from a mere 1,500 in 1956 to 152,000 in 2006, a one-hundredfold increase; the universities are creating scientific networks with the private sector. With 40 per cent of the European population living in a 500-km circle, the Ruhr Region is a major centre for European logistics (*Ibid.*, p. 2).

The Emscher Park Initiative

The shrinkage of the economy and the population base has resulted in chronically underfinanced public budgets. And this is exacerbated by the local government structure. With fifty-three local authorities located side by side, the challenge has been how to overcome parish-pump politics, provide services more efficiently and become competitive. A pioneering initiative to create a unified planning authority, the *Siedlungsverband Ruhrkohlenbezirk* (SVR – Ruhr Coalfield Planning Association) started as early as 1920 but became weakened by inter-city rivalries in the 1970s; its successor, the *Kommunalverband Ruhrgebiet*, did not have the same powers.

But the region's economic crisis was the trigger for a major initiative by the Nordrhein Westfalen *Land* government Ministry for Urban Development in May 1988: a plan for an international building exhibition, with the aim of transforming the landscape of the part of the Ruhr Region – covering 800 square kilometres, seventeen municipalities and about 2.2 million people, one fifth of the *Ruhrgebiet* metropolitan area with about 40 per cent of the population – over a 10-year period. *IBA Emscher Park* was duly launched in 1989 – ironically, a few months before the fall of the Berlin Wall. The 'International Building Exhibition' was an old German tradition, first developed as early as 1901, by cities seeking imaginative solutions for architectural or planning issues by inviting top international architects to propose solutions to the public. In 1952–1957 West Berlin had developed the mechanism to reconstruct several neighbourhoods simultaneously in its Hansaviertel, a celebration of the work of the modern architectural masters (Seltmann, 2007, p. 2). And yet another IBA in West Berlin, from 1979 to 1987, made a startling intervention in planning, rejecting comprehensive modernist urban renewal in favour of 'careful urban renewal' and 'critical reconstruction' that respected the qualities of the traditional urban form. But adopting the IBA concept for the regeneration of an entire region was a startling innovation.

To guide the process, the government created a state-owned private agency (*Ibid.*, p. 3). Under the directorship of Karl Ganser, and based in Gelsenkirchen, the *IBA Emscher Park GmbH* co-ordinated the 10-year long initiative which brought together local authorities, national and European funding and professional expertise in some 120 projects, with total funding of around DM5 billion (€2.6 billion), from Duisburg in the west to Hamm and Bergkamen in the east, ranging from re-naturalization of watercourses to building new housing, business parks and research centres (Almaas, 1999). Yet the remarkable fact was that the company had no funds of its own: all its projects used existing private and public funding available through regional, national and inter-European subsidy programmes. Nor did it have direct influence over local developers and municipalities: the projects were the responsibility of individual public institutions or private companies. Instead, the company guided the process, initiated discussions and competitions, moderated procedures and helped find public funding for projects. IBA staff might suggest projects to local authorities, or a municipality might apply for one of its initiatives to become an IBA project, the incentive being that the *Land* government would then give an IBA project funding and administrative priority. To accept a project, the IBA had to make certain that it reached a certain level of quality in respect of their overall aims, which included social, aesthetic and ecological criteria, and this was sealed in a contract. This generated a reciprocal element: since the scheme was fundamentally based on consensus, different city administrations found that they had to think beyond their geographical borders and to link up their different activities. Most projects were based on international competitions; many required cross-disciplinary teams of architects, engineers or artists (Seltmann, 2007, p. 3).

Central to the shared vision of the Park were five key elements, which represented a highly unusual and innovative combination. First was a park within a park, the *Emscher Landscape Park* (figure 7.16). This reserved 320 square kilometres – 40 per cent of the total Emscher Park area – barred to future development, as a large park area both separating the cities and penetrating inside them, in a complex pattern that defies mapping. Drawing on the historic 70-year old legacy of the SVR, a master plan defined seven regional greenbelts, to be planned and maintained by inter-municipal workgroups. In effect these form a layout of 'towns against a background of open country', the historic prescription that Raymond Unwin developed for London at the time the SVR came into existence. But the plan goes further than an English-style green belt: it is laid out for recreational use, complete with pedestrian signage and landscaped cycle paths. Within it, scores of local projects – ranging from small garden areas, through public art projects on top of old coal spoil heaps, to a 100-hectare brownfield reclamation – were developed as separate local contributions. A 400-km round tour with twelve museums attracts 2.5–3 million visitors a year. The locations are also used as bars, restaurants, art studios, or for parties and special events. A 230-km bikeway was built with over 200 bikes to rent, and was promoted under the theme 'from rail to trail'.

The second, closely associated, feature was a radical recasting of the entire ecosystem of the Emscher River basin. The 70-kilometre Emscher and its 250 kilometres of tributaries together collect the wastewater of more than two million people and thousands of companies, effectively constituting an open concrete-lined sewer system. But, until coal mining ceased, the risk of subsidence meant that it was not possible to divert all this waste into an underground sewage system. The central aim of the Emscher Park project was

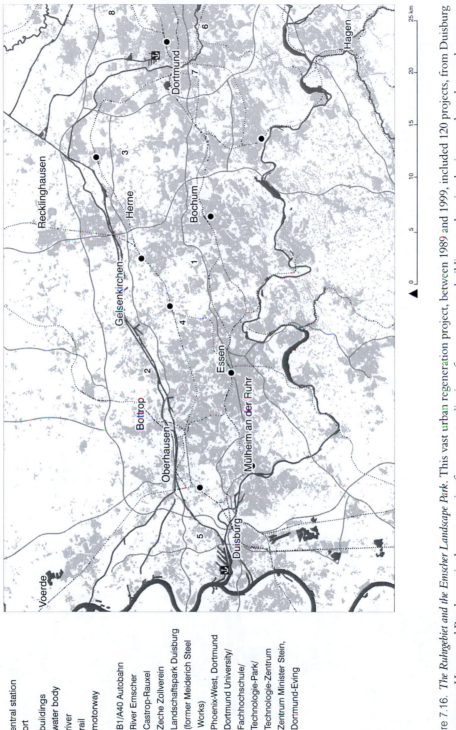

Figure 7.16. *The Ruhrgebiet and the Emscher Landscape Park.* This vast urban regeneration project, between 1989 and 1999, included 120 projects, from Duisburg in the west to Hamm and Bergkamen in the east, ranging from re-naturalization of watercourses to building new housing, business parks and research centres.

to do just that: to replace the open sewers by underground pipes, to remove the concrete river embankments so as to encourage rainwater seepage into the streams, and to construct local water treatment plants. This would not happen overnight: it would take 20–30 years, long after the end of IBA. The job was given to the *Emschergenossenschaft*, a private cooperative owned by the cities and large private enterprises, which charges all households and companies for collecting and cleaning the wastewater (*Ibid.*, p. 3).

Given these two elements, both centred on the green park background of the strategy, the third key theme concerned the treatment of the developed urban areas. They would no longer be seen as risky 'no-go areas', but as opportunities for new investments. Exploiting low land costs, key IBA areas – many close to city centres – would be developed by combining green spaces with new infrastructure and linking them to nearby urban development, creating attractive business areas and generating 5,000 new jobs (*Ibid.*, p. 4).

Within these areas, the strategy invented the fourth – and most startlingly visible – element of the entire IBA project, at least for the area's tens of thousands of visitors: the re-use of old industrial buildings. A central IBA idea was that these buildings were potentially valuable because they were part of the region's history, giving identity to its people and its cities, and offering countless opportunities for new uses if creative thinking were allowed to run riot (*Ibid.*). Two notable examples will give the flavour.

Essen: Zeche Zollverein. Opened in 1932, and designed by the architects Fritz Schupp and Martin Kremmer, the Zeche Zollverein was the largest and most

Figure 7.17. *Essen, Zeche Zollverein*. The transformed former coal mine in course of transformation into a major cultural and tourist attraction.

modern coal mine in Europe. It still employed 15,000 miners when it closed in 1986. One million square metres of space have been transformed, in a master plan by Rem Koolhaas, into a complex embracing a visitor centre and convention space; the Nordrhein Westfalen Design Centre and Design Museum in a former boiler house, designed by Norman Foster; the Ruhr Museum in the old coal washing facilities, designed by Rem Koolhaas; workshops for creative industries; a creative village with offices, studios, apartments, restaurants and a plaza; the Nordrhein Westfalen Centre for modern dance; the Triple Z Future Centre, with studios, offices and workshops for creative industries; the coking plant transformed into space for the arts and entertainment; and a public park with 40 hectares of pioneer forests and industrial nature (figure 7.17). In 2001 it was designated a UNESCO World Heritage Site as a representative example of the development of heavy industry in Europe (Kunzmann, 2010, p. 6).

Landschaftspark Duisburg. The vast Meiderich steelworks closed in 1985. One furnace was demolished, another sold to India. In 1989 the city of Duisburg decided to develop it; a competition among landscape architects followed the next year. Opened in 1994, today it is a successful public park with a mountain climbing training area, a panorama platform, a concert hall, an open air theatre, a discotheque, a training ground for rescue divers in a former gasometer, and spectacular open air events (figure 7.18) (*Ibid.*, p. 8).

Figure 7.18. *Landschaftspark Duisburg.* The huge Meiderich iron and steel complex has been preserved as a major visitor attraction including huge celebrity concerts: a classic example of imaginative urban regeneration. (*Photo*: CC by Carschten, 2010)

The fifth and final key element was housing. IBA generated about 7,500 new apartments, all on brownfield land. The projects covered a wide range, from the renovation of historic worker settlements to completely new settlements. Many had an experimental character – low-energy buildings, reusing rainwater, using new materials or integrating the residents in the process of planning and construction (Seltmann, 2007, p. 4).

The IBA Inheritance

When IBA closed in 1999, public and private organizations continued to work together on its further development. Responsibility for the Emscher Landscape Park was assumed by the Association of the Ruhr Municipalities and for the Emscher eco-system by the Emscher Cooperative (*Ibid.*, p. 6). In 2007 an extended regional grouping of three counties and thirty-five cities, with a population of 4.8 million, announced 'Concept Ruhr', a common strategy for sustainable urban and regional development to continue the work of IBA. There would be no less than 274 separate projects, financed by approximately €1.6 billion of public funding and €4.4 billion of private investment. Following the IBA model, they would all fit within the strategic guidelines for regional development, but will be carried out by the local authorities (*Ibid.*, pp. 8, 10).

More than a decade after the end of IBA, one of its major architects, Klaus Kunzmann, summed up some of its major achievements. The region's unique industrial heritage was being preserved and re-used. Problems were being turned into regional assets. The image of the region had changed, and a new identity was evolving. The huge landscape park – a 25-year project – was well under way. The re-naturalization of the Emscher was gradually happening. New economically successful locations had been created. Private developers were being attracted to revitalize old industrial structures. New jobs in creative and service industries had been created. High architectural and environmental standards had come to prevail. The IBA has become a globally acclaimed model for creative regeneration and its regional expertise in revitalizing brownfield land has become a marketable asset (Kunzmann, 2010, p. 15).

Perhaps the most remarkable expression of this follow-up strategy is the Technology Park Phoenix-West in Dortmund, about 5 kilometres to the south of the city centre, close to the district centre of Hörde (figure 7.19). Its 150-year history of steel production ended in 1998. The city is redeveloping the site on

Figure 7.19. *Dortmund Phoenix West*. A second technology park for the city will be dedicated to 'future' technology industries, laboratories, offices and start-ups, with a focus on prototype development – all embodied in a major extension of the Emscher Landscape Park.

classic Emscher Park principles: within the 110 hectare site, the development plan reserves 40 hectares for commercial uses, most for a 'technology park' dedicated to 'future' technology industries, laboratories, offices and start-ups, designed to attract micro- and nano-technologies, production engineering, software development and other IT industries and corresponding services, with a focus on prototype development. The remainder of the site will become part of the Emscher Landscape Park, part of a new generation of parklands including habitats of rare species that sprang up on the derelict site. Industrial monuments form distinctive landmarks and offer spectacular views of Dortmund and its surrounding area. In a particularly apt way, when it fully opens in 2015 – a quarter century after the Emscher Park initiative was launched – it will provide a triumphant symbol of the achievement.

Dortmund: A University Reinvents the Economy

In many ways, Dortmund – located at the eastern end of the *Ruhrgebiet* – is a microcosm of the region's problems and successes. A city of more than 580,444 inhabitants in 2010 – the biggest Ruhr city and the seventh in Germany (Kunzmann and Tata, 2003, p. 6) – its roots go back to the thirteenth century when the city was a member of the Hanseatic League. The city grew hugely during the second half of the nineteenth century on the basis of coal, steel and beer (*Ibid.*). But not long after World War Two these basic industries went into terminal decline; employment shrank from 80,000 in 1960 to 9,200 in 1997, and gains in the service sector, which now employs 75 per cent of all workers, failed to compensate (*Ibid.*, p. 9).

But then, the university came to the rescue. The *Universität Dortmund* is a new university in German terms, founded only in 1968, followed by the *Fachhochschule Dortmund* (University of Applied Sciences) in 1971. Both put their main emphasis on the natural sciences and technology – for instance, new materials, computational intelligence, telecommunications, statistics, logistics, microstructure – and environmental technologies. With 34,500 students, Dortmund is among the biggest university locations in Germany. But it is not a typical student city such as Münster, Freiburg or Göttingen. These cities – which are much smaller in size – are much more shaped by their student population (*Ibid.*, p. 12).

Equally important in Dortmund's dense and broad research landscape are more than twenty mostly public research institutes, including one institute of the *Max-Planck-Gesellschaft*, two institutes of the *Fraunhofer-Gesellschaft* and two institutes of the *Wissenschaftsgemeinschaft Gottfried Wilhelm Leibniz*. They are concentrated at three main locations: the University of Dortmund, the Technology Park area in the inner city, both with a technical or natural sciences focus, and a former coal-mine site in Dortmund-Eving, the *Zentrum Minister Stein*, mainly dealing with social and occupational issues (*Ibid.*, pp. 16–17).

In the 1980s, academics at the University of Dortmund conceived of a technology park based on the Silicon Valley model, which they then promptly implemented. The *TechnologiePark* and *TechnologieZentrum*, which is part of it, are home to many new industries and businesses. They are located next to the University of Dortmund just outside the city. Since its establishment in 1985, the Technology Park has rapidly developed into one of the successful locations of its kind in Germany. The close proximity to the university and its research institutes is a major factor, creating strong linkages and promoting knowledge transfer between science and industry. Some 230 companies, employing more than 8,500 highly-educated people, situated on a 35-hectare site, benefit from these linkages. Dortmund's economic structure is now shaped by a diverse service sector, a strong SME basis and technology-oriented businesses. It is not an overstatement to call Dortmund a 'Learning City' (Kunzmann and Tata, 2003, p. 18).

Kassel: A University Reanimates Its City

Dortmund is not the only German city where professors in a new 1970s vintage university helped to transform the economy. Kassel (figure 7.20) is a city of 200,000 people, 150 kilometres north of Frankfurt and just over an hour away on the high-speed ICE train. When it emerged as Germany's most dynamic city economy in the 2011 IW league table, the news hit the national headlines (IW, 2011). The title was not for the top-performing city – Munich came predictably first in that category – but the place that showed the most progress between 2005 and 2010, as measured by such criteria as reduction in unemployment, better levels of education and the development of local enterprises, plus quality of regional infrastructure and cultural institutions. The relevant comparison is if in the UK London emerged as usual as the top-performing place, but a city like Doncaster or Stoke on Trent won the prize for the most dynamic economy. So Kassel provides an interesting model for the many British cities that first lost their hearts to insensitive redevelopment and then experienced deindustrialization, and now face the question of what kind of urban renewal they should promote.

Local politicians were not slow in claiming the credit for Kassel's success. But, as ever, the critical factors underlying the positive development of a city or a region are complex and often part of long-term processes. In an important analysis, Helmut Holzapfel of the University of Kassel has analysed the origins of Kassel's remarkable success (Holzapfel, 2012).

By the 1960s, Holzapfel explains, Kassel had slipped down to a marginal position in Germany and in Europe. The Iron Curtain divided Europe, and the border of the Federal Republic of Germany – then only West Germany – against the Communist East German Democratic Republic was just 50 kilometres to the east. A proper transport connection hardly existed: there were only a few border

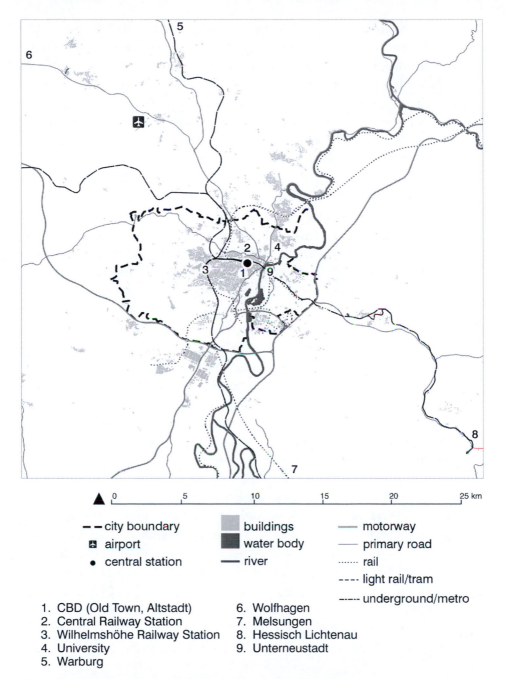

Figure 7.20. *Kassel map*. This mid-German city, transformed during the nineteenth century from a small princely capital into an industrial centre which suffered important wartime destruction, has been transformed by a major university that has encouraged important innovations including a new regional tram system.

crossings to the former GDR, all of which were very tightly controlled and unable to accommodate any real flow of traffic. Logically, the city's economic development stagnated.

On top of that, Kassel – a major industrial target – had been virtually destroyed by the RAF in the Second World War. (Since they have a mordant sense of humour, they named a bar in the rebuilt city centre after Bomber Harris.) The city had been reconstructed in the 1950s according to the best architectural and overall urban planning principles of the post-war era: a modernist approach, dominated by an entirely new city street plan, in which the historic city simply disappeared. It was almost precisely contrary to every principle of early twenty-first-century sustainable urban development.

But then came a paradoxical outcome: in 1970 the city took a fateful decision to found a new kind of university: a so-called *Gesamthochschule*, a new concept in Germany at the time, centred on new-style interdisciplinary projects based on practical examples, which would bring both students and faculty into direct contact with political issues. Soon after the first courses began in 1974, both students and faculty enthusiastically embraced the ideas of the then-new environmental movement. Well-known environmentalists – the Swiss sociologist and economist Lucius Burckhardt and the Austrian-American author and philosopher Ivan Illich – taught there; the German natural scientist Ernst-Ulrich von Weizsäcker, also deeply engaged in the movement, was university president from 1975 to 1980. They engaged in conflict with established interests in the city, as they began to organize opposition to nuclear power and to new *Autobahn* projects. This, Holzapfel argues, provides a perfect illustration of the formulation of the French theoretician Henri Lefebvre (who borrowed it from Michel Foucault): urban change emerges as a *heterotopia*, an alternative or antithetical reality to the existing order (Lefèbvre, 2003 [1970]).

Transport policy was the central example. During the 1960s various tramlines were closed down in the city; a further line followed in 1971. Then, in 1977, an intensive debate began on the possible shutdown of additional parts of the network. In a joint initiative supported by union members, citizens and the university, protests against this plan coalesced: a radical counter-proposal was developed, calling for the expansion of the tram system. From 1980, it gained increasing support. A new mayor, Hans Eichel, was elected in 1975 and served until 1991, later becoming German Federal Minister of Finance; he was far more open than his predecessor to expansion of the tram system, and gained support from the Green Party, which after 1981 became a significant force in the city council.

Transport experts in the university then began to develop a radical proposal: to use the existing rail system of the German national railway – *Deutsche Bahn* – to connect the tram system to the neighbouring towns in the surrounding region. In the city of Karlsruhe in southern Germany – to be analysed in an excursion in Chapter 9 – a similar model had been in development as a research project since 1983, with trams operating on existing rail lines since 1992 in the neighbouring city of Bretten. In 1990, one of the university's former Vice Presidents, Professor Rainer Meyfahrt, moved to the local tramway company, the KVG, and subsequently became its managing director. He asked Thomas Rabenmüller, a graduate of the new university, then working for the Frankfurt local transport planning authority, to come back to Kassel to prepare a plan for a radically new regional organization for local transport. In 1995 the *Nordhessische Verkehrsverbund* or NVV (North Hessian Transport Authority) came into being, and Rabenmüller was named its first managing director.

Step by step the tram system was enlarged; new, passenger-friendly trams were purchased. Modern forms of marketing were employed, attracting more and more customers to use the system. Kassel improved on the Karlsruhe tram-train idea by using low-floor trams, accessible to the disabled. Some trams were even equipped with diesel motors (bivalent operation) making it possible to use rail lines that did not have overhead lines for electric power. Operation of trams on rail lines began in 2001. In 2006, the first *Regiotram* service began in

Figure 7.21. (a) and (b). *Kassel: Two ends of the RegioTram.* The regional tram-train system, fully inaugurated in 2007, takes trams from the city centre over rail tracks to small towns and villages in the surrounding countryside, connecting them into an integrated city region.

the wider region, and in August 2007 a tunnel at Kassel's main railway station created a new connection between the city tram network and the railway system, making it possible for passengers from the surrounding region to travel to their destinations in the city centre without having to transfer (figure 7.21(a) and (b)).

Kassel's transport policy revolution was originally advocated by its proponents for social and ecological reasons; economic success was not the central aim. But, Holzapfel asks, has the new transport infrastructure contributed to the city's ranking as Germany's most dynamic city? To this the answer is a decided yes: there is no question that the *Regiotram* and the expansion of the local Kassel tramway system have had a major influence on the city's economic development. First, approximately 20 per cent of the production activities for the new trams took place within the Kassel region, which is a central area for rail production in Germany. The expansion of the rail system was mainly contracted to construction companies from the region. The new network supports the development of trade and business in the metropolitan centre of Kassel and the connection of the university with the surrounding area. Without the expanded capability of the tram system, it would hardly have been possible for the 20,000 students and 2,800 university employees to reach university destinations in the centre of the city. The *Regiotram* has been shown to increase the value of houses and flats in the surrounding region, close to the *Regiotram* lines. And the improved overall regional accessibility has had a positive influence on the growing economic success of the area (Sintropher, 2011).

Innovations often are the product of opposition or conflict. Holzapfel's relatively brief history of Kassel's reforming university shows that the tram system was not the only example. Organic farming, supported and promoted through university research, arose out of a critique of industrial agriculture; today it has proved a significant economic success. The critique of nuclear power in Germany led to funding and support for solar energy in the Kassel region, which in turn encouraged the manufacture of electronic components for solar power systems, now an important industrial sector in Kassel; SMA Solar Technology, with some 5,000 employees, was founded by former university employees. In addition, the university has had a wider influence in creating a supply of well-trained employees in the region. Thus it has played a central role in the overall positive development of the entire region.

University thinking also played a role in developing new and radical concepts of urban regeneration, which shaped an entire quarter of the city. The idea of 'critical reconstruction', first applied by the International Building Exhibition in Berlin in 1979–1987 (and embraced by Berlin's mayor in 2001) started from the standpoint that instead of iconic buildings, planning should seek to restore the historic pattern of streets, spaces and densities along with efforts to promote a social mix, using a variety of developers and architects. The concept had an immediate and major impact on Kassel, where key individuals in the university – notably the planning professor, Karl Friedhelm Fischer – became involved in redeveloping a huge area, on the opposite side of the river Fulda from the city centre, known as *Unterneustadt* (Lower New Town). In municipal ownership, it had been left as a large car park after wartime destruction. In 1992, the university, city council and housing associations came together to start the process of 'refounding the Unterneustadt', trying to restore its qualities before wartime destruction.

Underlying this approach, which can also be seen in the new Freiburg community of Rieselfeld or in Tübingen – another university city – is an interesting philosophy, which Karl Fischer explains is the basis of 'Teutonic' as opposed to Anglo-Saxon ways of thinking (Fischer, 2011). This relies on legally binding land-use plans (*Bebauungspläne*) that lay down the basic rules, within which architects can freely express themselves. Hence there is an accepted division of responsibilities between planners who deal with cities, and architects who handle buildings. Municipal autonomy is guaranteed by the national constitution, and cities exert considerable influence on the directions development should take. The land-use plan specifies mixed land uses with a wide range of different building types and densities. Then, sites are sub-divided and marketed as parcels, often on the basis of competitions, to smaller builders who respond to niche markets, using different architects. The resulting network of streets, which stretches over some 2.8 hectares, accommodates nearly 4,000 inhabitants (figure 7.22).

Such a philosophy has some important implications for economic growth, which the Kassel experience bears out. First, locating both the university and a

Figure 7.22. *Kassel Unterneustadt*. The new riverside mixed-use urban quarter next to the city centre, the outcome of ideas developed in the local university whose professors live in many of the new homes. (*Photo*: CC by Dietmar Walberg, 2008)

rebuilt residential area in the inner city means that there is much more spending power concentrated close to the centre, and higher densities of buildings not only support high-quality public transit systems, but also a greater choice of quality shops and restaurants. Second, the building blocks tend to be owned and managed by professional firms. Third, the structure accommodates many small inner-city firms that support the construction process, reinforced by an apprenticeship system that trains five times the British number every year, which encourages the introduction of modern methods of construction and production into the urban development process.

The original radical social goals of the reform university, such as the demands of the philosopher Ivan Illich that the world's wealth be distributed in a radically different manner, have not come to fruition – today's university has come much closer to mainstream German society. To what extent Kassel's success may serve as a model, to what degree this success will prove to be sustainable, and whether we should measure success according to other criteria than purely economic ones – these are questions that must be discussed not only in Kassel but throughout Europe and the developed world.

Conclusions

From these very varied cases, eight factors emerge in helping to explain Germany's economic success.

1. Municipal Leadership. Municipalities, not developers, lead development in German cities. Public wellbeing, not land values, shapes the outcomes. Taxes go first to the cities, which then reimburse part to regional and national governments. It is the cities that make development plans, not private developers. Berlin is the capital, but it does not dominate Germany as London dominates the United Kingdom. The country's urban structure, reflecting its nineteenth-century origin as a federation of independent kingdoms and city-states, is fundamentally polycentric – as can be readily seen in pictures from satellites at night. The great German cities have long had many of the trappings of capitals, such as banks, opera houses, and universities, and vie with each other in making their centres more attractive without having to refer to the national central government. They run many of the utilities, which makes it much easier to invest in sustainable infrastructure.

2. Highly Connected Cities. Compared with the UK, Germany like France has invested much more in transport infrastructure over the decades, connecting this polycentric urban network. An early system of motorways, ironically built for purposes of military aggression, made it easy to shift goods with large commercial vehicles, giving German firms an early advantage. The high-speed train network connects all the main cities, while modern suburban rail and tram systems link high-quality city centres both with their suburbs and with surrounding small towns and villages, turning cities into city regions that brilliantly combine compact urban form with freedom of access. Advanced transport and energy infrastructure has not only provided a strong home market for German manufacturers, because German governments have provided resources to invest in them, but has also enabled them to export services. It is significant that while *Deutsche Bahn* has taken over some British train franchises, the reverse has not happened.

3. Knowledge-Based Economy. There has been a commitment to universal education in Germany since 1807, with an early tradition of strong technical universities and independent government-financed research institutes, and a much greater respect for applied knowledge, which underpins both business and city success. These great research institutes have also been more effective in transferring innovations into products than UK science parks, where researchers and businesses often operate in different worlds. An intensive system of technical high schools and apprenticeships creates a far broader base of well-qualified workers. They find work in the great array of family firms that make up the *Mittelstand* (small and medium enterprise) companies which specialize in advanced science-based manufacturing, and which form the backbone of the German economy.

4. Engineering Excellence. Where the UK relied for centuries on its empire, which provided secure sources of supply and customers for its products, often based on iron and coal, Germany has had to rely on advanced engineering. The German government has supported applied innovation. Successive innovations in industries such as cars or electrical machinery gave German industry a competitive edge based on quality rather than price. This is neither new nor exceptional. Prince Albert is said to have promoted the Great Exhibition in 1851 from a concern that UK manufacturers were starting to lag behind their German counterparts, and the gap still exists in many sectors.

5. Regional Finance. Innovation and leadership have been boosted by easier access to finance, because banking is not concentrated in one city. Though 75 per cent of German banking activity consists of large universal banks which resemble their UK counterparts, the remaining 25 per cent is made up of specialized banks which provide a limited number of specific services, mainly to businesses. German banking is more decentralized than British banking, with regional banks whose record is bound up with local business success, not mergers and acquisitions. Their record is not totally unblemished, and state intervention has arrived relatively late, causing them to tighten lending. But, over the longer term, they have been more willing and able to help industry than their British equivalents.

6. Urban Pride. Though German city planners made the same mistakes after World War Two as those in the UK did, surrounding them with concrete ring roads, German cities reversed direction much faster, pedestrianizing their entire city centres and followed a pragmatic approach that cost much less to implement. A process of 'critical reconstruction' has recreated buildings and whole streets from areas that had been left derelict, as in Berlin or Kassel. City centres have retained their attraction for shopping, culture and leisure.

7. Climate of Innovation. German cities have been in the forefront of adapting rapidly and flexibly to changing needs. Whether it is the eco-extensions in Hamburg or Freiburg, the renewal of housing estates in Berlin and Leipzig, the celebration of the Ruhr's industrial heritage as a park, or the tram-trains of Kassel, cities are working to boost their economies and the wellbeing of their citizens. The planning system favours innovation because it is quite specific about what can happen and where, but is flexible on matters of design and use. There is a greater spirit of cooperation, reflected for example in the collaboration between adjoining authorities in the *Ruhrgebiet*.

8. Intelligent Spatial Planning. Cities faced with fundamental economic change have responded with an intelligent approach to applying knowledge through spatial clusters of new industries, as in Leipzig and Dortmund. This is fortified by intelligent planning at the national level, as with the *Erneuerbare Energien Gesetz*, the Renewable Energy Act of 2000 establishing the feed-in tariff, which boosted solar power. In 2011, 20 per cent of German electricity in Germany came from renewable sources and 70 per cent of this was supported with feed-in tariffs.[2]

Notes

1. See http://www.spinnerei.de/from-cotton-to-culture-2.html.
2. See http://en.wikipedia.org/wiki/Feed-in_tariff.

8 | Building Sustainable Suburbs in the Netherlands

In a search across Europe for best practice in sustainable urban development, there are several good reasons – despite a great deal of high-quality competition – for putting the Netherlands in first place. How could this small country, with just over a quarter of the UK's population and one-sixth of its land mass, have achieved so much, of such outstanding urban quality, in so amazingly short a time?

The reasons can be stated at the outset – though it will take the rest of this chapter to demonstrate them. First, for over half a century the Dutch have developed and perfected a system of well-articulated planning that proceeds systematically and effectively all the way down from the formulation of a national spatial strategy to delivery on the ground at the local level. Further, they have done this even though – a lesser-known fact outside the Netherlands itself – their inherited system of sub-national planning is not ideally fit for the job. It has three different tiers: national, provincial and municipal. National government provides the overall policy framework (long-term goals, general strategies) through a national spatial development plan, first produced in 1958 and subsequently revised approximately every 10 years, but executive planning powers are in the hands of 415 municipalities (as of 2012), ranging from major cities like Amsterdam and Rotterdam to hundreds of smaller rural units. In between, the twelve provinces are supposed to ensure a minimum level of coordination between local development initiatives and to check their consistency with national policy directives. This structure has been in place since 1848, when it was created almost single-handedly by Johan Rudolf Thorbecke (1798–1872), a celebrated nineteenth-century Dutch politician; to this day it is known as the 'House of Thorbecke'.

It has become almost a national icon, but it is not ideally adapted to twenty-first-century urban reality. This is most evident in *Randstad* (Ring City) Holland, the huge polycentric urban complex in the western heart of the country, which is home to 6 million people, nearly 40 per cent of the Dutch population. The Randstad takes a unique form: an approximately horseshoe-shaped line of physically separate cities, approximately 180 km in length. It incorporates three big cities – Amsterdam (784,000), Rotterdam (612,000) and The Hague (498,000) – as well as four other important cities: Utrecht (313,000), Almere (191,000), Haarlem (149,000), Dordrecht (119,000) and Leiden (118,000). Each is separated from its neighbours by a green zone, even though this is sometimes wafer-thin in the extreme western part of the horseshoe. All the cities look inwards into a central area of open space, carefully preserved by regional planning, which has earned the whole complex the nickname (in the words of the British planner Gerald Burke) of Greenheart Metropolis. Administratively, it is divided up among some 115 municipalities and four provinces: all of South Holland and much of North Holland, Utrecht (the province) and the newly-reclaimed polder province of Flevoland. It thus fits uneasily within the three-tier structure.

Unsurprisingly, there have been calls for the establishment of a fully-fledged metropolitan authority for the Randstad – but the Thorbecke national icon has been resistant to all reform. Instead, there have been patches here and there: merging municipalities, and attempts at inter provincial cooperation. One was *Regio Randstad*, an initiative dating back to the early 1990s, in which the four Randstad provinces, the four largest cities and their respective city regions undertook joint activities and engaged with national government in discussions of Randstad-wide concern; it does not appear very active. Another is the *Vereniging Deltametropool* (or Deltametropolis Association), a think tank and interest group that continues to promote a metropolitan development perspective for the Randstad area. And there are many other, often informal, arrangements covering smaller parts of this vast urban region – but nothing that approaches a Randstad authority.

So, despite all the formal difficulties – perhaps because the Dutch combine a can-do, must-do attitude (a product, doubtless, of the constant threat of incursion by the sea) with a pragmatic ability to overcome conflicts and reach agreement on critical issues – they have shown amazing capacity to move from strategic planning to effective high-quality delivery within a relatively short time span. The most striking and relevant illustration is the Fourth National Spatial Strategy Supplementary Volume of 1991– in Dutch, *Vierde Nota Ruimtelijke Ordening Extra*: VINEX for short.[1]

VINEX and the Ten-Year National Housing Plan

Around 1990, the Netherlands and the UK awoke to the fact that they both had a housing crisis. In the UK there was endless argument: it was the end of the Thatcher era, free-enterprise critics argued that her ministers had failed to deliver on the promise to set the builders free to build, the government commissioned a report from surveyors Gerald Eve which eventually concluded that to do anything really effective, the entire planning system would have to be virtually dismantled. The government, by then led by John Major and in ideological retreat from the excesses of high Thatcherism, demurred.

Typically, the Dutch did it differently. Ever since the late 1950s, the government's Department of Housing, Planning and Environment, VROM (*Volkshuisvesting, Ruimtelijke Ordening en Milieu*)[2] had produced a report every 10 years, charting the course of development for the decade ahead: in effect, a National Spatial Development Strategy. In a country that had become notable for the quality of its spatial planning, VINEX was one of the most influential reports ever to appear from VROM for it called for a huge national programme of new housing developments close to existing cities. These almost inevitably came to be called VINEX locations.

VINEX was thus the basis for a 10-year housing programme, running from 1996 to 2005 but still being completed, which has more than a passing resemblance to the UK 2003 Sustainable Communities Plan (ODPM, 2003). Generated by a right-of-centre government, like the Thatcher/ Major administrations in the UK, it took a resolutely free-market line – but with a particularly Dutch flavour. So the public sector, in the form of the local authorities, took the lead: the central government provided money to decontaminate land and provide access, but otherwise the schemes had to be self-funding. And the implementation of the plan was to come through agreement between VROM, the provincial governments and the municipalities – though, in the case of the largest cities, the report itself suggested where development should take place. The aim was, quite simply, to get a lot of housing built in a short time. And in this it proved phenomenally successful, producing no less than 455,000 new homes, including 285,000 (62 per cent of the total) in so-called VINEX housing units built in some ninety 'suburban' or urban extension schemes, with the remainder within city boundaries, on field sites and other types of urban in-filling; in total increasing the Dutch housing stock by 7.6 per cent.

But quantity was not enough: the houses had to be in the right places, close to existing cities so as to minimize invasion of valuable greenfield land, above all in the 'green heart' of the Randstad, and also to minimize travel to the cities and secure maximum use of public transport, walking and bicycles. The report laid town four key principles:

◆   Strengthen existing shopping centres and facilities by generating a larger potential customer base.

◆   Limit the threat of large-scale exodus from the larger cities.

◆   Protect open areas by concentrating development around existing larger and medium-sized cities.

◆   Offer better opportunities for use of public transport, walking and cycling between housing, employment and services, so as to limit the need for car use; this to be achieved both by investment and by planning to bring these elements closer together.

More subtly, it aimed to lure higher-income households out to the new locations, thus freeing up housing in the cities for lower-income residents – but also providing a share of cheaper rented housing in the VINEX locations themselves. The government, in implementing agreements with regional authorities, indicated that a maximum of 30 per cent social housing in the housing developments could be provided, but many authorities sought to achieve exactly that figure.

Among the ninety locations, there were twenty-five major VINEX schemes, dotted all over the country but with a marked preponderance in the Randstad, as in Vathorst and Nieuwland next to Amersfoort, the majority next to their parent city boundaries, in the form of urban extensions. The Dutch do not refer to such locations as 'suburbs', a term with rather negative connotations for them, but as *buitenwijk* (outskirts). What immediately strikes the visitor is how deftly they have been inserted into the existing, often very complex, pattern of development and open space within the Randstad. Whether the new developments are located in an old brownfield port area, like IJburg in Amsterdam, or in an urban extension at the border of the city, like Vathorst, or in a semi-independent satellite town, like Ypenburg next to The Hague, they are all close to the centre of the nearest major city and well connected to it by good public transport – typically with journey times of half an hour or less.

Amsterdam: New Residential Islands and a New Sustainable CBD

VINEX became celebrated among planners worldwide, for its novel policy prescription that all employment centres should be divided into three categories (figure 8.1). 'A' centres, in the hearts of the cities, were locations with excellent access by public transport from places near and far, though car access was limited and should be further limited: they should be the main concentrations of dense service employment. 'B' locations, on the city fringes, enjoyed less spectacular but still adequate access by rail or tram, but also good access by car via radial and orbital motorways; they were suitable for secondary concentrations that needed more space, for instance exhibition and conference centres or stadia. 'C' locations required a lot of space for activities like freight logistics, but needed

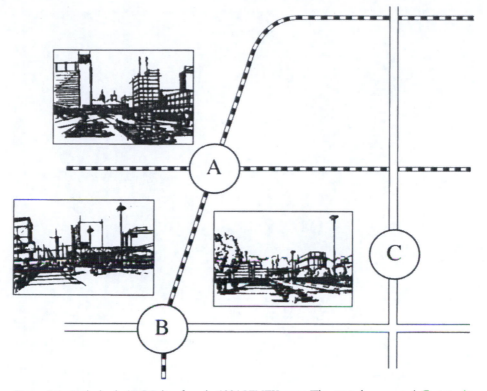

Figure 8.1. *Netherlands ABC Policy, from the 1991 VINEX report.* The central concept: *A-Centres*, city centres with top-quality public transport; *B-Centres*, edge-city locations combining good public transport and motorway access; and *C-Centres*, essentially logistics locations next to motorway interchanges. But in Amsterdam the B-Centre won out over the A-Centre for commercial development.

few employees; they alone should be allowed and even encouraged to locate near motorway interchanges, away from rail lines.

This threefold distinction was fine – in theory. But in Amsterdam (figures 8.2(*a*) and (*b*)) there proved to be a problem. The city planners wanted to redevelop the old docklands immediately north of the historic nineteenth-century train station, abandoned as a result of containerization, to create a major mixed-use commercial-residential zone on the islands where the old warehouses had been. This, within easy access of the station, was a classic 'A' location. But, with a few exceptions, commercial developers were not interested. They preferred another location, next to the Zuid (South) station close to Amsterdam's Schiphol airport, and on a new rail line, the Zuidtak, opened in 1993 in the median strip of a new motorway bypassing Amsterdam on its south side, and giving direct access from Schiphol airport to the eastern side of the Netherlands.

This area had first seen development as long ago as 1961, when an exhibition centre, the RAI, moved out from the city to a peripheral location conveniently located at the city end of the national motorway system. It steadily grew to

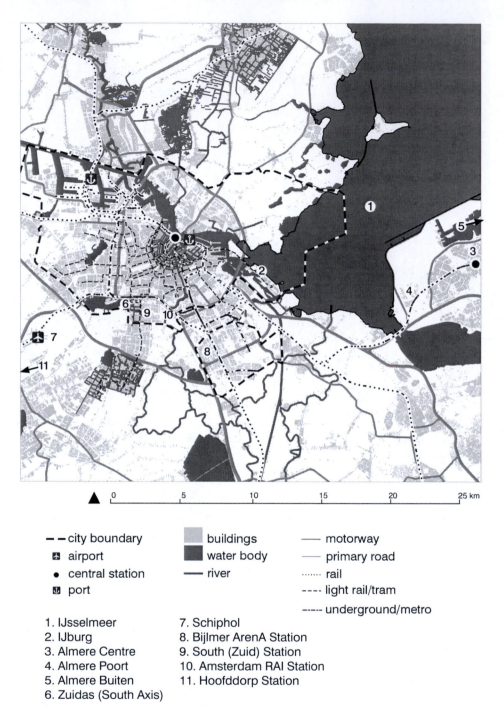

city boundary buildings motorway
airport water body primary road
central station river rail
port light rail/tram
underground/metro

1. IJsselmeer   7. Schiphol
2. IJburg   8. Bijlmer ArenA Station
3. Almere Centre   9. South (Zuid) Station
4. Almere Poort   10. Amsterdam RAI Station
5. Almere Buiten   11. Hoofddorp Station
6. Zuidas (South Axis)

Figure 8.2 (*a* (*above*)) and (*b* (*opposite*)). *Amsterdam map.* (*a*) The historic city centre bordered by the old docklands area to the north of the Central Station, originally proposed as an A-Centre for commercial development – but (*b*) Amsterdam Zuid, the B-Centre, was preferred by developers and commercial interests, so the docklands became a high-quality inner-city residential regeneration area. Also shown is Almere, a new town of the 1970s on reclaimed polder land, predicted to become the fifth city of the Netherlands by the 2030s.

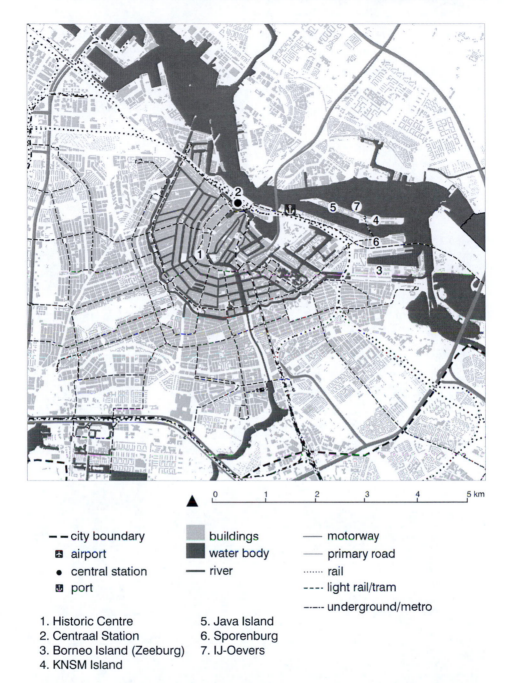

0   1   2   3   4   5 km

- – city boundary
- ✈ airport
- ● central station
- 🚢 port

- ▨ buildings
- ▨ water body
- — river

- — motorway
- — primary road
- ······· rail
- - - - light rail/tram
- —··— underground/metro

1. Historic Centre
2. Centraal Station
3. Borneo Island (Zeeburg)
4. KNSM Island

5. Java Island
6. Sporenburg
7. IJ-Oevers

become one of the biggest exhibition and conference centres in the world, and in 1985 was followed by a World Trade Centre. By the mid-1990s, with unequalled motorway, rail, city tram and metro links, it represented a classic 'B' location, and eventually Dutch planners accepted the fact. They developed the revolutionary concept of a new 10 kilometre linear central business district, the *Zuidas* (southern axis), along the ring motorway and rail line from the airport through Zuid station to Bijlmer, a station on Amsterdam's east side, originally opened in

1971 and totally rebuilt in 2007 to serve The Arena, home of Ajax Amsterdam football club. With extraordinary speed, this has effectively become the major central business district of Amsterdam, leaving the old centre to serve the city's huge tourist trade and assisting it by massively reducing pressures for physical development, which had been evident during the 1960s and 1970s (figures 8.3(*a*) and (*b*)). The Dutch may be very hands-on planners but they are also realistic and pragmatic: what is good for business is good for the Netherlands.

Figure 8.3 (*a*) and (*b*). *Amsterdam Zuid Station*. (*a*) Aerial view of the site today. (*Photo*: Irvin van Hemert Luchtfotografie). (*b*) Model of future development around the station, according to the 'dock' model. (*Source*: Projectorganisatie ZuidasDok)

Thus the diligent pilgrim inquiring after Dutch planning practice needs logically to look in succession at the two related arms of what has become a balanced and highly successful strategy: the mainly residential reconstruction of the IJ-Oevers (the banks of the River IJ) on the north side of Centraal station, and the new business centre of the Zuidas on the city's south side.

The IJ-Oevers. These consist of four artificial peninsulas in Amsterdam's Eastern Docklands, created (rather like their equivalents in the London Docks) over a long period from 1874 to 1927 to accommodate large passenger and cargo ships sailing to the former Dutch East and West Indies, the Americas and Africa. But, as in London and many other cities, after World War Two the docks began to decline as passengers chose to fly rather than sail, general mixed cargo was replaced by container and bulk transport, and new docklands in the west of Amsterdam were opened. In 1975, the Eastern Docklands were earmarked for residential development by the city council, with plans for high-density housing for around 18,000 people. The high-density approach went along the lines of the 'compact city' and made the scheme feasible, taking into account the huge investment required in preparing the land for development (including new infrastructure such as bridges, roads and public transport). In 1986, with a new city council at the helm, the focus moved away from predominantly social-sector housing, towards market-led development: the council wanted to stimulate private housing and luxury rented houses to attract higher income groups to the area, and the new policy became mixed-tenure housing.

High architectural standards and attractive urban realm were also important, as well as the reuse – and thus revitalization – of existing harbour buildings to preserve the area's history. In 1989, the plan for the Eastern Harbour District area was finalized, laying out the conceptual framework for 8,000 new dwellings. Significant government grants were made available, provided the development met certain requirements for density, housing mix and programme. By the time the development of Borneo and Sporenburg islands was being planned in 1992, the requirement was for a density of 100 units per ha, 70 per cent owner-occupied housing, and an aspiration to provide family units with ground level entrances to counterbalance the earlier phases. In order to maintain high densities but adhere to these low-rise objectives, the architect-planner Adriaan Geuze replaced the usual gardens with roof terraces and mini-patios.

After an overall master plan for the streets and densities was agreed by the Amsterdam Planning Authority, individual plots were made available to the public. Owners commissioned their own architects to design individual houses, resulting in sixty unique dwellings with different ceiling heights, canal frontages and interior layouts (all meeting relevant building control requirements and fitting the master plan). The dwellings had to be both durable and sustainable – for example, car parking spaces were restricted and roof gardens encouraged. High architectural standards were achieved – partly, it can be argued, because the

Dutch seem to display a greater interest in architecture and urban design than the British do (figures 8.4, 8.5 and 8.6).

The Netherlands has long been one of the most advanced European countries in its integration of public transport, cycling, urban development and land use, but in the last 10 years it has become increasingly sophisticated. Three aspects are particularly notable:

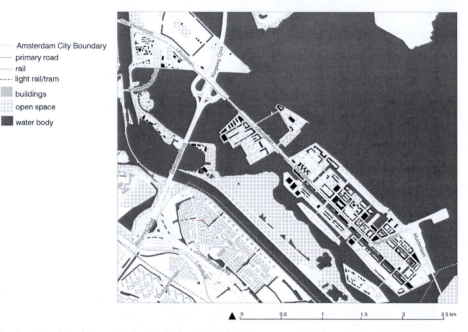

Figure 8.4. *IJburg figure ground*. The final stage of development of the former Amsterdam docklands.

Figure 8.5. *IJburg*. The dramatic island site, at the start of redevelopment. (*Photo*: CC by Debot from nl, 2005)

Figure 8.6. *IJburg*. Medium-rise, medium-density residential development in a dramatic waterfront setting. (*Photo*: CC by Marion Golsteijn, 2012)

1.   Total integration of different modes (walking, cycle, bus and tram, Metro, stopping train, intercity train, high-speed train and air) through a hierarchy of train stations.

2.   Replanned train stations with a wide variety of retail and other services on the station transit from one mode to another.

3.   Planned large-scale urban development around the stations, including both urban redevelopment for new employment and services and new residential zones.

The strategy for the southern axis (*Zuidas*) of development on the south side of the city, exploiting its extraordinary accessibility for all modes of transport including car, train and air, is dramatically illustrated by the five Zuidas stations: *Amsterdam Bijlmer ArenA*: a new (2007) station, designed by Nicholas Grimshaw, on a major regeneration site next to the problematic 1960s Bijlmermeer housing project, with a new arena and back offices; *Amsterdam RAI*, near the RAI exhibition centre; *Amsterdam Zuid*, where there is now an ambitious proposal to deck over the railway as the basis for intensified office development, making this the city's effective CBD (figure 8.3); *Schiphol Airport*, the world's most effective integrated air/rail interchange; and *Hoofddorp*, the location of the airport's logistical and associated services, beyond which is the start of the new *HSL Zuid* (High-Speed Line South).

Almere: Almere Poort and a Self-Build Community

Almere is a major new town and a VINEX location, built on land in the newly-reclaimed polders, facing out towards the inland IJsselmeer some 25 kilometres north-east of Amsterdam. Since construction of the first house in 1976, it has grown to a population (in 2011) of 191,000, the same size as Milton Keynes (with which it is twinned); by 2030, with 350,000 people, it is projected to become the fifth largest city in the Netherlands. Developed along the route of a railway line into Amsterdam, which was built in the late 1980s as a part of the settlement of the reclaimed polder, the community has an interesting variety of self-build houses with impressive eco-standards (figures 8.7(*a*) and (*b*)).

In the 1990s a large number of people in the Netherlands became interested in self-build houses which were more environmentally sustainable in their construction and operation. As a result, many formed their own groups, one of which negotiated with Almere Council for a parcel of land for sixty to sixty-five houses. The idea was promoted by Adri Duivesteijn, a Labour Alderman and former Dutch MP, who saw it as a way for people to own their own homes at a time when prices had become unaffordable for many. The city drew up the master plan, which links Almere through to its attractive coast on the IJsselmeer,

Figure 8.7 (*a*) (above) and (*b*) (opposite). *Almere*. typical single-family homes in a waterfront setting at Almere Buiten. (*Source*: TCPA)

but dispensed with design controls. The basic infrastructure was put in by the municipality – important, since on this reclaimed polder all the homes have to be piled. Individuals, and in some cases groups, agree to buy a plot at a price based on its size. They appoint an architect, in some cases choosing a design that is already approved (and costs no more then €170,000), and select contractors, who are usually small builders.

In developing the houses it was realized that at least half the group could not take the financial risk that their house might prove unsellable in the open market. They therefore teamed up with the local Registered Social Landlord (RSL) which provides affordable housing for the Municipality of Almere, to develop the housing cooperatively. The RSL took over the investment risk, contract negotiations with builders and other technical aspects. The housing group advised on the green technologies (such as green roofs, solar panels, rainwater recycling) to help develop the housing. Walls were also better insulated with radiators embedded in them, which is more efficient and cuts heating bills. The RSL found this aspect of the partnership fruitful as a way to develop new techniques to apply to future housing development.

Interestingly, people were attracted as much by the sense of community or location as by the eco-standards. As the first householders moved in, they were able to specify or build their own parts of the house, such as the kitchen or shower room. The school was only a 400 m walk/cycle away – important because most younger Dutch children still come home for lunch. Another difference in Dutch culture is the tendency to shop daily at smaller stores rather than the big weekly/fortnightly shop as often happens in the UK, which means that shopping is often carried in panniers on the back of a bicycle.

Then the international financial crisis led to cutbacks in house building in the Netherlands, prompting the municipality to undertake a massive extension of the original experiment by providing serviced sites for people to commission and build their own homes. In Almere Poort, which is one of the last areas of the city to be developed, 2,000 homes have been built; another 5,000 live there in what is effectively a building site that will eventually provide 14,000 homes. With plots still selling strongly at three to five a week, these already accounted for some one-third of the housing being developed in the city in 2011, as completions in the city as a whole have dropped from 3,000 to 1,200 a year. Property values are set by the level of comparable and competing sites, and the value of the land is determined from a curve, based on some 20–30 per cent of the final value. Social housing plots are sold for €30,000 each, and the sales price is capped at €175,000, so land is under 20 per cent of the total cost, with the requirement that it is kept as social housing for 25 years.

Creating a place of such distinctiveness has helped generate positive publicity for Almere, a new town whose image has suffered from being over-shadowed by nearby Amsterdam, and which has attracted a higher level of immigrants. It has reinforced the city's reputation for innovative design, for example, the imaginative *Het Klokhuis* (The Apple Core) designed by children for a television programme of the same name, which provides a landmark. A commitment to good design is also shown in the way the city's shopping centre has been redesigned by celebrated Dutch architect, Rem Koolhaas with housing above sloping streets, a new theatre overlooking a lake, and exciting housing overlooking new waterways. The combination of contemporary and traditional design side by side helps overcome the sense of everything being new, and also attracts a wider mix of people.

As well as enabling people to get more space than they could otherwise afford, and build the home of their dreams, the new homes cost much less to run. This in part stems from higher levels of insulation, but also every home is connected to the district heating system, which soon will use waste heat from a power station in Amsterdam. In addition extensive use is being made of solar power in Almere, including a 'sun island' with an array of solar collectors feeding heat into the district heating system.

As in other new settlements there is no through traffic; parking is away from the houses. Vehicles can deliver heavy items to the house, but not park there. There is a mixture of young and older people in the development and there is a culture of having low fences between back gardens, which facilitates community interaction. The housing group maintains the common areas (as 'super caretakers') and is developing a community centre in the middle of the housing. This new settlement has greatly improved the area's image and appeal.

Amersfoort: Vathorst and Branded Neighbourhoods

A 40-minute journey takes one from Almere, south-eastwards to Amersfoort, a city of 147,000 people just outside the conventional definition of the Randstad, where two motorways cross. Vathorst, Amersfoort's third new urban quarter (the others are Nieuwland and Kattenbroek), is a VINEX location of around 560 ha located immediately to the north of the city (figure 8.8). It is in effect

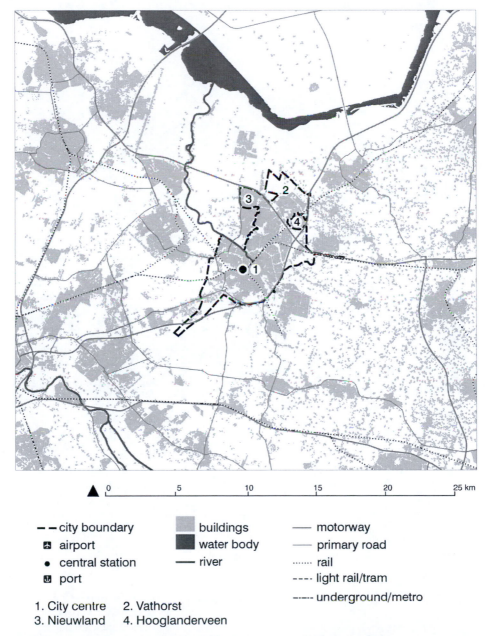

− − city boundary	buildings	—— motorway
✈ airport	water body	—— primary road
• central station	—— river	······· rail
⚓ port		- - - - light rail/tram
		-·-·- underground/metro

1. City centre 2. Vathorst
3. Nieuwland 4. Hooglanderveen

Figure 8.8. *Amersfoort map*. The new VINEX developments at Vathorst and Nieuwland are planned as urban extensions, well connected to the central city by high-quality bus systems.

a contiguous satellite, which has been promoted under the motto '*a world of difference*'. When complete in 2018, the area will contain seven distinctive neighbourhoods housing a total of 30,000 residents in over 11,000 houses, with a business park, a shopping centre, a railway station, and access to many other community facilities, all within a sustainable, eco-friendly environment. Infrastructure and community facilities are being developed in tandem with the housing and are available as soon as residents move in as temporary buildings are used to house shops, banks and other facilities (figure 8.9). The development

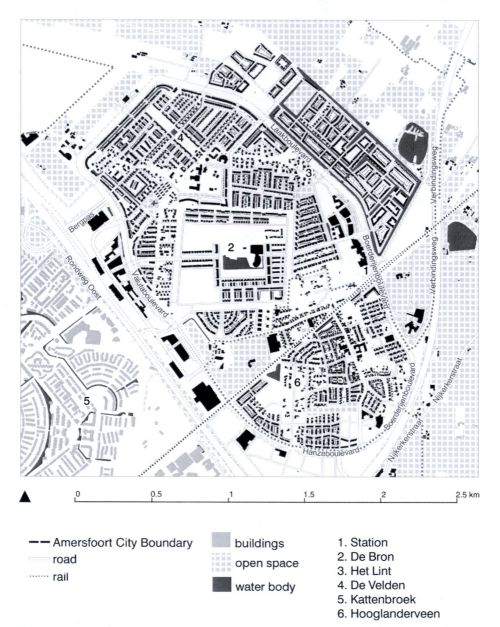

Figure 8.9. *Vathorst figure ground*. The train station, completed ahead of demand, is directly connected to the residential areas by bus feeder routes.

will include five or six primary schools, a secondary school and an agricultural college, ten football pitches, ten tennis courts, a skateboard park, swimming pool, two health care centres, a library, a theatre, five catering establishments as well as live/work units to attract businesses such as osteopathy and dentistry. A new industrial estate and a business park are expected to create around 5,000 jobs, and fibre optic connections to every new house will facilitate home working.

The municipality, which initiated the development, determined that it should all take place on its terms. A joint development company (*Ontwikkelingsbedrijf Vathorst* – OBV) was established, with the council as one shareholder, and the other a consortium of five companies which owned the land in the area but which the city admired because of good work they had done previously. OBV obtained a €250 million loan from the Dutch Municipal Bank and Local Government Funding Agency, BNG (*Bank Nederlandsche Gemeenten*), at relatively low interest rates (5 per cent) to be repaid over 15 years from the proceeds of land sales. Homes are sold or let in the conventional manner by property developers or estate agents. Social housing is developed by the Municipality of Amersfoort.

Two different master planners have been employed: Kuiper Compagnons and West 8. As a result, architectural variety is to be found across the development area (e.g. traditional forms contrasting with more modern houses with flat roofs), with different densities, scenery and structure. Amersfoort also pioneered the principle that now applies throughout the Netherlands: that there should be a complete balance of housing, in terms of values, in each neighbourhood of 500 units to avoid social polarization. For every 500 houses there is a mix of types of housing, 30 per cent of which must be affordable/subsidized and 60 per cent of that must be for social rent.

The overall density is 44 dwellings/hectare, but varies between 35/hectare at the periphery up to 100/hectare in apartment towers near Vathorst's railway station. There is an average 400-m walk to a bus stop from every house, with a maximum of 600 m, while a road runs round the edge of each neighbourhood. Houses in Vathorst have generous space standards: a small house has a floor area of 80 m² floor area and a large house 200 m² (figures 8.10(*a*)–(*d*)).

The master plan seeks to encourage the maximum use of bicycles and to make cycling an attractive alternative to the car. There is limited car access from the ring road around Vathorst into the centre. The Dutch government – via the Dutch Railways – pledged to pay for a 'standard' rail station, plus access roads. OBV added to the sum to upgrade the rail station, and to build it in advance of the population needed to support it. For the first 3 or 4 years the OBV also subsidized the local bus service, which is now self-sufficient.

Within the overall master plan it was agreed that 40 per cent of the area would be green space, in addition to the green space surrounding the existing village Hooglanderveen. The master plan is designed with residential areas that are individually branded, for example through their location alongside canals,

Figure 8.10 (*a*)–(*d*). *Vathorst*.
Representative views showing
the use of water features.

and with very different architectural styles. As a result it is highly walkable, and cyclists have priority.

Traffic calming, such as narrow roads and the use of humps, means that cars move slowly in residential areas. There is a wide cycle path with planting to separate it from the road and very little street furniture, which helps to promote an image of less clutter and more space. These and other design features persuade residents and visitors to treat the environment with respect and promote community interaction.

Despite the intentions of the master plan, which included building the new station on the main railway line, most people who moved in from outside use their cars to get to work and take children to school. This has created a congestion problem at times (in part because the site is bounded by two motorways), despite the greater use of bicycles. As in the UK, in the Netherlands this reflects the reality that often both parents work and have constricted timescales.

The OBV and the Municipality of Amersfoort set up an ongoing art project to encourage public participation (*Vario Mundo*). This charitable trust brings people together and helps to forge an identity for the new settlement. Most of the funding is from the municipality of Amersfoort with some contribution from OBV via land price increase as the Vathorst development proceeds. Many public art projects take place throughout the development area (twenty-two per year) and at these people have the opportunity to choose the artwork or suggest it. This choice is realized through voting at blocks throughout the residential area or on a dedicated website. Every phase of the development involved artists who worked with the new residents to achieve a sense of belonging and ownership through the creation of art.

Extensive use is made of district heating and combined heat and power (CHP) in Valhorst. Ground source heat pumps are installed in every house in one of the new neighbourhoods of 700 homes. In Vathorst, homes have an energy performance coefficient 10 per cent higher than the national average. A range of other energy performance measures is set and it is down to the individual developer to decide how to reach these using low-carbon technologies such as solar panels, CHP systems and extra insulation.

The municipality aims to achieve a water system with high ecological and recreational potential which is integral to the spatial planning and design of the area. Natural waterways form the basis for the design and are embedded in the master plan. Houses are built along the waterways with landing stages for small boats included. In Vathorst they say 'Make water your friend not your enemy'. To the west of the village of Hooglanderveen a former refuse dump is being transformed into a large water feature, *De Bron*, fed by clean seepage water, which will provide facilities for swimming, sailing and fishing. A high sand ridge separates it from another water system. *Het Lint*, a residential area on top of this ridge, will provide a wide variety of plot sizes, plot orientations and architecture, in which existing agricultural buildings will be maintained.

De Velden, surrounding Hooglanderveen, De Bron and Het Lint, will become a residential area built alongside existing canals and wooded banks.

The DHV Group, the water consultant and engineering service provider, describes how the eight different areas within the master plan of Vathorst set different targets for water: in the green and nature areas, the water system must be of high quality and design, replicating the natural characteristics of waterways and lakes; whereas in the business park area, a more functional design is accepted. It is expected that 65 per cent of the houses will have views of the water or will be situated on the waterfront.

Ypenburg: Integrating Transport and Development

Some of the most intensive VINEX development has occurred in a relatively small area bordered on the west by The Hague, on the south by Delft and Rotterdam, and on the east by the small city of Alphen aan den Rijn (figure 8.11). This was somewhat controversial territory as it is part of the green heart of the Randstad and was historically occupied by intensive glasshouse agriculture (in Dutch, *Tuinbouw*). But skilfully, Dutch planners have fitted in a lot of compact new housing in the form of small new towns, developed as extensions to the existing cities and connected to them by new public transport lines – a classic illustration of the Dutch ability to integrate transport and land-use planning.

Dutch planners have taken the principle of the tram-train (Chapter 9) several stages further. First, they have developed the concept itself, combining an old rail line and several tramlines into a single metro-plus-tram system: *RandstadRail*. Second, they have integrated this new system with street-running trams at key interchanges both inside and outside their major cities. And third, they have used the resulting integrated system as the basis for a series of VINEX developments.

The starting points came at the three ends of the eventual system. First, in The Hague two tramlines ran in parallel to the coast, along the streets from the city's western suburbs, and joining to run through the city centre. Second, a quite separate tram network operated in the small city of Zoetermeer, some 15 kilometres inland. Third, there was (and is) a sub-surface metro system serving the port city of Rotterdam, one line of which – the Erasmus line – connects the southern suburbs through the inner harbour, the site of intensive urban regeneration for over a decade, into the city centre and the central train station. Finally, connecting these elements was an old railway line between The Hague and Rotterdam, more direct than the circuitous main line that paralleled the coast through the university city of Delft, but terminating in a station in Rotterdam's northern suburbs – not a place that most customers wanted to go.

The planners' solution, achieved in 2006–2011, was to weld these disparate elements together in a particularly ingenious way. First, where the two tramlines in The Hague joined, they were buried under the centre of the city in 3 kilometres of tunnel, designed by the office of Rem Koolhaas with stations at

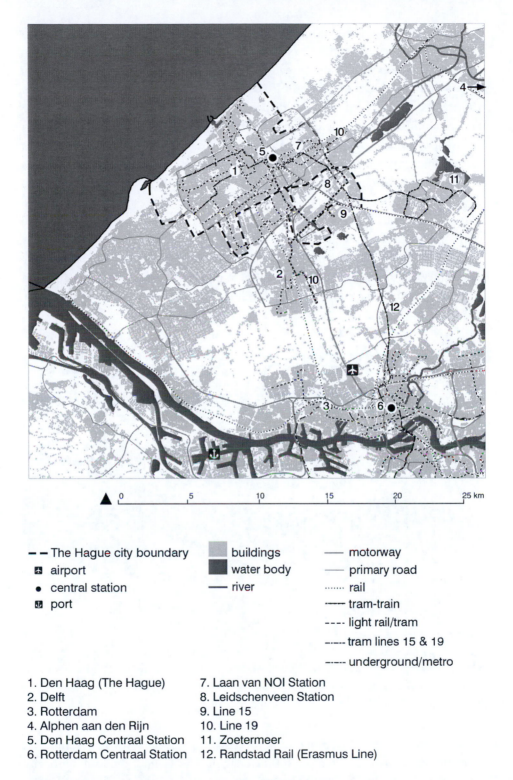

Figure 8.11. *Den Haag-Delft-Rotterdam map*. The VINEX development of Ypenburg, developed as an urban extension to The Hague, is connected to it by tram (Line 15) and to Delft and Rotterdam by another tram (Line 19) linking to the RandstadRail tram-train system.

key points, before emerging into the central train station and running out from there on a viaduct. Second, the existing heavy rail line from Den Haag Centraal to Rotterdam Hofplein, now downgraded to metro status, extended via a new urban tunnel in Rotterdam, completed in 2011, linking directly to Rotterdam Centraal station. Third, a short distance from the central station, these two lines combined into a single shared light railway between Laan van NOI and Leidschenveen stations, with common stops. A new train station for Ypenburg, on the direct national rail line from The Hague to Utrecht, was linked late in 2009 to RandstadRail at Leidschenveen by a tangential new tramline (Line 19) designed to link development sites in this fast-growing area to the east of The Hague (figure 8.12). Then, five stations further on, they split again, with the trams turning left, eastwards, on to the old Zoetermeer tracks and the metro trains running straight on, southwards, across open country to Rotterdam where, finally, in 2011 a new tunnel connected them under the city to the central station and on to the existing southbound metro line.

Figure 8.12. *Leidschenveen*. Interchange between RandstadRail tram-train (above) and Line 19 tram, lining to Ypenburg centre. (*Photo*: CC by Voogd075, 2010)

Ypenburg is a good example of a VINEX project. On a former, somewhat characterless Dutch air force site on the edge of The Hague, the local authority took the lead in the development process, commissioning a master plan by architect-planner Frits Palmboom (figure 8.13). The town was divided into five different 'theme districts' or neighbourhoods, each of around 2,000 homes

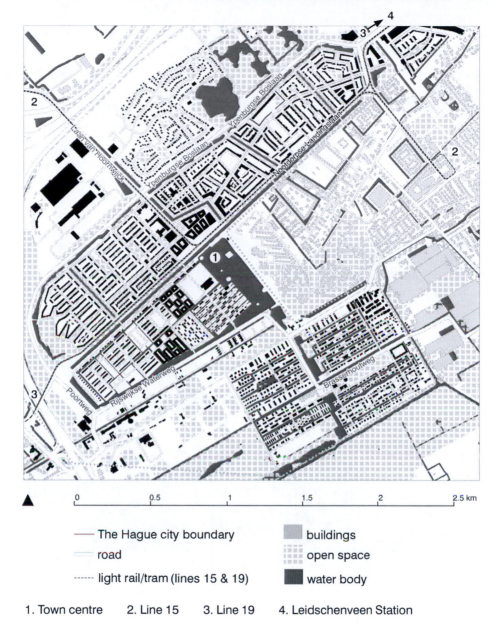

Figure 8.13. *Ypenburg figure ground*. The compact urban form is based around the two intersecting tram lines.

with a distinctive character, making up a total of some 12,000 units with around 30,000 residents: one has traditional urban villas, another housing that is reminiscent of old apartment blocks, while others are modern experimental architecture. The entire development, which is bordered on two sides by busy motorways, is protected from the noise by earth bunding (figure 8.14). No less than fifteen different developer/architect teams were selected to build the different neighbourhoods through limited competitions, with eighty teams in all. The local planners emphasize that the choice was based on quality not price, as it was thought that the better the quality, the greater the demand and hence higher the value. As with other Dutch schemes, the high quality of the transport infrastructure, including two new tramlines intersecting in the town centre, was made possible because the public sector ploughed back the uplift in land values as a result of the housing development. There are two large supermarkets, around forty shops, a library, childcare facilities, a medical centre and a sports centre. Underground refuse storage means that homes are not dominated by wheelie bins, and refuse sorting and hence recycling is made easier.

Figure 8.14. *Ypenburg*. A representative view, showing the earth bunding which reduces noise impact from the neighbouring motorway. (*Photo*: CC by Michiel1972, 2005)

Within the centre of Ypenburg, where flats had been built around a shopping centre, not all has worked out as planned; in particular older people have not been moving into the central apartments that were planned for them. However, overall, people tended to move within, rather than out of, the development, which is one indicator of success.

Conclusions

The Dutch urban experience offers valuable lessons: first in the processes they use, and secondly in the outcomes they have achieved.

Good Processes

In many ways the Dutch planning and development system is similar to that in the UK. But in the last two decades the Dutch system has increasingly proved an inspiration to the rest of Europe, with concepts which have been widely emulated: the Compact City, Integrated Public Transport, Choice-Based Lettings, and Traffic-Calmed Home Zones. Furthermore, as in the UK, 80 per cent of the funding for local government services comes via the central government, so there are similar concerns about how to finance major developments.

1. Universal Commitment to Planned Growth. The Dutch are clearly quite uninhibited about large-scale development: everywhere there is a great deal of new building to be seen along the main roads and around the railway stations. One clue to this is an astonishing degree of central control, maintained through the 10-yearly review by erstwhile VROM of the national spatial development strategy for the whole country. For half a century, despite political differences, this has been an accepted keystone of national policy. VINEX was merely a dramatic manifestation.

2. Contractual Agreements between Central and Local Government. The provinces and municipal governments were asked to implement the national strategy, by drawing up proposals for local housing growth, expressed as 'covenants'; in response, the government provided grants for land decontamination and towards connecting up sites. The process was relatively simple, with few controls over what was to be built other than the requirement to provide 30 per cent of social housing, and to concentrate housing where there was already infrastructure. A system of agreements was introduced, starting with the big Randstad cities, and first pioneered in Rotterdam.

3. Realistic Master Planning. The municipalities play a much more proactive role in both planning and development, and with greater financial freedom, than in the UK. This includes not only commissioning the master plan, but also investing in infrastructure. Because of the country's cultural history in having to keep water out and reclaim land (the so-called Polder mentality) major cities have their own development agencies that own much of the land, while smaller cities still take more of a lead than their British equivalents. The key to this is the municipal bank (BNG) that provides funding for infrastructure.

4. Balancing Infrastructure and Development. In all the new developments, transport infrastructure is provided from the very start, giving confidence to developers to proceed with implementation. Traffic has been rising rapidly in the Netherlands, and train travel has been increasing at 4 per cent a year, so this is important.

So as well as the major transport investments funded by the government and provinces, such as the RandstadRail tram-train system or the new high-speed line from Amsterdam and Rotterdam to Brussels, there has also been a huge programme of building local tramlines, as in Ypenburg, and Zoetermeer, or busways, as in Almere, to make it possible for people to get to work and to the main shopping centres without having to use their cars. By combining advanced civil engineering with good urban design, new infrastructure is welcomed, not resisted. This also reflects the educational system as well as cultural traditions, and is made easier by an ability to work as multi-disciplinary teams, with the local authorities playing the leading role.

5. *Importance of Land Ownership.* The relatively strong position of the municipalities comes from general trust in the planning system (with less scope, for instance, for appeals by landowners). It also stems from the fact that the local authority plays a pivotal role in land assembly, often owning key sites, or enabling different ownerships to be pooled. Though VINEX had led to private developers buying up sites in areas expected to grow, it was the municipalities that drew up the plans, and therefore set the basic principles for development. By mobilizing land for development, the Dutch have succeeded in finding innovative ways of catering for previously-untapped markets, including self-commissioned homes and various forms of co-housing, as well as social housing that appeals to a wider market. There is an important lesson for UK developers and house builders here.

6. *Delineation of Roles.* While the developments are carried out by experienced housing developers or housing associations, or by commercial developers, the master plan already exists and the basic infrastructure has already been provided. A contract is drawn up which provides security and hence minimizes risk, and thus getting the contract right is seen as critical. In the case of Almere new town, Rem Koolhaas was appointed following a competition, and (apart from designing some buildings himself, he was able to ensure that other world-class architects were involved – though not always with good results!). Great stress was laid – as in Zoetermeer – on getting the contracts for public-private partnerships right, as changes cost the municipality dearly, so there are clauses to cover the main risks, including linking development to infrastructure. Getting the phasing right is thus critical; notably, in Almere a requirement to ensure early development of cultural facilities, including an ice-rink and hotel, failed because it was separated from the rest of the scheme.

7. *Team Working.* Every VINEX location has a small multi-disciplinary team, the *Projectbureau*, which is responsible for the major schemes, and which is disbanded when the scheme is complete. This includes not just planners and property experts but also communications experts. A great deal was invested in

high-quality communications such as models and films, in visitor centres which were used to sell the individual units, so that people could see how their new home fitted into the grand plan.

8.   *Good Urban Design.* The master plans create new neighbourhoods that are a pleasure to walk and cycle around, though they generally have little in the way of facilities apart from schools; shops and other services are reserved for the town centre. The Dutch seem much more willing to adapt the physical landscape, with extensive reshaping of land – for example, to shield new housing from motorway noise. They also make imaginative use of water to break up housing areas, promote biodiversity, and minimize run-off.

9.   *Neighbourhood Management.* A number of policies for strategic neighbourhood management are helping to improve liveability and create a better public realm, especially in areas with high levels of immigration and unemployment. Two examples are the Opzoomeren programme and the 'Civic Wardens' initiative. *Opzoomeren* was introduced in Hoogvliet, a satellite town for Rotterdam in 1994, and has since been applied to 1,600 streets. It is about local government stimulating local communities in each street, square and courtyard to organize joint clean-up activities, plant flowerbeds, window boxes, and similar small-scale improvements, with a view to enhancing their immediate living environment. The key is seen as 'social etiquette' (going from aggression to self control) and there are now 250 cases where the process starts with a street party to identify the livewires. They then draw up rules for how the neighbourhood should be run, for example with regard to noise or rubbish. If agreed, the municipality then responds by funding some environmental improvements.

The *Civic Wardens Scheme* is a national public initiative where welfare benefit is used to cover the costs of the wardens who receive training in communication and social interaction skills, as well as IT and first aid. Local district authorities manage the schemes.

10.   *Good People, Good Team Work.* The Dutch have been able to attract and retain first-class people in their local authorities because of the proactive role they play in development, which assures continuity of staffing. This has been backed up by the use of competitions to secure more innovative approaches to design than conventional house builders would employ. This could also be the result of a 'can do' philosophy, reinforced by a lack of micro-control. The Dutch appear more adventurous, but also honest in acknowledging and learning from mistakes. They seem to be better at taking a team approach, having a positive attitude, and in maintaining spaces to higher standards. In part this is through taking care to involve everyone in the planning process, for example with architecture centres in the main cities. They use public-private partnerships widely, but without abdicating a sense of public control and stewardship for the

public realm; the local authority takes the lead. This is greatly helped by putting in public investment up front, assisted by developer contributions on a clear and predictable formula.

Good Outcomes

To sum up, many of the issues facing the Dutch are essentially the same as the ones faced in the UK. There has been a popular preference among families for moving to homes with gardens (though people without children, young and old, are happy to live in flats that are close to facilities). They too are concerned about the poor public behaviour of some young people and the problems of integrating people from different racial and cultural backgrounds. Congestion is also a concern which the Dutch government is tackling with extra 'rush hour lanes'. The climate is a big issue, particularly given the low-lying position of most Dutch towns.

1. *Environmental Sustainability.* The Dutch have built many more homes than the UK, and generally larger and to a better specification. In the new suburbs it is common to install CHP, wind turbines, and underground and separated refuse disposal systems, so there are many more places that have put 'eco-town' principles into effect. For example in Oosterheem, the final extension of Zoetermeer, there are fine looking eco-homes in a neighbourhood where the community took responsibility for looking after the public spaces, and where the drainage system creates a very attractive neighbourhood. In Ecolonia, the first stage of a 6,000 home development involved building over a hundred houses around a lake to test out different technical options.

2. *Design Excellence.* Though some of the new homes might seem clinical and soulless, there is no doubt that the Dutch have created new places with a distinct identity. The idea of 'branding' different neighbourhoods, as with manufactured goods, seems a powerful one. It has helped create a much broader market for new homes than in the UK, as new homes offer a distinctly better product than many of the old apartments. The Dutch seem adept at fitting larger homes into smaller plots, without cars dominating the layout. There is much more use of water (low-lying western part of the Netherlands has to form 8–10 per cent of the plan area for drainage and flood control) and tree planting as a means of creating a distinctive environment, and a conspicuous use of large areas of colour to brighten places up.

3. *Social Inclusion.* Though in practice the areas of social housing were clustered away from the private housing, they did not stand out. The Netherlands has achieved a much more equal society; recent well-publicized research for UNICEF into child wellbeing in rich countries showed that the Netherlands

provided the highest standard whereas the UK provided the lowest. In part this could be because people have more time to spend with their children, due to less time spent commuting, and in part to the efforts put into community engagement through the schools and neighbourhood activities. Homes are designed to enable people to grow older in them, and there are good social support systems, with a stress on voluntary work. Good public transport and low fares also help to pull communities together. That said, despite higher levels of economic growth and social equality, there are major spatial inequalities, both within major cities like The Hague, and between the older areas and the new suburbs. The new suburbs have attracted many of the white working and middle classes, leaving the main cities with a high concentration of immigrants.

4.   *Wealth Creation.* Finally investment in new housing has helped to make the Netherlands one of the strongest economies in Europe. Though the UK has a high level of consumer spending, it has suffered from chronically low levels of private and public investment. The disparities between London and the rest of the UK have continued to widen, whereas Amsterdam and The Hague are seen as part of a wider polycentric conurbation. Much of the new employment is on the edge of towns and cities, while the centres are increasingly places for living and enjoyment. Though – as in the UK – there has been a shift to service employment, and a loss of industrial jobs, there are still many major Dutch manufacturers, such as DAF (which took over Leyland Trucks).

Not Everything is Perfect...

Even in the Netherlands, the development process has not always been smooth. As we have seen, in Vathorst, the city of Amersfoort had to pay Dutch Railways to open a new train station 4 years earlier than they had planned – because they could not see the traffic justifying the investment in the early years. At Ypenburg, one of the planned two tramlines – connecting the development with the city centre – was operating early on, but another – Line 19, connecting to the new Randstad Rail train station – opened only in 2011. The delay, the planners said, had meant that the development had early on locked into a pattern of car dependence: people were leaving home at 6:30 to drive to the gridlocked motorways that surrounded the suburb. That underlined the importance of getting the public transport in very early, well in advance of the point where it would be economically viable: otherwise bad habits become set.

There was a related point of criticism: as in much planning in the UK, there was clearly a tendency to use motorways as natural boundary lines for new development. Both Vathorst and Ypenburg are in effect ringed by major motorways, with big spaghetti junctions close to residential areas. That meant high dikes and walls to reduce noise intrusion, which further isolated suburbs like Ypenburg from their 'mother city'; less clear was how much pollution was actually entering these areas, a matter of concern because of their large numbers of children.

There is one further question mark. The people in these places appear overwhelmingly to be white Dutch natives. The immigrants who have poured into Dutch cities over the last 30 years, and their children, seemed very much under-represented among the faces coming out of the schools in mid-afternoon. You might call this a success, if it meant freeing up inner-city housing for these newer arrivals. But, looking at the post-World War Two inner western suburbs of Amsterdam, now mainly populated by low-income residents with multiple social problems, there was a question: is the Netherlands becoming a spatially and socially segregated nation? The planners in Amsterdam evidently thought so: they are trying to regenerate the area to attract high-flying younger professional workers. But for the Netherlands, as for the UK, a problem of social and spatial inequality remains.

The country is also mired in recession, with budget cuts and a VAT rise, a freeze in civil-service pay, higher health-care contributions, cuts in tax benefits for commuter travel and a gradual rise in the pension age to 67, hitting disposable incomes. Unemployment has risen to over 6 per cent. As *The Economist* (23 June 2012) puts it, 'In effect, the Dutch have for the first time decoupled from the far stronger German economy'. The housing market has slumped, trapping 500,000 households – many of them in the VINEX developments – in negative equity.

Yet, despite all the reservations, overall VINEX has been a triumphant success. It is impossible to travel through these new neighbourhoods without marvelling at the huge scale and the generally high quality of the development. Effectively, a public corporation parcels out the land to private developers who competitively bid to build different residential areas – but all following neighbourhood master plans which in turn fit into the overall concept. That concept is generally a fairly conventional one: a central boulevard, sometimes quite wide, which makes allowance for a reserved central tramline or busway (the last, at Vathorst, somewhat alarmingly converging with other traffic on a series of roundabouts). Neighbourhoods are clustered on either side, built at a domestic scale with predominantly single-family housing all with small gardens; house sizes and densities vary, with one neighbourhood typically reserved for very up-market detached housing, others using higher-density terraced housing attractively designed next to canals. Especially at Vathorst, there has been a very conscious attempt to give each neighbourhood a distinctively different character. One, with a high share of subsidized rental housing, is built around a generous central public open space with an exceptionally attractive water feature: evidently, a magical space for children.

And VINEX has some major lessons for the UK. One is quality: the Dutch have demonstrated that public-private cooperation can achieve it, even to high eco-town standards. The other is where the new housing gets built. The Dutch have done it very deliberately, in or next door to their big cities.

In the Department for Communities and Local Government's Sustainable Communities strategy the UK is doing it differently, around middle-sized places distant from London, along the major transport corridors. There is nothing necessarily wrong about this: it is a continuation of a strategy begun 60 years ago with the first new towns and developed in the 1960s with new town additions to places like Northampton and Peterborough. And it does correspond to a different spatial order: the largest cities in the Netherlands, that archetypical polycentric nation, are one-tenth the size of London.

But the Dutch experience must raise doubts about the wisdom of building small eco-towns in isolated locations away from big cities. And the Department for Communities and Local Government announcement in 2010 on the second wave of eco-towns, which concentrates on local authority-led schemes within city boundaries or next door to them, rather uncannily seems to suggest that their planners quickly responded to what they have seen on visits to the Netherlands. It seems that they had learned one major lesson from the Dutch experience.

Notes

1. It was followed by a Fifth Strategy Report of 2001, which was killed in Parliament, and a further one, simply called *The Report on Space* (Nota Ruimte) of 2004.

2. Since 2010, VROM has been part of the 'Super Ministry' of Infrastructure and Environment (I&M).

11 — LILLE - Porte de Tournai - E. C.

9 | France Uses Transport to Develop and Regenerate Cities

For many long decades in the late nineteenth and much of the twentieth century, French cities languished in a deep torpor. The urban historian Anthony Sutcliffe, borrowing a phrase from the great German cultural critic Walter Benjamin, entitled his classic 1971 study of modern Paris *The Autumn of Central Paris: The Defeat of Town Planning 1850–1970*. A similar process of slow decay even more radically affected the great provincial cities of France, there reinforced by a long decline in economic strength and prestige that was expressed in 1947 in the title of a celebrated book by the right-wing geographer Jean-François Gravier, *Paris et le désert français*. Only in the 1960s, when the still-highly-centralized French planning system adopted the notion of designating them as *métropoles d'équilibre* with funds to boost them as independent counterweights to Paris, did they begin to show signs of recovery. But the real change came only in 1982, when the administration of François Mitterrand carried through a radical transformation of the historically-centralized French fiscal system, moving generous public funds from the central ministries in Paris to the newly-restructured councils of the twenty-one French regions, there to be used for investment in infrastructure as the basis of large-scale regional and urban regeneration. Not long afterwards, this was coupled with an administrative device, the *contrat de ville*, contained in a law of 1989 to implement the tenth national plan, which allowed the realization of major urban projects – in the environment, education, transport, security, sport and social services – through a new contractual relationship between the state, local governments and private partners. Together these triggered an astonishing 20-year frenzy of investment in France's great cities which has transformed them into some of the most modern and exciting places in Europe.

There was however one more intriguing piece to this urban puzzle. A special tax on employers, the *versement transport*, had been introduced, first in the Paris region, and then (from 1973) progressively extended to provincial urban areas. At first designed to support capital spending, it was increasingly also used to subsidize operating expenses. It was thus a hypothecated tax – something that, ever since the ill-fated Road Fund in Lloyd George's 1910 budget, has always been anathema to the UK Treasury. And, as any casual visitor can now see, it has been used to support massive investment in new public transport systems in every major French city – plus now, increasingly, many smaller cities too.

It so happened that devolution happened at almost exactly the same time as another major development which no visitor fails to notice: the opening, in 1981, of the first line of the *TGV (Train à Grande Vitesse) Lyon-Méditerranée* from Paris to Lyon. Followed by the first stage of the *TGV Atlantique* to Le Mans and Tours in 1990, by the *TGV Nord* to Lille, Brussels and the Channel Tunnel in 1994, by the extension of the original line to Marseille and Nîmes in 2000, and the first stage of the *TGV Est* in 2007, it has given France an unequalled network of super-fast, frequent trains connecting Paris to the major provincial French cities, and dramatically shrinking the effective distances between them. All this is evident to the millions of overseas visitors who have enjoyed travelling on the new services. What may be less evident is the way that, in the past 20 years, they connect seamlessly at the main train stations to fast-growing urban and regional transport networks that have been financed by the innovations in local and regional financing.

And in turn, this has been accompanied by massive investment in the physical quality of French towns and cities. The same processes of increased motorization and increased scale of operation have profoundly influenced shopping habits in France, just as in Britain: people drive to massive cut-price edge-of-town shopping warehouses like Carrefour and Auchan to do their weekly shopping, and many small shops have closed – though in all but the smallest villages, the *boulangerie* survives and is patronized once, twice or even three times a day. The cities and towns advertise their attractions to tourists on the motorways and *Routes Nationales*. The towns themselves have been transformed by careful schemes of *aménagement* which narrow the space available for cars while widening the pavements and providing local spaces to park. There is a palpable sense of local pride. The French National Town Centres Federation (a little like the Association of Town Centre Management in the UK) has published a ten-point manifesto which includes parking and public transport initiatives, promotion of diversification, and development of waste land. Its most innovative idea is the promotion of town centre payment cards allowing access to museums, transport and parking facilities.

In the tour that follows, we will see how these transport and planning policies and practices come together in four contrasted cities: first the capital of France's largest nineteenth-century industrial region, second France's fastest-growing major city (and capital of both its fastest-growing region and fastest-growing *département*) on the Mediterranean coast, and third an eastern border city that has become a symbol of European cooperation, Finally we make a short excursion over the border to learn how a German city preserved its trams and invented the idea of tram trains.

Lille and Roubaix Forge a Regional Identity

Sitting at the heart of north-west Europe, central point of a Paris–London–Randstad triangle with 100 million people within a 350 km radius, a major hub of local, regional and European transport networks (figure 9.1), the Lille metropolitan area is one of the great industrial power houses of Europe, offering uncannily close parallels with the great city regions of Northern England (Colomb, 2007, p. 19). But there is one key difference: since the 1960s it has been governed by an extraordinary strategic authority, *Lille Métropole Communauté Urbaine* (LMCU, previously CUDL, *Communauté Urbaine de Lille*), an intercommunal co-operative body, which – after a long series of false starts in the 1970s and 1980s – has largely been responsible for its extraordinary economic transformation (*Ibid.*, p. 22).

LMCU was born in 1966, when – to tackle the intense fragmentation of local power into 36,000 municipalities across France and to stimulate major provincial metropolises to counterbalance Paris – a national law required eighty-seven (now eighty-five) communes, led by the cities of Lille, Roubaix and Tourcoing, to establish a new type of 'metropolitan authority' (*Communauté Urbaine*), one of fourteen in France, to oversee the planning, coordination and management of key public services at the metropolitan scale. LMCU has over 2,300 staff, governed by an assembly of 170 local councillors selected by the individual councils of the member municipalities, and manages an area with a total population of 1.1 million, ranging from Lille with 226,000 to a country town with 179 people. Its original remit covered public transport, waste management, water supply, street and traffic management, to which were successively added strategic spatial planning, urban regeneration (in 1989), economic development (shared with individual cities), cultural and sports equipment, major cultural events and environment (in 2002), and (finally, in 2005) strategic housing renewal and provision. Many of these responsibilities are shared with the individual local authorities. In 2005, *Lille Métropole Communauté Urbaine* had a budget of €1.4 billion, coming from local taxes and central government grants: 73 per cent went to investments (*Ibid.*, p. 22).

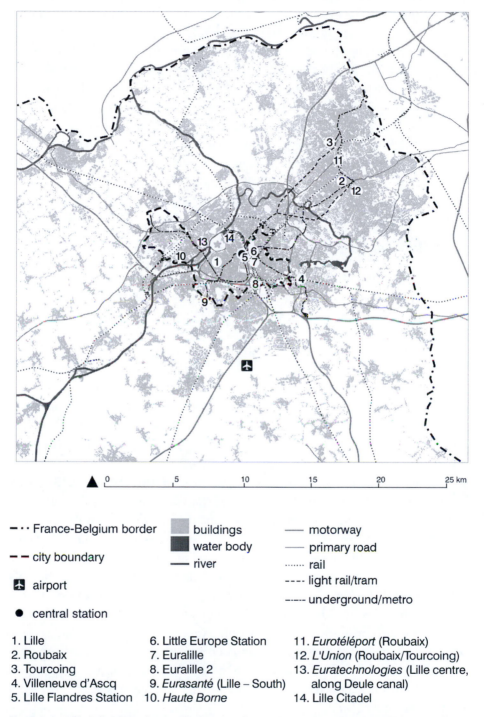

–·· France-Belgium border	▨ buildings	—— motorway	
– – city boundary	▮ water body	—— primary road	
✈ airport	—— river	······ rail	
● central station		---- light rail/tram	
		–·–·– underground/metro	

1. Lille
2. Roubaix
3. Tourcoing
4. Villeneuve d'Ascq
5. Lille Flandres Station

6. Little Europe Station
7. Euralille
8. Euralille 2
9. *Eurasanté* (Lille – South)
10. *Haute Borne*

11. *Eurotéléport* (Roubaix)
12. *L'Union* (Roubaix/Tourcoing)
13. *Euratechnologies* (Lille centre, along Deule canal)
14. Lille Citadel

Figure 9.1. *Lille: Lille Métropole map*. The largest urban agglomeration of northern France, embraces the cities of Lille, Roubaix and Tourcoing as well as a host of smaller communes including the 1970s new town of Villeneuve d'Ascq, and extends across the Belgian border to embrace French-speaking Mouscron and Flemish-speaking Kortrijk. The map shows the major regeneration initiatives under implementation across the area.

For two decades, from 1966 until 1989, LMCU played a limited technical role, focusing on motorway planning, and heavily influenced by the politics of small towns, and rarely addressing redistributive questions (Pradeilles and Chapoutot, 1981, pp. 39–58; Le Galès and Mawson, 1995, p. 383). Then every-thing changed. In 1989 Pierre Mauroy, Mayor of Lille and former Prime Minister of France (1981–1983), assumed the Presidency and achieved an historic political consensus between the Mayors of the four big cities – Lille, Roubaix, Tourcoing and Villeneuve d'Ascq. From then, LMCU began to play a strategic role, developing a vision for economic development and urban regeneration across the metropolitan region, implemented through a proactive strategy of development and regeneration to tackle major economic and urban problems and put 'Lille Métropole' on the European stage (Colomb, 2007, p. 28).

From Boom to Bust: The Collapse of Manufacturing

To understand the challenge facing LMCU in 1989, some history is needed. Together with Lorraine, this region was the cradle of the industrial revolution in France. Coal mining and steel making developed around Valenciennes, Douai and Maubeuge, on the great coalfield, the *Basin Minier*, of northern France and southern Belgium, while Lille, Roubaix and Tourcoing built their industrial prosperity upon textiles, to become the second largest textile region in the world after Manchester and south Lancashire (Fraser and Baert, 2003). Roubaix grew from 8,000 people in 1806 to 125,000 a century later, fed by massive migration from the neighbouring Belgian countryside; Roubaix-Tourcoing became 'The city of a thousand chimneys'. In 1911 Roubaix hosted the International Textile Exhibition, visited by 800,000 people (Colomb, 2007, p. 9).

But living conditions were exceedingly bad: in Roubaix in 1912, 50,000 workers were housed in 1,324 *courées* (courtyards), long and narrow alleyways with two rows of narrow two-room houses sharing one common toilet and water well, at densities up to 400 houses per hectare. Following massive slum clearance, 250 remain, overall in a very bad condition and mostly occupied by households on low incomes who cannot invest in maintenance, repairs or improvements. Small surprise that the French socialist party was born in Roubaix and that in 1892 Roubaix became the first socialist municipality in France, developing a policy of 'municipal socialism' promoting various programmes and services for the welfare of the working class in cooperation with associations and trade unions. Many social policy experiments in the fields of housing, hygiene and public health, later applied at national level, were born here in the first half of the twentieth century (*Ibid.*).

In 1900, and indeed much later, the region was still a series of separate towns. Initially the industrialists and their families lived in the inner city, close to their factories and to workers' housing. Just before World War One, a 14 km long '*Grand Boulevard*' linked Lille with Roubaix and Tourcoing; it included a tramline, brainchild of local engineer Alfred Mongy, which was promptly nicknamed *Le Mongy*. From the 1930s onwards, some of the industrial bourgeoisie left the city for surrounding towns and villas along the *Parc Barbieux*, the *Grand Boulevard*, Marcq and Croix. But, apart from discontinuous development along the tramline, it was only in the 1960s that rising car ownership led to urban sprawl and the creation of a British-style conurbation (Paris and Stevens, 2000, pp. 16, 51; Colomb, 2007, p. 18). Residential '*péri-urbanisation*' (edge city development) was accompanied by development of out-of-town shopping centres and the location of new business parks in rural areas (Paris and Stevens, 2000, p. 215).

Ironically, it was just at that point, in the early 1970s, that the region was hit suddenly by the crisis of the textile industry. After 30 years of sustained economic growth (*Les trente glorieuses*), France faced a sharp recession following the oil crisis of 1973–1974. The Lille urban region lost 130,000 jobs in textile manufacturing between 1945 and 1996; in Roubaix and Tourcoing alone, 50,000 textile jobs disappeared. The biggest mill, *La Lainière,* had 6,800 workers in the mid-1950s, producing 90 million tons of wool per year. It had 5,000 employees in 1982, 2,100 in 1989, 450 in 1996, and closed in January 2000, after 89 years of trading.

As a result, as elsewhere in Europe, the regional economy shifted massively from manufacturing to services. Liefooghe (2005) demonstrates how Roubaix and Tourcoing have become home to a highly specialized service cluster based on the presence of France's major mail order companies and head offices of hypermarket chains like *Auchan*, which emerged out of the restructuring and closure of the regional textiles industry, underpinned by a large variety of knowledge-intensive (and highly industry-specific) business services working for the mail order firms: logistics, advertising, graphics, photo studios, packaging, printing, direct marketing, call centres, software and so on.

But those who had lost jobs in manufacturing seldom found new ones in the retail and service sector. Older industrial workers and immigrants (especially from North Africa) who had been encouraged to come and work in the factories found themselves locked in poor housing conditions, long-term unemployment and with low prospects for mobility – a long-term spiral of deprivation which in many cases, through poor educational achievement and discrimination, turned into intergenerational poverty (Colomb, 2007, p. 12). The key problem is one of mismatch of supply and demand. In 2000, in the Lille arrondissement, unemployment of young people (under 25) reached 24.3 per cent. The region suffers from persistent long-term unemployment, high rates of unemployment among foreigners, and low educational/qualification levels. One-third of the unemployed in the Lille *arrondissement*, up to 40–50 per cent in some parts of Roubaix, lack qualifications (Colomb, 2007, pp. 15–16).

But deindustrialization, and the shift to the service sector, impacted to a very different degree within the region: the *Versant Nord-Est* (north-eastern side of the conurbation), around Roubaix and Tourcoing, demonstrates higher concentrations of deprivation and dereliction in comparison with the relatively more prosperous Lille and Villeneuve d'Ascq areas in the south. In Roubaix, deindustrialization and factory closures created many small pockets of physical decay – some with fine, but redundant, factory buildings – even in the city centre (*Ibid.*, p. 11). Retail also deserted the centre, as small shops closed down. By the mid-1990s, the centre was dead, unattractive and relatively unsafe, with very few retail and service opportunities left. The last cinema closed in 1998. In 10 years (1990–2000) house prices in Roubaix fell by 50 per cent in relative terms in comparison with those in the centre of Lille.

It took time for politicians to react. In the 1970s, energies and funding in LMCU focused on building a new town, Villeneuve d'Ascq, around the university, relocated from the centre of Lille to the city's eastern edge during the 1960s, and the development of a transport connection to it. To reinforce the idea of a very advanced high-technology campus, LMCU took a critical decision to develop a completely new, revolutionary automatic Metro system – the first of its kind in the world: the VAL (*Véhicule Automatique Léger*, Light Automatic Vehicle), with very small tunnels and coaches, thus reducing cost (Pradeilles and Chapoutot, 1981, pp. 81–82). The line, running through Lille from the western suburbs to Ville d'Ascq on the eastern side, opened in 1983 and attracted 100 million passengers by 1987. A critical element in the decision to proceed was the introduction of the new national tax on employers, the *Versement Transport*, which was forecast to provide 58 per cent of the capital cost (*Ibid.*, p. 115). In Jean-Claude Pradeilles's study, one interviewee commented:

> It's because of the *versement-transport*: with all that money, they couldn't do anything else: a tramway network, that was too difficult. (*Ibid.*, 145)

Even at this early date, a decision was taken in principle to develop a second line, northwards to Roubaix and Tourcoing (*Ibid.*, pp. 93–94). But nothing was done. Meanwhile the ageing Roubaix–Tourcoing tramway system – Le Mongy – went into increasing annual financial deficit from 1960 onwards, rising to nearly 7 million francs by 1971 (*Ibid.*, 64–75, 75–83).

1989: Pierre Mauroy and the Historic Compact

But then, in 1989, everything changed. Key political figures in LMCU at last accepted that the key to the long-term prosperity of the conurbation required a *balanced* spatial and economic development strategy in *all parts* of the city-region, including the areas which had suffered most from deindustrialization. Under the leadership of Pierre Mauroy, from 1989 onwards a 'metropolitan consensus' emerged within LMCU with the support of the Mayors of the four big cities (Colomb, 2007, p. 28). This consisted in a mutual recognition: on the one hand that, beyond old (and remaining) rivalries between cities, there was a need for Lille to become a strong 'core city' acting as the banner under which the wider city region would be marketed, with related flagship projects; on the other, that LMCU needed to commit itself to tackle the unbalanced development of the city-region and help deprived areas, to avoid a core-periphery situation which in the long-term would be detrimental to the overall prosperity of the city-region. This new agenda was sealed with a formal agreement between the Mayors comprising LMCU (Le Galès and Mawson, 1995, p. 384). A great deal of political and administrative effort was expended to achieve a commitment not only to large-scale prestige flagship projects and other economic development schemes but also to tackling the problems of disadvantaged groups and areas across the conurbation. Roubaix-Tourcoing accepted the backing of massive public investment in Euralille and the marketing of the city-region under the 'Lille Métropole' banner, while LMCU put significant resources into extending the Metro to Roubaix and Tourcoing (a decision made in 1990) as well as funding city centre and housing renewal in these two cities. In 1998 René Vandierendonck, the Mayor of Roubaix elected in 1994 and until then affiliated to the 'Centrist party', joined the Socialists at the regional election and thereby sealed the close relationship between Roubaix and LMCU.

Transport as the Key

Major transport developments played a key role in the evolution of the LMCU strategy and the resulting transformation of the LMCU economy. Two of these, the VAL Metro and the modernization of the tramway, were the direct responsibility and achievement of LMCU. The third, the achievement of the high-speed line from Paris to the Channel Tunnel and the new Euralille station, was a huge cooperative enterprise at national level in which, nevertheless, key CMU individuals played a vital role.

Construction of the second 32-kilometre Metro line linking Lille with Roubaix and Tourcoing was launched in the early 1990s and completed in 1999. The combined two-line Metro system, linking the four major cities of Lille, Roubaix, Tourcoing and Villeneuve d'Ascq, became the symbol of the polycentric conurbation. It carried 262,465 passengers per day in 2009 and has since then been adopted in Taipei, Chicago, and other French cities such as Toulouse.

In addition, the old tramway system was also modernized into a 22-kilometre tramline linking Lille, Roubaix and Tourcoing, and running underground to a major new underground interchange station with both Metro lines at Lille Flandres, which also included a new bus station above ground in front of the old station (Menerault, 2008, pp. 157–158). Roubaix now has six Metro stations and six tram stops. It takes 20 minutes to go by Metro from the centre of Roubaix to the centre of Lille. The metro, trams and buses serve the international and local railway stations. The huge investment required was funded mainly through a national payroll tax on employers, the *Versement Transport*. *Lille Métropole* also has eighty-nine urban and suburban bus lines including eight cross border routes (Colomb, 2007, pp. 28–29).

Finally there was the TGV. Lille had a central terminal station, Lille Flandres, as early as 1848 after the original city walls were torn down. In 1921 a plan by E. Dubuisson already proposed its replacement by a through station in the area of the old fortifications east of the city centre, an idea which lay dormant until picked up by Théodore Leveau in a project of 1951 and then in a plan by OREAM-Nord in 1971, which specifically proposed a through station for high-speed European trains, supplementing – not replacing – the old terminal station. This far-seeing plan already captured the idea of a multimodal interchange linking the new station both with the old tramway and with a new transit system serving the new town (Meneraut, 2008, pp. 155–157). Dropped when the Channel Tunnel project was abandoned in 1975, it saw new light on 20 January 1986, when President Mitterrand and Prime Minister Margaret Thatcher signed the Franco-British cooperation agreement on the construction of the Channel Tunnel. Pierre Mauroy immediately started to lobby French central government in order to secure Lille as the location of the future interchange station for north-west European high-speed train lines (Paris–London, Brussels–London and Paris–Brussels–Amsterdam). He was backed by a strong regional lobby of public and private leaders, and achieved the location of the future HST station in Lille in 1987. The City of Lille owned 70 hectares of former military land just a few hundred metres away from the old railway station. It was self-evidently an ideal location for the new high-speed train station. The new TGV station Lille-Europe, which opened in 1994, lies on the doorstep of Lille city centre, 5 minutes walk to the old station Lille Flandres and 15 minutes walk to the *Grand Place* (main square of Lille), and is connected to the Metro and the tram. This landmark decision gave a crucial impetus to the economic development of Lille Métropole. For decades, the Lille area 'was considered peripheral to the country, as remote from its cultural heart as the mountains of the *Pyrénées*' (Fraser and Baert, 2003). The high-speed train connection turned the city from a dead-end on the northern border of France into a strategic interface between the capital cities of north-west Europe.

However, largely for financial reasons, the opportunity to create a single through station was lost. The new station is 500 metres from the old one and the idea of a people mover was not followed up. So the two stations are connected only on the surface or by underground tramway or Metro – hardly convenient for passengers with baggage (Menerault, 2008, p. 158). A further complication is that the first east–west Metro line, opened earlier, lacks a station at Lille Europe. And – a more basic issue still – the Paris–Brussels high-speed line, extended since 2010 to Amsterdam and Cologne, bypasses Lille altogether to the south of the city, thus serving neither the city centre nor any of the poles of development in the 2002 strategy for the city region. For this reason Philip Menerault has proposed development of an entirely new Lille South station at the Eurosanté pole in the southern suburbs, not replacing but supplementing the present Lille Europe (*Ibid.*, pp. 160–161). But he emphasizes that TGVs could not stop there: SNCF and its Belgian and Dutch partners, obsessed by the commercial need to connect Paris with Amsterdam within three hours, would not countenance an additional stop.

In 1990, plans were launched for a major office and retail development, known as Euralille, to be built around the new high-speed train station, in order to boost Lille's position on the European stage. Euralille was built between 1990 and 1995 by a public-private partnership set up in 1990 on the model of the French *Sociétés d'Economie Mixte* (SEM), a common French institutional tool for major urban development schemes, which combines a mixture of smaller projects funded by private investors within a masterplan defined by the public sector and coordinated by a nominally mixed, though public sector controlled, management agency (Newman and Thornley, 1996). It includes offices, a large shopping centre, an hotel, a student hall of residence, a business school, a music venue, a convention centre and a large urban park, plus separate new housing developments in the vicinity (figure 9.2). The cost was estimated at around 5 billion francs (£500 million), of which 1.5 came from public funds and 3.5 from private investors. EU Structural Funds contributed to the financing of the convention centre. The contemporary architecture of the project, by leading architects such as Rem Koolhaas, Christian de Porzamparc and Jean Nouvel, was criticized by some, but was generally accepted by the local population as a new futuristic landmark symbolizing the vitality of the city. The shopping

Figure 9.2. *Euralille.* The office and retail complex planned around the Lille Europe high-speed train station, linking it to the old Flandres station at the edge of the city centre, with exotic structures designed by the celebrated *S, M, L, XL* architect Rem Koolhaas.

centre became an extremely popular venue, both for local and foreign shoppers, and attracts up to 30,000 visitors a day (50,000 on Saturdays), and generated a turnover of approximately 1.5 billion francs (£150 million) in 2000. It comprises 120 retail units, and created 1,200 jobs. Ninety-five per cent of the 50,000 m² office space built was sold by 2001. Over fifty firms settled in Euralille, including major companies such as Axa, Crédit Lyonnais, Compaq and Stanhome.

Ten years after its launch, Euralille thus met its primary objective to provide the Lille metropolitan area with a business centre of the same scale as those found in other major European cities. To increase the economic impact, a second phase, Euralille 2, was launched to form a new gateway to the city centre with a fresh urban façade on the ring road, between Lille Grand Palais and St-Sauveur station (figure 9.3). This is a 190,000 m² mixed-use scheme with public buildings (the HQ of the Nord-Pas-de-Calais Regional Council); the extension of the *Lille Grand Palais*; offices; hotels; sports and thirty-one leisure facilities and a new residential neighbourhood with 800 housing units in a green environment called the *Bois Habité*. In 2010, it was estimated that investments from the private and public sector in Euralille and Euralille 2 will amount to €1.8 billion (Colomb, 2007, pp. 29–30).

Figure 9.3. *Euralille 2.* The new office complex south of the original Euralille, designed to accommodate overspill demand as the city rapidly develops new advanced service functions replacing the old manufacturing base. (*Photo*: Jérémy Jännick, 2009)

Creating a Polycentric Metropolis

But there was another critical side to the historic compromise which Pierre Mauroy forged: in 1990, in addition to Euralille, LMCU decided to launch a number of new economic development nodes, spread across the conurbation, to ensure more spatial balance in the distribution of economic growth. The aim was to re-orientate the regional economy towards the growing economic sectors of a post-industrial economy: business services; information and communication technologies; biotechnologies; research and development. The strategy is based on functional specialization at different poles: communication technologies and textiles in Roubaix; executive and international business functions in Lille; logistics and transport in Tourcoing. These 'Poles of Metropolitan Excellence' are enshrined in the strategic spatial planning document for the city-region, the *Schéma Directeur* (figure 9.1). Each targets a different area of specialization:

◆ *Euralille* (Lille – Centre): a major business and retail centre around the new TGV station Lille-Europe.

◆ *Eurasanté* (Lille – South): a 300-ha business park and service centre on the university hospital site, designed to become an internationally recognized centre of excellence specializing in health-related and biomedical research and industries.

◆ *Haute Borne*: a science park dedicated to enterprises specializing in research, services and high technology. It contains nearly sixty research laboratories, five engineering schools, a large number of corporate headquarters and regional headquarters, and offers a full range of accommodation and services, among which a newly created Centre for Innovation and Exchanges interfaces between the universities and the business world.

◆ *Eurotéléport* (Roubaix): a technological park project dedicated to the development of companies producing or using IT and communication tools.

◆ *L'Union* (Roubaix/Tourcoing) a future centre for innovative textiles.

◆ *Logistical platform in Tourcoing* (International transport centre).

◆ *Euratechnologies*: a technological park for information and communication technology, started in 2007, along the banks of the Deûle canal, close to Lille town centre and main transport routes, also including an eco-friendly neighbourhood based on the garden city concept, with 2000 housing units for 5000 inhabitants (Colomb, 2007, pp. 32–33).

The strategy recognizes that the tertiary sector now represents 68 per cent of jobs, industry only 23 per cent, mirroring the national structure of the French economy. The Lille conurbation in the early twenty-first century has a working population of 500,000 people in a highly diversified economy. It still has significant strength in manufacturing, including specialized textiles (protection, sports, leisure, medical, building, transport, defence, agriculture), printing and publishing, mechanical and electrical industries, chemicals and pharmaceuticals and food processing, plus a dynamic retail sector (mail order sales, with 65 per cent of total national employment), retail and restaurant chain headquarters, and retail with a specialization in factory outlet bargain stores, telemarketing, and a major presence in the finance, insurance and IT sectors (689 company head offices employing more than fifty employees each; 450 bank branches, eighty credit establishments, thirteen foreign banks, six insurance companies headquarters; the second region in France for logistics and a major centre for e-business with a complete chain of subcontractors and service companies and express delivery companies; the ICT sector employs nearly 25,000 people, and the third university city in France, with four universities, twenty higher education institutions, about 100,000 students and researchers (concentration of university and high-tech research functions in Villeneuve d'Ascq). It has an increasingly significant tourism sector, with over two million visitors a year.

Sport and Culture as Agents of Regeneration

In 1994 Lille submitted a bid to be the French candidate for the 2004 Olympic Games. The city was selected over Lyon to represent the country. The bid then fell through, but boosted the self-confidence of local residents and united local networks of actors around a project of metropolitan importance. It also shifted the debate from Lille as a key regional metropolis in the French context to Lille as a metropolis in the European context (Paris and Stevens, 2000, p. 171). The momentum created by the Olympic bid was turned into another bid – to become European Capital of Culture. Both bids were initiated and supported by the *Comité Grand Lille*, an informal body created in 1993 on the initiative of Bruno Bonduelle, a leading local industrialist. The *Comité* brought together business and industrial leaders, academics, NGO representatives and some elected politicians. It discussed and recommended possible actions to improve the area's image and position as a major European centre – in such fields as culture, tourism, education and international partnerships. The Committee created a link between business leaders (traditionally Christian Democrats) and local politicians (mostly Socialists) on strategic ideas for the promotion of the city-region, focusing on common goals and not on political differences or the rivalries between individual municipalities. It also helped to secure business support for flagship events, such as European Capital of Culture. There was a clear strategy to spread the benefits of the year-long event across the whole city region, including Roubaix. The image of the city-region at national and European level changed significantly as a result, and Lille began to be perceived as a dynamic, creative, young city with lots of potential and many qualities. Media coverage at national and international level was significant. The year-long festival also established Lille as an important tourist destination in north-west Europe, attracting seven million visitors that year (Colomb, 2007, pp. 32–33).

Designation as European Capital of Culture in 2004 boosted development and promotion of the region's rich cultural and historical heritage, with a major Museum of Beaux-Arts; a Modern Art Museum in Villeneuve d'Ascq; the new Archives of Labour History and the Museum of Arts and Industry in Roubaix; a recently refurbished Opera House; a resident Symphonic Orchestra; an active, young music scene, the annual Carnival; the annual Fair (*Grande Braderie*) which attracts two million visitors; a stunning architectural heritage such as the Vieux Lille neighbourhood, dating back to the Flemish Golden Age of the sixteenth to eighteenth century (Baert *et al.*/ADULM, 2004; Paris and Baert, 2011).

The new 'metropolitan consensus', set out in the strategic spatial plan for the metropolitan region (ADULM, 2006), is based on a strategy of *Ville Renouvelée* (Renewed City), inspired by recent British approaches to integrated urban regeneration and renewal, which seeks an integrated approach to urban renewal – economic, social, environmental and cultural. It became a key element of French national urban policy based on the experience of the Lille region, embodied in the National Planning Act 2000 (*Loi Solidarité et Renouvellement Urbains*, modified in July 2003 with the *Loi Urbanisme et Habitat*). Bonneville (2005, p. 241) describes a central dilemma of urban regeneration: whether to concentrate on regenerating the most deprived neighbourhoods, running the risk that they will remain isolated ghettos, or to inject market forces into the process, thereby threatening the position of the existing deprived populations. But Colomb (2007, p. 35; 2012, pp. 94–95) shows that Roubaix has successfully managed to follow the second approach while attacking social exclusion and housing renewal, through an economic development strategy at the scale of the city-region plus a series of specific projects in the most deprived neighbourhoods. Some 4,000 ha of inner city neighbourhoods in various part of the urban region were designed as 'Priority neighbourhoods' in the 2002 *Schéma Directeur* and in the *Contrat d'Agglomération* (agreement between Central Government, the region and LMCU defining funding priorities in thirteen neighbourhoods over 15 years). These include nineteenth-century working-class residential neighbourhoods, former factories, brownfield sites, and some post-war housing estates. Most of Roubaix's territory is included under this designation (Colomb, 2007, p. 35).

Conclusion: Half Way to Success

Thus, over 20 years, the Lille conurbation has successfully managed, to a surprising degree, the transition from an industrial to a service-oriented economy. It also successfully promoted itself from being a secondary French city to a 'Eurocity' and a metropolis of significance for north-west Europe. In the city of Lille itself, the decline in inner-city population stopped in the 1990s, with a 6 per cent population growth between 1990 and 1999 and another 6 per cent between 1999 and 2008. Tourist flows have significantly increased in the last 10 years (40 per cent of tourists are from the UK and Belgium). In 1998, the region Nord-Pas-de-Calais came first among French regions for direct foreign investment, of which one-third is located in Lille Métropole. Claire Colomb's definitive account of the process (Colomb, 2007) identifies ten key factors underlying this transformation:

◆ Grasping the unique opportunity brought by the location of the high-speed train interchange station in Lille and changing patterns of accessibility in north-west Europe.

◆ Developing well-established institutional cooperation between the municipalities making up the urban region through LMCU, which has allowed for coherent decisions on investment and strategic planning at the city-region scale. Although decision-making within LMCU has not always been easy, since the early 1990s there has been a broad degree of consensus on the strategic development options to be taken to improve the positioning of the conurbation in Europe.

◆ A proactive, charismatic civic leader with good political and economic networks, Pierre Mauroy.

◆ Tapping into European and central government funding and programmes in the poorest part of the urban region; as well as in the financing of some major projects.

◆ Developing a public transport system that connects the cities of Lille, Roubaix, Tourcoing and Villeneuve d'Ascq, acting as the 'spinal cord' of the polycentric conurbation.

◆ Placing the emphasis on the polycentric development of the urban region through a network of public transport and the planning of major flagship projects in various locations, *Euralille, Eurasanté, Haute Borne, l'Union, Euro-téléport, Euratechnologies* – with each major city specializing in a certain type of activity.

◆ Developing a sub-regional economic strategy of clusters that deal with all the elements in the supply chain (*filière*) from design and training through to production and retail (*l'Union*, Roubaix).

◆ Encouraging an economic development agenda which is matched by a strong concern for social and economic cohesion in an urban region with very high socio-economic inequalities: the focus on the urban renewal of the most deprived areas of the urban region, through the *Ville Renouvelée* strategy, particularly benefited Roubaix.

◆ Developing cross-border networks to build synergy and links with Belgian cities.

◆ Promoting a proactive cultural marketing policy (European Capital of Culture 2004).

The job is far from complete. Lille Métropole still suffers from an unbalanced pattern of growth; Roubaix and Tourcoing still suffer from high unemployment and pockets of deprivation and dereliction. In August 2012, the French think tank Compas published the first results of an inquiry into poverty levels in the 100 biggest French cities; Roubaix topped the list for metropolitan France, with 46 per cent of the population below the official poverty level – three times the national level, and equal to that of Saint-Denis de la Réunion in the Indian Ocean (Compas, 2012). But the efforts to recast the entire metropolitan economy, away from the traditional economic base to the knowledge economy, remain some of the most remarkable in Europe (figures 9.4(*a*) and (*b*)). And transport investment, connecting people with new jobs, has played a critical role (Colomb, 2007, pp. 38–39).

Figures 9.4(*a*) and (*b*). *Roubaix.* The centre of this old textile-manufacturing city, slowly generating new service functions; interchange between two major investments of the 1990s, the modernized tramway (*Le Mongy*) and Line 2 of the automated *Métro*.

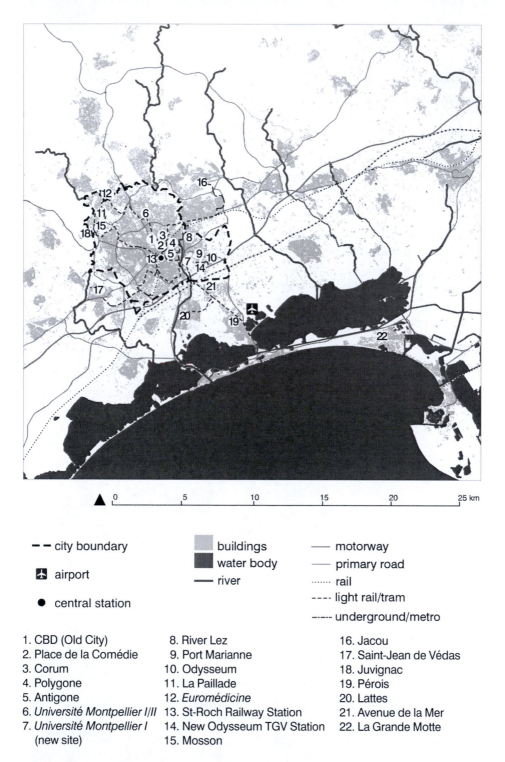

0   5   10   15   20   25 km

- – city boundary
- ✈ airport
- ● central station

▦ buildings
■ water body
— river

— motorway
— primary road
······· rail
- - - - light rail/tram
-·-·- underground/metro

1. CBD (Old City)
2. Place de la Comédie
3. Corum
4. Polygone
5. Antigone
6. *Université Montpellier I/II*
7. *Université Montpellier I*
   (new site)

8. River Lez
9. Port Marianne
10. Odysseum
11. La Paillade
12. *Euromédicine*
13. St-Roch Railway Station
14. New Odysseum TGV Station
15. Mosson

16. Jacou
17. Saint-Jean de Védas
18. Juvignac
19. Pérois
20. Lattes
21. Avenue de la Mer
22. La Grande Motte

Figure 9.5. *Montpellier map*. The fastest-growing major city of France over the last half-century, its attractive climate and strong knowledge base have been augmented by an extraordinary boosterism campaign led by a maverick mayor, the late Georges Frêche. The agglomeration extends beyond the airport to the Mediterranean littoral, now served by the city's newest tramway.

Montpellier Turns a Medieval City into a Technopole

At first sight Montpellier – capital of the Languedoc-Rousillion *Région* and the Hérault *Département*, located almost at the far southern end of France – could not present a greater contrast with Lille. Since the 1950s it has been one of France's most dynamic cities, rising steadily in the league table of French cities from twenty-fifth place in 1954, when it had a mere 97,000 people, to eighth in 2008 with 253,000. A wider Montpellier metropolitan area (*aire urbaine*), within an approximate 25-kilometre radius, had 510,000 people, making it the fifteenth largest in France; over the previous 7 years, it too had celebrated the fastest growth rate of any major urban area (figure 9.5 opposite). This extraordinary expansion has been fuelled by a number of forces: the arrival in the early 1960s of 15,000 French refugees from Algeria after it gained independence, the growth of tourism along the Languedoc coast, coupled with retirement migration from Paris and the north to Mediterranean France – both attracted by the climate[1] – and the development of a major complex of universities and advanced research. And it has been massively assisted by transport investments which have effectively and dramatically shrunk the 750-kilometre distance between Paris and the Languedoc Region: completion first of the A7 and A9 motorways in the 1960s and 1970s, and then of the *Ligne à Grande Vitesse Méditerranée* all the way to Avignon in 2001.

Much of this was directly or indirectly the result of deliberately planned and government-subsidized investment, from completion of *La Grande Motte* outside Montpellier between 1968 and 1975, the first major tourism complex in the Languedoc region – deliberately designed to attract trade away from the Spanish beaches – to the growth of the city's three universities. But Montpellier was a great medieval city, first mentioned in 985, with a university founded in 1160 (and with a charter from 1220) famous for its faculty of medicine, in which Dr Rabelais practiced in the sixteenth century, and which in 1809 was spun off as a separate *Université Montpellier 2* specializing in science and technology.[2] Louis XIV made the ancient walled city, in its commanding position on top of two hills, the capital of the ancient region of Bas Languedoc, which gave it elegant new eighteenth-century streets and squares outside the walls: most notably, the huge Place de la Comédie on the east side with an elegant Opera House on its south side (figure 9.6).

This ancient base was important because it allowed the city's planners to use it as an historic core around which, in the 1980s and 1990s, dramatic new developments could be inserted to accommodate the city's growth. The huge square was pedestrianized and a new conference centre, the *Corum*, built at the end of a pedestrian esplanade at its northern end. Then, to the east of the square, the planners used a sharp fall in level down to the River Lez to build a huge new covered shopping centre, the *Polygone*, with multiple layers of parking underneath and direct pedestrian access via escalators down to the lower river

Figure 9.6. *Montpellier, Place de la Comédie*. The centre of the eighteenth-century extension of the medieval core and the heart of modern Montpellier. (*Photo*: CC Christophe Finot, 2007)

level. And then, in the 1980s, they further extended this complex eastwards to the river in a huge high-density pedestrian neighbourhood, *Antigone*, designed by the celebrated (and controversial) Catalan postmodern architect Ricardo Bofill. Finally, on the other east bank of the river, development began at Porte Marianne (doubtless, if national pride ever allowed, to receive its own classical name in due order), which has become the new centre of the *Université Montpellier I/II*, with a new planned boulevard, Avenue Raymond-Dugrand, 'the new Champs-Elysées of Montpellier', eventually connecting to a huge existing edge-of-town leisure and shopping centre, *Odysseum* (figure 9.7). Directly accessible from the A9 motorway which bypasses this compact city on its southern border, Odysseum includes an aquarium, *Mare Nostrum* – which soon became a major tourist attraction – as well as a huge IKEA store (Mills, 2001, pp. 338–339). And, to follow, there will be Odysseum 2 on the other side of the motorway, due to open in 2013 with a theme park and 'urban hotel', Château Pourcel, a luxury hotel-restaurant complex around a giant 2,400 m^2 swimming pool designed by the Algerian architect Imaad Rahmouni.

The Master Planner: Georges Frêche

All this represents an epic series of planned *Grands Projets* in the classic French style, and almost without parallel even in France. And, appropriately, the whole process was masterminded by a major political figure whose career closely compares with that of Pierre Mauroy in Lille – but with one key difference.

Figure 9.7. *Odysseum*. The leisure shopping complex, an edge-of-town American import at the end of the first Montpellier tramway, achieved by Georges Frêche in the face of ferocious opposition from local city-centre business interests.

Georges Frêche (1938–2010), who was Mayor of Montpellier from 1977 to 2004 and president of Languedoc-Roussillon from that year until his death, was also a Socialist party deputy in the French parliament for the Hérault *Département* from 1973 until 2002, but deliberately never sought ministerial office. This was hugely shrewd: holding office when decentralization was the main political theme and Mayors were enjoying more and more power, able to wield huge influence as a backbencher and member of the central committee of the Parti Socialiste, presenting himself as the provincial outsider opposed to the Parisian élite, he was in the right place at the right time. Frêche had a consistent strategy to attract new residents: he wanted to bring in people who were young, well-qualified, consumers of culture and of leisure, who aimed to enhance their quality of life. Because he knew what he wanted and his opponents were weak, he had a considerable margin of political action (Arab, 2004, p. 290). Variously described as a master builder, a visionary and a feudal megalomaniac, he directly controlled the para-public organism that operated in the urban field, equally in the city and the fifteen *commune* districts: SERM (*Société d'Équipement de la Région Montpelliéraine*) (*Ibid.*, pp. 286–287). Through this he and his allies gained control of economic development, employment, financing of enterprises, real estate promotion and transport – all in opposition to the Chamber of Commerce and Industry, CCI (*Ibid.*, p. 291). This centralized and authoritarian system of government was then employed to establish an audacious urban policy, designed to raise Montpellier from a sleepy medium-sized city to a first-rank southern European metropolis (*Ibid.*).

As the *Guardian* obituary put it, 'While railing publicly against the outmoded anticapitalism of much of the French left, Frêche turned Montpellier from a sleepy southern outpost into one of the most commercially dynamic agglomerations in France, successfully courting major high-tech and financial-sector employers'. He established no less than eleven business parks around the city. Dell Computers, which employs 600 people in Montpellier, and Palm Computing Europe both chose Montpellier as home for their southern European operations, creating an image of a high-tech, thriving town, able to attract the country's best researchers and computer experts. Even the audacious projects, designed to attract criticism, had the deliberate effect of generating endless publicity, boosting the city's image and encouraging visitors – some of whom, at least, might later invest in the city. He fought ferociously for the Odysseum project, over two decades, against the opposition of city centre commercial interests and eco-warriors. Most audacious of all was his final achievement: La place du XXème siècle, at Odysseum, opened in August 2010 – the 'political holiday season', as *Le Figaro* acutely observed – not long before his early death from a heart attack, it is adorned with five enormous statues, each 3.3 metres high, of 'great men' including – in addition to more obvious candidates like de Gaulle, Churchill, Roosevelt and Jean Jaurès – Vladimir Iyyich Lenin (figure 9.8). When France's ruling UMP party complained, Frêche told them

Figure 9.8. *Homage aux Grands Hommes*. Statue of Lenin in the open-air theatre in the centre of Odysseum, confronting the massed forces of late capitalism.

they were lucky he had not chosen Stalin. Frêche engendered deep resentment on the part of local private interests, reinforced by violent criticism of an urban policy which the local Chamber of Commerce and Industry (CCI) gauged detrimental to the interests of the city centre where so much commercial activity was concentrated.

The Saga of Odysseum

His relationship with the CCI deteriorated to a rare intensity over the development of Odysseum (Arab, 2004, pp. 290–291). The strategy to extend the city's commercial heart progressively eastwards raised the question of opening a new pole of development far out, 4 kilometres from the historic core, close to the A9 motorway which forms the city's border on its southern side. SERM first looked to commercial partners and then, failing to find the vision it needed, alone took charge of decisions up to the point of commercial approvals. Three members of SERM played crucial roles: the Director-General, Director of Planning and 'Project Director', all followed closely by the Mayor and his Assistant Mayor for Urbanism (*Ibid.*, p. 371). The Director of Planning later told a researcher that he had read every available academic analysis of the effect of new development on city centre activity from 1977 onwards, and found nothing (*Ibid.*, p. 385). The Director-General asserted that the so-called leisure promoters simply did not exist, while so-called 'leisure champions' knew nothing; they had 'lead boots' (*Ibid.*, p. 387).

A critical event was a visit to the United States at Easter 1998, with Design International (DI), an architectural-planning practice which had designed a new kind of shopping-leisure complex, Coconut in Miami; the visit also included similar developments in Los Angeles, Las Vegas and Chicago. This provided the model: to unite on a single site land uses and activities previously seen as different and even incompatible – a huge hypermarket, an IKEA store, a multiplex cinema, an aquarium, a skating rink, bars and restaurants along new planned pedestrian streets, all served by a tramway (*Ibid.*, p. 376). SERM proceeded quickly to designate a ZAC (*Zone d'Aménagement Concerté*), a French planning procedure designed to allow public and private interests to coordinate activities in the service of a major new development. 'For the traders in the centre, the approval of the ZAC dossier in July 1998 … was a demarcation of war' (*Ibid.*, p. 379). The management of the *Polygone*, the huge shopping centre in the city centre, estimated a loss of trade of 25 per cent, and the CCI concluded that more jobs would be destroyed than were created (*Ibid.*). 'From their viewpoint, this new programme, described as megalomaniac and pharaonic, amounted to moving the city centre' (*Ibid.*).

Their attack on the Odysseum project took place on three different levels: an economic conflict of interest, a conflict on style of development ('frenetic urban development', 'unending urbanization', 'tentacular urban expansion' and *'folie des grandeurs'*); and a conflict on the methods of public action ('authoritarian exercise of power', 'refusal to discuss', 'expedient methods') (*Ibid.*).

The Key Role of Transport

Frêche also saw the critical importance of investment in transport, both directly in improving accessibility and also indirectly in terms of image making. So he jointly campaigned for the extension of France's original high-speed rail line, opened in 1981 from Paris to Lyon, onward to Marseille with a branch toward Montpellier, completed in 2001. And, inside the city, he enthusiastically embraced the French tramway revolution that had been launched with the funds made available by the *Versement Transport* in the 1970s.

Montpellier like almost every other French city had scrapped its tram network, focusing on the Place de la Comédie, in the 1950s, replacing the trams by buses operated by CTM, a private company. But December 1978 saw the founding of the *Société Montpelliéraine des Transports Urbains* (SMTU), a French *société mixte* with the city as its major shareholder and the balance of the shares held by private companies, which took over operation of the twelve line, 109 km network serving the city and one other commune. Then, in 1982, the city and fourteen other municipalities formed a District of the Montpellier Agglomeration, with certain planning powers, as the sole body with the right to organize urban public transport within its boundaries. At that point, SMTU established nine more lines to serve the other communes. By 1996, a network of twenty-seven lines with 247 buses covered 349 route-km during the day, plus a limited night network. Patronage grew markedly and then, after 1988, stabilized – in sharp contrast to the trend in many other European cities (Mills, 2001, pp. 339–340). Even so, despite bus priority measures, average network speed was only about 14 km/h in the mid-1990s, and patronage remained flat.

The first tramline (Line 1, the Blue Line), opened in July 2000, involved a radical reorientation of the entire urban transport system, to give the tram priority and facilitate bus operation. Most bus services were removed from the central area; one important bus route was replaced by the tramway, while the others now terminate outside the central area, necessitating a transfer from bus to tram. This use of a smaller number of high-capacity trams instead of a larger number of buses has reduced noise, air pollution and congestion and has also reduced operating costs, because of a reduction in vehicle-kilometres. But the new system was also critically designed to promote an overall and highly radical strategic planning framework that sought to develop an east–west linear city in place of the traditional concentric form. This was in accordance with the planned extensions of the city to the east of the historic centre, which aimed to reduce a long historical asymmetry in the city's development, while renewing some existing neighbourhoods. And it thus helped generate a positive feedback between tramway investment and urban development, by raising the numbers of people travelling along the east–west axis while simultaneously boosting the business case for the tramway (*Ibid.*, p. 341).

The new line achieved this objective by being deliberately routed to serve series of important traffic generators – from west to east:

◆ The high-density residential suburb of La Paillade (26,000 inhabitants), together with the Mosson football stadium;

◆ The science/technology park of Euromédicine;

◆ A hospital/university zone (with 10,000 jobs and 30,000 students) of the *Université Montpellier II*, the city's 200-year-old scientific and technological university, including Lapeyronie and other hospitals, the medical teaching unit, the Faculty of Science and Technology, the Faculty of Letters, and university halls of residence;

◆ The Corum (concert hall and congress centre) on the edge of the old town;

◆ Place de la Comédie;

◆ The main train station and the adjoining bus station for rural and inter-urban buses;

◆ The Polygone shopping centre;

◆ Antigone, the high-density residential development, including the new Olympic swimming pool and a city library;

◆ The first developments at Parc Marianne: apartment buildings, the Faculties of Economics and Management of the *Université Montpellier I* (soon to be combined with the city's other two universities in the new *Université Montpellier Sud de France*), and a new university library;

◆ Leisure facilities including a cinema multiplex opened in 1998, and adjacent 'big box' retailing, at Odysseum.

Many of these traffic generators (especially the Corum and those to the east of it) are within 100-200 metres of a tram stop (*Ibid.*, pp. 342–343).

Line 2 (the Red Line) followed in December 2006, in effect prolonging the east–west axis in two new directions: towards the north-east, and towards the south-west where it could have connected with a new TGV station at Saint-Jean de Védas, later rejected in favour of an alternative site at Odysseum – a story told below. The longest tramline in France, it was deliberately projected outside the central built-up area of Montpellier across green fields to serve a big-box retail centre (a Carrefour and a Leroy Merlin *bricolage* store) at La Condamine – a similar approach to that used in planning Line 1, and indeed tramlines in other French cities such as Strasbourg (figure 9.9(*a*) and (*b*)).

Figures 9.9(*a*) and (*b*). *Montpellier trams*. Tramlines intersecting in front of the main St Roch train station, and providing seamless interchange from TGV and regional rail services to all parts of the city.

The final agent of urban transformation was Line 3, the Green line, opened in April 2012[3] with trams designed by the fashion designer Christian Lacroix. Given a brief that the trams had to have a nautical flavour, Lacroix excelled himself in a feat of creative frenzy. The new trams, which change in the course of three cars from a surreal shade of reddish-black (or blackish-red) to a surreal shade of green (or perhaps turquoise) to another colour not easily describable, are all decorated with thousands of marine organisms, inspired (apparently, according to M. Lacroix) by Jules Verne's *Twenty Thousand Leagues under the Sea*.

They were deliberately marketed in YouTube clips as erotic objects.[4] This might seem whimsical, but it was very much the point. Like the trams that preceded it on Line 1 – with their flying swallows, from stylists Elizabeth Garouste and Mattia Bonetti, and Line 2, with their happy-go-lucky floral themes also from Mattia Bonetti – the new tram was being marketed very deliberately not as a means of transport (it is capable of selling itself very effectively on that count, without PR help) but as an integral part of a lifestyle. It said, in effect, 'come and relax riding around on me, in a city where the sun shines almost all year and the living is perennially easy'.

Running along a new north–south axis, the *Avenue de la Mer*, from the university quarter at Porte Marianne down to Pérols, almost on the sea, with a branch to Lattes, the new tramline will act as the basis for transformation over a 20 year period of a 5 km, 2,500 m² corridor, now occupied by time-expired buildings from the 1960s, with between 6,000 and 8,000 totally new homes where none now exist, 75,000 m² of new offices and 40,000 to 50,000 m² of new public buildings. It represents a major change in scale, because these developments will occur largely outside the Montpellier city limits, in the communes of Pérols and Lattes. And thus it represents a critical transition, earlier noticed in Lille, where the central city forms an alliance with bordering communities to develop strategic transport and land use planning on a city-regional scale: the *Écocité Communauté d'Agglomération de Montpellier: Castelnau le Lez, Lattes, Montpellier et Pérols*. Eventually, they plan for it to reach *La Grande Motte*, the giant ziggurat-like resort complex that launched the tourist trade on this, the late-developing half of Mediterranean France, 40 years ago.

The project is nothing if not ambitious: it aims, in the words of its website, to 'mainstream the hydraulic design of the project, build a city of biodiversity by integrating natural and agricultural areas, develop travel arrangements based on sustainable mobility, control energy efficiency and create a low carbon city with regard to the characteristics of Mediterranean climate, and more vaguely to organize the transformation of trade and urban renewal to achieve functional and social diversity'. It is part of a national government programme, announced in 2011, to support development of no less than ninety-three such eco-cities across France. Whether and whenever it will come to pass is still an open question: the line runs through largely undeveloped territory to terminate at an isolated roundabout where passengers interchange to regional buses for the remainder of their journeys, and local media report opposition by more distant communes to any further extension. So this remains a truly audacious investment – but there is a further massive complication.

The TGV Comes to Montpellier

This is another critical decision at national level: to construct the first section of the *Ligne à Grande Vitesse Languedoc*, which will eventually connect the existing high-speed line from Paris with the onward high-speed extension from Perpignan through the Pyrenees and onward to Barcelona, due to be completed some time after 2020. This first connection will be a 60 km by-pass (*contournement*) of Nîmes, to open in 2017, which unusually will carry both high-speed passenger and freight trains on the same tracks, and unusual also (for France) in being financed through a public-private partnership. The new line will further shrink time-distances between Montpellier and the other great cities of France: to Lyon in 1 hour 30 minutes, to Paris in 3 hours, to Lille in 4 hours 30 minutes. Critically, the new line will include new edge-of-town stations for Nîmes and Montpellier – and the Montpellier station will be located at Odysseum, in the core of the new Avenue Georges Frêche eco-city, serving as the basis for a new commercial subcentre. But in addition, by removing 230 freight trains a day from the existing line through the city-centre train station of St Roch, the new line will allow the fast-expanding regional train services, serving the wider Montpellier metro region, to be boosted by 30 per cent, offering a service of three or four trains every hour at peak hours.

In one important sense, therefore, transport planning in Montpellier has followed the same model as in Lille: a new high-speed line is being built to a new station that in time will form the heart of a new district of the city. The critical difference is that while in Lille the new and the old stations are less than 600 metres apart, in Montpellier they will be separated by no less than 3 kilometres. This is more comparable with the position in Lyon, where the first TGV line in 1981 was deliberately routed not to the old Perrache station in the city's ancient and congested core but to a new station at Part-Dieu, a similar distance away, which duly became the core of a new central business district. But it is not completely comparable either, because in Lyon, a much bigger city, the new station was placed in an inner urban zone in need of regeneration, while in Montpellier the Odysseum station will be in a fairly shameless edge-of-town location on a motorway bypass of the city – the kind of location that has been condemned by many French transport planners as a 'beetroot field station' *(Gare des betteraves)*. Time will tell whether this last great gamble of Georges Frêche pays off.

Almost inevitably they are renaming the boulevard, along which the trams run, after him. It will be an appropriate way to remember a politician who, remarkable in his own right, was also a very representative example of a French political type: an individual who moves effortlessly between the local and the regional and the national stages, developing and exploiting an incomparable range of political contacts which are used to further the interests of the city he (and, very occasionally nowadays, she) represents. It is a model which, with rare exceptions – the Chamberlains, always cited for lack of others – has never flourished in the UK. Looking at Montpellier, that could have been a bad thing for British cities.

Strasbourg Rejoins the European Tram Club

Our final stop in France takes in another of France's great regional capital cities – but this time with a very special history (figure 9.10). From Paris the TGV

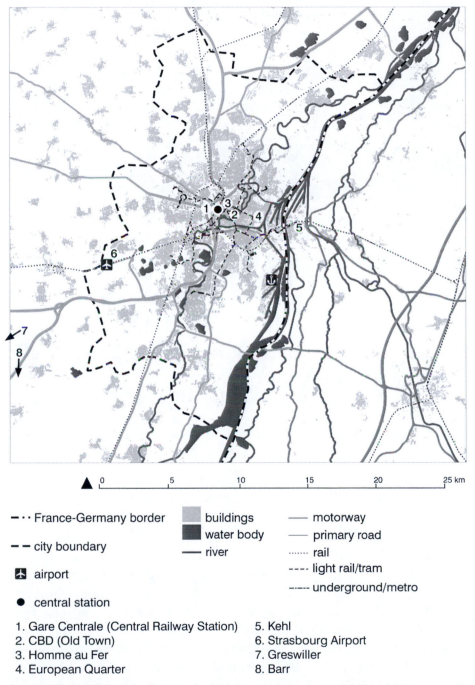

▲ 0   5   10   15   20   25 km

– ·· France-Germany border

– – city boundary

✈ airport

● central station

🟦 buildings

⬛ water body

—— river

—— motorway

—— primary road

······ rail

---- light rail/tram

-··-·· underground/metro

1. Gare Centrale (Central Railway Station)
2. CBD (Old Town)
3. Homme au Fer
4. European Quarter

5. Kehl
6. Strasbourg Airport
7. Greswiller
8. Barr

Figure 9.10. Strasbourg map. The capital of the Alsace region on the river Rhine marking the border with Germany, with major international functions that have boosted its growth, it has one of the most extensive tramway systems in France.

joins the new *Ligne à Grande Vitesse Est-Européenne*, the fastest rail line in Europe, across the plains of Beauce and Champagne. But after an hour's race at a speed of 200 miles per hour (320 km/h), the train slows to use the tortuous old line through the Vosges mountains before emerging into the Rhine Valley north of Strasbourg's nineteenth-century station, which received an impressive new glass façade in anticipation of the new TGV service that opened in 2007 (figure 9.11).

Figure 9.11. Strasbourg train station. The ingenious modern extension to the classical nineteenth-century façade, seamlessly connecting passengers from the TGV to the underground tramway below.

That mountain barrier – through which engineers have now started to drill a four-kilometre tunnel for the extension of the high-speed line, due to open all the way to Strasbourg in 2016 – is significant, because it is one of France's natural frontiers. For many years, the Rhine Valley beyond it was part of Germany. That was true in 1878, when Strasbourg's historic system was opened, and in 1894 when it was electrified; trams ran out from the city centre on to both banks of the Rhine. Bounced in 1919 into France, temporarily repatriated into Germany in 1940 and badly damaged during World War II, the network – now cut back to the French left bank of the river – closed in 1960 together with other major French cities at about that time, in the interests of modernization and reducing traffic congestion. Only four lines were left: two in Lille, one each in Marseille and St Etienne (Arab, 2004, p. 127). But in the 1990s, faced with increasing traffic and pollution, the city decided to build a totally new modern tram system. The first line, opened in November 1994 – together with lines in Nantes and

Grenoble – represented the rebirth of the tramway in France; a second line, started in 1995, opened in 2000 (*Ibid.*, pp. 127, 129).

But the real origins of the system lay 20 years earlier, during the 1973 energy crisis. In July that year the government sent *dossiers d'agglomération* to leading *Communautés urbaines* (Bordeaux, Grenoble, Nancy, Nice, Rouen, Toulon, Toulouse and Strasbourg – in Strasbourg comprising twenty-seven communes), heralding a shift to public transport. This was followed by the introduction of the *Versement Transport* for all communities of 300,000 people and over and for employers with more than nine employees (*Ibid.*, p. 142).

Throughout the 1980s there were fierce debates in French cities as to the best available urban rail system. Some cities – Lille, as we have seen, Toulouse, Rennes – opted for the automated (DLR-type) VAL system, which had the disadvantage of high construction costs due to the need to build a tunnel system. Other cities – Grenoble, Nantes, St. Denis/Bobingy, Rouen, and, of course, Roubaix-Tourcoing – preferred a much cheaper ground-level tram system. Strasbourg, doubtless looking across the Rhine, elected for the latter solution – but with an interesting variant at the central train station, where the need to tunnel under the tracks necessitated that the system be buried in an underground station.

Introducing Another Multi-Tasking French Mayor: Catherine Trautmann

The Strasbourg tramway was a key project of Catherine Trautmann, elected Mayor in 1989. In 1995, the year after Line A opened, Catherine Trautmann was re-elected, immediately announcing a go-ahead for Line B, which was duly opened in September 2000 – just before the 2001 municipal election (*Ibid.*, pp. 127–129). In 1995, the year of her re-election, the Strasbourg *Communauté Urbaine* was reorganized, but with Catherine Trautmann still President and Roland Ries (her first deputy in Strasbourg, and right-hand man) as first Vice-President with responsibility for transport (*Ibid.*, p. 175). Trautmann then became national Minister of Culture and Communications (1997–2000), relinquishing the posts of Mayor and President of the *Communauté Urbaine* de Strasbourg to Ries with an understanding that she could recover her positions on return. As minister she was chief patron of Line B (*Ibid.*, p. 175), determined to have it opened before the 2001 election (*Ibid.*, p. 177). Ironically, though it duly opened, she was defeated. In the best tradition of French multiple office-holding, she also served as an MEP between 1989 and 1997 and again after 2004. In 2008, when Roland Ries was elected Mayor of Strasbourg, she was elected second Vice President of the *Communauté Urbaine* (French Wikipedia).

Through subtle political management – a decentralized one, described as a 'conversation with the problem' involving both those with immediate concerns (locally elected councillors) and those less immediately involved (*Ibid.*, p. 266) – in a little over a decade, Strasbourg built France's largest tram network, extending over 55 km (figures 9.12(*a*) and (*b*)). Four routes radiate from the busy city centre, some reaching into semi-rural areas; a fifth bypasses the centre. The system has seventy stations, one underground (*Gare Centrale*) giving improved access to the trains on the other side of the SNCF station's new glass façade.

Figures 9.12(*a*) and (*b*). Strasbourg trams. The main interchange of tram routes at the Homme au Fer in the heart of the medieval centre, and on an ancient street nearby.

The majority of the system runs on reserved trackbed, which varies between paved surfaces and neatly cut grass. The system uses overhead power supply at 750V DC and standard-gauge 1435 mm gauge lines – an important detail, since it can provide for possible future tram-train extensions over the regional rail system. Most tram stops, apart from Gare Centrale, are simple waiting shelters with real-time digital information displays; but the central interchange station at Homme de Fer, in the heart of the city, is an impressive architectural design that has been imitated in other French cities.

The trams, with 267 places and sixty-six seats, have low-floor street access and are fully accessible for passengers with limited mobility and those with a baby carriage; all are air-conditioned. As well as impressive service frequency – the lowest line frequency is 15 minutes, with a standard frequency of 5–6 minutes between 06.30 and 20.00 – the multiple ticketing options (including a smart card), low fare levels and nine park-and-ride sites are all aimed at discouraging private vehicle use within the city.

The Tramway: Key to Quality of Urban Life

The city's decision was not a casual one. It was based on a central principle of improving the quality of urban life (*qualité de vie*) including systematic restriction of car use, pedestrianization of streets, and restoration of the city's historic urban spaces. From the start this was seen as an 'urban project', not just as a 'simple transport project' (*Ibid.*, p. 127). Urban design was central to the process, not an 'add-on' as elsewhere; this was unique (*Ibid.*, p. 245). In addition, the new system was to provide a backbone into which existing bus services would be reshaped and linked, providing feeders at key interchanges. This bus network has a length of 310 km, plus an additional 280 km in the smaller surrounding municipalities; timetables are synchronized with the tramway. And finally, bicycle travel would be systematically encouraged: there is a 160 m bicycle network, one of the largest of its kind in France. There are bicycle parking spaces at key tram stops and bus stops. In addition, these park-and-ride facilities are equipped with free taxi phones, and it is also possible to rent electro-cars. The main aim of the traffic plan, developed and implemented from February 1992 onwards, is to reduce car traffic. Crossing of the city centre by car is prohibited through traffic loops and bypasses; new underground parking facilities were installed in the outlying areas of the city centre and under the central square (Place Kléber). This and the Place de la Gare have been reshaped for the tram and buses, and for cyclists and pedestrians. Ecological compensation measures along the new routes of the tram include the planting of 1,400 new trees and transplanting 300 others.

The trams have played a major part in revitalizing the city's open spaces, especially the city centre. An attractive centre helps in attracting European institutions, and gave a further boost to the city's economy, which was already the second largest finance centre in France. The Dutch transport planner Hugo

Priemus comments that:

> Partly as a result of its exemplary public transport, the number of visitors to the central city in Strasbourg has increased. A synergy between urban vitalization and the improvement of public transport in Strasbourg has brought about a cost recovery level for the tram of more than 100%. Both the liveability and economic attraction of the city centre have been strengthened. (Priemus, 2011, p. 64)

The *Versement Transport* met about a quarter of the initial cost, more than the government grant. Once again, financial innovation enabled technical innovation, which produced social, environmental and economic benefits.

The Future of the Strasbourg Tramway: A European Project

In 2007, with the opening of a fifth line directly serving the city's European Quarter, Roland Ries developed the radical idea of a 'second European quarter' shared with Germany, prolonging Line D a short distance from its present terminus (at Aristide Briand) across the dock basin with a new train station on the border, located on the island between the branches of the river, and on to Kehl station in Germany. This would be accompanied by major urban regeneration and new construction to create a new 'European quarter' (Beyer, 2011, pp. 5–6).

But, beyond this, there is an even more ambitious project: a tram–train, extending the present system far out into the Alsatian countryside, to the foot of the Vosges mountains. To understand the significance, an excursion across the Rhine is first necessary.

Excursion: Karlsruhe's Regional Tram-Train System

In the corner of Europe where France, Germany and Switzerland meet, urban tram systems never entirely went away. Swiss cities like Basel and Zürich, neutral and immune from destruction during World War Two, saw no reason to remove them; German cities like Freiburg and Karlsruhe, as most others, simply rebuilt them amidst the ruins in order to keep their economies running. And, as the German economy recovered in the 1950s and 1960s, ancient vehicles were replaced by new ones and extensions took place. Then, in the 1970s and 1980s, in bigger cities like Frankfurt and Düsseldorf, to reduce congestion the tracks were put underground in the city centres and the entire network was rebadged as a U-Bahn system: a term borrowed from the metro systems in cities like Berlin, Hamburg and Munich, and useful because it gave these other places a kind of big-city aura. But the many medium-sized cities that kept their trams, like Karlsruhe and Freiburg, saw no need: it was more convenient to pedestrianize the central streets and to leave the trams sharing the space with the pedestrians and the bicycles, even when the result appeared occasionally chaotic.

One of these cities, Karlsruhe in Baden-Württemberg on the other side of the Rhine from Strasbourg, became the first European city to implement track-sharing for light and heavy rail vehicles. The 'Karlsruhe Model' has passed into rail vocabulary to describe street-to-main line operations and has inspired system developments in nearby Saarbrücken, Kassel, the Randstad Rail project in the Netherlands, the system centred on Mulhouse in France, and now the UK national trial on the Sheffield–Rotherham line.

Karlsruhe was and is an archetypal mid-sized German city with a population of just over a quarter of a million. As such, its tram system did not justify expensive conversion to a U-Bahn system; in addition, its suburban commuter rail system did not justify an equally expensive construction of a so-called S-Bahn network like those in Berlin, Hamburg, Frankfurt or Munich. But it was the centre of an extensive rail system connecting out to attractive and fast-growing towns and villages within about an hour's journey. Karlsruhe determined on a radical solution: to link all these places over the existing rail right-of-way, enabling passengers to travel into and out of the city centre without having to change vehicles, and thus to attract passengers in this very affluent corner of Europe out of their cars.

Deutsche Bahn (DB) operated several local services into the city, of which two, to Worth and Bretten, were identified as being particularly suitable for the experiment. The local Siemens engineering works was linked to the network in May 1989, and a line subsequently extended a further three stops to Kneilingen Nord.

The technical problems were considerable. Trams needed to run on both the urban network, electrified at 750 V DC, and on DB lines running on the standard German power system of 15 kV, $16\frac{2}{3}$ Hz AC. Car dimensions had to be made compatible, a heavy transformer had to be incorporated on the cars, a new wheel profile developed, together with a mobile footboard to allow the trams both to run on the streets and stop at station platforms. The original high-floor model has been joined by a second generation with a partial low floor called 'mid-high', established at 580 mm above the tracks, thus permitting direct pedestrian access from rail platforms 550 mm high.

The most difficult question was accident prevention: to develop a sufficiently crush-resistant building material, 5,000 rail incidents and accidents were studied, demonstrating that it was not the vehicles' rigidity but the stopping distance that counted. Tram-trains use railway speed control and ground-to-train radio transmission.

A world first, through-running of tram vehicles on a national heavy rail, occurred on 28 September 1992. Linking the Bretten area by use of the urban network and the infrastructure of the DB shared with conventional trains, the 'bimodal tramway' as it was then called, represented a revolution in urban transport. The commercial results were extraordinary: in the first three days of commercial service, ridership on the Bretten line, which had struggled to achieve

2,000 passengers daily, increased to over 10,000. Progressively the network has grown: first, beyond Bretten to Eppinghen and then Heilbronn, to Rastatt and Baden-Baden, and to Forchbach deep inside the Black Forest. Today the network totals over 400 km in length and operates 20 million train-km per year: 15 million on the urban network, 5 million on the tram-train. Distant centres such as Heilbronn, Pforzheim and Bad Wildbad have become part of the system, with main line running commonplace. The system's longest run is now a 210 km S4 service from Öhringen through central Karlsruhe to Achern, south-west of Baden-Baden (figures 9.13 (*a*), (*b*) and (*c*)). On each section of line covered

Figures 9.13(*a*), (*b*) and (*c*). Karlsruhe tram train. The S4 tramway, Europe's longest route, runs on national train tracks at the spa resort of Baden-Baden, runs on streets through central Karlsruhe past the eighteenth-century Pyramid (where however it is now being put underground) and then goes back on rail through open country to the city of Heilbronn. Applied successfully in Kassel (Chapter 7), the 'Karlsruhe model' will also be used by Strasbourg for a new route into the Vosges mountains.

by the tram-train, traffic has at least doubled. The subsidy per passenger is only 23.3 cents – a figure its operators are particularly proud of. Forty per cent of Karlsruhe's bi-modal tram-train passengers actually have cars at their disposal but have made the conscious decision to leave them at home.

Eliminating the passenger train-to-tram exchange is not the tram-train's only advantage. The relative lightness of the tram gives it a high power-to-weight ratio, which means excellent acceleration performance and breaking capacity, allowing more stops without a corresponding time penalty. The trams are relatively cheap to buy (typically €2.2 million) and operate (shorter training for drivers, simplified maintenance), allowing service levels to be enhanced. The entire system is now owned by the local authority and runs under the identity of the Karlsruher Verkehrsverbund (KVV).

But not all communities have welcomed the opportunity to join the network, exemplified by local opposition holding back projected extensions into central Rastatt and Baden-Baden. In addition, the main constraint is now capacity in the city centre. Around 2 kilometres of track with several junctions runs east–west along Kaiserstrasse, the main shopping street. Largely pedestrianized, the section carries an intensive service of tram-trains and trams due to the convergence of many routes: one per minute. And this figure is set to increase, as passenger numbers are steadily climbing: from 123.6 million people in 1997 to 176.6 million in 2010.[5]

To remedy this, the Combined Project (*Die Kombilösung*) has two linked elements: a 2.4 km rail tunnel under Kaiserstrasse with a 1.0 km branch tunnel for south-bound lines, with seven underground stations, making room for a rail-free 1.0 km pedestrian zone above ground, and a 1.4 km road tunnel underneath the parallel Kriegsstrasse, allowing an attractively landscaped tramline to be put on top. Of the €640.9 million cost, the German federal government will cover 60 per cent, the state of Baden Württemberg 20 per cent, and the construction company the remaining 20 per cent. Construction started in 2010. The rail tunnel will open in 2017, immediately reducing the number of trains and trams on Kaiserstrasse by 70 per cent.

There is a lesson for the UK. The eco-towns programme has returned the country back to the 1898 Ebenezer Howard vision of small, isolated garden cities set in the countryside. That is not the way they do it in Freiburg and other German cities, or now in French cities; there, urban extensions, close to city centres and linked to them by excellent public transport, are the rule. British visitors tend to come back convinced that they are right. The Karlsruhe tram-train concept, which they boldly pioneered in 1992 and is now spreading across Europe, extends an urban tram system on national rails to serve smaller towns and villages in a wide sub-region all around: the tram, the S4, runs one hundred miles from end to end (and they are now contemplating the need to fit toilets). That way, it is possible to build eco-towns as town or village extensions, all linked into a single regional system.

Postscript: A Return to Strasbourg

France was slow to adopt the tram-train principle. But a first project opened in 2010 in Mulhouse, a medium-sized Alsatian city 30 kilometres south of Strasbourg, and the regional capital is now following suit with a project to bring local rail services from Greswiller and Barr, at the foot of the Vosges mountains west of the city, via the Strasbourg airport at Entzheim, on to the tram system via a new 1.5 km link extension of the present Line F. The ultimate tram-train network will cover 44 km: 4 km urban, 25 km double track and 15 km single track. At a cost of €7 million per km, this is very cheap compared to the €20 million per km cost of an urban network. Out of six radiating lines, two have been selected, with approximately 10,000 commuters per day. The proposed service is mixed-mode, with guaranteed tram-train base-frequency (15 minutes) complemented by traditional (regional) trains occupying available paths. An old tunnel of the postal tramway, under Strasbourg central station, will be reused to link the urban network and the main-line rail infrastructure; the rail sections will be electrified at 25 kV, with seven new stations and eleven extra stopping points. The infrastructure costs are estimated at €151.6 million for the regional authority, €43.6 million for the urban community and €8.89 million for SNCF. Capable of operating at up to 100 km per hour, the train sets should have sufficiently acceleration to avoid slowing the line. Projections show that ridership will increase 2.5 times while public subsidy will be reduced by 40 per cent, lowering the per-trip price from €1.60 to €1.00.

Due to open in 2016, it could be prolonged from its presently planned Strasbourg terminus at the Place d'Island to Offenburg in a corresponding position on the lower slopes of the Black Forest (Beyer, 2011, p. 12). This would be an ultimate European project.

Conclusions

In France, a country stretching over an area twice the size of the UK, connectivity has always been a key issue. Over three decades since 1980 the country has led the way in not only connecting its cities together with a high-speed rail network, but also linking them up with their hinterlands. In 1980 France had fewer miles of tramway than the UK, whereas today it has five times as much, and even quite small cities are building their own lines, while existing systems are being extended.

De Gaulle famously observed 'How can you govern a country that has 246 different varieties of cheese?' The answer, since the historic Mitterrand reforms of 1982, has been devolution of powers from Paris on a grand scale. An important economic result has been that provincial cities have outperformed Paris, and their regions, as measured by growth of GVA per capita – in contrast to the UK situation. At the same time town and city centres almost everywhere have undergone a noticeable urban renaissance (even though some of the suburbs have been hit by racial tensions, with riots in the places that have been most cut off from opportunities). How has this process worked so well in places as diverse as Lille and Montpellier and Strasbourg? There are nine tentative conclusions:

1. *Municipal Leadership.* Elected Mayors concentrate on making their cities more successful, which usually means improving the quality of the public realm. Trams are one of the ways a city can not only reduce congestion, but also – just as important - boost its image. While they can not solve all the problems of economic decline (as old industrial places like Valenciennes illustrate), they do form a visible symbol of a city's resolve to modernize itself. Not only do city leaders sit in the French Senate, but a career in local government is the usual route to national politics. Pierre Mauroy, who was both Mayor of Lille and French Prime Minister, is said to have thought the role of Mayor was the more important. Georges Frêche declined public office in Paris, but worked behind the scenes on behalf of Montpellier. Roland Ries, asked by President Hollande in 2012 to become his Minister of Transport, declined on the ground that he still had important unfinished business in Strasbourg. But he remains chair of the Group of Transport Authorities *(Groupement des Autorités Responsables de Transport, GART),* an association of elected politicians responsible for transport. And here lies the real power.

2. *Strategic Planning.* Since 1983, when municipalities were given the powers to develop local plans, transport planning and development have been closely linked, as the Montpellier case study illustrates. Land is acquired by the municipality or a joint venture, often with more generous compensation than in the UK, and less weight is given to objections. The conurbation or city-region is regarded as an economic entity, with regions having an important role in the provision of infrastructure. Private developers play their part, but do not lead the process. The Lille case study shows the importance not just of combining local transport improvements with those for high-speed inter-city trains, but also of combining these with investment in the social infrastructure, so everyone feels they have benefited from growth.

3. *Public-Private Relationships.* French conurbations own the infrastructure and control their operations, which are then managed as an integrated system by private companies operating on a long-term franchise, but working closely with the municipalities. These management companies have gone on to win contracts in the UK (as have French energy and water companies) but the reverse has not applied. Private companies do not have the same freedoms in the UK (the result in part of the Napoleonic Code which underpins French law). Instead major construction projects have to secure a *Déclaration d'utilité publique* to show public benefits, which may necessitate a public inquiry before they proceed.

4. *Multi-Criteria Analysis.* Instead of believing that project assessment can be reduced to a single number through some form of cost-benefit analysis, greater reliance has been placed on the business case, and a municipality's capacity to bring the necessary funding cocktail together. The contracts between the cities and the government, which started with the first *Contrat de Ville* in Lille, are based on them being equal partners, not subordinates, in the pursuit of wellbeing. It is no coincidence that the French were among the first to look for alternatives to national income per capita as the principal measure of success, and have been the main proponents of the concept of 'social exclusion'.

5. *Local Taxes on Employers.* Devolution may have helped to overcome the 'stagflation' of the 1970s, and get the economy moving again. Instead of having to depend largely on government grants, municipalities have been able to tap local funding sources. The *Versement Transport* (VT), a hypothecated local tax on salaries of companies employing more than nine people that finances 70 per cent of public transport costs in Paris, helped get radical new infrastructure, such as the Lille Metro, started. The process of getting approval means that municipalities have to build good relations with employer organizations and neighbouring communes.

6. *Cost Control.* The French have managed to build more for less, and their rail system also benefits from most of its electricity coming from nuclear power. They avoid expensive costs by integrating tramway planning and building with underground services. In contrast the recent UK experience with building trams and railways has been a depressing tale of delays and cost overruns.

7. *Domestic Industry.* Behind the French enthusiasm for modern forms of transport is a concern to promote French industry, and to benefit from the latest advances in engineering technology. French cities like British cities must conform to EU competitive procurement rules, but the very scale of their procurement ensures that many of the contracts go to French tram and TGV suppliers like Alstom, which are then well-placed to secure export contracts – particularly as the products can be showcased to potential overseas buyers.

8. *Urbanism.* France not only pioneered ideas like the omnibus and the high-speed train, but walking and cycling are still seen as civilized ways of getting around. The quality of its city centres is consequently world renowned. Instead of planning being seen primarily as a form of regulation or control, the French concept of *urbanisme* (as opposed to *planification*) is essentially about creating liveable places. And their success is testified by the fact that rich and successful Frenchmen and Frenchwomen crowd into their cities. There is a downside, as in Paris: the least successful are exiled into soulless *banlieues*, which too easily become ghettos for the socially-excluded. The significant point remains: that city life is seen as the highest and best form of existence.

9. *City-Regional Cooperation*. The final lesson is an extension of the first, a political one: Lille, Montpellier and Strasbourg demonstrate the critical importance of the *Communauté Urbaine*, the device invented by the French government in the late 1960s in order to give greater weight to the country's great provincial cities. Slowly and hesitatingly at first, they achieved life in the late 1980s and subsequently, as powerful mayors - Mauroy, Frêche, Trautmann, Ries – provided the vital leadership, triggering the creation of powerful city-region federations, which attracted large sums for public investment in transport and urban regeneration. This was not done easily, as Roland Ries underlined in a recent interview (Ries, 2011; see also Dagnogo and Ries, 2011); it requires great political subtlety and sense of timing. But the agglomeration-wide tram networks of Lille, Montpellier and Strasbourg are testimonies to their success.

There is however one important reservation. Research by Xavier Desjardins and his colleagues at the Sorbonne has demonstrated that in three major French urban areas – Amiens, Rennes and Strasbourg – the peri-urban areas, outside the built-up agglomerations where the critical investment in tram systems has taken place, demonstrate a poor and worsening relationship between the pattern of urban development and the accessibility to rail-based urban transport; in other words, these areas are becoming steadily more car-dependent (Desjardins et al, 2011). Strasbourg however performs marginally better than the other two sample areas. And Strasbourg is going farthest of all, learning from its German neighbour to take the critical next step: a regional network that extends far into the surrounding countryside, linking small towns and villages in a new polycentric urban structure, the *mega-city region*, that promises to become the model of sustainable urban development in the twenty-first century. This is the specific solution commended by Desjardins in another paper, which commends the tram-train – illustrated by the Kassel Regiotram – as an answer to the challenge of serving peri-urban areas (Desjardins, 2011). Not only this: this is a city region that transcends national borders, inside a wider transnational region – embracing south-east France, south-west Germany and north-central Switzerland – that has become the prime global example of the learning region: an entity in which cities learn best urban practice – in transport, in regeneration, in urban design – from each other, in a constant process of iteration and further improvement. In the next chapter, we will travel far north to visit the only other such example in Europe: the Øresund region embracing Copenhagen and its near neighbours at the far southern tip of Sweden.

Notes

1. Opinion polls show that Montpellier is the place where most of the French would like to live, work and play. The main reason seems to be Montpellier's sunshine. The Languedoc-Roussillon region, of which Montpellier is the principal city, boasts more hours of sunshine (equalling 300 days per year) than any other in France (see http://www.jeremyjosephs.com/montpellier.htm).

2.   In 2009, on the 200th anniversary of the split, the two universities and a third, *Université Montpellier III Paul Valéry,* were reunited as the *Université Montpellier Sud de France*, one of a limited number of national *Pôles de recherche et d'enseignement supérieur* established by a law of 2006 to create internationally-competitive research universities in France.

3.   Simultaneously, a Line 4 opened. This involved no new construction, but joined parts of the existing three lines to make a circular route around the city centre.

4.   See http://www.dailymotion.com/montpelliervideo/xjwxfh_-tramway-christian-lacroix-ligne-3 _tech.

5.   http://www.diekombiloesung.de/fileadmin/user_upload/kombiloesung/PDF/Infoflyer-eng-105x210.pdf.

10 | Conserving Resources in Scandinavia: Stockholm and Copenhagen–Malmö

There is one obvious part of Europe to go next on our twenty-first-century Grand Tour. Stockholm and Copenhagen occupy the same distinguished positions in the Pantheon of modern European planning as Athens or Delos in European antiquity. Because urban growth came so late to Sweden and Denmark – at the end of the nineteenth century and in the twentieth – these cities were able to develop effective town planning controls almost from the start. Soon after 1900 Stockholm, still a small city of 100,000 people, began to buy land all around, so as to guarantee properly planned development. In the 1950s and 1960s, its 1952 General Plan provided the basis for a network of planned suburbs systematically located around a new Underground rail network. Today, with 872,000 in the city and 2.1 million in the entire metropolitan area, Stockholm remains the most comprehensively planned city in the whole of Western Europe. In the immediate post-World War Two period, Copenhagen became renowned worldwide for its growth management strategies. Its famous 1948 Finger Plan developed an alternative to Abercrombie's green belt/new town strategy for London, guiding growth into satellite communities along tram extensions and regional rail lines. The strategy has controlled Copenhagen's growth for 60 years, as the city population has stabilized at 500,000 while the wider metropolitan area has grown from just over 1 million to 1.8 million. And it has now been dramatically extended into the concept of an international metropolis, uniting Copenhagen with Malmö by the world's first regional metro service and thereby creating a model for the world's first international sustainable metropolis.

But the chief reason for this northern tour is that – despite doughty competition – Danish and Swedish cities have established an enviable reputation for setting and achieving extraordinary environmental standards. Scandinavian people have always faced the reality of long, hard winters. In Sweden, winter and its ending are the stuff of celebration and of legend. Go to Sweden's national museum in Stockholm, and the place of honour in the hall of the central staircase is occupied by *Midvinterblot*, a painting specially created for this space by the artist Carl Larsson in 1915. Inspired by his visit to the Danish national museum, it depicts a Norse legend in which the ancient Swedish king Domalde was sacrificed in order to avert winter famine. Swedes celebrate Yule, a pagan festival that has been partially Christianized, as well as Walpurgis Night and the succeeding May Day, the end of winter. These festivals express their deep sense of the passing of the seasons, from a midwinter when the sun scarcely rises, to a midsummer where the twilight lingers all night long. And Sweden, a country where long harsh winters ally with rock-strewn landscapes and thin acidic soils, was for centuries a poor country, forced to husband meagre resources. From this has stemmed a tradition of good building to conserve energy and keep the winter out, as well as a deep care for conserving limited natural wealth.

Stockholm's Planned Satellite Towns

For professional visitors to Stockholm, a key starting point for any study tour is a pilgrimage on the city's 108-kilometre Tunnelbana system (figure 10.1) which radiates out from the central interchange station, T-Centralen, in the heart of the comprehensively-reconstructed city centre, to one of the planned satellite towns (figures 10.2(*a*) and (*b*) and 10.3). These are located at approximately 1 km intervals, each designed around a planned centre for shopping and other services. They are organized on the principle of local pyramids of density: higher densities around the stations, so that the shops have the maximum number of customers within walking distance, in the immediately-surrounding high-density flats, and then falling away at greater distances. And in turn the centres and their surrounding residential areas are ordered according to a hierarchical principle; between four and six units are planned as a single cluster, with local 'C' centres serving 10,000–15,000 people, mainly within walking distance of a station, and a single central sub-regional 'B' centre serving the entire cluster, with 15,000–30,000 people within walking distance and another 50,000–100,000 served by underground, feeder bus or private car; these together typically make up a total population of 50–60,000, equivalent to a typical Swedish provincial town. And each cluster is physically defined by a local green belt, wrapping around each unit and around the entire cluster. Finally, the satellites are designed as 'ABC communities' – *Arbete*, *Bostad*, *Centrum* (workplace, dwelling, centre): they are not pure dormitory towns but also employment and community centres, thus

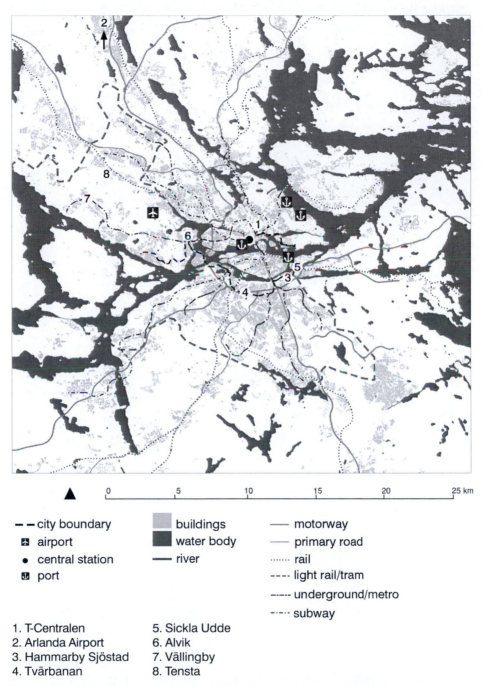

| 0 | 5 | 10 | 15 | 20 | 25 km |

- – city boundary
- ✈ airport
- ● central station
- ⚓ port

buildings
water body
— river

— motorway
— primary road
······· rail
---- light rail/tram
----- underground/metro
-·--· subway

1. T-Centralen
2. Arlanda Airport
3. Hammarby Sjöstad
4. Tvärbanan
5. Sickla Udde
6. Alvik
7. Vällingby
8. Tensta

Figure 10.1. *Stockholm map*. The compact nineteenth-century apartment city, on the two areas north and south of the medieval Old Town (*Gamla stan*) on its island (*Staden mellan broarna*, The Town between the Bridges), expanded hugely after 1950 with the construction of planned satellite towns along the city's new Metro (*Tunnelbana*) lines.

reducing commuter flows into the centre but also producing contra-commuting flows away from the centre.

Nearly a third of the dwellings were built by public housing corporations, almost a third by cooperatives and similar non-profit makers, a little less than a third by private builders: the great majority, 90 per cent, consist of apartments.

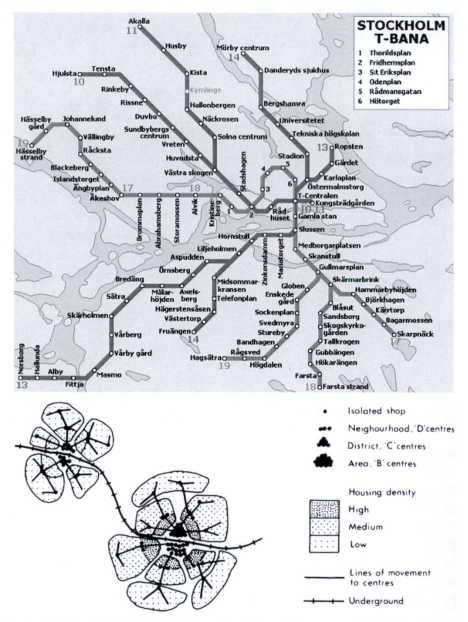

Figures 10.2(a) and (b). *Stockholm Tunnelbana*. The city's new Metro system, built during the 1950s and 1960s, was deliberately planned to serve the new satellite towns proposed in the 1952 General Plan. Each typically had five units: four lower-level 'C' centres serving 10,000–15,000 people, mainly within walking distance of a station, with one central sub-regional 'B' centres serving the entire complex, with 15,000–30,000 people within walking distance and another 50,000–100,000 served by underground, feeder bus or private car.

Figure 10.3. *Vällingby Centre*. Vällingby, first of the new satellites, was built in the mid-1950s. Its attractive pedestrian shopping centre, designed with facilities appropriate to a town cluster of around 100,000 people, was successfully modernized in 2001–2008.

About 95 per cent of all dwellings were financed with public aid; and of course there was no upper income level for families housed there. As Stockholmers would proudly tell visitors in that golden age of the Swedish welfare state model, in places like Vällingby and Farsta everyone lived together: the Prime Minister next door to the refuse collector, the company director next to the disabled welfare recipient.

Fifty years after that heroic satellite-building age, Stockholm's metropolitan area has expanded to encompass a far larger metropolitan area beyond the Tunnelbana termini, including separate medium-sized towns within a 50–100 kilometre wide belt around Lake Mälar, such as Ensköping, Västerås, Eskilstuna and Örebrö (and also Arlanda Airport, 40 km north of the city centre), all served by a new concept in transport planning as a basis for long-term development, pioneered by Copenhagen as well as Stockholm during the 1990s: the Regional Metro, linking up longer-distance suburban train lines to provide a new level of express commuter services as well as specialized services connecting to these two cities' airports. This was the first case in which a regional development plan was deliberately structured around the existence of high-speed links.

The Shift to Orbital Transit and Inner-City Regeneration: Hammarby Sjöstad

In the 1990s, just as the Regional Metro was accepted as a key feature of a new plan for the whole Mälardalen metropolitan area, a decade-long debate began to rage in Stockholm over the Dennis package, a radical congestion charge system which included construction of two new toll road systems – an inner ring around the central and inner areas, and an outer western tangent – and tolls on access to the central area, together with public transport improvements including a new orbital tram line. As well as helping to finance the investments, the tolls would secure a predicted decrease in inner-city car traffic of no less than 34 per cent. The proposal was abandoned and then, in 2006, reintroduced for 6 months on an experimental temporary basis. Local consultative referenda asking whether permanently to implement the congestion tax were held in the city and several surrounding municipalities in September 2006. Stockholm voted 53.0 per cent to 47.0 per cent in favour; the other municipalities all voted against. A general election was held on the same day and the new conservative government of Fredrik Reinfelt decided to implement the congestion tax permanently, but with the revenue going entirely to new road construction in and around Stockholm instead of entirely on public transport. It was reintroduced in August 2007, and since then the debate has calmed down, largely because the environmental impact on central Stockholm is perceived as beneficial.

But meanwhile, ironically, Stockholm had completed a large part of the planned orbital tramline: *Tvärbanan*, the Crossways line, running for 11.5 kilometres through the inner western suburbs from Sickla Udde in the south to Alvik in the west, with seventeen stops, linking to the southern and western branches of the underground and commuter rail systems. Fully opened in 2002, it carried 44,000 passengers per weekday in 2007. There are proposals to extend it further to the north and east, producing more extensions with the underground and commuter rail systems. The new line is significant, because just as it was being constructed there was a shift in planning priorities to inner-city regeneration. It passes through the main axis of *Hammarby Sjöstad* (Hammarby Lake City) (figures 10.4(*a*) and (*b*)), a 160-hectare site about 3 kilometres south

of the city centre, which was under construction as it was finished, and which depends on its existence just as fundamentally as, half a century ago, the satellite towns depended on the *Tunnelbana*.

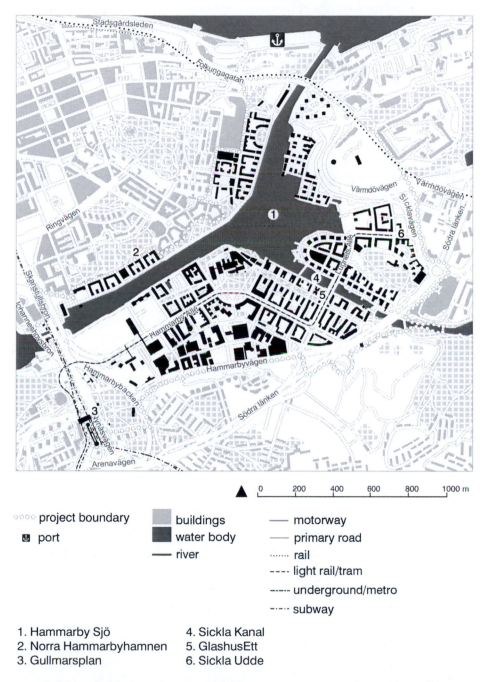

○○○○ project boundary	▨ buildings	—— motorway
⚓ port	■ water body	—— primary road
	—— river	······· rail
		---- light rail/tram
		—·— underground/metro
		—··· subway

1. Hammarby Sjö   4. Sickla Kanal
2. Norra Hammarbyhamnen   5. GlashusEtt
3. Gullmarsplan   6. Sickla Udde

Figures 10.4(a) (opposite) and (b). *Hammarby Sjöstad.* Aerial view and figure ground of this new town in-town, built on an old industrial site about 3 kilometres south of the medieval Old Town, on an attractive waterfront site. (*Photo:* Ola Ericson imagebank..sweden.se)

Hammarby, an inner-city location only 5 km south of Stockholm city centre, marks a significant change in emphasis, reflecting similar reversals elsewhere in European cities: a shift away from outward growth and towards inner-city regeneration. Like so many other such sites, until the 1980s Hammarby was *Södra Hammarbyhamnen* (roughly *South Hammarby Port*), a mainly industrial zone and part of the port of Stockholm. But then the factories closed, and the city had to decide what to do with the site.

New plans for most of the neighbouring Södermalm area – Norra Hammarbyhamnen, on the opposite side of the Hammarby Sjö lake – opened the possibility for redeveloping the entire area around the water. A general plan, featuring an extension of the planned Tvärbanan light rail link eastwards, from Gullmarsplan T-Bana station through the area, was developed.

Then came a major boost, with Stockholm's bid for the 2004 Olympic Games. The core area of Hammarby Sjöstad became the Olympic Village with a strong emphasis on ecology and environmental sustainability, promoted as one of Stockholm's unique selling points. It lost to Athens, but development was already kick-started and the momentum for change became irresistible. The city decided that the ideas it had developed for an Olympic Village were too good to jettison, and Hammarby was transformed into an eco-town.

It thus does not neatly compare with other models like Vathorst, Nieuwland and Kattenbroek in Amersfoort described in Chapter 8, or with Vauban and Rieselfeld in Freiburg to be considered in Chapter 11. They are all urban extensions at the edges of their respective cities; Hammarby is unambiguously an infill regeneration scheme at the edge of the dense nineteenth-century inner city of Stockholm. Yet, viewed on the map or on arrival, there is a superficial physical similarity, especially with the Freiburg schemes: in all three, a frequent tram service – in this case, part of the planned new orbital line circling the inner city – runs in the centre of a boulevard lined with ground-floor shops and apartments above, with two or three blocks of housing on each side (figures 10.5(*a*) and (*b*)).

A key difference is that with a land area of 160 hectares and an eventual total of 10,800 apartments, Hammarby is considerably bigger than Rieselfeld (72 hectares) or Vauban (42 hectares). It is also denser, with 100 residential units to the hectare in the residential areas or 67.5 over the whole land area. This means that unlike the Freiburg schemes, which maintain a quite rigid height limit of four storeys, Hammarby rises to four or five storeys along the waterfronts, and to six or even eight storeys along the main streets. The master plan aims deliberately at an inner-city feeling, in terms of street width (18 metres, with double that width along the main boulevard), block sizes (70 by 100 metres), density, and land-use mixture. It gives a good feel along the waterfronts but can feel oppressively high and claustrophobic along some of the interior streets and in the interior courts.

Figures 10.5(a) and (b). *Hammarby Sjöstad*. Views of developments on the waterfront and on an attractive linear park with natural drainage, representative of the area's high environmental standards.

The Master Plan

Hammarby Sjöstad lies just outside the conventional perimeter of inner-city Stockholm which is marked by the Hammarby Sjö lake. But the City Planning Bureau team, directed by the architect, Jan Inghe-Hagström, who drew up the master plan, intentionally created a design that follows standards for Stockholm's inner city in terms of street width (18 m), clearly defined and architecturally varied city blocks (70 x 100 m), density, land use with boulevards, and commercial spaces in the ground floor of the buildings. The location, next to the Hammarby Sjö lake and a canal, Sickla Kanal, has allowed much of the development to take place directly along the water.

The planners then combined this traditional city structure with an architectural style that responds to its specific waterside context, promotes the best of contemporary sustainability technology and follows modern architectural principles, maximizing light and views of the water and green spaces and using glass as a core material. The main boulevard connects key transport nodes and public focal points, and creates a natural focus for activity and commerce. Along this central axis, the ground floors of nearly all the buildings have been designed as flexible spaces, suitable for shops, leisure or community use. Additional opportunities for commercial uses are also provided through intermittent two-storey pavilions along the Sickla canal. This structure has proved attractive to a wide variety of businesses.

The tram service along this central spine is central to the entire development. There are four tram stops in the heart of Hammarby Sjöstad, bringing residents within about 5 minutes to the interchange with the *Tunnelbana* network and there are plans to extend the tram further eastwards and northwards, to connect directly to one of Stockholm's main transport hubs. Three new bus routes and one night bus also serve the area. In addition to new bus and tram infrastructure, a free ferry link across Hammarby Sjö has been introduced, taking 5 minutes to cross the lake, and running every 10 to 15 minutes from early morning until midnight. Bicycles can be taken on board. Finally, residents have access to a carpool in the area. There are twenty-five cars in the pool and some 450 residents have joined the scheme.

The master plan also deliberately seeks to enhance the geographical setting of the site. It is bordered by a hilly nature reserve to the south and by the lake, which is the central focus, its 'blue eye' and its most attractive public open space. Pedestrian boardwalks, quays and linear parks provide a varied perimeter to the waterfront and residents have access to boat moorings in the summer. A network of parks, green spaces and walkways runs through the district. Where possible, the natural landscape has been preserved. The original reeds and rushes remain along the waterfront, in between which there are secluded walkways out into the water. Birch trees create the landscape for a beautiful waterfront park and rocky oak-woodland defines the edge of the district. Following the new Swedish prescription for competition in school education – followed now by the UK's academies - the two state schools (6–16 years) are joined by one private school as well as one pre-school and nursery.

The quality of it all is extraordinary. And the key is local authority leadership, which has permeated every stage from the development of the master plan to actual building on the ground, facilitated by the fact that the city had already acquired most of the land. Starting with the strategic master plan, the area was divided into twelve sub-districts, to be implemented as a series of development phases, six of which were complete by early 2009. For each sub-district, detailed master plans are then generated through a design process called 'parallel sketches'. The City selects three or four private-sector architect/master planners to 'test' the strategic master plan and draw up more detailed proposals for the sub-district. The City's chief planner for Hammarby emphasizes that wherever possible, they try to choose new architects for each sub-district, and to encourage young architects and up-and-coming firms to take part. The City evaluates the sketches and assimilates the best features from each to arrive at an agreed detailed master plan.

To complement the detailed plan, the City planning and design team then prepares a design code for each sub-district, in close partnership with the chosen developers and architects for each plot. This is spelt out in almost agonizing detail, covering items like *district character*, traditional European inner city combined with modern architecture influenced and inspired by the natural environment, spelt out in the land-use mix, density, built form, public spaces and relationship to the water; *layout, form and structure,* including guidelines for each block, key landmark buildings, public spaces and pedestrian routes; *architectural style* with a lot more about height, form and style; *building types* each with details of apartment sizes and stairwells; *building design* including: façade materials, and details like window and balcony arrangements and roof types; *building elements* with yet more guidelines and dimensions for entrances, balconies, windows and roofing; *apartment standards* showing layout, daylight, height of rooms, access to outdoor space, sound insulation and accessibility requirements for entrances, balconies, terraces and outdoor space; and lots more on *standards for additional services*, like storage, laundry provision (inside the apartment, or shared), garages and refuse collection; *building colour* for each block and key landmark buildings; *design of courtyards and open spaces*: including a 50:50 mix of green and hard space; *design of public spaces, parks and streets*, including landscaping, paving, lighting and street furniture; and, on top of all that, *detailed architectural and design principles for each plot*, with 3-D images of each block. All this detail forms an appendix to a development agreement between the City and the developer-partner, aiming to establish a level of quality on which both the City and developer can agree. Each small plot or even an individual building within the sub-district – typically between four and eleven plots, depending on the size and complexity of development – is then taken forward by an invited consortium of developers and architects to ensure architectural diversity and a fine urban grain to the development, while conforming to the overall unifying code.

Certainly, the results so far are impressive – even spectacular. Generous use of glass as a core material maximizes sunlight and views of the water and green spaces. Aquatic areas act as storm water drainage, encouraging biodiversity, the creation of new habitats, informal amenity areas and formal areas of public open space.

The 'Hammarby Model'

At the heart of the Hammarby project is a very clear environmental concept, politically-driven and now internationally-renowned. It includes targets for decontamination, use of brownfield land, provision of public transport options to discourage car use, energy consumption, and recycling of water and solid waste. In particular, Hammarby has piloted a new 'Hammarby model' (figures 10.6(*a*) and (*b*)) for recycling energy, waste and water management, which has been

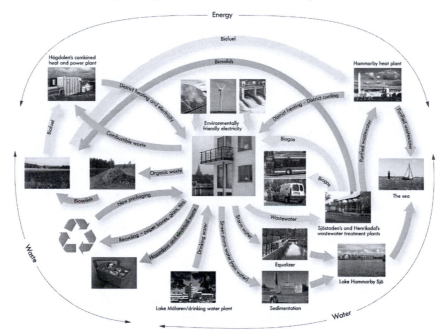

Figures 10.6(a) and (b). *The Hammarby Model*. The celebrated diagram demonstrating the way in which all development is based on recycling of natural resources, and the suction pipes that convey solid wastes from every locality, underground, to the central recycling depot.

developed jointly by the private company Birka Energi, Stockholm Water Company and the City of Stockholm Waste Management Bureau. The target for the project is to be twice as environmentally effective as normal new-build projects in the inner city. For example, new apartments in Hammarby Sjöstad should use half the amount of water compared to new apartments in the inner city.

Overall, Hammarby claims to tick almost every box as one of the world's exemplary eco-towns. It collects four different kinds of domestic waste through tubes, looking a bit like the tubes one finds on a ship's deck, located next to every residential block – convenient, though use maybe less than comfortable on a Stockholm January morning. There the waste is shot underground to a treatment plant, where it is used to generate combined heat and power. In turn the plant's heat pumps send out wastewater that is used for cooling. The system, run by Birka Energi, operates efficiently with a maximum pipe run of 2 kilometres.

Sewage is cleaned and purified at a large sewage plant just outside the area and the waste recycled into biogas. Heat produced through the purification process is recycled for use at a district-heating unit. Hammarby Sjöstad also has its own pilot sewage treatment centre, which opened in 2003. The unit recycles nutrients from sewage for use on agricultural land. Surface water is cleaned locally. Any combustible waste produced is recycled into heat energy for use in the apartments. Biodegradable waste is composted nearby.

Some apartment blocks are heated by solar panels – though these are a far from universal feature, and of course solar energy is scarce in the long Stockholm winter. The quality of housing construction is traditionally very high by necessity; some of the housing, at least, appears to approach PassivHaus standards.[1] Hammarby is aiming to cut water consumption by a third, simply by using eco-friendly installations like low-flush toilets and air mixer taps, and to reduce the quantity of heavy metals and non-biodegradable chemicals. It collects storm water into its local canals – which also form a central design feature of the whole development – before dispersing it into the lake. This method, which we will later find in Malmö, is becoming almost a feature of contemporary Swedish urban development.

To educate and encourage residents to make full use of all the environmental features of the area, an environmental education centre – *GlashusEtt* (the Glass House) – has been built in the centre of the district. The centre provides an opportunity for Stockholm Water, the City's street cleaning department and the Finnish energy company, Fortum (who have taken over Birka Energi), to showcase the range of technical solutions used across Hammarby Sjöstad. The Glass House also provides advice to local residents on environmental issues and organizes presentations for study visits and regular exhibitions. The centre cost around £2m to build, underwritten by the City of Stockholm, with approximately one-third funded by a local investment programme grant. Ongoing revenue funding for the centre (approximately £110,000 a year) is split equally between Stockholm Water, Fortum and the City of Stockholm's land development bureau.

The Stockholm Experience: Three Key Questions

Hammarby thus presents an extraordinary battery of technologies, about as impressive as one will find anywhere in the world. And the transport system, which takes residents to a *Tunnelbana* connection within 5 or 6 minutes – and will eventually loop round further parts of the development, to an interchange station at the edge of the city centre – is reducing car dependence: Hammarby residents own an average of only 0.7 cars per household, way below the Swedish average. There is a lesson here: after major debates, the city put the trams in right from the start, even though they would not initially pay their way. Thus they established sustainable travel patterns from day one, impossible to achieve once the new residents had defected to the Volvo showrooms.

Thus, purely in terms of environmental sustainability, Hammarby is as good as it gets. And the residents appear to like it. A 2005 survey of residents, to which 805 replied, revealed that they were very satisfied with the environment. Though approximately 66 per cent of households owned a car, similar to the average for the inner city, two-thirds of all trips were made by public transport, bicycle or walking and only a third of trips were by car; 8 per cent of residents were members of the car pool, which was used mostly for shopping trips; the ferry was used as a link for a quarter of all trips; and their highest priorities were a ferry link directly into the centre of Stockholm and an extension of the tram directly into the inner city.

But there are three key questions. The first concerns the applicability of the model. Typically, Stockholm inner suburbs, like those of Paris, have high residential and employment densities, which may not be the case in cities in other countries – especially those built in the Anglo-American-Australian lower-density suburban tradition. Here, an orbital tram route like the *Tvärbana* is unlikely to be viable, so a very large number of non-radial journeys may be inadequately catered for. There has to be another answer.

A second concerns demography. The Stockholm City planners imagined that Hammarby would attract younger singles and DINKY (double income, no kids) couples and older empty nesters whose children had left the family home; instead, it has proved unexpectedly attractive to couples with young children, who now swarm all over the limited amounts of open space, wearing the grass away and putting a strain on the school planners. Thanks to Sweden's new school model, private and charitable schools compete vigorously with established city schools for the parents' favour, so the system seems to be coping (apparently with the city schools winning). But the child density seems uncomfortably high for such an urban environment. Of course, the playgrounds are well designed; this is Sweden. But it is not child-friendly in the same way as Vauban – as we shall see in Chapter 11.

The third concerns social sustainability. Fifty years ago, all the satellite towns were built by the City, on City-owned land, with a combination of public rented housing and cooperative units which produced a remarkable social mix. Hammarby too is built on City-owned land, and follows an overall City master plan – the same model that we found in Amersfoort and will find in Freiburg. But with this critical difference, symbolizing the ideological difference between Stockholm 1965 and Stockholm today: the individual blocks are then developed by commercial developers, for profit, with a combination of for-sale and rental units. Sweden now has a UK-type system of national housing benefits that attach to the household, not to the housing – so in theory, here too, people with very different social positions and income levels could live cheek-by-jowl together.

But evidently that is not true in practice. The restaurants and cafés and shops along the lakefront are distinctly upmarket, looking as if they have been airlifted out of the San Francisco Bay Area. The children in the play areas, and their mothers, are overwhelmingly golden-haired; there is next to no evidence of the great migration, product of generous Swedish asylum policies that has brought hundreds of thousands of people from the beleaguered parts of the world into this city over the last 30 years.

Where were these other Stockholmers? The answer is that they occupy apartments at lower rents, farther away, in the satellite towns – many in one of them, Tensta. Built at the end of the 1960s when the Stockholm planners sacrificed quality to speed of construction at a time of housing shortage, it is a vast apartment complex of concrete blocks, very monotonous, built in a hurry before the Tunnelbana came. It proved hard to let; asylum-seekers filled the empty flats. Today, immigrants and their children make up two-thirds of the population and more than nine in ten of the children in the schools; two in five households are on social welfare.

The town centre is dominated by a huge Lidl store; all around, men sit chatting just as they might in some distant Bosnian or Iraqi village from which they came. This is a ghetto, as stark as any in Europe. Of course it is a Swedish ghetto: the apartment blocks with their forests of satellite dishes are well maintained, the gardens in between them well tended. But Stockholm, the Stockholm of the 1950s when the ruling Social Democratic party began to realize its long-term dream of building the People's Home, seems very far away. Stockholm in the twenty-first century may again be providing a model for the world, and for that reason the planners should continue to undertake their pilgrimages. But the Swedish dream of an egalitarian utopia has gone, perhaps forever.

Copenhagen–Malmö: Transnational Model Metropolis

Five hundred kilometres south of Stockholm is one of the most remarkable metropolitan areas in the world. The Öresund (in Swedish; in Danish, Øresund) is a strip of water, at its narrowest only 4 kilometres wide, separating the Danish island of Zealand on which Copenhagen stands, from Sweden's southernmost province of Skåne. Together they have become world-famous through their fictional detectives, Kurt Wallander and Sarah Lund, who obsessively stalk their prey through the streets of the Danish capital or the broad fields of Skåne – or, occasionally, invade each other's territories via the new bridge. The intervening strait has given its name to the wider Öresund region, which stretches over more than 20,000 square kilometres and is home to 3.6 million people – 2.5 million Danes, 1.2 million Swedes – making it the biggest urban area in Scandinavia, and generating fully a quarter of the combined GDP of Sweden and Denmark (figure 10.7).

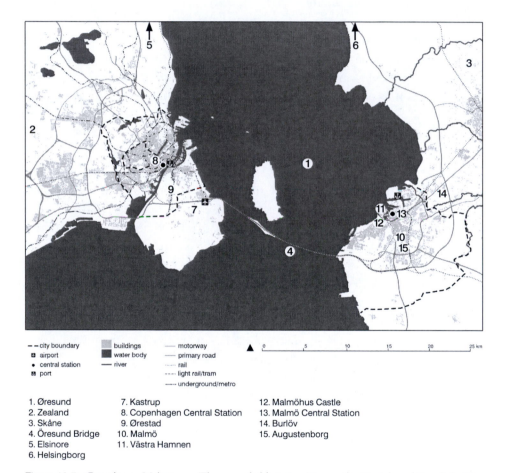

– – city boundary	▨ buildings	⋯⋯ motorway
⊞ airport	■ water body	—— primary road
● central station	—— river	⋯⋯⋯ rail
⊞ port		- - - light rail/tram
		⋯⋯⋯ underground/metro

1. Øresund
2. Zealand
3. Skåne
4. Öresund Bridge
5. Elsinore
6. Helsingborg
7. Kastrup
8. Copenhagen Central Station
9. Ørestad
10. Malmö
11. Västra Hamnen
12. Malmöhus Castle
13. Malmö Central Station
14. Burlöv
15. Augustenborg

Figure 10.7. *Copenhagen-Malmö map.* The remarkable twin cities on the Danish and Swedish sides of the Øresund, now linked by the new bridge connection.

But, until 2000, it was really a concept rather than an actuality, without a physical link and divided between two nations with two languages, two national governments, two systems of local government (both, since a Danish reform of 2007, based on regions),[2] and even – since neither country has yet joined the Eurozone – two currencies. Only a joint committee of politicians from both sides of the water, the Öresund Committee, worked to forge closer links between the two sides.

But on 1 July 2000 all that changed, when the King of Sweden and the Queen of Denmark jointly opened the new 18-kilometre €3 billion Öresund Bridge linking Copenhagen's 510,000 people with the 281,000 inhabitants of the neighbouring Swedish city of Malmö (figure 10.8). Curiously, the decision to build the bridge – and to build it to connect Copenhagen and Malmö, not at the narrowest crossing between Elsinore and Helsingborg – was taken almost overnight and undersigned by both governments in 1991, confirmed by the two parliaments in 1992–1993, and approved by a Swedish court decision in 1995, only weeks before construction started (Matthiessen, 2000, p. 172).

Figure 10.8. *Öresund Bridge*. The new connection between Copenhagen and Malmö, opened in 2000, carrying a lower-deck rail line between the two city centre stations via the Copenhagen Katsrup international airport. (*Photo*: CC Nikos Roussos)

The new link embodied huge ambitions on the part of urbanists and planners on both sides of the strait. First, it was designed to change traffic flows in northern Europe, by concentrating them through the region. But the ambition went much further: it was to integrate the two sides into a single functional economic region, thus increasing regional productivity, economic growth and competitive dynamism. This vision was largely the invention of a Swedish economist and futurologist, Åke Andersson, who in 1985 had published a remarkable book, *Kreativitet: StorStadens Framtid* (*Creativity: The Future of the Metropolis*), which for the first time identified creativity as a major driving force in the post-industrial urban economy. Andersson was increasingly concerned that Swedish policy had taken a wrong direction by trying to divert growth into remote northern areas which lacked the necessary creative synergies for success in the new economy; he argued for a concentration of investment in the Greater Stockholm region, Sweden's biggest metropolis.

But soon after this he began to work with a Danish geographer, Christian Wichmann Matthiessen, on a study of the Öresund region, culminating in the publication in 1991 of a jointly-authored book, *Øresundsregionen: Kreativitet –*

Integration – Vækst (*Öresund Region: Creativity – Integration – Growth*). Essentially this developed the argument further: in a rapidly globalizing world, and after the creation of European economic and monetary union in 1992 and Sweden's impending entry into the EU in 1995, economic advantage would flow increasingly to very large metropolitan regions which alone could exploit the economies of trade and transport links – Copenhagen's Kastrup airport, the largest international airport in Northern Europe, has direct flights to more than 120 destinations – and develop a rich intellectual infrastructure of universities and research centres. To achieve these potential advantages, it was essential to weld the two halves of the Öresund region into a single transnational metropolis. As Matthiessen has explained, to weld the two sides into a single political unit was effectively impossible but to create a functional economic region, in a very advanced part of Europe, was perfectly feasible; forging a cultural unity was much harder, but conceivable over time (Andersson and Matthiessen, 1991; Matthiessen, 1993; Matthiessen, 2004, p. 33).

What has been the practical result? Matthiessen has followed progress through his research on global knowledge centres, measured by the research output from universities and research institutes across the world. He concludes that between 1996–1998 and 2004–2006 the Copenhagen–Lund region fell marginally from fifteenth to seventeenth place, that a core region comprising London–Oxford–Cambridge and Paris dominates the European map of knowledge generation, and that within a North European band Copenhagen–Lund and Stockholm–Uppsala constitute second-level centres in relation to a dominant Amsterdam (Matthiessen *et al.*, 2010, pp. 1884, 1889). So, at least initially, the bolder ambitions of the Andersson-Mathiessen strategy have not yet been realized. But strangely, the region has achieved something different and outstanding: it has raised itself to a leading point in Europe for sustainable urbanism. And, though there is no discernible element of conscious competition, this is equally evident in both sides of the water: in Copenhagen and in Malmö.

Copenhagen

Over the space of a generation, Copenhagen (København) has become one of Europe's most attractive capital cities; small and welcoming, it is a city where people rather than cars set the pace, with a multitude of pedestrianized thoroughfares, green spaces and cycle lanes (figure 10.9). The wave of modern buildings along the harbour front aside, architecturally much of the city centre dates from the seventeenth and eighteenth centuries: a cultured ensemble of handsome Renaissance palaces, parks and merchant houses laid out around the streets, waterways and canals. But today's city centre reflects the dramatic transformation following the regeneration and rethinking of the city's planning and development over the last 15 years, which has made it one of the most 'liveable' cities on the planet.

Since 1980, as in Stockholm, planning has shifted away from urban growth strategies to emphasize sustainable regeneration in the old harbour and industrial areas close to the city centre and around the old harbour, which – as in so many

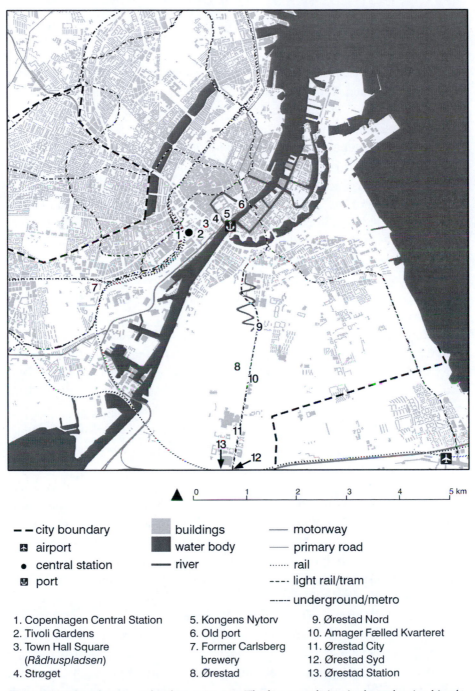

– – city boundary	buildings	—— motorway
✈ airport	water body	—— primary road
● central station	—— river	······· rail
⚓ port		- - - - light rail/tram
		----- underground/metro

1. Copenhagen Central Station	5. Kongens Nytorv	9. Ørestad Nord
2. Tivoli Gardens	6. Old port	10. Amager Fælled Kvarteret
3. Town Hall Square	7. Former Carlsberg	11. Ørestad City
(*Rådhuspladsen*)	brewery	12. Ørestad Syd
4. Strøget	8. Ørestad	13. Ørestad Station

Figure 10.9. *Copenhagen central and inner city map*. The key central sites in the pedestrian-bicycle-friendly central area, and the linear new town, Ørestad, linking the centre with the airport via the new Metro line.

cities across Europe and the world – has seen its port traffic move outside the city. Linking this reconstruction to the wider concept of the international metropolis is Ørestad, a 'new town in town' linking the old harbour area to the airport area and the approach to the Øresund Bridge.

Climate Proofing

Copenhagen has taken the challenge of climate change very seriously. It hosted the United Nations' Climate Change conference in December 2009, having taken the UN's Agenda 21 to its heart, and now plans to be the world's first 'eco-metropolis' by 2015. The Danes have made up for their lack of natural resources by using energy efficiently, and 98 per cent of Copenhagen residents are connected to a district combined heating and power (CHP) system, the main source of energy savings. Many of these CHP plants are owned by cooperatives – a distinctive feature of the Danish approach. A remarkable 48 per cent of waste is incinerated, another 34 per cent recycled and 14 per cent composted; waste meets 30 per cent of annual heating demand.

Denmark pioneered commercial wind power in the 1970s, and amazingly this small country produces almost 50 per cent of the wind turbine power in the entire world. Internally, in 2008 wind power generated 18.9 per cent of electricity production and 24.1 per cent of electric generation capacity; in 2012 the government adopted a plan to increase the share of electricity production from wind to 50 per cent by 2020, involving an investment of some €600 million. The Middlegrunden offshore wind farm – the world's largest when built in 2000 – is 50 per cent owned by the 10,000 investors in a cooperative and 50 per cent by the municipal utility company.

All the municipalities in the Copenhagen region have signed up to the Copenhagen Climate Catalogue, which is based on the government empowering, engaging, and resourcing its cities. The aim is to achieve a 20 per cent reduction in CO_2 emissions by 2015 and to be carbon neutral by 2025. This will include making more use of biomass, removing plastics from waste incineration, and developing a smart grid.[3] There was a 20 per cent cut in emissions between 1990 and 2009, at a time when GDP rose by 66 per cent. Now the focus is on reducing carbon emissions in a number of ways, including particularly transport. Copenhagen expects to be able to export energy, and already does this with wind power.

Carbon neutral transport is also being promoted, with measures to narrow the streets, and thus remove even more parking, promote public transport, with new metros, and carbon free transport. Work is being done on harnessing hydrogen, and the City plans to promote itself as a city of green enterprise. As in the United Kingdom, there has been a stress on developing brownfield sites, but in a much greener way. The City's Blue Plan has developed the Copenhagen waterfront from an industrial wasteland to an urban harbour. It has opened up access to the water with a swimming pool, beaches and public access to 40 km of piers and quays. Similarly the post-war suburb of Ishoj is being given a new image as a result of measures such as using the waste from building the metro to create new beaches, while nearby a power plant uses municipal waste. There is also an innovative contemporary art gallery to help boost its attractions.

Copenhagen's Biking and Walking Strategy

Eco-pilgrims visiting the city invariably arrive into Copenhagen Central Station via a train from the airport or via the tilting X2000 high-speed train from Stockholm, and follow a time-honoured path past the Tivoli Gardens and through the central Town Hall Square (*Rådhuspladsen*) into the pedestrianized city centre, and on to the regenerated old harbour area (figures 10.10(a) to (d)).

Copenhagen's main shopping street, *Strøget* (literally 'the stroke' or 'straight line') is 1.8 km long, the longest pedestrian shopping area in Europe. Stretching from Rådhuspladsen to *Kongens Nytorv* (King's New Square), it is actually a succession of streets stretching out from a central axis. It was pedestrianized as early as the mid-1960s after a fierce controversy. Elsewhere in European cities, pedestrianization had been introduced only after construction of an elaborate inner distributor road system to take the diverted flows of car traffic. Proponents

Figures 10.10(a) to (d). *Copenhagen*. Following the work of the architect-planner Jan Gehl, the central business axis of the city, leading from the Town Hall Square to the regenerated Old Harbour, has been pedestrianized and adapted to mass bicycle traffic since 1970, while massive regeneration has occurred along the waterfront.

of the scheme, including the architect-planner Jan Gehl, argued that this was unnecessary. They proved right: the traffic effectively 'vanished'. Today it is one of the most successful shopping streets in Europe.

Copenhagen is widely celebrated as the bicycling capital of the world, with some 37 per cent of trips to work made by bike. There are 460 km of cycle tracks and every day 1.3 million kilometres are cycled in Copenhagen with 36 per cent of all citizens commuting to work, school or university by bicycle – a figure the city plans to raise to 50 per cent by 2015. The City invests some €10–20 million a year in cycling facilities and the process of change has taken 40 years. As it was unsuccessful in implementing a congestion charge, it has had to achieve a modal shift in more subtle ways. The City's engineer progressively cut the amount of parking spaces by 3 per cent a year – enough to make a difference over time but not enough to create too much opposition. This has provided space for a combination of measures, including extensive cycle lanes as well as wider pavements on the main streets, some shared surfaces on minor streets, removing roundabouts, creating a 'green loop' in which cyclists and pedestrians have the shortest and most direct access to the city centre, providing cycle storage on the suburban trains, and ensuring that offices provide changing facilities. Inside the central area there is a system of free bicycle hire; a system later taken up by Paris in its *Vélib* scheme and then by London with its Boris bikes. Together these measures are designed to produce a '5 minute city' where everything is close at hand, with a third of the movements by public transport, a third by bike, and only a third by car. The results have been spectacular: though car ownership rose by 40 per cent between 1995 and 2004, usage only went up by 10 per cent while bicycle use increased nearly 50 per cent; thus, kilometres cycled have increased by twice as much as kilometres driven, while bus rapid transit has reduced journey times by 23 per cent.

New Town in Town: Ørestad

Ørestad is a remarkable concept: a linear new town in town, only 600 metres wide but 5 kilometres long, on the island of Amager just 5 kilometres from the city centre and close to the international airport, using the new automated Copenhagen metro as the primary public transport axis to connect the area with the rest of Metropolitan Copenhagen (figure 10.11). The metro (line M1), paralleling the main north–south axis, Ørestads Boulevard, has six stops in Ørestad. Ørestad is divided into four districts: Ørestad Nord, Amager Fælled Kvarteret, Ørestad City and Ørestad Syd. The Øresund motorway E20 and the Øresund railway cut west–east through Ørestad at the main metro interchange station, Ørestad, separating Ørestad City and Ørestad Syd. From here, regional and inter-city trains on the Øresund railway link reach the airport in 5 minutes and, in the opposite direction, Copenhagen Central Station in 7 minutes.

Ørestad was developed under special legislation, passed in 1992. The land,

Figure 10.11. *Ørestad*. The remarkable linear new town under development along the new automated Copenhagen Metro line, between the city centre and Kastrup airport.

which had been largely owned by the military (and used for firing practice) was taken over by a development corporation, *Ørestadsselskabet I/S* (Ørestad Development Corporation), founded in March 1993, and owned 55 per cent by Copenhagen municipality and 45 per cent by the Danish state. The winning project of an international architectural competition, held in 1994, produced an overall master plan for Ørestad, dividing the area into four districts. The Finnish design office APRT and Danish KHR arkitekter established a joint venture and presented a final plan in 1997. It provides for a mixed-use new town with 310 hectares of space, in which housing and businesses co-exist side by side. Development, which started some 10 years later, was planned to take some 20–25 years at a cost of about €175 million.

The first office building was completed in 2001, funded by the Norwegian local authorities' pension fund, and others followed soon after, attracted by the location close to the city centre and airport. The first residential buildings were completed 3 years later. The metro, funded from the future increase in land values through the linear development on either side, was built and opened before the first person moved into the new town in 2005. By the start of 2008 over half the area had been sold to developers, each of whom was allocated around 120–150 units, resulting in great diversity of designs and concepts. Social housing companies developed some of the buildings, and the results look indistinguishable from the privately-owned blocks. When complete in 2025–

2030, Ørestad is planned to house at least 20,000 residents; employment, about 10,000 in 2010, is expected to rise to 60,000–80,000 people. And already 20,000 students are in the area's colleges and universities.

Some 10 km of canals snake their way through the site, and the drainage and rainwater system recycles water into lakes and wetlands. The design provides for a large central park, partly to meet the concerns of the existing residents on the other side of the canal, and the buildings slope down towards them. As about 70 per cent use public transport to get to work, the need for parking was halved. Residential parking is largely provided under the buildings, and there is an ingenious multi-storey car park with housing above which looks a pleasure to use.

The centre of the new town, Ørestad City, is situated 4.5 km west of Copenhagen Airport Kastrup and 5 km south of Copenhagen city centre, focused on a new station where the metro interchanges with the main railway line out to Sweden. It is dominated by the Ferring office building and the largest shopping centre in Scandinavia: Field's. Major buildings include the Copenhagen Concert Hall (Jean Nouvel), Cabinn Metro Hotel (Daniel Libeskind) and Copenhagen Towers (Foster and Partners).

There are criticisms that the town feels dead at weekends, when all the workers have gone home, and the large open spaces could feel intimidating. It has proved difficult to get cafés and restaurants to open up, which makes it feel very different from Copenhagen's amazingly lively central area. Maybe, as the second series of the TV series *The Killing* features the area rather obsessively in almost every episode, Copenhageners and visitors will follow Sarah Lund into these streets.

Malmö

Malmö is Sweden's third-largest city, with a population of 286,000. It is the commercial centre of southern Sweden and has a truly cosmopolitan quality: its residents speak some 100 languages, and belong to 174 different nationalities (28 per cent of inhabitants were born abroad). It has a relatively 'young' demographic, with 50 per cent of people under the age of 35.

Malmö, until 1658 part of Denmark, grew throughout the 1200s onwards from the size of a small village into a fortified town, but it is not an 'old' city as such. During the sixteenth century, it flourished as a centre of trade and commerce – a trend that was to continue into the nineteenth and early twentieth centuries, when it mutated into a successful industrial city. But then, from the 1960s, its industry began to suffer competition from the newly-industrializing four tigers of South East Asia. Malmö, a major shipbuilding centre, suffered massive deindustrialization in the 1980s. In 1986 the Swedish government decided to close the Kockums shipyard for the production of civilian vessels, and the huge dock was filled in to accommodate a new Saab plant. But hardly had the plant opened, when a merger with General Motors resulted in its closure. Finally, following the merger of Kockums Malmö and Kockums Karlskrona at the end of the 1990s, the production of military vessels was transferred to Karlskrona. Though Malmö continued to serve as the Kockums HQ office, with a focus on design, planning and development, in all 25,000 jobs were rapidly lost. In the mid-1990s it had an unemployment rate of 22 per cent.

Malmö's decline, and the environmental, social and economic issues that came with it, stimulated proactive thinking about the vision for the city's future. This led to a huge programme to regenerate the old industrial area, with a strong commitment to sustainability. Compared with a major British city, a Swedish local authority like Malmö has both a greater incentive and greater fiscal power to take initiatives: the City Council owns some 40 per cent of all the land in the city, and about two-thirds of its revenue comes from the local share of the income tax, which represents 28 per cent of the total. A City-owned housing society owns some 20,000 homes, and has been a major force for innovation. The City Planning Office proudly proclaims how Malmö has entered into a 'dynamic development period', driven by the opportunities generated by the new Öresund Bridge. The city is currently attracting around 7,000 new residents a year, 3,000 of them Danes, the great majority of whom commute across the bridge into Copenhagen each morning. Malmö is now seen as a national success story, and the city expects to grow by 100,000, or a third in population.

Västra Hamnen

In particular, the closure of Kockums shipyard presented a dramatic opportunity for the transformation of an old industrial area into a new district in the city: *Västra Hamnen* (the Western Harbour), the City of Tomorrow (figure 10.12). Its location is critical. In one direction it looks east to *Gamla Stad* (Old Town), the historic city centre next door, with all the communication and service facilities, culture and recreation of a compact city centre, and to the nineteenth-century train station, reinforced by the completion of the city tunnel in 2011, which turned the station from a terminus into a through station and slashed commuting times to Copenhagen by over 10 minutes. In another direction, to the south, it adjoins the most attractive parks and recreational areas of Malmö, including Malmöhus Castle. To the north and west, it is close to the magnificent Ribersborg beach and enjoys panoramic views across the sea. Thus, looking out to the sea, the new 175-hectare quarter – 44 per cent of which was already complete by 2012 – will become an extension of Malmö's inner city, with high-density housing (at a planned density of 57 units per hectare) for an eventual population of 10,000, plus schools, service facilities, parks and playgrounds in sheltered locations, wharves, squares, bathing areas and urban parks.

This unique opportunity came through an international trade fair, Bo01, in 2001. The City had won the right to hold an international Building Exhibition

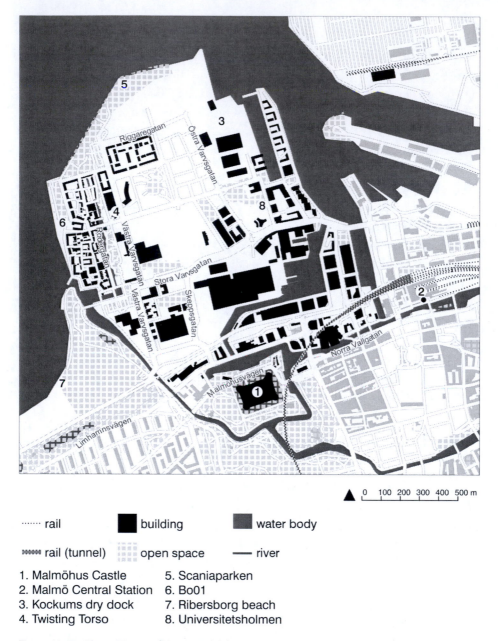

0 100 200 300 400 500 m

······ rail   ■ building   ▮ water body

ⁿⁿⁿ rail (tunnel)   ░ open space   — river

1. Malmöhus Castle   5. Scaniaparken
2. Malmö Central Station 6. Bo01
3. Kockums dry dock   7. Ribersborg beach
4. Twisting Torso   8. Universitetsholmen

Figure 10.12. *Västra Hamnen figure ground*. The ongoing regeneration of the former shipyard area, next to the central railway station, for a variety of uses including a new university and a model environmental residential area, Bo01.

or Expo in 1996. It stalled for 2 or 3 years, but building began in earnest between 2003 and 2007. The key was that – as in Stockholm's Hammarby – the City Council acquired two-thirds of the site, and then commissioned a master plan that divided the first phase of 25 hectares into a series of plots. There were eighteen different developers and twenty-three architects, including houses built by many different countries – not, unhappily, including the UK. Despite early problems, including the Expo going bankrupt, development continued thanks to the Mayor's determination: by 2012 there were over 2,500 homes housing 4,300 people, well on the way to the eventual target of 10,000. It won widespread plaudits for the quality of its public realm, especially the intimate spaces between the buildings, as well as for the great variety of the buildings themselves (figures 10.13(a) to (d)). The scheme has been very popular, with about 70 per cent rented, the rest owner-occupied.[4]

One important goal was to establish a robust and easily-understood structure that would convey the essence of the area. A tree-lined boulevard, which forms a long, unbroken roof of tree tops, links the area around Malmöhus Castle with

Figures 10.13(a) to (d). *Västra Hamnen.* The Bo01 residential development on the waterfront of this regenerated industrial area close to the centre of Malmö, offering outstanding quality which is now attracting commuters from Copenhagen. (*Photo:* (a) CC Fredj)

the sea at the northern end of the site. This tree-lined route will not just be a place for walks and exercise. It will entice residents and visitors with various activities, such as cafés, games of boules, ice-cream stands and many more reasons for lingering on the way. An east-to-west canal route is being built at right angles from the Bo01 Expo area to the huge Kockums dry dock, with the 180-metre, 40-storey 'Twisting Torso', Santiago Calatrava's remarkable residential tower, as its predominant feature. These intersecting main routes and the surrounding water and park landscape will form the basic framework for the new Västra Hamnen district. New, smaller districts, each with a character of its own, will grow up in between. Early development has been deliberately concentrated on some of the smaller districts, in order to provide a strong sense of place early on. There is emphasis on the area's proximity to water, reviving the contact that this city has traditionally had with the sea. Everyone has easy access to the seafront. The historic Scaniaparken, on the landside, is being regenerated and a stronger link will be formed with next-door Ribersborg beach.

Interestingly the Council has shifted from setting down Stockholm-style briefs to negotiating with groups of developers – in the next phase thirteen developers are involved, developing between five and eighty units – in a 'Good developer dialogue'. It intends to apply the German principle of *Baugruppen*, or cooperatives that co-commission homes, with a principle that the design of future phases should change every twenty-five buildings in order to engender variety. Noticeably, in recent sections the landscaping is much less ambitious, and water is no longer retained above ground. The apartments – those with sea views are let at nearly double the rents of those facing inland – attract a wide range of residents, including affluent commuters as well as eco-enthusiasts.

One central feature is the university at Universitetsholmen, where new university buildings have been constructed at record speed. In the former shipyard area, where not many years ago were only Kockum workers, we now see students, business people and residents bustling about their lives and jobs. Within a few years, the hope is that several thousand people will be working in spin-off knowledge-economy jobs.

The World's Leading Eco-City?

Malmö, often called the 'City of Parks', is rated by some as one of the world's greenest cities due to its innovative use of renewable resources and its goal to become the world's leading eco-city. There is a very strong emphasis on energy conservation. In summer solar panels accumulate energy which is pumped into an underground aquifer to release in the winter months; conversely, in winter cold water is stored underground for release as air-conditioning in the summer months. Wind turbines supply electricity for 70,000 households, at a cost of about £315 per home. The Sysavs waste-to-energy system produces 1,300,000 MWh of heat and 250,000 MWh of electricity each year, meeting 60 per cent of total heat demand in Malmö and the neighbouring community of Burlöv. The goal is to reduce electricity consumption by 20 per cent by 2020 and by a further 20 per cent by 2030, when it is intended that the city will have become completely carbon-neutral. All homes are insulated to high standards, and no less than 98 per cent of households have access to district heating, providing 60 per cent of total need. The percentage of solid waste going to landfill has been slashed from 55 per cent in 2000 to a mere 2.4 per cent in 2011. Waste is put in a 'recycling house' and food waste is turned into biogas, which is used to run the buses. All the city buses will run on biogas by 2017. Forty per cent of all commuter and school trips are by bicycle, using a 425-km bikeway network. There are only 0.7 parking spaces per home, largely provided underground or in a multi-storey 'parking house' and there is a carpool.

Water gives the Västra Hamnen neighbourhood much of its character, being held on green roofs and ponds, before going into open channels, which support a lush landscape, and then into the sea. There are at least ten 'green points', such as nesting boxes or wild flowers, in every courtyard in each housing development. Older buildings, such as the former foundry and nearby buildings next to the bascule bridge, are being preserved and will be used for club, cultural and leisure activities for everyone in Malmö. The old industrial districts – the former Kockum dock with its slipway, the historic shipyard crane (now, sadly, exported to Korea), the former aircraft factory – will either be replaced by big space-using activities – an exhibition area for Malmö's trade fair area, which moved here from the stadium area – or developed as mixed-use areas, consisting of residential, office, commercial and educational uses.

Västra Hamnen, including Universitetsholmen, has the highest priority in the city's strategic development programme, and will be the city's most attractive redevelopment and building area for business and housing during the 2010–2020 decade. The Swedish government has chosen the area as a national example of urban sustainable development, gaining great recognition both nationally and internationally, along with the *ekostad* (eco-town), Augustenborg.

Augustenborg: A Model Estate Renewal Scheme?

In 1998 the Malmö City Council launched one of Sweden's largest urban sustainability projects. Augustenborg, located on the edge of Malmö, but linked to the centre by frequent buses and suburban trains via the nearby Persborg Station, is a huge housing estate, built in the 1950s, which had gone from being a desirable place to live to a place with a bad name. Its 3,000 residents, most of whom were born abroad, live in relatively small flats. Environmental measures have been used to save resources and regenerate the area. In the process, turnover of the housing units has dropped by 20 per cent as has environmental impact, and unemployment has fallen from 65 per cent 12 years ago to 45 per cent now.

The character of the estate has been transformed through extensive landscaping, and an elaborate system for conserving rainwater, in green roofs and in ponds before it passes through surface channels and on to underground sewers. Heating costs have been cut by 35 per cent and total energy costs by 25 per cent. Old steel sheeting material which caused damp has been replaced with 100mm of external insulation. Fifteen 'recycling houses' enable residents to sort their waste into clearly marked containers. At first food waste was composted but now it is turned into biogas. As well as a new school, prefabricated so it can be reassembled elsewhere, there is an impressive works department building, covered in a green roof and solar panels.

Copenhagen–Malmö: Eight Key Lessons

In their different ways Copenhagen and Malmö offer inspiring lessons for other cities embarking on sustainable urban development – in particular, because they have succeeded in tackling some of the issues which prove most intractable in cities elsewhere. There are at least eight major lessons, starting with a much stronger role for local authorities, and ending with a much greater commitment to equality.

1. *Dynamic Municipal Leadership.* The two cities have been the economic dynamos for their countries, and have led the way in adapting to higher environmental and quality demands. Three out of four new jobs in Denmark have been created in Copenhagen, and multi-cultural Malmö is now the fastest-growing city in Scandinavia. City councils and their mayors have set visions in both thematic and spatial terms for a region that has a combined population of 3.7 million, and is now a major player on the European stage. Copenhagen is growing by a thousand people a month, and has set out to be the world's leading environmental city under the theme 'Copenhagen Together: a metropolis for people'. Development is concentrated along new railway lines, the old port, and former Carlsberg brewery. Similarly Malmö – half an hour away across the new Øresund Bridge – responded to the closure of its shipyards with a vision of setting a national example of sustainable urban development in the Western Harbour, along with a transition to a knowledge-based society, with a new university. The City Council has also pursued social sustainability by upgrading failing estates, and through technical education. That council is still in power today.

2. *Smarter Public Finance.* Scandinavians have opened up markets to competition (for example, housing societies are now independent businesses), without letting the banks get the upper hand. Planned developments have concentrated new buildings in places with the right infrastructure. Cities have benefited from having reserves of development land. As well as using municipal banks to enable local authorities to borrow for capital projects, major infrastructure projects such

as the Copenhagen Metro have been undertaken through a joint company set up between the national government and the City of Copenhagen. Finance has been raised through 40-year bonds repaid by selling off land for development. Land value uplift in the new town of Ørestad is effectively paying for Copenhagen's new metro line, while Malmö has attracted a multiplicity of private developers to build what the city wants. The incentives come in part from the fact that in Sweden local authorities receive the first 28 *öre* of each *krona* raised through income tax, which means that those most able to pay contribute the most to financing city projects.

3. *Thriving Green Economies.* The Scandinavians are not only concerned about conserving natural resources, but have made a profitable business out of it. The post-war success of the Scandinavian economies has in part been due to opening up export markets for their building products and systems (and trade makes up half the Swedish GNP). High levels of insulation were a natural response to their harsh climate and lack of cheap carbon fuels. Thus Swedish windows were the first to be triple-glazed. Prefabricated houses have substantially cut energy consumption, and made use of natural resources, for example by using timber frame construction, and lots of wood. Constructing wind turbines was a natural spin-off from the technologies and skills used for building ships. Waste is reused, reduced or recycled, and, for example, used to support district heating systems, though bio-digestion, or to power Malmö's buses with ethanol. By investing in the public realm, including extensive neighbourhood 'greens' and 'sustainable urban drainage systems', Swedes and Danes have been able to restore housing estates, which in the UK would have been demolished, into safe and attractive urban places.

4. *Super Connectivity without Car Domination.* In a series of measures to tame the car, while promoting high accessibility, the Danes and the Swedes built the Øresund Bridge between the two countries, using high car tolls on the upper deck to subsidize rail travel below, integrated buses and railways, and created extensive systems of bikeways that are safe and efficient. As well as concentrating development in the most accessible places, councils have sought to control car traffic. Copenhagen has led the world not just in excluding cars (Strøget, the main shopping streets, is a mile long), but also in promoting cycle use. Thirty-seven per cent of trips to work now involve a bike, and suburban trains are designed to carry bikes, while offices provide shower and changing facilities. Space has been progressively taken away from the car and given over to cycling or walking, and street cafés have flourished as a result (some 5,000 in Copenhagen). Main roads are progressively being turned into quality streets, cutting car use, congestion, and pollution. Parking under buildings keeps cars in their place.

5. *Functional and Efficient Design.* The quality of Scandinavian design is world-

famous, as individual craftsmen designers have successfully made the transition into volume production. New settlements have won widespread acclaim for the high standards of their housing, and initiatives like the Hammarby Sjöstad 'water cycle' in Stockholm, where nothing is wasted. Instead of trying to build one-off 'icons', the focus has been on economic forms of mass construction, epitomized by IKEA with its flat-pack system, and prefabricated elements. Regulations appear to be much less complex. Apartment living is much more common than in the UK, with large balconies providing outdoor space. The master plan for Malmö's Western Harbour stresses 'sustainability, mixed use, the creation of meeting places, and attractiveness'. Malmö's new university has taken over redundant buildings, and is located in the heart of the Western Harbour, not on a peripheral greenfield site. There has been a 'BuildingLiveDialogue' with developers, rather than relying on rulebooks, as is the tendency in the UK. The idea of Living or Green Roofs shows how designing with nature can be both functional and look good.

6. *Comprehensive Technical Education.* The great stress on skills has been encouraged through Labour Market Boards that consider the demand and supply for each type of job. Education is geared to enabling people to participate in society, and there are strong pressures to conform. By siting new universities in development areas such as Ørestad or Malmö's Western Harbour, the state has been able to inject capital as well as people into regeneration. It also seeks to equip people with the skills needed for the new economy, and the hope is the children of immigrants will pass on what they know to their parents. There are real problems, reflected, for example, in the rise of the far right in Sweden, and occasional riots in areas with a predominance of immigrants in Malmö, with issues over access to jobs. But there is also a determined effort on the part of local authorities to avoid the rise of 'racial ghettoes' with access to education, housing and transport being key.

7. *Commitment to Sustainable Economic Development.* Sweden, a country where in the nineteenth century a quarter of the population were forced to emigrate to the USA, now has the highest economic growth rate of any OECD country. Norway is ploughing the proceeds from North Sea oil back into diversification, while Finland continues to develop its knowledge-based economy. While Scandinavian national government policies have shifted from a left-of-centre welfare state model towards a right-of-centre liberal free-market model with a shrunken welfare state (partly in response to popular perceptions of the impact of immigration), they have done so only to a limited extent. National governments have embraced exceptionally strong policies to encourage sustainability in response to the challenge of global climate change, while individual cities have sought to go even further. In particular, local government still plays a leading role in shaping city development. The exodus to new suburbs is being countered

by developing new urban quarters that meet the highest sustainability standards alongside upgraded public transit systems. Swedish and Danish city councils have also taken action to make their city centres truly memorable, through extensive pedestrianized streets and bikeways, outdoor cafés (with blankets to fend off the cold), and the greening of post-war estates as a means of changing their image. Above all they have invested in developing a sustainable infrastructure in terms of transport, energy, water and waste, and have made regional planning work.

8.   *A Cooperative Philosophy based on a Belief in Human Equality.* Under-pinning the extraordinary Scandinavian record is a continuing moral philosophy that stresses the 'common wealth' rather than individual consumption. Sweden and Denmark score highly in surveys that measure both environmental and social sustainability. Though some of the old security is breaking down, as recent television dramas bring out, there is a continuing commitment to an equal society that seems to be linked to much higher ratings for happiness than in the UK (Wilkinson and Pickett, 2009). Women pursue active careers but family life is valued, aided by flexible working patterns and outstanding childcare provision.

Scandinavian Cities and the European Project

Thus Scandinavian cities are leading Europe in many aspects of sustainable urban development – but in turn, they are increasingly part of a pan-European mutual learning movement. The Swedes are applying the lessons from German *Baugruppen* in the next phases of Malmö's Western Harbour. The professionally-led top-down model of development, exemplified alike by Vällingby in the 1950s and by Hammarby Sjöstad half a century later, is being subtly transformed into a cooperative model forged in Germany.

This symbolizes the fact that though Sweden and Denmark remain outside the Eurozone, they share a continuing commitment to the construction of Europe. Just as in 2000 the Øresund link joined the two countries both physically and symbolically, so the new Fehmarn link from Denmark to Germany, due to open by 2021, will further reinforce their integration into Europe. So, to see Europe's urban future, look at the Øresund region – before heading south, to the last remarkable place on this tour.

Notes

1.   See http://www.passivhaus.org.uk/standard.jsp?id=122.

2.   In Denmark: Capital region (*Region Hovedstaden*, twenty-nine municipalities) and Zealand region (*Region Sjælland*, seventeen municipalities); in Sweden, Scania region (*Region Skåne*, thirty-three municipalities).

3.   See http://en.wikipedia.org/wiki/Smart_grid.

4.   See http://www.itdp.org/documents/092211_ITDP_NED_Vastra.pdf.

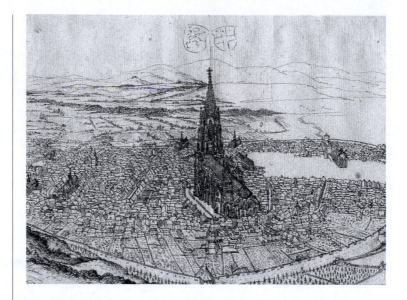

11 | Freiburg: The City That Did It All

Freiburg has come to represent some lonely pinnacle of European urban excellence: the city that took on every challenge – economy, housing, transport, environment – and did best at it. In 2008, the Department of Communities and Local Government's Eco-Towns Challenge Panel thought that Freiburg represented some kind of yardstick, some universally-applicable measure, of what a sustainable twenty-first-century community should be. Subsequently the Academy of Urbanism voted it best European City in 2009, beating Valencia and Bordeaux. Its *Freiburg Charter*, first published in 2010 and in a new edition in 2012, has become some kind of holy grail for believers in sustainable urbanism (Academy of Urbanism and Stadt Freiburg, 2012). Though it is not unique – other German university cities such as Tübingen and Kassel are also producing exemplary development – what stands out in Freiburg is the role that visionary leadership can play in changing a city's direction. So though visitors tend to flock to Vauban as the city's model neighbourhood, it is only an expression of a concept that animates everything the city does, from power generation to building codes. And, though some other European cities can also claim to be trying to do the same, Freiburg has been doing so for longer, with single-minded consistency, than any other place on the planet.

What kind of place is this new Jerusalem? A city of some 230,000 people in the far south-west corner of Germany, a stone's throw from the French border and a mere half-hour train ride from the Swiss city of Basel, it enjoys a wonderful location where the Black Forest meets the flat Rhine valley plain (figure 11.1).

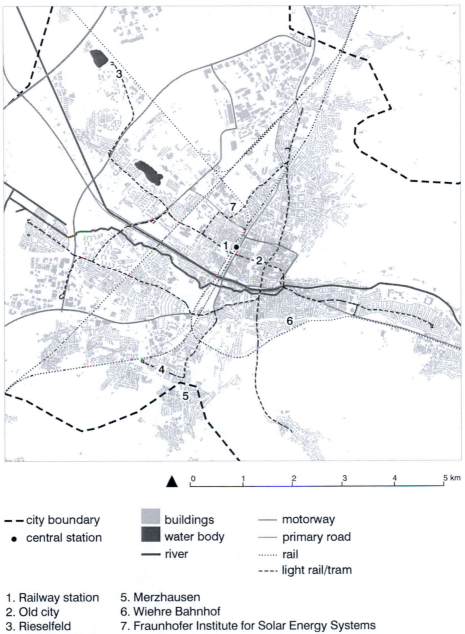

— — city boundary
● central station

▨ buildings
▮ water body
—— river

—— motorway
—— primary road
······· rail
- - - - light rail/tram

1. Railway station
2. Old city
3. Rieselfeld
4. Vauban

5. Merzhausen
6. Wiehre Bahnhof
7. Fraunhofer Institute for Solar Energy Systems

Figure 11.1. *Freiburg map*. The compact university city, located where the flat Rhine valley floor (left) meets the slopes of the Black Forest (right). Its medieval city core, reconstructed after World War Two damage, is surrounded by nearby suburbs served by tram or bus – the 'city of short distances' – including the celebrated Vauban (on the south-west corner) and Rieselfeld (on the north-west extremity).

The sunniest city in Germany, it has a wonderful climate, cool and crisp in winter, warm and balmy in summer. It is an exceptionally attractive city, even by the high standards set by other German cities, with beautiful pedestrianized city-centre streets – many with the original *Bächle*, gullies with running water – set between medieval buildings painstakingly rebuilt after World War Two bombing. Outside the line of the city walls bounding the medieval city and the railway on its west side that bisects the modern city stretch compact nineteenth- and twentieth-century suburbs, culminating in the two jewels in Freiburg's crown: the planned suburbs of Vauban and Rieselfeld, each at the end of a tramline that connects them to the centre in 15 minutes. Beyond them is a wealth of green space: 6,420 hectares of forests, 586 kilometres of forest trails, 408 hectares of parks, green areas and playgrounds, and even 700 hectares of vineyards. An ancient city, founded in 1120 by the local duke as a free market town (Freiburg: Free Borough), it also boasts one of Germany's oldest universities, founded by the Austrians and dating back to 1457.

This historic background is significant, because the university, which is in the middle of the city and has 21,000 students – making it larger than most British universities and a major player in the city and its politics – acts as a magnet, bringing a steady in-migration of new students and young professionals. Freiburg is part of the *Land* (State) of Baden-Württemberg, a major industrial powerhouse of Germany – Mercedes-Benz is based in the state capital of Stuttgart – which is why the region did not feature in Chapter 7's tale of economic restructuring. But it is not itself a manufacturing city: rather it is an archetypal example of the twenty-first-century knowledge economy. It is also relevant that Baden-Württemberg in general, and Freiburg in particular, are affluent places: Freiburg's GDP per capita is above the EU average, though lower than Stuttgart, the State capital.[1] This makes the city interesting: it may act as an indicator of the way that other cities may go as they too graduate into affluence.

Germany in the past – during the Weimar republic in the 1920s – took a world lead in developing radical new approaches to almost everything, including urban planning and design. It has long had an exceptionally strong environmentalist movement, which can be traced back to naturalist movements a century and more ago. This began to play a major part in the city in 1975, when a tiny collection of Freiburgers fought a proposal for a nuclear power station nearby, part of a national policy to go nuclear in the wake of the 1973 oil crisis. Forced to develop an alternative solution, they began to think furiously about renewable energy. So it is rather as if some Oxford or Cambridge students had formed a tiny environmentalist cell that gradually took over the city. Progressively, as the Greens won more seats on the council, the city initiated greener and greener policies, years in advance of almost anywhere else in Germany – and therefore, by definition, in the world. A Socialist mayor, Dr Rolf Böhme, was elected in 1982 and remained in office until 2002, overseeing many of the innovations that made the city famous worldwide. Then, Freiburg became the first major

German city with a green mayor: Dieter Salomon, born in Australia but brought up in Bavaria, who came to the university and got his PhD in 1991, becoming a student activist in the process, was elected mayor in 2002 with over 64 per cent of the vote on a second ballot.

But long before that, and equally significantly, in 1984 the city appointed a young planning officer, Wulf Daseking, who remained continuously in post for nearly three decades, retiring in August 2012. In many places that might be a recipe for tired and mediocre leadership. Instead, Daseking – who held the position of *Oberbaudirektor*, head of planning and building, and now holds a chair in the university – steadily developed his eco-vision for the city, attracting in the process one of the most talented and dedicated teams of planners of any city in the world, some forty strong. That vision is important, because in Freiburg everything – building policies, planning policies, energy policies, waste policies – fits together as parts of a wider whole. Böhme and Daseking are not global household names, even in Germany, though they surely ought to be. But they represent something absolutely special, which is long-term vision allied to sustained delivery.

What is remarkable is that this small university city has simultaneously tackled the five major challenges outlined for the UK in Part One of this book and has supplied answers at least as interesting as any of the other model mainland European cities visited in Part Two. It appears literally as 'the city that did it all'. In the sections that follow, we look at Freiburg's responses to each challenge and then ask how it managed to achieve this remarkable outcome.

Boosting Economic Growth

Freiburg was placed fourteenth in the 2011 *Institut der deutschen Wirtschaft Köln* (IW) economic ranking of German cities, thanks largely to its strong labour supply and good employment structure. By 2011 the cluster promoted as 'Green City Freiburg' claimed some 12,000 jobs, contributing some €650 million of regional added value (Green New Deal, 2011).

By then the city had six university research institutes, including two Fraunhofer Institutes (see page 92), and also offices of the Steinbeis Foundation that promotes the transfer of innovation. By 2007 the Fraunhofer Institute for Solar Energy employed some 500 staff, and another 100 were employed making solar panels and a similar number installing them. By this time the city was generating almost as much solar energy as the whole of Britain, with some 3,000 people employed in the sector, largely in research (Stadt Freiburg, 2006). As a result of such initiatives Baden-Württemberg, despite its paucity of natural resources, has become a highly competitive region, with 4.8 per cent of its GDP invested in Research and Development (R&D) in 2009 – a European record (BWCareer, 2012). What distinguishes German cities like Freiburg from their UK equivalents is not just the higher spending on research, but the way government funding has enabled German companies to gain a comparative advantage in conquering new markets.

One important lesson from Freiburg's remarkable economic growth is that investment in linking university and other research to the creation of attractive modern urban environments pays off. Another is the stress placed on high levels of technical education and training. Significantly the university and the city council meet every month to discuss common issues. Because the city is so successful and also so attractive, graduates tend to stay, so the investment in their education is not dissipated elsewhere. The city continues to grow, because homes are reasonably affordable, and there is easy access to a choice of jobs. In turn, a talented and committed workforce enables Freiburg to compete successfully in the global knowledge-based economy, while minimizing its environmental impact: a virtuous circle of sustainable growth.

Liveable Housing in People-Friendly Neighbourhoods

Freiburg does so well today in large part because, as is already evident, it is such a pleasant place to live. It has been cited as Germany's fastest-growing city, expanding at about 1 per cent a year when many German cities have been shrinking. Freiburg has to build 850–1,200 homes a year just to keep pace with demand. There is a saying that 'it is better to be unemployed in Freiburg than to have a job in the north'. About 4 per cent live in the central area, 70 per cent in the city proper, and the rest in outlying villages. So the city is much denser than most comparable places in the UK, though not unlike many English historic towns.

A distinctive feature of the German housing market, which helps explain the low rate of house price inflation, is the predominance of rented apartments. Four-fifths of Freiburg homes are rented, compared with a 70 per cent average for German cities. According to a report from Savills, of the 20.8 million units in the total apartment stock in Germany, some 3 million are in the hands of owner-occupiers, while approximately 8.8 million units are owned by small, private landlords (Savills, 2012, p. 3). The largest proportion is accounted for by professional commercial landlords with some 8.9 million apartments. This group is dominated by three types of owner: private housing companies (3.9 million apartments), municipal housing companies (2.4 million apartments), and housing associations (2.1 million apartments) (*Ibid.*). There is no direct equivalent of the UK's social housing sector, but in Freiburg's mixed-tenure communities, a third of the new housing goes to those who cannot afford to buy. And the widespread use of cooperative building groups (*Baugruppen*) has made home ownership much more affordable.

The historic centre was almost completely rebuilt after the wartime bombing, and much of the housing immediately surrounding the centre, as in other German cities, is made up of post-war four-storey walk-up apartment buildings, which are not always ideal for families. The city planners also laid the foundations of a very high-quality public transport system, including extensions of the historic tram system as the basis for the creation of new planned suburbs within easy reach of the centre. The urban character is further enhanced by good urban design and extensive landscaping. But what most strikes visitors to these new suburbs is their family-friendly character (Falk, 2007). And this is based on a strong sense of vision: Wulf Daseking talks of building communities that anticipate future needs, *'where young people can rent spacious apartments and not have to mow the lawn'* (Daseking, 2009).

At one level the vision is astonishingly simple. The strategic plan aims to keep the city compact, a *'city of short distances'*, by redeveloping brownfield land rather than invading greenfield – which in any case would be difficult, because the city is surrounded on three sides by the Black Forest, which is effectively a national park. But this policy has been aided by the fortunate accident of two brownfield windfalls on the urban periphery: an old sewage works, Rieselfeld to the north-west, and an old French army barracks, Vauban, to the south-west. Both have become new urban extensions, within a short (15 minute) tram ride of the city centre. And, because Freiburg had resolutely resisted the trends of the 1950s and 1960s, keeping its trams when other German as well as British cities were scrapping theirs, it proved relatively simple and economic to build the short extensions that were needed.

The principles of the master plan were straightforward. The vision in both Vauban and Rieselfeld was to produce low-energy developments. There would be no tall buildings: the city took a key decision that high-rise blocks were a mistake for families, because the basic principle must be that parents should be able to call to their children from the top floor. The planners wanted a variety of apartments, limited areas for parking, a denser city, and a layout that used green wedges to bring people together, not separate them. They also wanted to restrict development outside the built-up areas to protect agriculture. The vision in both Vauban and Rieselfeld was to produce low-energy developments. The maximum building height, 12.5 metres, basically accommodates four- or five-storey structures (the top floor invariably reserved for storage), allowing parents to keep an eye on their children. Inside the new neighbourhoods, the design could not be simpler, a 'fishbone' of rectangular grids of streets and green public places, with the buildings – some town houses, others apartments – either parallel to the main street carrying the tramway or at right angles to it (figures 11.2 and 11.3).

There are some small local shops: chain stores are kept out of the city centre except for one large *Kaufhof* department store. Schools and kindergartens are set in the residential areas, close to where people live. In Rieselfeld, which is twice as big as Vauban (Rieselfeld: 72 hectares, 12,000 people; Vauban: 38 hectares, 5,500 people), there is a large Mediothek, providing a cafe, library, computer facilities, and a film club. In Vauban, there is a flourishing community centre where people can hold meetings or organize entertainments or just drop in for a casual

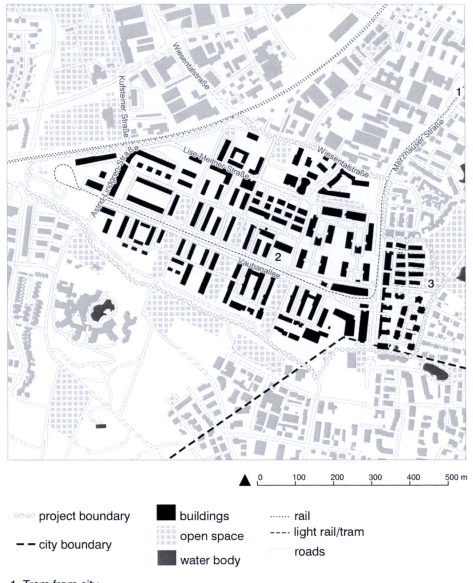

0   100   200   300   400   500 m

○○○○ project boundary   ■ buildings   ┈┈ rail

− − city boundary   ▦ open space   ---- light rail/tram

▦ water body   ▭ roads

1. Tram from city
2. Community centre
3. Privately developed area

Figure 11.2. *Vauban figure ground*. The extremely simple plan concept: a central boulevard, carrying tram tracks and with local shops and services, lined on both sides by housing around green open spaces resembling London squares, divided from each other by narrow alley-like streets, traffic-calmed, for local vehicle access.

drink or meal. Cars are banished from the residential areas, save for loading and unloading in home zones shared with pedestrians including children at play (figures 11.4(*a*) and (*b*)): they can be housed only in communal underground basements or in large multi-storey garages on the periphery (figure 11.4(*c*)), so that it is invariably faster and more convenient to take the tram or go by bicycle.

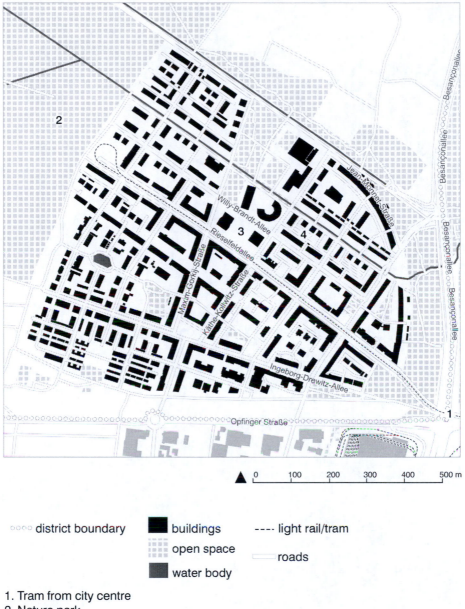

ooo○ district boundary ▪ buildings - - - - light rail/tram

open space ▭ roads

water body

1. Tram from city centre
2. Nature park
3. Mediothek
4. Public housing

Figure 11.3. *Rieselfeld figure ground*. This second planned suburban development, on the north-west extremity of the city, shares the same features as Vauban, but is twice the size.

But this introduces another key idea: within a quite rigid overall master plan, the city encourages maximum local bottom-up implementation by local neighbourhood groups. And here there was a basic difference in the gestation of the two new suburbs. Rieselfeld was essentially about creating better neighbourhoods for families: originally half the housing was to have been social

Figure 11.4(*a*), (*b*) and (*c*). *Vauban traffic calming*. The narrow alleys between the residential 'squares' are relentlessly traffic-calmed for the safety of residents, especially children; homes have their own local bicycle storage, but cars are garaged in communal spaces either under the blocks or in peripheral garages. (*Photos: (a)* and (*b*) CC Claire7373)

housing, reduced to a quarter (figure 11.5) because of government cutbacks. Few developers were prepared to invest, following the withdrawal of housing subsidies. The site was a low-value location as it had been a sewage works, and was close to the poorest part of town. So the municipality, which was the landowner, provided serviced sites, on the basis of groups collecting together and submitting a preliminary design. The concept, pioneered by the architect Rolf Disch[2] in the next-door village of **Merzhausen**, worked. Neighbours got to know each other, and by the time they moved in had already formed a community. The owners usually wanted more environmental measures, and worked with local firms, which was good for the economy. The schemes provide homes at up to 25 per cent below the usual price, and so appeal to people who could not otherwise afford to own their own home. Designs are customized to individual needs but with the same façade shared between several adjoining homes, which were typically three-storey terraces with living space in the roof. There is generally much more space than in the British equivalent. Well over a hundred different builders have been involved, with about 20 per cent developed by cooperatives. The city borrowed the money to pay for planning and installing infrastructure, and then recovered the investment when the plots were sold.

Figure 11.5. *Rieselfeld public housing*. A whole sector (originally planned to be one-half of the entire development, later reduced to one-quarter due to expenditure cuts) is reserved for subsidised social housing, which shares the same design features as the remainder of the development.

Vauban was led by environmental activists, where during the 1990s – the French having abandoned their barracks after the end of the Cold War – there was a running battle between the city and a group of *Fundis* – fundamentalist eco-freaks – who squatted the site, and the city. This was eventually resolved by years of painstaking mediation, though even today the visitor is greeted by defiant slogans from a small residual group, still holed up in their army surplus vehicles behind a wire fence. In the process, Freiburg developed a remarkable idea, albeit one derived from the community architecture movement of the 1970s: each individual piece of the development, consisting of a superblock of buildings around a semi-public open space, would be undertaken by a local Building Group (*Baugruppe*, see above) working together with their own architect.

However, this basic principle also extended to Rieselfeld: that is, involving the people who were to live in the two communities in their design by the extensive use of cooperatives; coops which not only commission blocks of houses, but also help design and manage the communal spaces. Rieselfeld was promoted as 'a huge space for innovative ideas'. Vauban became known as the solar capital, to be developed in a cooperative and participatory way. But this mode of development depends vitally on one precondition: the city acquires the land and builds the necessary infrastructure before development takes place, using investment funds through a trust. The city's investment is then recovered by selling off sites to builders and individuals. This has worked triumphantly, because good location and brilliant design have generated huge demand, effectively allowing the process to self-fund itself. And, by engaging the future residents in the design process from the start, many of the development risks are simply removed, generating strong built-in neighbourliness and accumulated social capital as soon as the first residents move in.

To achieve community participation from the start, no less than nineteen working groups were involved on the city's land-use plan, which was agreed in 2006. Over a period of 6 months the technical officers took part in many weekend and evening meetings with groups to discuss all the different aspects. A design competition for Rieselfeld attracted eighty-five proposals, and a panel made up of experts, politicians and local groups was set up to judge them. The law required one of the top three to be selected. Competitions were also used for all the major elements, such as the church, cultural centre, the schools and the sports hall. The city then laid down requirements in the form of development briefs for what was to be paid, and what could be built and when. As a result, in both Rieselfeld and Vauban much of the development was by small builders and cooperative groups. The process of finding others to join a group, appointing an architect, drawing up proposals, and raising the finance inevitably brought people together and gave them a huge stake in the community's success.

A standard house type, 'the Blue House', emerged and became a blueprint for many of the developments that followed. But there are some interesting variations, as a book documenting thirty-four *Baugruppe* projects brings out in its subtitle '*an experiment without rules*' (Schelkes *et al.*, 2005).

◆ One 180-unit area, Wiehre Bahnhof, was 100 per cent produced by *Baugruppen*.

◆   In one case in Vauban, a scheme was developed for seven flats and a retail unit without residents being lined up, with three basic dwelling types and a simple white and grey façade. This scheme brought different reactions from the neighbours, who often had coloured houses.

◆   One scheme for six passive houses[3] used a low-energy building fabric of timber construction, 90 per cent of which was prefabricated, and 300 mm insulation in the walls (figure 11.6). This enabled assembly in as little as 6 weeks. The scheme has a basement, and there is a communal heating system and heat recovery as well as solar panels, resulting in homes that are very cheap to heat.

Figure 11.6. *Vauban passive houses*. Using low-energy timber construction, 90 per cent of which was prefabricated, this small-scale scheme was assembled in only 6 weeks. (*Photo*: CC Claire7373)

◆   Another scheme for eleven maisonettes and one flat in a four-storey multi-family block, plus three terraced houses was all built to low-energy standards, had no load-bearing inner walls – which allowed for flexible interiors, but was extraordinarily well-insulated outside. It was undertaken by a neighbourhood group without professional project management. The scheme was completed in nine months, fast by British standards.

The city takes a hard-headed commercial approach to development, and draws on private investment advice.

If you own the land you go to a bank and set up a trust account. Build the streets. You don't have to build the whole amount from the start. You take into account the interest to be paid. We planners being too stupid for this we took two employees into our group to balance the books. (Daseking, 2009)

All loans have to be repaid, grants are limited, and only 5 per cent of the housing in Rieselfeld is funded by the municipality. But the city aims to get a good return on its investment. In one case, it paid €130 per square metre for land valued at little more than half that (€80 per square metre) – but then its investment triggered seven times as much in private investment, so it got a good return. Here as elsewhere, the city could acquire the land because the owner would never have been able to do anything else with it without its approval. Further, because the local authority has control over the development process, it can secure substantial economies. Beneath the edges of the roads – most only 4 metres wide – run the pipes that carry heat, water and power, and take away sewage. So less than a quarter of the area is given over to traffic, and much more can be used for common open space. Daseking explains:

We have a law that owners cannot build just what whatever they want. We can specify the housing mix. When the developer comes, normally with land without planning permission worth €50 a square metre, (after planning approval) the value goes up to €350. The law in Germany permits the owner to take two-thirds of the uplift. The public purse gets the other third, which can not be taken in money – only in kind, through installing social infrastructure like a kindergarten or social housing. (Ibid.)

Land for building is disposed of in small plots (190–210 m²), with limits on the number of plots that any one group can buy so as to favour small builders and cooperative groups. 'Give plots of six flats to groups of people to engage their own architects and six months later demonstrate what they were going to build and how they were going to pay for it' (*Ibid.*). In Vauban less than 30 per cent was built by larger investors. Seventy per cent of the plots were sold to private owners, resulting in some 175 different projects, which explains the extraordinary visual variety compared with similar new developments in the UK. The price is based on the floor area to be built on the site. In one example the land value worked out at €430 per square metre, relatively low for Freiburg. The average unit size was 900 m² and the plots included a share of the communal space. Those who have built their own homes have benefitted from the uplift in values when they come to sell, but so too has the city, which can use its share to develop further phases.

In Freiburg as a whole approximately 150 *Baugruppen* projects have provided some 2,000 dwellings, with an investment of €400 million. The costs have generally worked out at under €2,000 per square metre for a specification far more advanced than in the UK; many would satisfy Building Code Level 6. The coops save around a third on the usual price of a house, possibly because there is no developer's profit. In Vauban and Rieselfeld they account for as many as one in four of the units. The general principle is '*you can do it if you want to*', with considerable freedom on what people can build within the height limits.

The local authority acquired Vauban for a reasonable price (equivalent to 20 per cent of the ultimate value), the result of its highly contaminated state reflecting its previous military use. It worked up master plans and then borrowed the cost of installing infrastructure from banks at the favourable rates available to local authorities through a trust. As well as the Freiburg Bank there are some 2,000 other banks in Germany, which means there is plenty of choice. Furthermore, the State reconstruction bank KfW (*Kreditanstalt für Wiederaufbau*) also specializes in funding sustainable forms of building. A significant part of Vauban was initially given over to student housing in the old barracks. Other parts were developed early on by pioneers, and some grants were provided to test out energy saving principles.

The outcome in both Vauban and Rieselfeld is urban development of a quite extraordinary quality: there is a uniform background of height and massing, with four- or five-storey residential blocks aligned at right angles to a central axis served by a new tramway extension (figures 11.7(*a*), (*b*) and (*c*) and 11.8), and a universal devotion to good contemporary architecture (significantly, a street name in Vauban commemorates Walter Gropius) that produces a contemporary version of Georgian London squares. Each superblock has huge variations in detailing, both within individual terraces and even more so between one complex and another. The plot ratio in Vauban is 1.4 to 1 for some 20 hectares of the development, and, significantly, roads take up only 23 per cent of the

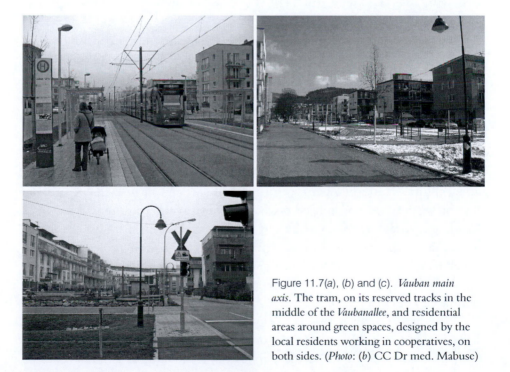

Figure 11.7(a), (b) and (c). *Vauban main axis*. The tram, on its reserved tracks in the middle of the *Vaubanallee*, and residential areas around green spaces, designed by the local residents working in cooperatives, on both sides. (*Photo*: (*b*) CC Dr med. Mabuse)

Figure 11.8. *Rieselfeld main axis.* As in Vauban, the tramline in its central reservation is lined on both sides by residential developments with local shops and services including a *Mediothek* (idea store).

area, with a net density of around 40 dwellings to the hectare, a little higher in Rieselfeld.

The buildings are generally quite simple, often made up of concrete panels, and therefore inexpensive to build. The richness of detail, which comes from the balconies and bike/waste sheds, is multiplied in the semi-public or communal spaces enclosed by the blocks, where imagination – especially in treatment of children's play areas – has run riot (figures 11.9(*a*), (*b*) and (*c*) and 11.10(*a*) and (*b*)). Truly, this is a children's paradise – as visitors on sunny summer days testify. These are magical places where, as Colin Ward once memorably said, children can play out their childhood (Ward, 1978). And that includes the spirit of adventure. Thirty-two per cent of residents in Vauban in 2006 were under 17, and visitors see children everywhere, thanks to the communal play areas. Housing tenure is mixed on a block by block basis. Perhaps the most chastening point was when, in Rieselfeld, a visiting group of British professionals saw a wonderful space with a pond in the centre, fed naturally by drainage (figure 11.10(*b*)). No local authority in England would ever dare do that; someone said: 'contrary to health and safety'.

The overall lesson is that new city quarters can be developed that are as attractive and valuable as historic ones, provided there is sufficient long-term investment up front in the public realm and infrastructure – a lesson well understood by the private landlords who built Bloomsbury and Mayfair in London, or the development corporations that built the better English new towns, such as Milton Keynes. Private developers have seen the value of following a similar approach (figure 11.11). But it does call for a very different

Figure 11.9(a), (b) and (c). *Vauban green areas*. Within the general planned framework, there is a huge variety of different treatments.

Figure 11.10(a) and (b). *Rieselfeld green areas*. Notable features are the spaces looking out to the nature reserve which borders the development on its outer (west) side, and the use of natural drainage to recycle rainwater into an attractive children's play area.

Figure 11.11. *Vauban private development*. Still controversial, this section of the planned suburb, on the other (east) side of the tram route from the city, shares the same high architectural standards.

approach to planning, one that is more strategic but much less regulatory, and which enables a much greater number of builders to create a rich and diverse community, where collaboration is valued.

The Freiburg *Baugruppe* model of development is increasingly being seen as a solution to the problem of providing affordable high-quality housing. It is being applied to difficult sites, as in the centre of Mannheim, and also – as we have seen – in the Western Harbour at Malmö. But the UK has been slow to react: by 2013 the successes were limited to innovative cohousing schemes in Stroud and Lancaster, though sites are starting to be made available, for example on council-owned land in Cambridge. The UK government has provided some pump-priming capital funding as part of its housing strategy (DCLG, 2011). But the essence of the model depends not only on the ability to obtain serviced sites, but also on having a sympathetic landowner who is prepared to wait for groups to get their schemes and funding together. It also helps if there are architects or other building professionals able to act as catalysts and enablers, which is easiest in historic and university cities where there is an appetite for something more sustainable and better value than the standard suburban home. In Freiburg it has been found that although better architecture and construction can add 8–14 per cent to the cost of new homes, it is more than repaid through energy savings.

Boosting Public Transport and Reducing the Need to Use the Car

Freiburg's title as Germany's 'environmental capital' and its most sustainable city is fully justified by its remarkable revolution in urban transport, which has gone completely counter to worldwide trends. Over the last three decades, Freiburg's coordinated transport and land-use policies have tripled the number of trips by bicycle, doubled transit ridership, and reduced the share of trips by car from 38 per cent to 32 per cent. Since the early 1990s, the level of motorization has levelled, and per capita CO_2 emissions from transport have fallen, in spite of buoyant economic and population growth (Buehler and Pucher, 2011, p. 45). In 2006, Germans owned 30 per cent fewer cars per capita than Americans (560 vs. 780 cars and light trucks per 1,000 inhabitants), and Germans drove less than half as many kilometres by car (11,500 vs. 24,000 km per capita) (*Ibid.*, pp. 45–46). Germans not only drive less, but the German vehicle fleet is also more energy-efficient and less polluting.

But Freiburg did remarkably better even than this. There, motor vehicle ownership did not increase at all between 1990 and 2006, remaining at 420 cars per 1,000 inhabitants – 23 per cent below the German average in 2006 – and car use decreased. Between 1982 and 2007, the share of car trips in Freiburg fell from 38 per cent to 32 per cent, during a period in which the car's mode share was increasing rapidly almost everywhere else in the world. At the same time, the share of bicycle trips almost doubled, from 15 per cent to 27 per cent, and public transport's share rose from 11 per cent to 18 per cent. Freiburg's combined 68 per cent share of trips by public transport, bicycling, and walking is between two and ten times higher than in North American cities and 10 per cent to 30 per cent higher than in other German cities (*Ibid.*, pp. 49–51) (figures 11.12(*a*) and (*b*)). As a result, Freiburg is a quiet city, where, in the words of a councillor from Cambridge, '*you can hear the birds sing*'.

Freiburg's highly competitive public transport system – a 3,000-kilometre network of light rail, buses and urban railways, run by the regional transport

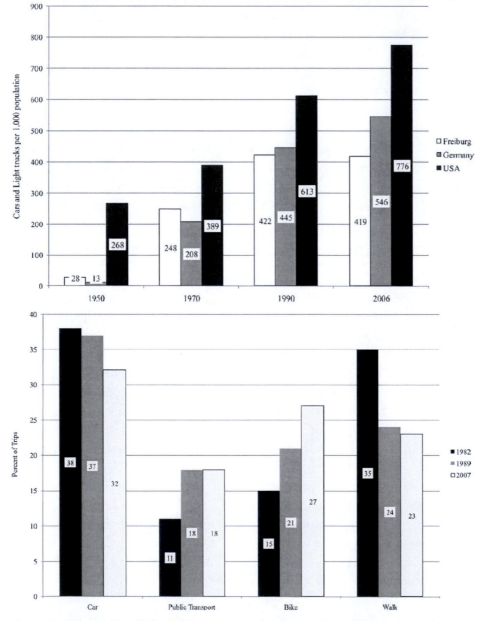

Figure 11.12(a) and (*b*). *Vehicle trends in Germany and Freiburg.* (a) Since 1970 car use in Germany has flattened in comparison with the United States – but in Freiburg it has risen notably more slowly than in Germany as a whole, and since 1990 has actually declined: a remarkable reversal. (b) The decline in car use in Freiburg has been matched by sharp rises in the use of public transport and bicycle, though walking has declined. (*Source*: 'Sustainable Transport in Freiburg: Lessons from Germany's Environmental Capital', Ralph Buehler and John Pucher, *International Journal of Sustainable Transportation*, 2011, **5**(1), pp. 43–70, reprinted by permission of Taylor & Francis)

association – requires little subsidy because it is so well used, thanks in part to the city's compact urban form. Farebox revenue covers 89 per cent of the running costs – higher than anywhere else in Germany or Europe. A monthly ticket for the whole network costs around €50. Following heavy bombing in the Second World War, the railway station was completely redeveloped to form a transport hub, with hotels and offices alongside. The backbone of the city is its tramlines. At the interchange at the main railway station is a bicycle park with space for 1,000 bikes, where you can also get your bike repaired. The trams run on grass verges in the residential areas, contributing to a 40 per cent noise reduction and decreasing the area of impervious surfaces and run-off, as well as being aesthetically pleasing (Field, 2011, p. 102).

Rieselfeld was connected to the tram system before the first housing was occupied, and Vauban's tram replaced buses after a few years. Car ownership is consequently relatively low in places that could easily have become car-dependent. Residents who decide to own a car can purchase a space in one of the underground car parks or at a multi-storey one on the edge of the development for €18,000 ($25,000); those who wish to live car-free pay a one-time fee of €3,700 ($5,000) to preserve open space at the edge of the development in lieu of a parking space. A recent survey showed that there are 150 cars per 1,000 inhabitants in Vauban, compared to roughly 420 for the City of Freiburg and over 560 for Germany (Buehler and Pucher, 2011, p. 56, quoting Forum Vauban, 2009). In Rieselfeld there is some on-street parking, and blocks have underground parking, which is limited to twelve cars. There are also car sharing clubs. The result of policies to minimize car dependency has been an average ownership of 1.2 cars per home, which is reduced by 45 per cent near to tramways.

As a result, Freiburg is a city of neighbourhoods and of short distances. Vauban and Rieselfeld are only two examples out of many. They have places for different sorts of living, in which rich and poor live together with schools and cultural centres and market places and leisure areas all found within a short walk. Daseking fervently believes that this model – the decentralized, integrated, socially stable city, closely bound to a freely-available public transport system – represents the future of the twenty-first-century European city.

Protecting the Environment and Conserving Natural Resources

Freiburg's international reputation as a 'Green City' has not only been used to brand the city - and hence help attract visitors and students - but is also being applied more widely, as builders and investors learn from demonstration projects that environmental initiatives can pay off in faster occupancy and building rates.

Vauban promoted a number of such innovative schemes, such as using solar power to cool offices; and an early building, the Heliotrope built by Rolf Disch for himself, rotates to face the sun. These early eco-pioneers shared similar values of civic commitment, collective building, and living with ecological awareness'. Both Rieselfeld and Vauban sought to include small shops and community facilities in line with Freiburg's philosophy of being a 'city of short distances'. While both wanted to include office employment, only Vauban has been successful. This does not matter, however, as Rieselfeld is next to one of the city's main employment areas, and is well connected to the centre. Drawing on the inspiration of 'model projects', the city sought to apply environmental policies to everything it does, not just isolated developments.

The general Freiburg standard is one-third less energy consumption than is required by German law. The results provide possible benchmarks or targets for situations where the context is similar. Despite all their efforts (and Freiburg accounts for over half the solar installations in Germany), renewables in 2012 only accounted for 10 per cent of electricity consumed in the city. Far more important is energy saving through high levels of insulation, careful siting of homes, and efficient technologies. Thus half the energy consumed by buildings in Freiburg is produced locally, which doubles the overall efficiency from 40 per cent to 80 per cent, and enables waste heat to be reused through combined heat and power (CHP) or co-generation. A thermal waste treatment plant supplies electricity to 25,000 households. Where flats have been refurbished, energy costs have been reduced by as much as 85 per cent.

A new climate and energy strategy in 2007 reinforced the commitment to avoid nuclear power by first saving energy, then securing energy efficiency in generation, and finally developing renewable sources of energy. Tomas Dressler of the Solar Region Association attributes this strong environmental policy to four factors:

◆ Clusters of environmental practitioners (over 700 are employed in solar related activities).

◆ An Environmental Protection Authority within the municipality with sixty staff working on nature, water, waste management and energy, i.e. not fragmented between national agencies.

◆ Participation in international initiatives such as Expo 2000 at Hanover, which led to the city promoting itself as a Solar Region.

◆ Involvement of all the stakeholders in getting the message across, from the regional energy company to the soccer club, and including schools.

Freiburg has saved both carbon emissions and heating costs by generating most of its energy locally. There are fifteen medium and large-scale district heating plants, which together produce half the city's energy and heat requirements in an eco-friendly and economical way. The new quarters of

Vauban and Rieselfeld have their own plants, which are sited close to the blocks of housing they serve. These are mainly fuelled by imported gas and oil. The developments were required to consume less than 65 kW/m² (a third less than German law requires) and they are moving to 55 kW/m².

As one of the sunniest places in Europe, Freiburg has taken the lead in promoting solar energy from photovoltaic panels. There are several hundred projects which provide another attraction for visitors. One of the most impressive has been installing solar panels up the side of a large office building by the railway station, thus converting it into a power station. Although renewables currently produce 10 per cent of the electricity used by the city, the target is to more than double the amount from solar power, and it could easily be 40 per cent. Photovoltaic panels made in Freiburg are guaranteed for 25 years. Some houses in Vauban generate more than they consume (Passiv Plus). In one of the pioneering blocks, a family occupying 90 m² has an energy bill of €90 a year, compared with a national average of €2,400. The block was built by a community of twelve young households, and even generates methane from its own waste (gas is otherwise not supplied to the homes). As noted above, solar energy is also being used to cool buildings, for example the Solar Ship office complex in Vauban.

Renewable sources of energy are now supported nationally by a national feed-in tariff, which enables small producers to sell back their surplus to the grid at twice the usual price. This provides a payback in less than 12 years. The incentives are funded through a tax on energy producers as this is seen as a key sector for the future German economy. Thus in some way or other most people are engaged in efforts to save energy.

The astonishing progress of sustainable development in Freiburg has been due to the close relationship between research and implementation. Thus the Fraunhofer Institute for Solar Energy Systems was originally set up here in 1981, and in 1992 the city won the award of German Capital of the Environment. In the same year, the city council decided that on land it owned it would only permit construction of low-energy buildings, and that all new buildings must comply with certain 'low energy' specifications: as well as solar panels and collectors on the roof, providing electricity and hot water, passive features use the sun's energy to regulate room temperatures.

Energy is also saved by minimizing waste. The key principle is to avoid waste in the first place, for example through returnable packaging. Household waste has to be sorted and collected from four different containers – cardboard, paper, organic, and the remainder – plus recycling sites in residential areas for other materials such as furniture, glass, garden waste, and harmful substances. These are located in the new developments in communal areas, along with bicycle storage. As a result waste has been reduced by a factor of six over 17 years and in 2012 amounted to about 114 kg per resident a year. Only the residual waste is incinerated in a plant that serves seven city and rural districts, and provides electricity for 25,000 homes (Stadt Freiburg, 2012).

As water represents the greatest long-term problem in tackling climate change, Freiburg's ecological rainwater management begins with the avoidance of excess surface drainage, for example by integrating water-permeable surfaces and green roofs in the construction plan. It integrates seepage areas in new built-up areas. In Vauban, because of contamination which required the removal of all topsoil, the water is treated locally to remove contaminants before being released back into the small river that runs along the edge (figure 11.9(b)). In Rieselfeld the Sustainable Urban Drainage System supports streams and ponds that add to the attraction of the neighbourhoods (figure 11.10(b)). As a consequence, even though densities are quite high by suburban standards, the feeling is one of the country suffusing the town.

How Freiburg Did It: Generating Mechanisms for Collaboration and Innovation

For a visiting British professional planning group, the typical reaction to Freiburg oscillates wildly between cosmic depression and euphoric elation. Depression, because places like Vauban and Rieselfeld seem light years in advance of anything that has been achieved in Britain: as the German model – also visible in nearby Karlsruhe – spreads out by osmosis to neighbouring countries and cities like Strasbourg and Mulhouse in France, and Basel in Switzerland, it begins to seem as if this corner of Europe is creating something truly amazing in terms of new styles of urban living and working, so far in advance that the rest of us will have to run to catch up. But elation too, because they show that such things can be made to happen (Falk, 2011).

What then are the keys to Freiburg's remarkable success? Buehler and Pucher, who have examined the city's transport policies in depth, conclude that there are seven key lessons (Buehler and Pucher, 2011, pp. 60–62).

1. *Implement controversial policies in stages, often choosing projects everybody agrees on first.* Thus residential traffic calming was initially implemented in neighbourhoods whose residents complained most about traffic.

2. *Plans should be flexible and adaptable over time to changing conditions.* Over the last 40 years, Freiburg has phased and adjusted its policies and goals gradually. In the late 1960s, the city took the initial decision not to abandon its tram system. Then, in the early 1970s, it approved the extension of the light rail system – which finally opened in 1983. Once it proved successful, more lines followed.

3. *Policies must be multi-modal and include both incentives and disincentives.* Freiburg has simultaneously made public transport, cycling, and walking viable alternatives to the car, while increasing the cost of car travel. Improving the

quality and level of service of alternative modes of transport made car-restrictive measures politically acceptable.

4. *Fully integrate transport and land-use planning.* Policies promoting public transport, cycling, and walking rely on a settlement structure that keeps trip distances short and residences and workplaces within reach of public transport.

5. *Citizen involvement must be an integral part of policy development and implementation.* For example, citizen groups worked with the city administration to redevelop Vauban as an environmentally friendly car-free neighbourhood. The city's latest land-use plan has been developed with input from 900 citizens. Over time, public opinion in Freiburg has become more and more supportive of sustainable policies.

6. *Support from higher levels of government is crucial to making local policies work.* Starting in the 1970s, the German Federal government reduced funding for highways and provided more flexible funds for improvements in local transport infrastructure – including public transport, walking and cycling. Similarly, the State of Baden-Württemberg provided funds for the initial trial of Freiburg's flat-rate monthly travel ticket.

7. *Sustainable transport policies must be long term, with policies sustained over time for lasting impact.* Freiburg started its journey towards sustainable transport in the early 1970s. The initial expansion of the light rail system took over a decade. Some policies can be implemented quickly, but changes in travel behaviour and a more sustainable transport system take much longer. So planners should curb their expectations for quick success (Buehler and Pucher, 2011).

Their verdict can be extended to embrace the totality of the city's winning policy combination.

8. *Set clear long-term goals, and pursue them consistently.* The city's political and professional leaders have to exercise their democratic right and responsibility to set a long-term course. They are dedicated to making lives better for their residents and workers. They achieve this not by setting unrealistic targets or going for the latest architectural fad, but by benchmarking themselves against both competing and comparable cities. And they have to work resolutely through setbacks and challenges. Daseking (2009) refers to the need for a '*strong Lord Mayor who takes the ship through a storm*'.

9. *The city has to take control, but always enlist the support of the people.* Daseking says, 'if nothing else the city council owns the streets', and the basic philosophy is 'we do it our way' (*Ibid.*). There is a cooperative and independent spirit, but a

city's culture also is influenced by its leaders. The *Freiburg Charter for Sustainable Urbanism*, a collaborative effort between the city and a group from the Academy of Urbanism (Academy of Urbanism and Stadt Freiburg, 2012), shows how the policy process starts with long-term vision, but also involves communication and participation, cooperation and partnership. Daseking sums up the spirit: '*I was the captain, and I said we are going to negotiate with developers to get things done as we wanted*' (Daseking, 2009). The contrast with the usual UK development process could not be more striking. Daseking, asked for his final words of wisdom to take back to the UK, replied: '*Don't let the developers near. They won't develop*' (Comment to TCPA visiting group, September 2008). But he is not averse to harnessing the desire for private profit where it can help.

Further, there is a strong emphasis on creating mixed communities, but social housing tenants are rigorously checked out to exclude problematic neighbours. Key to the success of both Vauban and Rieselfeld has been the way residents have been engaged in the design (with professional help) and subsequent management of the communal areas. While there is some maintenance provided by the City, most of the work is done by the residents, who look after the spaces in front of their homes just as UK households care for their front gardens. The city retains ownership of the streets and public open space.

In Rieselfeld key projects have included construction of the church (shared by Protestants and Catholics) and the sports hall. About a sixth of Rieselfeld's population belong to the sports association, and from the start an active residents' group, called Kiosk, has helped people to get to know each other. The schools function as community hubs and are not cut off by walls and fences as in Britain. One primary school in Vauban has been designed to be turned into offices when demand falls off, as predicted. Shops also help people to socialize, and apart from a small supermarket, none is very big. There are over twenty in Vauban, some currently used as craft workshops. There is an excellent restaurant and bar in one of the barracks buildings that functions very much as a social centre.

10. *Work subtly and flexibly to achieve cooperation with a great variety of investors and communities.* Resources have to be conjured up through a variety of techniques including spotting opportunities, devising winning strategies, packaging funds, building agreements, and making deals. Freiburg had to raise the funds to acquire key sites and upgrade its infrastructure, and this called for more than conventional land-use plans. Of course it helped to have local banks that could see the potential demand for what the city was doing, but in the end nothing succeeds like success. Hence the process was essentially incremental or step-by-step.

11. *Be proud of your achievements and publicize them, making your citizens even prouder.* Freiburg takes part in national and international events, such as International Building Exhibitions, and promotes the city's achievements through well-

illustrated publications and good websites. Titles like 'greenest city' are won by making the most of your strengths, and a lot of discussion and soul-searching, not just an occasional newspaper article.

12. *It does not even have to cost the city money.* Rieselfeld and Vauban are so-called *Entwicklungsmaßnahme*; they were built without any contribution from the city budget, by selling plots, which paid for all the necessary physical and social infrastructure. The procedure was actually quite simple: the planning department made a programme, they discussed it with the city council, a competition was launched, based on the result a business plan was drawn up, a loan was obtained from a bank to start the project, then all the plots were sold and the money repaid.

13. *Continuity is vital.* Developing a new quarter or regenerating an old one inevitably takes time. No one person has all the necessary skills: it is vital to build and sustain a winning team, which includes achieving early wins, attracting talent, building capacity, learning from experience and reassuring supporters. It is no coincidence that Wulf Daseking spent nearly 30 years in charge of the planning department, or that only two Lord Mayors have been elected over that time. This means being able to outlive political swings and financial ups and downs, without compromising on quality or sacrificing the basic strategy. Daseking's analogy of being the captain of a ship involves not only setting course, but also changing tack as circumstances change. It is difficult to maintain a sustainable course in a democratic society where tensions and conflicts and changes of leadership are always bound to occur, but – as Freiburg triumphantly demonstrates – it is possible.

Notes

1. See http://epp.eurostat.ec.europa.eu/tgm/table.do?tab=table&init=1&language=en&pcode=tgs00005&plugin=1 and http://epp.eurostat.ec.europa.eu/tgm/table.do?tab=table&init=1&language=en&pcode=tgs00006&plugin=1.

2. Born in Freiburg, Rolf Disch is an architect and solar energy pioneer. In 1994, he built Heliotrope in Freiburg, the world's first house to create more energy than it uses.

3. The term *passive house* (*Passivhaus* in German) refers to the rigorous, voluntary, *Passivhaus* standard for energy efficiency in a building, reducing its ecological footprint. See http://en.wikipedia.org/wiki/Passive_house.

Part Three:
Lessons from Europe

12 | Learning the Lessons

What can we learn from Europe? How can we all re-learn the lost art of urbanism? At first sight, it may seem daunting. Drawing out general lessons from this wide range of case studies, in European cities and countries that demonstrate such a variety in their systems of government and mode of governance, does not at first sight appear at all easy. But strangely, perhaps precisely because they were chosen as examples of best practice, they exhibit a number of quite extraordinary similarities and consistencies. We can identify these key features that seem to run like a red thread, or threads, through most or all of them.

They divide into two clear groups. First, *lessons in what needs to be done* – and has, in these exemplary places, already been done. This is fairly easy, because the lessons have clearly appeared in the chapters of Part Two, in particular their summary conclusions. Second, *lessons in how to do it*: the structures and mechanisms that have been used in Europe's best-quality cities, and that need to be in force to achieve similar outcomes in other places. This is somewhat harder, because it introduces the critical question: how far is it ever possible to transfer lessons from one nation or city, with its distinct socio-economic-political systems and relationships, to another? And, at this point, it will be necessary to introduce another question: what steps have UK governments taken to address these issues, and how far have they demonstrated any sign of success or any promise of future success? The answers to these questions will constitute most of the rest of this chapter. But finally, there must be a summary, headline-fashion, of the lessons that need to be learned.

The 'What?' Questions

The *'what needs to be done?'* lessons emerge easily enough from the case studies in the preceding five chapters.

Recharge urban economies to create good new jobs to replace old ones that are being lost.

Germany, Europe's most economically successful country at the start of the 2010s, has shown a phenomenal capacity to grow new jobs in new activities stemming from industrial innovation, much of it coming from the country's celebrated *Mittelstand* – the extraordinary number of small and medium-sized firms, some very old, some much newer – that, as we saw in Chapter 7, base their success on the ability to identify new needs in the modern economy and then to fill them. Two archetypal examples from the transport sector appeared in the account of Kassel, hailed as Germany's most dynamic city in 2011: a firm that makes the bellow-like connectors in bendy buses and bendy trams, and another that makes equipment allowing Europe's high-speed trains to change electrical and control systems as they cross from one country to another.

Such firms demonstrate Germany's outstanding competence in advanced engineering: firms both old and new, large and small, quickly respond to demands from newly emerging markets, in effect constantly creating and recreating new sub-industries like environmental engineering and advanced transport engineering. They are thus early into these new markets, establishing a strong presence in them and progressively honing the quality of their products. One of the oldest and largest, Siemens, produces a bewildering range of products from medical equipment – CT and MRI scanners and a huge range of other diagnostic and therapy systems – to the latest ICE-3 high-speed trains that have become the familiar workhorses on European railways from Germany to Spain. At the other extreme is a small company like Herrenknecht, founded by Martin Herrenknecht in 1975 with a staff of one and now, as mentioned in Chapter 7, employing 6,000 and selling its tunnel-boring machinery to railway, road, water and sewer companies worldwide. This is a highly specialized company, but again its essence is very advanced engineering for exacting institutional markets. Large or small, their products have high unit costs, so they are expensive. They have to embody the most advanced technology combined with reliability. They are bought by large institutional buyers (hospitals, railways) which themselves embody great technological competence; these are among the world's most sophisticated and exacting purchasers. The standards are high but the potential profit is huge.

To a considerable degree, but far from exclusively, these firms tend to be located in the economic powerhouse of southwest Germany, in the *Länder* of Bavaria and Baden-Württemberg. Some of the most famous, like Mercedes-Benz and Bosch, were founded here; others, like Siemens and many others, relocated here from eastern Germany (including Berlin) at the end of World War Two and later, as the result of Russian occupation and the nationalization of the parent firm. The critical question is what gives them their unique advantage in highly competitive global markets. That will need to await an answer in the second half of this chapter.

But others are located in older industrial cities in other regions that have seen their fair share of drastic industrial change. Kassel, as Chapter 7 showed, is an old industrial city with traditional industries that were contracting, thus resembling other such cities across the United Kingdom and across Europe. But it has fought back by marshalling its inherited skills and employing them to fill new niches. That required a deep basic human infrastructure – human capital – in the form of a two-century-old tradition of strong technical universities, implanted in Kassel in 1970 when a new university was established there. But it needed more than that: the professors in the new university began immediately to challenge the established wisdom of the day in matters of transport policy, helping generate a revolution in the city administration and making it a pioneer in radical new approaches that dissolved the conceptual barrier between trams and trains. Likewise, simultaneously its architectural and planning professors argued for a new approach to city development, based on a return to traditional urban forms, which proved highly successful in regenerating an inner-city area next to the city centre. In another old industrial city facing decline of its basic industries, Dortmund, professors in another new 1970s university successfully fought for the radical concept of a science park where university research discoveries would be spun off into profitable innovations in new companies.

Not every city was as lucky as that – though in Leipzig, an east German city that suffered perhaps the worst single episode of deindustrialization in all Europe after the country was reunited in 1990, the venerable university – one of Europe's oldest – has experienced a huge revival that has attracted students from all over Germany and all over Europe. Leipzig's lesson is particularly that the city deliberately enlisted academic research to write a strategic policy of cluster development in industries where the city could be expected to make a strong showing: cars, logistics, information technology, and the media. Through a hard-nosed policy of public relations, financial incentives and deliberate political implantation, the city now has two highly-successful car plants, a burgeoning logistics industry facilitated by an excellent motorway network rebuilt in the 1990s and by a 24-hour airport, and a flourishing electronic media centre where a television company has deliberately encouraged the formation of a network of suppliers and specialized services.

Berlin, the capital city, offers yet another lesson. Here, the euphoric hope that the city would return to the primacy it had enjoyed in the golden age of the 1920s all-too-soon evaporated, requiring the mayor to develop a radical alternative strategy: based on the slogan *Arm, aber Sexy* (poor, but sexy), the city deliberately exploited its parlous position to market its empty buildings, low rents and funky atmosphere to creative people who began to flood in from all over Europe, many arriving as tourists and staying as residents. Within a decade the strategy has proved so successful that it has now produced its own counter-reaction: by 2011–2012, rising rents have been threatening the very spaces in which these creative people have found their homes and work and play spaces. Not so, as yet, in Leipzig, where three visionary entrepreneurs bought a vast derelict industrial complex and then, denied loans by the banks, used their own scant resources to turn it into one of the largest creative complexes in Europe.

Likewise, finally, back in the former West Germany, where the people who created the Emscher Park deliberately pursued non-economic priorities to turn most of their area into a permanent park and clean up its waterways, then seized upon derelict industrial buildings that had no apparent value and turned them into brilliantly successful tourist attractions that have created a new economic base for the region. And exactly the same spirit is seen in Hamburg, where a city-led company prioritized high-quality urban redevelopment along the city's waterfront in order to attract affluent residents and creative businesses back into the city centre. These examples demonstrate a key common quality in German urban regeneration: don't do it on the cheap, don't surrender the process to predatory developers in search of cheap speculative profits, but instead lead the process through strong public companies that develop long-term policies that bring firmer growth in the long run.

Build enough good-quality housing to meet demands from all kinds of households, large and small, rich and poor.

Here the outstanding examples come from the Netherlands and Scandinavia. In the Netherlands, the government's VINEX programme achieved agreements with local authorities that generated 455,000 new homes in just 10 years. They were built in carefully chosen locations, some of them brownfield regeneration sites in derelict industrial or dockland areas – as in Amsterdam and Rotterdam – but the majority as satellite towns adjacent to major cities, linked to them by excellent public transport (rail, tram, bus) that was built in advance to guarantee that it would be there as the first residents arrived.

In Sweden, two outstanding mixed-use housing developments utilized derelict inner-city industrial sites. Hammarby Sjöstad in Stockholm is a vast waterside site once occupied by a steel works, only 5 kilometres from the city centre. Outstanding for its environmental standards (to be discussed below), it embodies relatively high-density apartment housing built next to open park or water spaces, all centred on a single spine road that includes a tramway (linked within a few minutes to a Metro interchange) and local shops. It has proved extraordinarily (and surprisingly) attractive to affluent middle-class households with young children, who appreciate the communal atmosphere and the easy access to jobs and services in the city centre.

In Malmö, the Västra Hamnen (Western Harbour) development occupies an analogous site next to the historic city centre and main train station, deserted by a local shipyard which closed down. Again exploiting a waterfront situation which directly faces out to the Öresund, with spectacular views of Copenhagen and the new bridge that connects the two cities, its high-density apartment housing around planned open gardens with children's play spaces has also proved outstandingly attractive to young families with children, some of whom appreciate the easy access via a new rail link to the bridge for commuting to Copenhagen city centre. Both these developments, like their Dutch counterparts, have been master planned by public corporations that have maintained a strong control over the quality of the entire development, while in effect leasing individual development sections to private developers – a model that will merit a closer look later in this chapter.

Create sustainable neighbourhoods with homes, jobs, shops, schools and services within easy reach on foot or by bicycle, connected to the rest of the city and the region by good-quality public transport.

Here, Hammarby, Vauban and Rieselfeld demonstrate remarkable similarities in overall concept and detailed design. In all three, a central traffic spine carries a tram system as well as traffic that feeds the entire development through short connecting streets at right angles to the main axis. Housing is designed off these connections around communal open spaces, which often embody small ponds that act as water collectors; in Hammarby, the lakefront provides additional open space. Walking and bicycle travel receive privileged treatment throughout. There are local shops along the main traffic axis within a short walk of all homes; higher-order and more specialized shopping is provided in the city centre, a short journey away by tram or Metro. There is some provision for local jobs, but it is assumed that most people will work elsewhere in the city. In Freiburg, radial tram routes connect one suburb with another via the city centre; in Stockholm, the tram system is part of a growing orbital line that is eventually planned to connect middle-ring centres around the city.

A similar approach is seen in Ypenburg, the Dutch VINEX settlement outside The Hague, essentially a satellite new town, with two tramways along traffic spines that meet and cross in the town centre, one from The Hague city centre, the other an orbital route connecting with similar satellite developments around The Hague, which also links at the edge of Ypenburg with a new tram-train line between The Hague and Rotterdam.

Build high-quality transport systems, in advance of development, to ensure that new housing areas are connected to jobs, shops, schools and services from the very start.

This, as just seen, is the approach in the tramway spines at Hammarby, Vauban, Rieselfeld and Ypenburg. Great attention was paid to investment in tramways ahead of development, or at very least before it was finished – a feature that local planners regard as essential if inhabitants are not to lock early into habits of car dependency, though this proves difficult to avoid. In the Dutch satellite of Vathorst outside Amersfoort, the development authority financed the Dutch railway system to build and open a new train station well in advance of demand; they also built in a BRT (bus rapid transit) system along the main spine of the development, similar in character to the tramway spines in other places.

French cities tell a different story. There, with few exceptions, cities scrapped their tram systems in the 1950s and 1960s. But from the 1990s onwards, in city after city they restored them. Interestingly, here the trams were seen not merely as agents of mobility but as part of a total concept of urbanity. Combined with generous treatment of public space and restrictions on obtrusive and polluting car traffic, they are a part of urban image creation and place marketing. And, especially through collaboration among neighbouring municipalities in *Communautés Urbaines*, cities like Montpellier, Lille and Strasbourg extended accessibility far beyond the city limits into surrounding regions. The most extreme example of this extension however came not in France but in Germany, where – first in Karlsruhe and then in Kassel – a remarkable urban innovation, the tram-train, allowed trams to run off the city streets on to national rail tracks, thus allowing them to serve small towns and villages within the entire surrounding city-region. These new networks have brought residentially-based growth to many small rural towns and villages in these wider regions, through a sudden and dramatic improvement of access to jobs and services in the heart of the core cities. Their success is beginning to inspire imitations across Europe, notably in the tram-train line in Mulhouse (opened 2010) and the similar line in Strasbourg (due to open in 2016) as well as the Randstad Rail network which unites an extension of the Rotterdam Metro network with the tram system in The Hague, as a device to assist widespread development of new satellite communities immediately outside these cities.

Manage the environment to conserve resources and recycle waste.

Swedish cities have produced some of the most commendable developments in terms of energy conservation and waste management. Hammarby Sjöstad in Stockholm and Västra Hamnen in Malmö demonstrate in various ways high construction standards that minimize energy use and energy loss, and that maximize recycling of both solid and liquid waste. They do so by prescribing very high standards, well above national norms (though these too are outstanding), and then incorporating them in master plans to which individual developers must conform; in addition, Hammarby's solid waste disposal system involves total pre-investment in underground infrastructure that permeates every corner of the development. Augustenborg in Malmö demonstrates how a 1960s housing scheme can be retrofitted to achieve many of the same features, particularly in its treatment of wastewater which not only meets environmental standards but also constitutes a charming design feature throughout the area's open spaces. Many of the same features are replicated in the Freiburg suburbs of Vauban and Rieselfeld. And here, again, the key is overall master planning that embodies environmental sustainability as a central feature of the design, investing in the essential infrastructure ahead of the development of individual plots by developers.

Create places where people want to live and where they feel good about living.

This, in a sense, is the easy part. If planners take the right steps ahead of development, and during the process, the result can be – and often is – a development that is not only good to live in, but is outstandingly so. And this is abundantly evident to anyone who makes a study visit to these places. They radiate a good feeling in the attitudes of their inhabitants, not least in their children, for whom they appear such attractive places in which to grow up. Partly this reflects the fact that they seem to have been deliberately designed to be child-centred. The locations of the schools in the middle of residential areas, the careful attention to providing walking and biking routes between home and school, the abundant common play spaces all bespeak this concern. Physically they vary quite considerably, from pure English-style garden cities in the Dutch examples, through terraced housing in Freiburg, to denser apartment living in Stockholm and Malmö. And these appear to represent different social and spatial lifestyle preferences, which should be respected so long as they are not imposed through artificial constraints, whether by the market or by regulation. It should be no part of any prescription for good cities or better lives to try to make the British live more like their continental neighbours, any more than it is for making those neighbours more like us; it is about shared and shareable lessons for planning which could apply here as well as there. And the interesting common fact is that, despite an initially very different feel, they all seem to work in very much the same way.

The 'How To?' Lessons

What is more difficult is to identify the *'how to do it?'* lessons: the key features that have allowed these good things to happen. But, probing more deeply, these too demonstrate a considerable family resemblance from one good-practice European city to another.

Rebalance the national economy by generating a strong science base in the regions.

The model here has to come from Germany. As suggested in Chapter 7, part of the phenomenal long-term success of the German economy is its strength in advanced manufacturing, and this in turn rests in large part on two long-established national institutions: the Max Planck Society for the Advancement of Science, and the Fraunhofer Society for the Advancement of Applied Research. A key question is how this model could be re-engineered for the very different context of the UK.

The Max Planck Society dates as far back as 1911, when it was founded as the Kaiser-Wilhelm Society (Kaiser-Wilhelm-Gesellschaft [KWG]); already, by the interwar years, it had become one of the world's outstanding research centres. Renamed after World War Two in celebration of the great German quantum physicist who had been its president until he was forced out by the Nazis, it is a formally independent non-governmental and non-profit association of research institutes, nearly eighty in number, publicly funded by the Federal and the sixteen state governments to conduct basic research in the natural sciences, life sciences, social sciences, and the arts and humanities. With a total staff of around 13,000 permanent employees, including 4,700 scientists, plus around 11,000 non-tenured scientists and guests, they had a total budget (in 2006) of about €1.4 billion, 84 per cent of it from state and Federal funds. In 2006, the *Times Higher Education Supplement* ranked it No. 1 in the world for science research, and No. 3 in technology research (behind AT&T and the Argonne National Laboratory in the United States).

Though the UK too has developed national research institutes such as the Royal Aircraft Establishment at Farnborough or the Atomic Energy Research Establishment at Harwell – both incidentally defence-related in origin, both located in the South East England 'Golden Triangle' of higher education and research, both swallowed up in major spasms of reorganization and losing their distinct identity in the 1990s – overall there is no comparison with the Max Planck structure; fundamental research is heavily concentrated in the universities. A tentative approach to build on the Max Planck concept, while creating a strong research base in regional universities outside the 'Golden Triangle', was the Science Cities initiative of 2004–2005. Six cities – York, Manchester, Newcastle, Bristol, Nottingham, and Birmingham – were designated to increase rates of innovation and leverage economic growth; Gordon Brown declared that they would help make Britain 'a world leading location for the next wave of research and development' (Brown, 2005, q. Webber, 2008, p. 12). But bizarrely, they had unclear objectives and no funding. Chris Webber's review, based on thirty-five semi-structured interviews with key participants, concludes that Newcastle, the university that made perhaps the biggest effort and achieved the biggest funding from the EU and the Regional Development Agency, was unrealistic in expecting a powerful life sciences cluster to develop in the city: while Newcastle University performs very well in research it does not rank alongside the likes of Cambridge, Oxford and others either in research performance or economic impact. The central issue is that Oxford, Cambridge and London house England's top research universities: in 2007 the Shanghai Jiao Tong University international ranking of UK universities put Cambridge at second place, Oxford ninth, Imperial College London twenty-third, University College London twenty-fifth and the next, Manchester, forty-eighth (Webber, 2008, fig. 8, p. 21). The universities in the 'Golden Triangle' receive a disproportionate share of public sector research funding, around 45 per cent, while the Core Cities together receive only 28 per cent; the four leading universities (Oxford, Cambridge, UCL and Imperial) alone received 28 per cent of HEFCE (Higher Education Founding Council for England) funding in 2010/11 (Goddard and Vallance, 2013, pp. 79–80).

The economic impact of universities also varies significantly. Of the twenty universities sampled in a 2007 study, five – Oxford, Cambridge, Imperial, Bristol and Southampton – generated 55 per cent of the venture capital backed spin-outs and attracted 75 per cent of the spin-out related venture finance between 2001 and 2006 (Webber, 2008, q. Library House, 2007). And top universities in smaller cities are likely to have a proportionally larger impact on overall economic growth than top universities in larger cities. Cambridge, Oxford, Southampton and York receive a much higher amount of research spending per head of population than larger cities like London, Birmingham, Newcastle and other core cities (Webber, 2008, pp. 21–22).

Webber reaches extremely negative conclusions about the Science Cities initiative. First, city-regions need to tackle the wider barriers to innovation in their economies – in areas like transport, housing and planning. In many city-regions, dealing with pressing problems in these areas could have a greater impact on rates of innovation than introducing dedicated policies to support innovation. Second, he proposes, the designated Science Cities should drop the brand if they see fit. Everywhere, except for York and Newcastle, there are signs that the brand is not working – especially in Manchester. Third and critically, city-regions should be more realistic about university-led economic growth. In most of them, university-related business activity will only ever be one part of a much wider growth story. Economic strategies and investments need to reflect this reality (Webber, 2008, p. 2).

The most proactive of the Science Cities, Newcastle, drew up a plan to invest £700 million in redeveloping the former Newcastle Brewery on Gallowgate to become Science Central, an 'Innovation Machine', generating clusters of highly-specialized research jobs. But in October 2008 an OECD report on the North East regional economy (OECD, 2008) concluded that the scheme was 'unlikely to meet the expectations' for change in the regional economy. One of its key elements, the International Centre for Life (ICFL), included the Institute for Genetic Medicine (IGM), focusing on stem cell research and working in association with Cels, a snappily-named entity set up by the Regional Development Agency to develop a commercial cluster in the area. But in 2008 one of the key researchers, Professor of Regenerative Medicine Colin McGuckin, resigned in a disagreement over research priorities. The development of Science Central was delayed by the collapse of the local property market following the 2008 financial crisis and the subsequent recession. Then, in 2011, the new Coalition government refused an £8 million request from One North East, the Regional Development Agency, for Science Central, followed by the resignation of the chief executive. The new government shut down One North East, forcing the university and the city to buy the RDA's share at near-market prices; the City Council and University scrambled together £1.5 million of funds, and the government's Regional Growth Fund contributed £6 million, but in 2013 the scheme remains unfinished (Goddard and Vallance, 2013, p. 98). A further and perhaps final blow came with the government's Catapult initiative for scientific research applications, described below, which placed the stem cell research centre in London. Goddard and Vallance (2013, p. 122) conclude that 'the aspirations for development in the region based on the growth of medicine and bioscience clusters have yet to materialise on any significant scale in terms of new firms or employment created'.

Create institutions to translate scientific research into innovative products and services.

The other half of the German industrial achievement (Chapter 7) is the Fraunhofer Society, founded in 1949 and named after the scientist-engineer-entrepreneur Joseph von Fraunhofer. With sixty institutes across Germany, each focusing on a different field of applied science, it employs around 18,000 people, and has an annual research budget of about €1.65 billion. Though some basic funding comes from the Federal and state governments, which together 'own' it, more than 70 per cent of its funding comes from contract work, for government sponsored projects, or from industry. It has proved outstandingly successful in bridging the so-called 'valley of death' between university research and its practical commercial applications.

Very belatedly, the UK has started to try to replicate the Fraunhofer model. An important official report in 2010 from Dr Hermann Hauser, the celebrated Austrian-born scientist-entrepreneur closely associated with the growth of 'Silicon Fen', drew attention to the fact that in other OECD economies a variety of non-university research organizations like the Fraunhofer Institutes, ITRI in Taiwan, and ETRI in South Korea, perform tasks that business and universities, left to their own devices, often cannot or will not perform in sufficient quantity and/or quality (Hauser, 2010). These organizations account for significant shares of R&D performance, both in applied R&D and in fundamental research, estimated as 40 per cent of publicly funded R&D in the EU and about 14 per cent of all R&D (Hauser, 2010, Table 1, p.11). But the UK lacks clear prioritization, long-term strategic vision, or coordination at a national level in promoting such Technology Innovation Centres (TICs). The current UK approach, it concluded, has often resulted in sub-optimal and dispersed investments with the lack of long-term funding certainty.

Hauser therefore concluded that the UK government should commit to funding a network of elite business-focused national TICs in areas where the UK has the potential to gain substantial economic benefit. It should work with the UK's innovation agency, the Technology Strategy Board, and private and public sectors to develop a strategic vision for their development over the next 10 years. Decisions on the location of these TICs, whether totally new or building on existing centres, must take into account their national nature, track record, the location of UK research excellence (in universities and elsewhere), alongside industrial capability and absorptive capacity. Funding – of the order of £5–10 million per annum per TIC – must be sustained over a period of 10 years. Finally, Hauser suggested that like their German equivalents they should have a name. He proposed Clerk Maxwell Centres, after James Clerk Maxwell whose unified theory of electromagnetism is the basis of the whole IT industry.

Both the outgoing Labour government and the incoming Coalition government accepted the Hauser Report, with a commitment to invest over £200 million over 4 years in a network of new technology and innovation centres, now to be called *Catapults*, designed to transform research rapidly into commercial success. Created and overseen by the Technology Strategy Board, each Catapult will focus on a specific area of technology and expertise. Once fully established, the centres will receive broadly equal funding from the core Technology Strategy Board grant, from research and development grants won by the Catapult in collaboration with business, and from contract research funded fully by business – the so-called third-third-third model.

The first centre, focusing on high-value manufacturing, opened in October 2011. Interestingly it is not a single geographical centre, but embraces seven members employing 625 staff, supported by public investment of over £140 million over a 6-year period:

◆ Advanced Forming Research Centre, Glasgow (billet forging; sheet forming; precision forging);

◆ Advanced Manufacturing Research Centre, Sheffield (AMRC) (machining; materials and component testing; hybrid and metallic composites; assembly);

◆ Centre for Process Innovation, Wilton, Sedgefield (chemical processing; biotechnology; printable electronics);

◆ Manufacturing Technology Centre, Coventry (automation and tooling; fabrication, joining and assembly; additive and net shape; process modelling);

◆   National Composites Centre, Bristol (design and manufacture of composites);

◆   Nuclear Advanced Manufacturing Research Centre, Sheffield (fabrication of civil nuclear components);

◆   Warwick Manufacturing Group, Coventry (lightweight product system optimization; energy storage and management; digital verification and validation).

Two of the constituent centres are thus in the Midlands, three in the north of England, and one in Scotland; only one is in the south. However, in March 2012 it was announced that the second centre would be in cell therapy and would be located in London, chosen for its rich cluster of hospitals and clinical infrastructure, logistics, universities, talent and a reputation as an international business hub with proximity to the financial sector – a final blow to Newcastle's ambitions. A third area – offshore renewable energy – will have its headquarters in Glasgow and an operational centre near Narec, the National Renewable Energy Centre, near Blyth in Northumberland. The plan also identified a further ten promising candidate areas: complex systems; digital media/creative industries; future cities; future internet systems; photonics; resource efficiency; sensor systems; smart grids and distribution; space; and transport systems and integration. A fourth – Connected Digital Economy – will be a single centre, based in London. Thus, so far, two of the four centres are London-based.

The Sheffield AMRC, a key part of the first centre, has already built up a reputation over a decade of activity. Symbolically located on the site of Orgreave colliery, scene of a huge battle between police and picketing miners in 1984, when it was a British Steel coking plant that converted coal into industrial fuel, it has over sixty member companies, from global aerospace giants to local SMEs. Run by the University of Sheffield and backed by major private sector players, led by Boeing together with Rolls-Royce and BAE, it is developing breakthroughs in machining technology – in basic terms, taking a lump of metal and turning it into a high-quality product through drilling, cutting and grinding. It employs around 200 highly qualified researchers and engineers, working with more than sixty individual companies on specific projects, and collaborating on generic projects for the benefit of all members, in two purpose-built centres on the Advanced Manufacturing Park (AMP) in South Yorkshire.[1] It is currently preparing for further growth as part of the new University of Sheffield Advanced Manufacturing Institute.[2] The key, according to Jamie McGourlay, a Rolls-Royce representative at AMRC, is that before centres like this happened, universities made breakthroughs that had no commercial home, while companies could not justify the cost and time of imaginative research and development. At Orgreave, these problems are reconciled. The university runs the centres; the industrial groups provide materials, expertise and funding (Milmo, 2012).

It is a promising story. But there are at least three reasons for caution. One, as already seen in Webber's report, is that the total UK research base is still disproportionately concentrated in the 'Golden Triangle': the new Catapults, even supposing they are mainly located north of Birmingham, will depend on a narrow research base. The saga of Newcastle's attempt to promote stem cell research is a cautionary lesson here. The second is that compared with their German model, the Catapults will be sparsely funded. Compared with the €1.65 billion annual funding of the Fraunhofer centres – of which about 30 per cent, €495 million, comes from public sources – total funding for the Catapults is only £200 million a year over 4 years – about half as much. The third, critically, is that the money is being salami-sliced – as witnessed by the division of the first centre among no less than seven different locations. Admittedly, the German Fraunhofer funds are also divided, among no less than sixty centres – an average of €8.25 million, of public funds per centre. The Fraunhofer 'system' seems to have worked wonders in Germany; time will tell whether the Catapults achieve the same in the UK.

Meanwhile, quite unexpectedly, in May 2013 the Secretary for Business Innovation and Skills, Vince Cable, celebrated the launch of a UK branch of Fraunhofer. Having just created a centre for applied photonics at the University of Strathclyde, supporting sectors such as security, healthcare, energy and transport, it hoped to establish other centres around the UK, potentially in technologies such as web science, bioenergy and plastic electronics. Cable commended its 'proven track record in bringing new ideas and technologies to market' and thought it would make a 'valuable contribution to the innovation landscape across the UK' (Groom, 2013*b*). But a key question was how his department could find core funding, at a time of continuing public expenditure cuts, in addition to its existing commitment for the Catapult centres. It looked like an odd case of backing two horses in mid-stream with a very rapid current. But he may have felt that he could not look this particular gift horse in the mouth.

Develop universities, especially newly-founded ones with non-traditional faculty structures and educational remits, to challenge conventional policy wisdom and to suggest radical new initiatives.

Universities are the places where planners and other urban professionals are educated. So they play a critical role in the successes and the failures of professional planners in the decades that follow. But the best universities can and should teach much more than professional competence: they should be the sources of radical new ideas that challenge the received wisdom. They should work side by side with focused research and development centres, like Max Planck and Fraunhofer, but with a different remit.

Germany provides the best examples, as seen in Chapter 7. In the former West

Germany, two new universities established at the start of the 1970s to provide a new source of economic growth and employment for old industrial cities with problems, Dortmund and Kassel, structured themselves on non-traditional lines, stressing unconventional approaches to intellectual problem-solving and novel solutions. In both, within less than two decades there were remarkable outcomes. Dortmund borrowed a model already developed in the Anglo-Saxon academic world – first at Stanford in California, then at Cambridge in England – creating a science park next door to its new campus in order to spin off university research into commercial applications. Kassel's professors developed a critical approach to conventional wisdom on the environment. Rapidly taking on board the teaching of European and American thinkers who were arguing that there were environmental limits to economic growth, they developed alternative policy prescriptions, especially in transport, which eventually culminated in the tram-train project.

But, interestingly, an older university – in fact one of Germany's oldest, Freiburg University – went exactly the same way at the same time. And, since this was a much smaller city where the university played a dominant political role, in effect the university captured the city; a young PhD rose to become mayor and worked to transform the city into a global model for sustainable urban growth, celebrated across the world. Finally, in Leipzig another venerable university quickly escaped from the shackles of communist orthodoxy to play a central role in rebuilding the cultural life of the city. Its circumstances, one could argue, were unusual. But in many other cities across Europe, universities have played a key role as urban catalyst. Small wonder that in the quest of Malmö to rebuild its economy after it lost its industrial base, a new technical university is playing a central role.

Generally, the new universities and polytechnics established in Britain in the 1960s and 1970s have not performed this vital role of urban catalyst. Nor did the older-established nineteenth-century civic universities in the great cities. Coventry did not follow Dortmund, Central Lancashire did not become another Kassel, Salford did not emulate Leipzig. Too often the new universities and polytechnics simply sought to compete with the older-established universities in traditional course structures and approaches. Centralized research funding, which emphasized traditional academic excellence at the expense of all else, actually encouraged this process after the polytechnics became universities in 1992. Only belatedly, in the 2013 REF (Research Excellence Framework) has the funding agency emphasized the impact that innovative research can have. It remains to be seen whether the result will be a British Dortmund or a Kassel.

Create new locally-based banks with a dedicated mission to fund local businesses and home ownership.

In many of the European model cities visited in Part Two, a key feature is the presence of local funding institutions, such as the German *Sparkasse* – or savings banks, over 1,000 in number with 13,000 branches, or the 420 local municipal banks. As well as assisting the German *Mittelstand* of small businesses, they make it much easier for private landlords or building groups (*Baugruppen*) to access funds for building new homes. In other European countries, too, there are national banks that specialize in funding infrastructure projects put forward by municipal and regional governments, such as the *Caisse des Dépôts et Consignations* (which, long ago, Louis Napoleon used to rebuild Paris). Many, such as the Swedish *Kommunbank* or the Dutch *BNG*, are effectively run by and for municipalities. Such institutions are better placed than distant Treasury officials to assess local demand, and thus the viability of projects. They can afford to develop the competence to assess both the projects and the borrowers. Their support can provide the sense of security needed by other investors, who want to avoid going it alone in fields they do not properly understand.

As with successful municipal investments in the past, such as Birmingham's Exhibition Centre, which was then used to underpin investment in the Convention Centre, it is important that local authorities bear part of the risk. If they are not supportive, investors will go where more confidence is being expressed. The American system of municipal bonds, while undoubtedly leading some cities into virtual bankruptcy, is also credited with helping many others to invest in projects such as Portland's tram system, the MAX (Metropolitan Area Express), which has helped the city to counter sprawl, apply European best practice, and encouraged a host of other cities to invest in tram projects.

But a major question arises. There is an upsurge of support in the UK for strong regional banks on the nineteenth-century model, when a commercial bank like the Midland or a mutual society like the Leeds Permanent or the Bradford and Bingley was the norm. And undoubtedly they would be closer to their customers, whether these were small businesses seeking finance to expand, or home buyers seeking a mortgage. But would they necessarily be more effective, or more efficient? The saga of failed German *Landesbanken* and Spanish *cajas* – both prominent among the casualties of 2007–2008 – is not reassuring. The report of the Independent Banking Commission (ICB), chaired by Sir John Vickers, shows that a significant proportion of the banks that suffered the largest proportionate losses in the 2007–2010 crisis were smaller European regional banks such as Dexia, a Franco-Belgian bank that had to be nationalized by the Belgian government, Hypo Real Estate, a Munich-based holding company for several German real estate banks, and various individual German *Landesbanken* (ICB, 2011, figure 4.11, p. 112).

The Spanish story is particularly chastening: Bankia, the bank that was at the centre of the Spanish state financial crisis of 2012, was itself founded to take over a host of regional *cajas* that had failed, leaving behind a record history of mismanagement: Caja Madrid, Bancaja from Valencia and smaller savings banks from the Canary Islands, Catalonia, Rioja and the towns of Avila and

Segovia in central Spain. They were typical of the *cajas* that accounted for half of Spain's banking system by assets before the crisis began. They began as regional businesses and were in most cases closely connected to politicians in the areas where they operated, so that Caja Madrid and Bancaja were influenced and run by the Popular party now in government. Above all, they were heavily exposed to property, having financed the homebuilding bonanza in the decade up to 2007 and lent freely to developers, construction companies and house buyers. One of the many investment bankers involved in the July 2011 market flotation of Bankia stated that 'Fifty per cent of the banking sector in Spain – which was the *cajas* – did not have the corporate governance or the management skills to withstand a crisis' (Mallet and Johnson, 2012). Bankia's fall not only exemplified all the political and managerial weaknesses of the Spanish financial system, it was also so large as to be 'systemically important'. Its failure would threaten the entire banking network and it was therefore 'too big to fail'. On 25 May 2012, José Ignacio Goirigolzarri, an experienced banker brought out of retirement to rescue Bankia, requested €19 billion in new emergency capital, on top of earlier state aid of €4.5 billion to help clean out bad loans. Bankia 'restated' its 2011 results to reflect a net loss of €3 billion instead of the reported net profit of €309 million (*Ibid.*).

The key therefore must be to devise a new structure for local banks, which avoids the record of mismanagement that has brought down such institutions elsewhere. The ICB report concluded that the UK banking system needed major reform. Most of its recommendations concerned macro-financial issues, not of direct concern to local urban development or regeneration. But some, concerning structural reform, are highly relevant. The most important was that by 2019 at the latest, retail banking should be ring-fenced from wholesale/ investment banking (ICB, 2011, p. 12). But this still left two related questions: should UK banking continue to be dominated by a very small number of big banks, or should it be required to deconcentrate? And should it continue to be dominated by for-profit commercial banks, rather than the mutual societies which historically played such a significant niche role in British banking, but which have been encouraged to turn themselves into commercial banks over the last quarter century?

On both these questions the Commission took a firm view – one which could significantly change the face of British banking. It concluded that there was a long-standing problem of insufficient competition in UK retail banking, stemming from a concentrated market structure and significant barriers to entry, coupled with poor conditions for consumer choice, particularly in the so-called Business Current Account (BCA) and Personal Current Account (PCA) markets (*Ibid.*, para. 7.66, pp. 197–198). It recommended specifically that the government should reach an agreement with the effectively nationalized Lloyds Banking Group (LBG) to create a new entity with a share of the PCA market of at least 6 per cent. (*Ibid.*, paras. 8.31–8.32, p. 214). The Commission also recommended that it should be made easier for small banks to enter and to compete effectively with the big ones, specifically by establishing a current account redirection service to smooth the process of switching current accounts for individuals and small businesses (*Ibid*., paras. 8.57–8.58, p. 221).

The Commission studiously refrained from commenting on the virtues of commercial banks versus mutual societies, save for one perhaps-significant paragraph:

> The precedent in building society legislation appears to provide a particularly good basis for the risk management functions of ring-fenced banks. Building society regulations have operated effectively for a long time. A number of former building societies failed in the crisis or were taken over as a result of poor business models, sometimes associated with their treasury-related activities. However, evidence to the Commission suggested that problems that occurred in the treasury function only did so following the lifting of the relevant restrictions after demutualization. In principle a ring-fenced bank should be able to undertake its necessary risk management within the building society regulatory framework, although the types of permitted instruments might need some extending given the wider range of services which may be provided by ring-fenced banks. (*Ibid*., para. 3.53, p. 60)

UK building societies originated in the eighteenth century: they had their heyday in the period from 1890 to 1980, when there were hundreds, many locally-based. But after a Building Societies Act of 1986, which allowed them to 'demutualize' if 75 per cent of their members voted in favour, many societies merged, the great majority of them demutualized, and were taken over by banks. By 1999 about two-thirds of their business had been demutualized; by 2011 the number of mutual societies had fallen to forty-seven. Ironically, after a quarter-century in which neither major political party had expressed any opposition to the process, in June 2012 Vince Cable publicly condemned their destruction, arguing that the existence of 1,000 building societies in the 1930s had created a 'virtuous circle' of more mortgage lending, thus promoting a wave of house building. He blamed the shortage of mortgage lending on the destruction of building societies, calling it 'one of the great acts of economic vandalism in modern times'. 'Demand has to be created, it does not emerge simultaneously. There is scope here to both create demand and solve a pressing supply need at the same time' (Treanor and Jowit, 2012). Almost immediately, the government proposed that the remaining building societies might be helped by a relaxation of rules to help them act as an important alternative to the big banks. They would be exempt from the Independent Commission for Banking proposals that would force banks to ring-fence retail and small business activities (Goff, 2012). This would meet popular demand. Since the start of 2012, Move Your Money UK (http://www.moveyourmoney.org.uk/) estimated that an average of 80,000 savers a month had been leaving the big banks – a total of almost half a million since the start of 2012 (Heather Stewart, *The Guardian*, 7 July 2012).

At that point came major news: the Co-operative Banking Group agreed in principle to acquire the so-called 'Verde' business of LBG, with 632 branches and an estimated 4.8 million customers, thus creating a major High Street bank with almost 1,000 branches, representing nearly 10 per cent of the UK bank network and 11 million customers – more than meeting the recommendation from the ICB. Subject to approval from the erstwhile Financial Services Authority (FSA), HM Treasury and the European Commission, the deal was expected to be complete before the end of November 2013. The Co-operative proudly proclaimed itself to offer a 'customer-centric, member-led, ethically driven, banking model'. Without the need to provide high shareholder returns, it could avoid risky trading in favour of simple products: mortgages and deposits. And, as part of a wider group that includes supermarkets and funeral parlours, the Co-op was committed to selling its products in a 'fair and honest way'. Its model – mutual ownership by its 7 million members – promoted loyalty. The week after the announcement saw a 25 per cent rise in its customers.[3] And the move was enthusiastically extolled by Vince Cable. In a major speech in September 2012, he announced that the government was working to set up a government-backed institution, currently in gestation, which 'could operate through alternative providers such as the new challenger banks like Handelsbanken, the Co-op and Aldermore and non-bank lenders boosting their lending capacity as well as corralling existing provision such as co-investment and guarantees to support business expansion'. The measure of the new institution's success, he said, would lie not merely in its own direct interventions, but also in how far it succeeded in shaking up the entire wider market in business finance, helping to ease constraints for high-growth firms.[4]

But it proved a false hope: in May 2013 came the dramatic announcement that the deal with Lloyds had collapsed. Concerned about the Co-op's lack of capital, Moodys, a credit-rating agency, downgraded the bank on 9 May. It then emerged that, buying the Britannia building society in 2009, with its large commercial real-estate portfolio and buy-to-let mortgages, it had acquired big risks. In 2012, its profits plunged from £54 million to a loss of £670 million. Ironically, it could not seek help from other parts of the group, its reserves of cash and capital were thin, and its model means it cannot speedily raise equity. At the end of 2012 it reported a capital ratio of 8.8 per cent, lower than all the big-four banks. 'In the end', *The Economist* commented, 'the Co-op turns out to be an old story: a British bank with too little capital that may need government support'.[5]

One particularly disappointed person was Vince Cable. Hearing the news of the collapse on a visit to Brazil, he commented:

> I think it is very disappointing. I was really hoping this would happen… We do need more competition and we need more diversity in business lending, and having the Co-op, a mutual, a new player in the small business lending, would have been a big step forward.[6]

The official Labour Party response, outlined by Ed Miliband immediately after the collapse, was close to Cable's vision: to establish a network of regional banks, based on the German model of community banks, to help small business get access to finance could reinvigorate and rebuild trust in the banking sector. Labour had already published plans for a British Investment Bank, focused on providing long-term funding for small and medium sized business, particularly start-ups. But the new proposal went further: a network of lenders in every major region of England, based on the German *Sparkassen* model, with a civic duty to promote local growth and lending only to local businesses. This remains the objective. Achieving it may not be easy, as both the Co-op collapse and the failure of some German *Sparkassen* illustrate. But, these cautions aside, it remains a vital foundation for a stronger German-style banking system focused on investing in local growth. A few past failures must not detract from the massive overall success of the German model.

Free the cities from the dead hand of Treasury control, fundamentally decentralize the structure of government so that it more closely resembles that in every other democratic country – including our European neighbours.

For too long, the great British cities have been tied to the apron strings of Whitehall and in particular the obsessive centralist traditions of the Treasury, creating by far the most centralized bureaucratic state in the Western world. Simon Jenkins has observed that:

> Unlike most countries of Europe, Britain has continued the steady centralisation of state power begun in the two world wars of the 20th century. Local participation in politics has declined and local democracy withered to an extent that baffles Germans or Americans. While the aggrandisement of the state is opposed by politicians out of power, it continues unchecked when they assume it. This is reflected in incessant measures to reorganise the NHS, criminal justice, local government, defence and education, each one increasing the size and cost of government. (Jenkins 2012*b*)

This simply does not happen in the other countries of Western Europe. There, cities have autonomy in policy-making and detailed management of their own affairs, accompanied by significant local sources of public finance that make them partly independent of higher (national or regional) levels of government. Some countries, such as Germany and Austria, established Federal systems of government in their constitutions after World War Two. Others, such as Spain, developed systems of autonomous regions, with considerable local devolution, later on. Interestingly, in all these cases local autonomy came as a reaction to life under totalitarian regimes. In extreme cases, as in the cases of Hamburg and Berlin, this was because cities were constituent *Länder* within the German Federal system of government, enjoying the same rights and powers as Bavaria or

Nordrhein-Westfalen. But other cities lacking this exalted status, such as Leipzig or Kassel, nonetheless were guaranteed autonomous powers by the constitution, accompanied by independent sources of government. In one extreme case, the *Ruhrgebiet*, the State government of Nordrhein-Westfalen took the initiative in setting up the Emscher Park IBA (International Building Exhibition) and created a management structure for it in the form of a Development Company, but notably this company had no powers or funds of its own and depended entirely on its ability to win cooperation from the constituent cities.

Likewise, in non-federal countries like the Netherlands, Denmark or Sweden, the cities enjoy considerable autonomy in their management, though they are also involved in communal organizations covering a wider area, discussed below. In the Netherlands the national government in The Hague set up the VINEX programme but then implemented it in close cooperation with the municipalities – not an easy task, since outside the limits of the big cities most municipalities are small and many of the developments involved cooperation between two or more of them, a painstaking and time-consuming process. However, in all these cases the end-result was the creation of strong dedicated agencies to carry forward the planning and development process.

Another factor, in Spain and in Belgium, was nationalist pressure from regions that demanded almost complete autonomy, if not downright secession, from a central state – pressure that has of course been paralleled, and partly recognized, in the United Kingdom. But the most interesting case is that of France.

Historically, the British in particular have always regarded France as the most extreme example of a centralized state in Europe: *La France est une République indivisible, laïque, démocratique et sociale* as the constitution of the Fifth Republic put it in 1958. True, this also stipulated that the county's organization was 'decentralized', but this was barely observable in practice: the myth was that, by Napoleonic decree, every school in France taught the same lesson at the same time. That may never have been true, and it was the arch-centralizer Charles de Gaulle, author of the Fifth Republic, who in 1962 famously complained 'How can you govern a country which has 246 varieties of cheese?' (Mignon, 1962). But France fundamentally recast its system of government in 1982, under President François Mitterrand. The *Loi Deferre* abolished the Napoleonic system whereby centrally-appointed *préfets* had controlled their departments and regions (the *tutelle administrative a priori*), transferring prefectural powers to new elected assemblies and their chairs. Importantly, with this went a significant transfer of tax revenues.

No such reform ever took place in the UK. 'Britain's provincial cities', Simon Jenkins writes,

> have been weak links in the chain of revival from deindustrialisation. Their lack of mandated
> champions, the absence of clearly accountable leaders, has enabled central government to

deaden their enterprise. Police forces, schools and colleges, hospitals and clinics, social services – locally accountable in most of Europe – have become elephantine nationalised industries, with all the brittle bureaucracy and inefficiency that implies. (Jenkins, 2012*a*)

Opponents of decentralization, he notes,

> … always deploy catch-22. Local politicians are not up to scratch, they say. They cannot be trusted with discretion, let alone over local taxes. As a result, ever more power must be taken from them, their quality worsens and fewer people vote for them, stripping them of any claim to more power. This is the vicious circle of the democratic deficit. Councils become agencies of nationalised services, and MPs and police chiefs become de facto mayors. Ministers must answer in parliament for why a patient is sent home from hospital after midnight. (*Ibid.*)

The Treasury mandarins might of course adduce the example of the seventeen Spanish autonomous regions, faced in 2012 with accumulated debts and excluded from financial markets. In July 2012 Valencia became the first to request formal aid from Madrid, which at the time was desperately trying to limit total public spending in order to counter a rise in Spanish 10-year bond yields above a sustainable 7 per cent level (in which, by year's end, it had succeeded). Though thirteen of the regions agreed to caps on spending at a meeting in Madrid in August, two of the biggest, Catalonia and Andalucía, did not. Catalonia, the biggest contributor to Spain's economy and its most indebted region, was required to keep its debt burden within a limit of 22.81 per cent of GDP in 2012 and 23.6 per cent in 2013, but flatly declined even to attend the meeting to agree the limits. Clearly, this is not an outcome any UK government could face with equanimity. But the Spanish case is special: as Emilion Gonzalez, Professor of Structural Economics at the Autonomous University of Madrid, puts it, 'This isn't a decentralization; it's a reproduction of the model of the central state in the seventeen regions', producing – for example – fifty-six autonomous public universities where twelve or fourteen should suffice (Anon, 2012).

The answer, of course, is to devise structures of regional and local autonomy that specifically prohibit such outcomes from emerging. No one might want to follow the example of many American states, whose constitutions forbid any kind of counter-cyclical debit financing. But Germany, where both Federal and state government deficits have specific limits, could clearly provide an acceptable model to follow.

This was the main burden of Michael Heseltine's report, *No Stone Unturned*, published in October 2012 (Heseltine, 2012). 'With central government reserving for itself the power to make the vast majority of economic decisions – creating itself as a functional monopoly – local authorities have been relegated to service providers', Heseltine said. And, 'as Whitehall has taken more powers so its distrust of local decision makers has increased … the involvement of local business people in the governance of their communities has dwindled, and their energy and innovation has been lost' (*Ibid.*, para. 2.4). The Whitehall monopoly, he went on, 'is dysfunctional on two counts': too many decisions are taken in London without a real understanding of the particular, and differing, circumstances of the communities affected; and, 'with responsibilities divided up between policy departments, no one in government is tasked to look holistically at the full range of issues facing a particular area' (*Ibid.*, para. 2.5). Therefore, he concluded, 'We need to brigade the separate funding streams which support the building blocks of growth into a single funding pot for local areas... These include significant parts of the skills, infrastructure, employment support, housing, regeneration and business support budgets held by central government' (*Ibid.*, para. 2.29). If the government had used this approach for the current spending review period, he calculated, the total funding available would have been approximately £49 billion (*Ibid.*, para. 2.30). And:

> competitive funding is key to unleashing the entrepreneurial spirit in local areas. It injects a surge of excitement and incentivises communities to seek a wider and much more ambitious vision to anything they had thought of before. A healthy rivalry between areas comes into play. (*Ibid.*, para. 2.33)

But what are these areas? Heseltine goes on to make a further key recommendation:

> Matching LEPs [Local Enterprise Partnerships] to functional economic market areas is vital as it ensures that the full range of barriers to growth in a local economy is considered together. It ensures that each LEP is in the best position to identify and align local action to support growth. (*Ibid.*, para. 2.56)

He even supports the recommendation of the Redcliffe-Maud Commission, in 1969 for unitary authorities across more of England, based on the new LEP geography (*Ibid.*, para. 2.77), with conurbation-wide mayors where localities wanted this (*Ibid.*, Recommendation 15).

Nearly six months later, the government proudly proclaimed that it was accepting the overwhelming majority – 81 out of 89 – of his recommendations. Specifically, from 2015, it would create a new Single Local Growth Fund to include the key economic levers of skills, housing and transport funding, with competition through a local Growth Deal with every Local Enterprise Partnership (LEP), 'with the allocation of the Single Local Growth Fund reflecting the quality of their ideas and local need'. But details were left to the summer 2013 Spending Review – where George Osborne promptly shrank the pot from £49 to £2 billion. And the government said it expected that every LEP would receive something, but also warned that less developed LEPs – or those without 'effective governance and joint working across the LEP area' – would have to work within 'central controls on how the single local growth fund can be spent'. A return to Redcliffe-Maud was one proposal that got firmly scotched – but the Treasury indicated that it would look for LEPs to create a combined authority, and stated that it would bring forward legislation to allow directly elected conurbation mayors to be created where an area wanted to do so.

Cities working cooperatively (often through strong political leaders) with neighbouring local authorities, either formally or informally, for strategic planning and transport across entire city-regions. Strong city-region administrations with independent financing, not dependent on central government subventions, to build urban infrastructure, especially transport infrastructure providing the critical accessibility to unlock new development or regeneration opportunities.

It is evident almost at first sight that virtually all of the best-practice case-study places have enjoyed heavy investment in infrastructure, including streets and sewers and services, in advance of housing construction. In particular, as already underlined, top-quality public transport investment has taken place well in advance of demand, thus long before it would be justified in a conventional cost-benefit analysis. This, clearly, has been an article of policy for these cities. It represents a radically different approach from the narrow economic calculations employed in the United Kingdom and some other countries. In France, for instance, tramway investments are made not merely to improve accessibility, but also as part of a general programme of investment in the urban public realm (CETE Nord Picardie, 2011). And this has had measurable results.

The Core Cities Group (CCG) and British Property Federation (BPF) have pointed out that the UK ranks only thirty-fourth in the world for its infrastructure, behind Saudi Arabia and Malaysia, and sixth amongst the G8 countries. A mere 1.5 per cent of UK GDP is spent on infrastructure compared to 6 per cent in Japan and 3 per cent in France, resulting in France having 20 per cent greater productivity despite its less flexible labour markets (Core Cities and BRF, 2010). In other European countries, notably Germany and France, many more cities have invested more heavily in tramway systems than in the UK (though, as said earlier, in Germany, the explanation is that cities never scrapped them whereas in France, they were removed and reinstated), and rail-based public transport (rail, metro and tram) in those countries recorded huge gains in patronage during the period, to levels exceeding those in the UK.[7]

The cases of Montpellier, Lille and Strasbourg, in Chapter 9, demonstrate that during the 1990s and 2000s strong city mayors used the mechanism of the *Communauté Urbaine*, established in French law as early as 1966 but not used vigorously in early years, to establish strategic pacts with smaller neighbouring *communes* in order to pursue transport and urban regeneration strategies that benefited the entire city-region. Invariably these involved strengthening the nodal position of the central city by extending the national TGV network to serve either the existing station or a new dedicated TGV station, which in turn became a hub for regional train services and city-regional tramway systems (and, in Lille, a new Metro). In turn these invariably triggered large-scale development around the new hub but also at other key locations within the city-region. These mayors thus used their political clout but also their persuasive powers to bind together *communes*, hitherto often mutually suspicious, in pacts that brought new growth to the entire region. They could have not done so without the powers that the 1966 reform gave them. But the most interesting and relevant point is that these powers were in an important sense passive and permissive. They were waiting for the right moment and the right person to invoke them.

The tram-train networks in Karlsruhe and Kassel, discussed in Chapters 7 and 9, were inevitably more complex to bring into being, since they involved a difficult technical and administrative set of agreements between cities and their local tram systems, on the one hand, and the national rail system, Deutsche Bahn, on the other. Further, each was based on a regional transport network (*Verkehrsverein*) that had already been created to coordinate services and fares across a wide region within the catchment area of the central city – itself no mean achievement. They also involved the cooperation of a number of local government units – cities and counties – that fortunately had been reorganized some years earlier to create larger and more coherent units. This unique experience will undoubtedly prove useful to cities in other countries across Europe, which are now planning to develop similar networks.

There is an obvious application to the UK, which has long suffered from under-investment in infrastructure, not only because much of the infrastructure is ageing, and needs to be modernized, but also because of the implications of reducing carbon emissions to comply with government commitments. But private investors are interested only in completed schemes with proven returns. In 2012 came belated recognition of the problem from the government. Following provisions in the 2012 Budget, in July 2012 the then-Cities Minister Greg Clark announced City Deals with England's eight core cities: Greater Birmingham and Solihull, Bristol and the West of England, Greater Manchester, Leeds City-region, Liverpool City-region, Nottingham, Newcastle and Sheffield City-region. In February 2013 deals were signed with another twenty authorities. The deals pass new powers to city-regions in return for setting ambitious targets and addressing governance issues, including the pooling of various investment streams into a single capital pot. The 2012 Budget provided up to £150 million, available from 2013–2014, for larger scale projects in Core Cities to be financed through Tax Increment Financing (TIF), a device successfully used in the United States since the 1950s – originally for urban renewal, latterly for a variety of purposes including housing, urban revitalization, and economic development - allowing local authorities to borrow against future growth in business rates (Anon, 2013; Sear, 2012; Dye and Merriman, 2006, p. 18).

In the UK, the Core Cities Group and the British Property Federation, which have both campaigned for TIFs, have pointed out that the Treasury may enjoy wider fiscal benefits from a TIF scheme: higher stamp duty revenues resulting from rising property values, higher income and corporate tax revenues due to more economic activity, and lower health, security and benefits costs as the community enjoys the social benefits of regeneration. The full increased revenue from business rates in the designated area will also be available to the Treasury after the funding cost for the infrastructure has been paid off (Core Cities and BRF, 2010).

The model, already announced ahead of the 2012 Budget, came from Greater Manchester and involved a variation on TIF known as 'earn-back'. Greater Manchester's ten councils will create a 'Revolving Infrastructure Fund', allowing the consortium to 'earn back' a portion of additional business rates, over and above that allowed by the forthcoming reform of local government finance – up to £30 million a year – allowing it to invest £1.2 billion in improving infrastructure such as transport, on a payment-by-results basis. Most of this up-front £1.2 billion initial investment will be raised by the councils through prudential borrowing against business rate revenues and a levy on those authorities. In return, the government has committed in principle to allowing a maximum of £30 million a year to be 'earned back' from the Treasury over a 30-year period, the precise amount each year to be determined by the city's 'growth performance' linked to changes in rateable values of commercial properties across the city-region. The 'earned back' funds will be reinvested in further infrastructure improvements with schemes in the Greater Manchester Transport Fund, including the Metrolink tram extension to Trafford Park, first in line for investment.[8]

Greg Clark – by now elevated to become Chief Financial Secretary to the Treasury – quoted an estimate from the eight cities that over the next 20 years the eight deals would create 175,000 jobs and 37,000 new apprenticeships.[9] Sir Bob Kerslake, head of the home civil service, said the government had tried to pursue a 'city-region approach' in the deals. One will see the Leeds city-region join Greater Manchester in establishing a combined authority, in return for a 10-year funding allocation for transport in the city with money paid upfront. Eight authorities in the Sheffield city-region also want to form a combined authority and have begun a formal process. Newcastle is looking further to take steps towards forming a North East Combined Authority.

Later, the government would undertake to promote new and farther-ranging deals including rural areas as well as urban areas (Drillsma-Milgrom, 2012). This is significant because unless the deal can be extended outside the eight core city-regions, the real danger is that a new regional imbalance will emerge: within each region, between the cores and the rest.

An associated and deeper problem is that since the TIFs are based only on anticipated rises in business rates, they ignore the much wider uplift that could come from residential development. Quite apart from all the problems that arise from the reluctance of successive governments to revalue residential property, this means that local authorities wanting to promote residential development – whether in outer South East England where demand for new housing is greatest, or in northern seaside resorts that could benefit from better rail connections to key business centres like Manchester or Leeds – will be unable to join in the resulting value uplift. The obvious remedy would be to extend the scheme over time to include residential value uplift.

But there is, of course, a more fundamental objection still: that, like previous schemes from UK governments, it essentially depends on borrowing from future revenue to pay for current expenditure. The attraction is that it does not add to the total of current government capital expenditure. The snag is that eventually, however long deferred, the expenditure has to be paid for. Other European countries, that are not afraid to spend serious government money to improve their national infrastructure, do not suffer from this strange British inhibition. It remains a question as to why the UK remains the odd man out. The Heseltine review has challenged this orthodoxy head-on – but, interestingly, this is one of the few recommendations which the government has effectively rejected. The long battle for city-regional government, going back to the tragic failure to implement Redcliffe-Maud, is not yet won.

Ensure release of sufficient housing land, in parcels of sufficient size and with already-developed master plans, at a fair price, for immediate development.

As seen in Chapter 3, since the 2007–2008 crisis UK housing construction, already inadequate to meet existing and projected demand, has plummeted to unprecedentedly low levels. But better access to housing finance, to kick-start stalled housing schemes, will not in itself work and may perversely have contrary effects. George Osborne's 2013 budget prominently featured a 'Help to Buy' scheme, to run until 2017, with two elements - an 'equity loan' scheme, whereby new or existing homeowners who are able to raise a 5 per cent deposit can borrow up to a further 20 per cent from the government interest-free and a new mortgage guarantee of up to 15 per cent on homes worth up to £600,000. As commentators – culminating in no less than the outgoing Bank of England governor Sir Mervyn King, and a visiting high-level delegation from the International Monetary Fund – pointed out, it carried a clear risk: that, with housebuilding at the lowest peacetime level for eighty years, the incentives would bring a surge in demand that would meet a fixed supply, leading to the obvious outcome: a price surge.

And this would be felt with particular force in and around London. The latest survey, from analysts Hometrack, shows that though nationally house prices rose by 0.3 per cent in March 2013 – the highest growth since March 2010 – the major driver was London where prices rose by 0.7 per cent in the month, followed by the South East and East Anglia. Thus the big risk is not the outcome feared by the CPRE, the rumble of nearby concrete mixers, but that they will remain silent as house prices remain out of reach for first-time buyers. As King commented, 'This scheme is a little too close for comfort to a general scheme to guarantee mortgages. We had a very healthy mortgage market with competing lenders attracting borrowers before the [financial] crisis, and we need to get back to that healthy mortgage market'.[10] Any stimulus to the demand side must be accompanied by an equally significant increase in supply.

Cities in other European countries evidently manage their urban development better than British cities. But that is not because they have more stringent powers of regulation or land ownership. Swedish planning powers were modelled on the UK 1947 Town and Country Planning Act, and contain the same basic provision that no development can occur in contradiction of a current town plan. Stockholm once had huge land reserves within the city limits and beyond, in the wider region, but it is now running out of land: it is now too expensive to buy more. The Swedish capital's role is changing from developer to that of an intermediary with private developers who invest in infill projects, ensuring that redevelopment protects the public interest. Dutch property laws are similar to British ones, and the great majority of all land in and around Dutch cities is privately owned.[11]

Indeed the best-practice model cities in Part Two tended to represent special cases. Hammarby resulted from an agreement between the city and the private owners. Vauban and Rieselfeld represented brownfield sites that the city of Freiburg either owned or could buy from the state. Generally, planners in these cities work with similar powers and similar constraints to their UK counterparts.

In the UK, David Lock has reviewed the long and extremely dreary history of successive attempts by government, ever since the historic 1947 Town and Country Planning Act, to capture development value uplift for the public purse (Lock, 2012). The latest attempt is the Community Infrastructure Levy (CIL) but, he comments, 'the way it is being calculated locally seems highly variable and politically contentious' (*Ibid.*, p. 14). And local experiments like the Milton Keynes tariff 'have not taken root nationally or been subject to public examination' (*Ibid.*). This is connected indirectly to another major issue: the 'stuck sites', properly allocated reserves of development land that have not been developed. Though no one can say for sure that developers are holding land banks in the expectation that values will rise, 'it is obvious that there is no need for developers to rush to build on some sites' (*Ibid.*).

Lock poses two answers to the problem. One, a left-of-centre government is elected and moves to compulsorily purchase development land as a matter of course, coupled critically with a change in the compensation law to wipe out 'hope value'. 'Compulsory purchase based at the value of its existing use', he writes, 'would be the predictable socialistic destiny' (*Ibid.*). The radical right-of-centre alternative would be for a local planning authority to state how much development land it needed, set down locational criteria and invite bids from developers: an 'auction' of development rights (*Ibid.*). This is the proposal of Tim Leunig, Reader in Economic History at the London School of Economics and a radical right-of-centre policy advisor, who suggests that councils would evaluate sealed bids on the basis of both the offer price – in particular, the gap between the offer price and the value with planning permission – and standard good planning principles. The gain would pass to the local authority and its citizens in the form of lower local taxes or better services. Leunig asserts that around Cambridge, one of the country's hottest development spots, the gain could be as much as £1 million per household (Branson, 2012, p. 18).

Lock suggests that there is a third way: John Walker, former Chief Executive of the Commission for the New Towns, has proposed that councils come together with landowners or developers to form strategic land and development companies. They would bring forward sites on a joint venture basis, with both sides sharing the risks and the rewards. Lock suggests that clever landowners and developers, faced with more radical solutions, will be highly motivated to join with councils in such bodies (Lock, 2012, p. 15).

These suggestions are not mutually exclusive: they could be combined in different variations. But a central problem for all of them – and also a potential solution – is hope value: the additional value, over and above the value of land in its existing use, that developers are willing to pay in the expectation that they might win planning permission for its development. Lock himself has bitter personal experience of how this forced the Milton Keynes Development Corporation, and the bodies that developed the second generation of new towns in the 1960s, to pay far more for compulsory purchase of the land than their predecessors who built the first generation new towns in the 1950s – simply because the owners of the land were able to claim that development would have happened here anyway, new town or no new town. This was a monstrous perversion of the central provision of the 1947 Act: that all values arising from the development of land were nationalized, and indeed compensation was paid to owners for lost development values. The Conservatives rescinded this provision in 1954, but not for new towns and similar major developments – hence the constant war of attrition, during the 1960s and 1970s, by landowners who argued that they should be compensated because they had paid hope value.

The drastic answer is surely to return to the central principle of the 1947 Act: all development value accrues to the state, and no hope value is payable. But this could be interestingly combined with an incentive: landowners could be free to reach deals with local authorities up to some appointed day, for instance one year after the passage of legislation. After that local authorities would assume control, and offer packages of land with full planning permission at auction on land already master planned (the Dutch principle), or alternatively develop themselves or in partnership with a selected developer on terms reached by agreement. The underlying principle throughout would be that after this appointed day, developers could continue to make reasonable profits from the development process, but not from land speculation.

Strong city planning departments (or city agencies) with real planning powers and a willingness to take a positive lead, particularly in developing overall master plans as a framework for development or regeneration of specific areas. Planners equipped with real competence across all aspects of their profession. Willingness, even eagerness, on the part of these departments or agencies to engage with the private sector, or with citizen groups, in the subsequent detailed development process. But they do so from a position of strength through their control of the master planning process.

This, without doubt, is the most important single conclusion to come from the places we visited on our Grand Tour. Whether the precise agent is the city planning department (as in Stockholm or Freiburg) or a dedicated public agency (as in Hamburg, Leipzig or the Dutch VINEX developments), the key to success is a well-staffed and well-led planning office with a dedication to the task and the professional competence to draw up master plans and engage in complex arrangements for implementation with the private sector and with community groups. In every successful case, the detailed case studies show that from the start the public agency took the lead: it drew up a master plan, usually in considerable detail as to layout of streets and buildings and open spaces – even down to the detailed height and massing of individual building blocks – before inviting private or communal agencies to make their proposals for detailed development of individual elements. The result can be clearly seen in all these cases: it is the coherence and elegance of the three-dimensional plan for the entire development, within which other agencies may make significant variations in detail – for instance in the façades of buildings, producing extraordinary variety within uniformity.

But it does require continuity of personnel and of purpose, over years and sometimes – as in Freiburg – over decades. The best cities, like Stockholm and Freiburg, have offices staffed by planners equipped with real competence across all aspects of their profession, from urban design to project finance. They are thus able to take a positive lead in every aspect of the planning process, from overall city strategy through detailed urban design to negotiation with the private sector. They are confident in taking the lead in the process, because they know their business.

This does not at all mean that the process is one of centralist top-down public control. The city planning office, or its deputed agency, has to be aware of the ultimate commercial viability of the planning scheme and its individual parts. This is vital because the city will have invested very large amounts of public money in the basic infrastructure – transport, water and sewerage, flood control – that must precede the development. If it proves that the expectations are wrong, the city must be able and willing to modify the process. This is particularly true, because inner-city regeneration involves attracting new residents back into areas that they have long deserted for the suburbs. They may surprise the planners, when for instance – as in Hammarby – parents with young children express a new willingness to live in the city.

There is no reason at all why this model should not be followed in British cities. As already emphasized, the legal powers are essentially similar. And, in the most celebrated cases – the reconstruction of the East End of London in the 1950s and 1960s by the former London County Council, using powers of comprehensive development, or the construction of twenty-eight new towns between the mid-1940s and the early 1990s, including such notable examples as Stevenage, Harlow, Peterborough and Milton Keynes – a similar model was followed as in the examples in this book, with similarly creditable results. But lamentably, the competence of the average UK planner is less than it was half a century ago, in that golden age of British planning. In 1967, the peak year for housing completions in the UK, planners were busy at work on regional plans for the South East and the West Midlands and the North West, starting Milton Keynes and Peterborough and Telford and several other new towns, and were beginning the first sub-regional plans based on the new systems planning methods. The government had a vast phalanx of professional planners embedded in the precursor of today's CLG. It was, in retrospect, the high water mark of a belief in a total, centralized, top-down, expertly-based but also benign planning. Afterwards, British planning went on a long downward slide. While knowledge of such vital aspects as urban design and real estate development was widespread in UK planning half a century ago, it has largely dissipated. Rather remarkably, the average qualified planner has no competence in urban design and is not equipped for the delicate and vital task of arguing with a prospective developer about the figures in the latter's spreadsheet and the basis for them. It is lamentable, but the truth, that British planners have lost the art of urbanism. They could not achieve a Hammarby or a Vauban or an Ypenburg without enlisting an army of consultants. Planning education needs to restore these areas of competence, through a broad-based general education coupled with deeper specialist understanding, if it is to take the lead again.

Planning has survived, as it has before. There are local plans and there is a planning process. And the new National Planning Policy Framework may achieve what previous prescriptions have failed to achieve, and what the expert inquiries have called for: a planning system that achieves a due balance between the need for development and the need for conservation. Time will tell. But meanwhile we are a very long way away from the bright confident world of the late 1960s when the planning system led the process. Planning and planners have been residualized into a purely passive role. And that stands in stark contrast to the models we have seen on our tours in the places that have got it right. We once led the world in the art of intelligent planning, but now we are sadly diminished.

It is not that we lack the powers: it is that we have lost the will, and with it the energy and the competence that once made British planning the envy of the world. Once, other Europeans came to us to discover how to plan good cities; now we go to them. But there is no reason at all why we should not repeat the trick again. We should be asking how the Aire Valley eco-town in Leeds could become an English Hammarby Sjöstad, or the Cambridge region could use its Bus Rapid Transit to produce a bus-based version of the Kassel Regio Tram, with a series of small eco-towns connected by excellent public transport, or Luton and its region could use its new BRT network to reproduce the pattern of new settlements linking The Hague and Rotterdam.

Indeed, we should be considering the device the Germans invented early in the twentieth century and have so successfully employed in Berlin and then in the Emscher Park: the International Building Exhibition (*Internationale Bauausstelling*, IBA). This is a tradition, little known in the United Kingdom – there is no English entry in Wikipedia – which produced the remarkable Hansaviertel in Berlin in 1957, followed in Berlin in 1977–1987 by a decade-long IBA that took a radically new line, rejecting comprehensive modernist destruction-plus-redevelopment for a more sensitive approach of 'careful urban renewal' and 'critical reconstruction', seeking to recreate the qualities that had made the old city so liveable. This approach proved immensely influential over the years that followed, both in the reunified Berlin and in other German cities like Kassel. The latest, IBA Heidelberg (2012–2020), will focus on the relationship of knowledge and urban development, establishing a ten-year laboratory to explore the implications of the knowledge society for European cities. Managed by a local agency, financed by local government but independent from it, it will be located on the former headquarters of the US army in Germany, and an inner-city railway yard (Kunzmann, 2013). The UK has never adopted an IBA approach, with one outstanding exception: Lansbury, the first neighbourhood in London's East End to be rebuilt after wartime destruction, was part of the 1951 Festival of Britain celebration (albeit completed a year late). The UK badly needs to recapture and re-celebrate that example, showcasing a new generation of British urban design.

Work to achieve a broader policy framework that will allow and encourage these policies to happen.

This is the hard part, because the most contentious. Coming out of the fiscal crisis of 2007–2008, a host of new books has appeared advocating governments worldwide to adopt radical changes in economic policy, running quite counter to the currents that have dominated the Western world since the 1980s: in particular, they propose Keynesian counter-cyclical public spending during the present period of recession, and a return to the much more egalitarian distribution of income that characterized western economies during the 1950s and 1960s (Krugman, 2012; Wapshott, 2011; Lansley, 2011; Skidelsky and Skidelsky, 2012;

Stiglitz, 2012). They illustrate, if nothing else, the truth that economics is not an objective science like physics; the old name that David Ricardo[12] gave it, *Political Economy*, is more apposite. But, confusingly, it is not just a matter of conflicting ideologies: these books also demonstrate that it is possible to adduce evidence as to whether it is better in recessions to cut or to expand public expenditure, or whether being richer makes people feel happier.

Much of their content is some way from the central theme of this book, except in the sense that everything is in some way related to everything else. But not entirely: the policies advocated in this final chapter are by definition political, and they do relate more than incidentally to the wider framework of economic and social policies that governments set for themselves in different countries and at different times. Specifically, it is difficult to separate the qualities of the best places in this book from a certain bundle of political philosophies that have been immensely influential in mainland European counties since World War Two, but whose origins go back before that. Outstanding among these was the *social market economy*, described by the Skidelskys as 'The chief secular fruit of Catholic social theory' (Skidelsky and Skidelsky, 2012, p. 187).

> Developed by a group of anti-Nazi intellectuals in the 1940s, its main purpose was to rebuild a heavily cartelized, shattered and compromised German economy on the basis of family businesses, thus securing the goal of dispersed ownership of assets, which was seen as an indispensible condition of freedom. Stiff inheritance taxes would ensure just initial conditions for all, 'co-determination' of employers and workers in large plants and at national level was needed to ensure the trust of all strata. These ideas were endorsed first by the Christian Democrats in 1948, then by the Social Democrats in 1959. The theory of the social market economy helped shape the social model of the European Union. (Skidelsky and Skidelsky, 2012, p. 188)

This has a parallel, they show, in the Protestant world with the secular 'New Liberalism', developed in the UK before World War One, and with Social Democracy, an offshoot which 'added a strong egalitarian commitment to New Liberalism in a "mixed economy" of private and public sectors. With many variations on the basic model, it found political homes in Britain, France, Italy and Scandinavia' (Skidelsky and Skidelsky, 2012, p. 190). In 1991, in his influential book *Capitalisme contre Capitalisme*, the French economist and banker Michel Albert characterized this model as 'Rhineland capitalism' in opposition to the Anglo-Saxon Reago-Thatcherite free-market model (Albert, 1993). Since then, of course, in all these European countries these distinctive socio-political philosophies have been strongly influenced by the political tide in favour of free-market solutions (Wooldridge, 2013). But, as compared with the UK and the USA, it is possible to see clearly that they have remained strongly influential as basic assumptions about the very basis of social relations. And it is impossible to ignore the influence on such developments as Hammarby, Västra Hamnen,

Ypenburg or Vauban. It might be possible to imitate such models while totally ignoring the spirit that helped bring them into being. But it would be a thankless task, and most likely an unprofitable one.

What Can We Learn?

The lessons are clear because they are so consistent – sometimes almost uncannily so – from country to country and from city to city. Europe's leading best-practice cities have triumphantly rediscovered the lost art of urbanism. So have cities elsewhere in the world, not visited in this book for lack of space. Their lessons are freely available – at least, to those prepared to read, to visit and to see. The harder part may be to apply them.

Harder, because deeply entrenched administrative structures and cultural traditions get in the way. Other countries have had similar obstacles, but have worked hard to remove them. We need to learn from them.

There are six outstanding final messages. They represent a kind of non-party political agenda for urban regeneration in the United Kingdom – and, some of them, perhaps for other countries too. They are:

1. *Free the cities.* For too long, the great British cities have been tied to the apron strings of Whitehall and in particular the obsessive centralist traditions of the Treasury, creating by far the most centralized bureaucratic state in the Western world. The overwhelmingly important first conclusion is that *cities must be allowed to grow up and earn their own livings, independent of Treasury pocket money.*

2. *Goad city leaders to grow city-regions.* In the largest and densest conurbations, cities by themselves cannot do the job. They need to cooperate, French style, to plan and invest across entire city-regions. London provides the outstanding model in all of Europe. Small wonder that its economic trajectory soars endlessly, removing it ever farther from the melancholy state of the rest of urban England. Emulation is the answer.

3. *Invest adequately in urban transport and urban quality* on the French model. Tramways in the larger cities, BRT networks in the smaller ones, should be under construction across the country, accompanied by small-scale urban improvements that cost relatively little but achieve a big effect in urban imagery and urban place marketing. The coming campaign for a European infrastructure investment programme, centrepiece of a Keynesian counter-cyclical economic programme that has been delayed for far too long, will provide the critical opportunity.

4. *Establish (or relocate) state-financed research institutes,* whether or not associated with universities, in key locations within those regions most needing economic

regeneration. Following the German model, these should include both funda-mental research institutes and other centres, in association with private capital, for applying research results to commercial innovation.

5. *Recast universities* to make them agents of technical and cultural change, on the German model. It should not be difficult to do: Germany has been doing it for two hundred years. The polytechnic tradition, brilliantly invented by Tony Crosland in 1965 but then scandalously allowed to wither and then even more woefully to be swept away by John Major in 1992, needs to be rediscovered and reconfirmed.

6. *Create (or recreate) regional and local banks, motivated not by speculative profit but by the desire to serve their local entrepreneurs and housebuilders, through provision of capital for sound new enterprises.* Despite the massively emblematic failure of the Co-operative takeover of the retail functions of the Lloyds Banking Group, this remains a major objective shared by the Labour Party and at least some key members of the Coalition.

7. *Create new forms of housing tenure* to supplement and provide an alternative to those now available. In particular, rediscover the co-partnership tenancy movement that was so outstandingly successful in creating garden cities and garden suburbs in the decade before World War One, but which was then destroyed by the dead hand of the Treasury. Use these new forms to create a new generation of garden suburbs within easy reach of the great cities, connected to them by convenient public transport, on the Dutch VINEX model.

8. *Work to achieve a broader policy framework that will allow and encourage these policies to happen.* More contentiously, develop changes in economic policy, based on expansionary deficit funding in times of recession and, even more fundamentally, a return to a more egalitarian distribution of income: a return to the principles of the social market economy in Germany and of Social Democracy in Britain, France, Italy and Scandinavia during the 1950s and 1960s.

The models are there before our eyes. We merely need to remove the blinkers that are obscuring them, and to clear our minds for forging fresh solutions. But in doing so, we need constantly to keep in mind one central caution. As Ebenezer Howard wrote at the foot of his famous diagram of Social City, the group of Slumless Smokeless Cities,

A DIAGRAM ONLY. PLAN MUST DEPEND ON SITE SELECTED.

Yes, Hammarby Sjöstad could provide a model for an in-town eco-town in the Aire Valley in Leeds. And yes, Vauban and Rieselfeld could be inspirations for sustainable extensions to Northampton or Peterborough. And yes again, Ypenburg and other Dutch VINEX extensions could inspire new urban clusters in Thames Gateway and elsewhere. But never precisely: the geographical circumstances will never be precisely the same. And this is above all true when we take into consideration the critical factor of regional spatial scale. There is no urban area in Europe that remotely compares with the South East England Mega-City Region. The equivalent area in France, the Paris Basin, is larger in area but most of the small towns within it have minimal functional connection with Paris; in fact, as the geographer Ludovic Halbert has demonstrated, the real functional Paris is a relatively minute area embracing the historic city and its near suburbs including the five contiguous new towns started in the 1960s (Hall and Pain 2006). The nearest comparison is with Randstad Holland (Chapter 10), but even here the central cities (Amsterdam, The Hague, Rotterdam, Utrecht) are tiny compared with London and the so-called Green Heart does not present the same absolute spatial constraint to urban extensions as does London's Green Belt. So the most popular formulae that have emerged here – urban extensions at the ends of short tramlines, whether on urban brownfield or new greenfield – cannot easily be applied in the London case. For good or ill, the vast polycentric urban complex that is South East England has evolved over 70 years, since the Abercrombie 1944 plan and the 1947 Town and Country Planning Act, into a region not quite like any other.

Fully to work out the implications of this fact, and to forge appropriate solutions even in outline, would require another book. Fortunately, that book exists. In *Sociable Cities* (Hall and Ward, 1998), the late Colin Ward and I explored solutions for huge urban complexes in South East England: a City of Mercia between Northampton, Wellingborough, Kettering and Corby, a City of Anglia linking Cambridge, Huntingdon and Peterborough, and a City of Kent embracing Folkestone, Dover, Deal, Ramsgate, Margate and Whitstable.

Not long after the publication of this book, the publishers will issue a new and revised edition of *Sociable Cities*, which will specifically seek to embody the lessons learned here in a revised vision for the future of these three sub-regions. That will provide the acid test of their applicability in different geographical contexts, and finally also a justification for the utility of this Twenty-First-Century Grand Tour.

Notes

1. See http://www.amptechnologycentre.co.uk.

2. See http://www.amrc.co.uk.

3. http://www.co-operativebank.co.uk/servlet/Satellite/1342592967915,CFSweb/Page/CFSCtpl Standard. http://www.guardian.co.uk/money/2012/jul/07/big-five-bank-customers-anger?newsfeed =true.

4. http://www.bis.gov.uk/news/speeches/vince-cable-industrial-strategy-september-2012.

5.   See http://www.economist.com/news/britain/21578109-challenger-britains-big-four-banks-loses-its-appeal-brink.

6.   See http://www.bbc.co.uk/news/business-22276082.

7.   See http://www.urbanrail.net/eu/euromet.htm and http://epp.eurostat.ec.europa.eu/cache/ITY_OFFPUB/KS-CD-11-001/EN/KS-CD-11-001-EN.PDF.

8.   See http://www.communities.gov.uk/news/corporate/2110432 and http://www.guardian.co.uk/local-government-network/2012/jul/11/city-deals-greg-clark-local-governance-finance.

9.   See http://www.gregclark.org/greg-in-parliament/.

10.   See http://www/bbc.co.uk/news/business-22581191.

11.   See http://depts.washington.edu/open2100/Resources/1_OpenSpaceSystems/Open_Space_Systems/Stockholm_Case_Study.pdf; http://www.eui.eu/Documents/DepartmentsCentres/Law/ResearchTeaching/ResearchThemes/EuropeanPrivateLaw/RealPropertyProject/TheNetherlands.PDF; and http://www.eui.eu/Documents/DepartmentsCentres/Law/ResearchTeaching/ResearchThemes/EuropeanPrivateLaw/RealPropertyProject/Sweden.PDF.

12.   David Ricardo (1772–1823) was a British political economist, stockbroker and MP. His book *On the Principles of Political Economy and Taxation* was first published in 1817.

References

All websites cited below were accessed in May 2012 or later.

Academy of Urbanism and Stadt Freiburg (2012) *Freiburg Charter: Requirements on Urban Development and Planning for the Future*, 2nd amended edition. Freiburg: Stadtplanungsamt.

Accenture (2012) *Carbon Capital*. London: Accenture.

ADULM (Agence de Développement et d'Urbanisme de Lille Métropole) (2006) *The Urban Regeneration of Lille Métropole. Le renouveau urbain de Lille Métropole*. Lille: ADULM.

Albert, M. (1993) *Capitalism against Capitalism*. London: Whurr.

Almaas, I.H. (1999) Regenerating the Ruhr (IBA Emscher Park project for regeneration of Germany's Ruhr Region). *The Architectural Review*, **205**, February, pp. 13–14. Available at: http://findarticles.com/p/articles/mi_m3575/is_1224_205/ai_54172205.

Andersson, Å.E. (1985) *Kreativitet: StorStadens Framtid*. Stockholm: Prisma.

Andersson, Å.E. and Matthiessen, C.W. (1991) *Øresundsregionen: Kreativitet – Integration – Vækst*. Copenhagen: Munksgaard.

Anon (2012) Régions au bord de Gouffre. *Midi-Libre*, 27 July.

Anon (2013) English cities: freedom at last. *The Economist*, 2 February. Available at: http://www.economist.com/news/britain/21571193-englands-big-cities-are-getting-surprising-taste-autonomy-freedom-last.

Arab, N. (2004) L'Activité de Projet dans l'Aménagement Urbain: Processus de l'Elaboration et Modes des Pilotage. Le Cas de la Ligne B strasbourgeois et d'Odysseum à Montpellier. Doctoral thesis, Ecole Nationale des Ponts et Chaussées.

Bader, I. and Scharenberg, A. (2010) The sound of Berlin: subculture and the global music industry. *International Journal of Urban and Regional Research*, **34**(1), pp. 76–91.

Baert, T., Le Bailly, S., Le Bailly de Tilleghem, S., Joseph-François, D., Klein, R. and ADULM (2004) *Architectural Guide to the Lille Metropolitan Area*. Paris: Le Passage.

Ball, M. (2012) *European Housing Review 2012*. London: Royal Institution of Chartered Surveyors.

Banham, R. (1971) *Los Angeles: The Architecture of Four Ecologies*. New York: Harper Row.

Banister, D. (1996) Energy, quality of life and the environment: the role of transport. *Transport Reviews*, **16**(1), pp. 23–35.

Banister, D. (1997) Reducing the need to travel. *Environment and Planning B*, **24**(3), pp. 437–449.

Banister, D. (2005) *Unsustainable Transport: City Transport in the New Century*. London: Routledge.

Banister, D., Dreborg, K., Hedberg, L., Hunhammer, S., Steen, P. and Åkerman, J. (1998) Development of Transport Policy Scenarios for the EU: Images of the Future. Paper presented at the 8th World Conference on Transport Research, Antwerp.

Banister, D. and Stead, D. (1997) Sustainable Development and Transport. Paper presented at the Expert Group Meeting of the URBAN 21 Project, Bonn.

Banister, D., Watson, S. and Wood, C. (1997) Sustainable cities – transport, energy and urban form. *Environment and Planning*, **24**(1), pp. 125–143.

Barker, K. (2003) *Review of Housing Supply. Interim Report – Analysis*. London: The Stationery Office. Available at: www.barkerreview.org.uk/

Barker, K. (2004) *Barker Review of Housing Supply*. London: HM Treasury. Available at: http://www.barkerreview.org.uk/.

Barker, K. (2006) *Barker Review of Land Use Planning. Final Report – Recommendations*. London: HMSO. Available at: http://www.barkerreviewofplanning.org.uk.

Barling, D., Sharpe, R. and Lang, T. (2008) *Towards a National Sustainable Food Security Policy: A Project to Map the Policy Interface between Food Security and Sustainable Food Supply*. London: City University London.

Barlow, J. (2000) *The Private Sector Housebuilding Industry: Structure and Strategies into the 21st Century*. London: Council of Mortgage Lenders. Available at: www.cml.org.uk/cml/filegrab/pdf_pub_resreps_26full.pdf.pdf?ref.

Barton, H., Grant, M. and Horswell, M. (2011) Suburban solutions: the other side of the story. *Town and Country Planning*, **80**, pp. 339–345.

Bathelt, H. and Boggs, J.S. (2003) Towards a reconceptualization of development paths: Is Leipzig's creative industries cluster continuation of or a rupture with the past? *Economic Geography*, **79**(3), 265–293.

Bathelt, H. and Boggs, J.S. (2005) Continuities, Ruptures, and Re-bundling of Regional Development Paths: Leipzig's Metamorphosis, in Fuchs, G. and Shapira, P. (eds.) *Rethinking Regional Innovation and Change. Path Dependency or Regional Breakthrough?* New York: Springer, pp. 147–170.

BBC News Business (2012) *Energy bill Q&A*. 29 November. Available at: http://www.bbc.co.uk/news/business-20458326.

Beyer, A. (2011) L'enjeu transfrontalier de l'extension des réseaux de tramway urbain à Strasbourg et à Bâle, in Hamman, P. (ed.) *Le Tramway dans la Ville. Le Projet urbain négocié à l'Aune des Déplacements*, Rennes: Presses Universitaires de Rennes, pp. 253–267.

BIS (Business, Innovation and Skills) (2010) *Local Growth: Realising every Place's Potential*. Presented to Parliament by the Secretary of State for Business, Innovation & Skills by Command of Her Majesty, 28 October 2010. Cm 7961. London: Stationery Office.

Blake, N., Croot, J. and Hastings, J. (2004) *Measuring the Competitiveness of the UK Construction Industry*. Volume 2. London: Experian Business Strategies for DTI.

Boddy, M. and Parkinson, M. (eds.) (2004) *City Matters: Competitiveness, Cohesion and Urban Governance*. Bristol: Policy Press.

Boeijenga, J. and Mensink, J. (2008) *Vinex Atlas*. Rotterdam: 010 Publishers.

Bonneville, M. (2005) The ambiguity of urban renewal in France: between continuity and rupture. *Journal of Housing and the Built Environment*, **20**, pp. 229–242.

Branson, A. (2012) Interview: Tim Leunig, motivational thinker. *Planning*, 1 June, pp. 18–19. Available at: http://www.planningresource.co.uk/news/1134415/tim-leunig-motivational-thinker/.

Breheny, M. (1997) Urban compaction: feasible and acceptable? *Cities*, **14**(4), pp. 209–217.

Breheny, M. (2001) Densities and sustainable cities: the UK experience, in Echenique, M. and Saint, A. (eds.) *Cities for the New Millennium*. London: Spon, pp. 39–51.

Breheny, M. and Rookwood, R. (1993) Planning the sustainable city region, in Blowers, A. (ed.) *Planning for a Sustainable Environment*. London: Earthscan, pp. 150–189.

Brown, G. (2005) Chancellor of the Exchequer's Budget Statement. 16 March.

Buchanan, J., Froud, J., Johal, S., Leaver, A. and Williams, K. (2009) Undisclosed and Unsustainable: Problems of the UK National Business Model. CRESC Working paper 75, University of Manchester. Available at: http://www.cresc.ac.uk/sites/default/files/wp%2075.pdf.

Bueler, R. and Pucher, J. (2011) Sustainable transport in Freiburg: lessons from Germany's environmental capital. *International Journal of Sustainable Transportation*, **5**, pp. 43–70.

BWCareer (2012) Intensity of Research and Development: Baden-Württemberg a European Leader. Available at: http://www.bw-career.com/index.php?id=144&tx_ttnews%5Btt_news%5D=396&tx_ttnews%5BbackPid%5D=29&cHash=a00a12f1a3a609c96191ab737d61fc32#.

Callcutt, J. (2007) *The Callcutt Review of Housebuilding Delivery*. London: DCLG. Available at http://www.communities.gov.uk/archived/publications/housing/thecallcuttreview.

Calthorpe, P. (1993) *The Next American Metropolis: Ecology, Community, and the American Dream*. New York: Princeton Architectural Press.

Carmona, M. (2004) *Smaller Towns Report: Delivering Retail-Led Renaissance in Towns and Smaller Cities*. London: British Council for Shopping Centres.

Carmona, M., Cadell, C., Falk, N. and Hall, P. (2000) *Living Places – Urban Renaissance in the South East*. Technical Report. London: DETR.

Centre for Cities (2008) *Cities Outlook 2008*. London: Centre for Cities.

CETE Nord Picardie (2011) Appraising Territorial Effects of Tram-based System: Results of the State of Art. Presentation by Hasiak, S. and Richer, C. at the SINTROPHER Workshop, Valenciennes. Available at: http://sintropher.eu/fileadmin/editors/Workshops/Valenciennes_2011/WP2/WP2_SINTROPHER_synth%C3%A4se_phase_1_CETE_.pdf.

Champion, T. and Townsend, A. (2011) The fluctuating record of economic regeneration in England's second-order city-regions, 1984–2007. *Urban Studies*, **48**, pp. 1539–1562.

Christaller, W. (1966 [1933]) *Central Places in Southern Germany*. Translated by Baskin, C.W. Englewood Cliffs, NJ: Prentice Hall.

Clark, C. (1951) Urban population densities. *Journal of the Royal Statistical Society, A,* **114**, pp. 490–496.

Clark, C. (1957) Transport: maker and breaker of cities. *Town Planning Review*, **28**, pp. 237–250.

Collins, P. (2013) Five questions for Britain. *Prospect*, February, pp. 26–29.

Colomb, C. (2007) *Making Connections: Transforming People and Places in Europe. Case study of Roubaix, Lille (France)*. York: Joseph Rowntree Foundation.

Colomb, C. (2011) Culture in the city, culture for the city? The political construction of the trickle-down in cultural regeneration strategies in Roubaix, France. *Town Planning Review*, **82**, 77–98.

Colomb, C. (2012) *Staging the New Berlin: Place Marketing and the Politics of Urban Reinvention Post-1989*. London: Routledge.

Committee on Climate Change (2011*a*) *Adapting to Climate Change in the UK: Measuring Progress*. Adaptation Sub-Committee Progress Report 2011. London: Committee on Climate Change.

Committee on Climate Change (2011*b*) Renewable Energy Review. Available at: http://www.theccc.org.uk/reports/renewable-energy-review.

Committee on Climate Change (2012) *How Local Authorities can Reduce Emissions and Manage Climate Risk*. London: Committee on Climate Change. Available at: http://www.theccc.org.uk/reports/local-authorities.

Committee on Climate Change, Adaptation Sub-Committee (2012) *Climate Change – is the UK Preparing for Flooding and Water Scarcity?* London: Committee for Climate Change. Available at: http://hmccc.s3.amazonaws.com/ASC/2012%20report/1586_ASC%20Report%202012_Bookmarked_2.pdf.

Compas (2012) Premières Estimations du Taux de Pauvreté des plus grandes Communes de France. (By François Cousseau, Louis Maurin and Violaine Mazery). *Compas Études*, No. 2, August. Available at: http://www.compas-tis.fr/download/compas_etudes_2_aout_2012.pdf.

Connolly, K. (2010) Anarchists in Berlin turn anger on new 'bourgeoisie'. *The Observer*, 10 January.

Conservative Party Central Office (2009) Control Shift: Returning Power to Local Communities. Green Paper no. 9. London: Conservative Central Office. Available at: www.conservatives.com/.../Returning%20Power%20Local%20Comm...

Cook, B. (2013) Tackling the energy crisis. *Planning*, 22 February, pp, 17–19.

Core Cities Group and the British Property Federation (2010) *A Rough Guide to Tax Increment Financing*. London: Core Cities Group. Available at: http://www.bpf.org.uk/en/files/bpf_documents/A_Rough_Guide_to_Tax_Increment_Financing.pdf.

Council of Mortgage Lenders (2009) *Market Commentary*. Available at: http://www.cml.org.uk/cml/publications/marketcommentary/160.

Dagnogo, C. and Ries, R. (2011) *Mobilité durable, la nouvelle révolution des transports*. Paris: Fondation Jean Juarès.

Daseking, W. (2009) Cambridge Masterclass, 17 June 2009. London: URBED.

Davis, I. and Harvey, V. (2008) *Zero Carbon: What does it mean to Homeowners and Housebuilders?* Amersham: NHBC Foundation.

DCLG (Department for Communities and Local Government) (2004, 2007, 2010) *Indices of Deprivation*. London: DCLG. Available at: http://www.communities.gov.uk/communities/research/indicesdeprivation/deprivation04/; 07/; 10/.

DCLG (2006) *Policy Planning Statement, PPS3: Housing*. London: DCLG. Available at: www.communities.gov.uk/.../planningandbuilding/pdf/1918430.pdf.

DCLG (2007) *Homes for the Future: More Affordable, More Sustainable*. CM 7191. London: The Stationery Office. Available at: www.communities.gov.uk/documents/housing/pdf/439986.pdf.

DCLG (2009) *Sustainable New Homes – The Road to Zero Carbon: Consultation on the Code for Sustainable Homes and the Energy Efficiency Standard for Zero Carbon Homes*. London: DCLG. Available at: http://www.communities.gov.uk/publications/planningandbuilding/futureofcodeconsultation.

DCLG (2010) *Evaluation of the National Strategy for Neighbourhood Renewal: Final Report*. London: The Stationery Office. Available at: http://www.communities.gov.uk/publications/communities/evaluationnationalstrategy.

DCLG (2011) *Laying the Foundations: A Housing Strategy for England*. London: The Stationery Office. Available at: http://www.communities.gov.uk/publications/housing/housingstrategy2011.

DCLG (2012) *House Building: March Quarter 2012, England*. London: DCLG. Available at: www.communities.gov.uk/documents/statistics/pdf/2145660.pdf.

de Goei, B., Burger, M.J., van Oort, F.G. and Kitson, M. (2008) Testing the super-region. *Town and Country Planning*, **77**(11), pp. 458–464

DECC (Department for Energy and Climate Change) (2010) *The Green Deal: A Summary of the Government's Proposals*. London: DECC.

DECC (2011*a*) *Planning Our Electric Future: A White Paper for Secure, Affordable and Low-Carbon Electricity*. Cm 8099. London: Stationery Office.

DECC (2011*b*) *UK Renewable Energy Roadmap*. London: DECC.

DECC (2011*c*) *Transport Energy Consumption in the UK since 1970*. London: DECC.

DECC (2012) *The Green Deal: A Summary of the Government's Proposals*. London: DECC. Available at: http://www.decc.gov.uk/assets/decc/legislation/energybill/1010-green-deal-summary-proposals.pdf.

DEFRA (Department for the Environment, Food and Rural Affairs) (2006) *Food Security and the UK: An Evidence and Analysis Paper*. Available at: http://statistics.defra.gov.uk/esg/reports/foodsecurity/foodsecurity.doc.

DEFRA (2011) *Water White Paper – Water for Life*. Cm 8320. London: The Stationery Office. Available at: http://www.official-documents.gov.uk/document/cm82/8230/8230.asp.

Desjardins, X. (2011) Quand le tramway sort de la ville. Reflexions sur la pertinence territoriale des tramways regionaux a partir de l'exemple de Kassel. *Transports urbains*, No. 119 (Novembre), pp. 16–22.

Desjardins, X., Seguret, S. and Beaucire, F. (2011) Urbanisation et corridors ferroviaires: quel degré de relation? in Pumain, D. and Mattel, M.-F. (ed.) *Données urbaines*, 6. Paris: Economica, pp. 75–80.

DETR (Department for the Environment, Transport and the Regions) (2000) *Our Towns and Cities: The Future: Delivering an Urban Renaissance*. Cm 4911. London: The Stationery Office.

Diacon, D., Pattison, B., Strutt, J. and Vine, J. (2011) *More Homes and Better Places: Solutions to Address the Scale of Housing Need*. Coalville: BSHF. Available at: www.bshf.org/scripting/getpublication.cfm?thePubID=25E04994...

Dorling, D. (2011) *Injustice: Why Social Inequality Persists*. Bristol: Policy Press.

Dorling, D. and Thomas, B. (2005) *People and Places: A 2001 Census Atlas of the UK*. Bristol: Policy Press.

Drillsma-Milgrom, D. (2012) Clark launches City Deals. *Local Government Chronicle*, 5 July. Available at: http://www.lgcplus.com/briefingsservices/economic-development/

clark-launches-city-deals/5046680.article?blocktitle=Latest-Local-Government-News&contentID=2249.

Dye, R.F. and Merriman, D.F. (2006) Tax increment financing: a tool for local economic development. *Land Lines*, **18**(1), pp. 1–7.

Dykstra, C.A. (1926) Congestion deluxe – do we want it? *National Municipal Review*, **15**(7), pp. 394–398.

Echenique, M., Barton, H., Hargreaves, T. and Mitchell, G. (2010) *SOLUTIONS Final Report. Sustainability and Land Use in Outer Neighbourhoods*. Available at: www.suburbansolutions.ac.uk.

Echenique, M., Hargreaves, A. and Mitchell, G. (2009) Spatial planning, sustainability and long-run trends. *Town and Country Planning*, **78**(9), pp. 380–385.

ECOTEC (1993) *Reducing Transport Emissions Through Land Use Planning*. London: HMSO.

ECOTEC in cooperation with NordRegio and Eurofutures (2007) *State of the European Cities Report: Adding Value to the European Urban Audit*. Available at: ec.europa.eu/regional_policy/sources/.../urban/stateofcities_2007.pdf.

Environment Agency (2011) *The Case for Change: Current and Future Water Availability*. Report – GEHO1111BVEP-E-E. Bristol: Environment Agency.

Ertürk, I., Froud, J., Leaver, A., Moran, M. and Williams, K. (2011) City State against National Settlement: UK Economic Policy and Politics after the Financial Crisis. CRESC Working Paper 101, University of Manchester. Available at: http://www.cresc.ac.uk/publications/city-state-against-national-settlement-uk-economic-policy-and-politics-after-the-financial-crisis.

European Environment Agency (2012) *Towards Efficient Use of Water Resources in Europe*. Available at: http://www.eea.europa.eu/publications/towards-efficient-use-of-water.

Eurostat (2011) News Release 37/11: Recycling accounted for a quarter of municipal waste in 2009. Available at: epp.eurostat.ec.europa.eu/cache/ITY.../8.../8-08032011-AP-EN.PDF.

Falk, N. (2007) Lessons from Freiburg: pointers for 'eco-towns' provided by the Vauban and Rieselfeld extensions of Freiburg. *Town and Country Planning*, **76**(10), pp. 336–339.

Falk, N. (2008) *Beyond Eco-Towns: The Economic Issues*. Manchester: URBED Available at: http://www.urbed.coop/projects/beyond-eco-towns.

Falk, N. (2011) Masterplanning and infrastructure in new communities in Europe, in Tiesdell, S. and Adams, D, *Urban Design and the Real Estate Development Process*. Chichester: Wiley-Blackwell, pp. 34–53.

Farthing, S., Winter, J. and Coombes, T. (1997) Travel behaviour and local accessibility to services and facilities, in Jenks, M., Burton, E. and Williams, K. (eds.) *The Compact City. A Sustainable Urban Form?* London: E&FN Spon, pp. 181–189.

Field, S. (2011) Vauban, Freiburg, Germany: case study, in Foletta, N. and Simon, S. (eds.) *Europe's Vibrant New Low Car(bon) Communities*), New York: ITDP, pp. 96–106. Available at: http://www.itdp.org/documents/092611_ITDP_NED_Desktop_Print.pdf.

Fischer, K. (2011) Learning from Europe: Myths and Models of Urban Design. Lecture at University of Sydney. Available at: http://tv.unsw.edu.au/EF160EB0-79D5-11E0-8BD10050568336DC.

Fogelson, R.M. (1993) *The Fragmented Metropolis: Los Angeles, 1850–1930*. Berkeley, CA: University of California Press.

Foletta, N. and Simon, S. (eds.) (2011) *Europe's Vibrant New Low Car(bon) Communities*. New York: ITDP.

Forum Vauban (2009) *Planning a Sustainable Community*. Freiburg: Forum Vauban, e.V.

Fraser, C. and Baert, T. (2003) Lille: from textile giant to tertiary turbine, in Couch, C., Fraser, C. and Percy, S. (eds.) *Urban Regeneration in Europe*. Oxford: Blackwell.

Gallent, N. (2009) The future of housing and homes. *Land Use Policy*, **26**, Supplement 1, pp. 93–102.

Gallent, N., Hamiduddin, I. and Madeddu, M. (2011) Selecting and Allocating Land for Housing Development: Politics, Expedient Sites, Regional Planning and Localism. London: RICS. Available at: http://www.rics.org/site/scripts/download_info.aspx?file ID=10870.

Garreau, J. (1991) *Edge City: Life on the New Frontier*. New York: Doubleday.

Glazer, N. (1988) *The Limits of Social Policy*. Cambridge, MA: Harvard University Press.

Goddard, J. and Vallance, P. (2013) *The University and the City*. London: Routledge.

Goff, S. (2012) Move to relax building society rules. *Financial Times*, 6 July. Available at: http://www.ft.com/cms/s/0/ab0402c6-c782-11e1-a850-00144feab49a.html#axzz20Q 5il6cK.

Goodhart, D. (2013) White flight? *Prospect*, February, pp. 30–31.

Goodier, C.I. and Pan, W. (2010) *The Future of UK Housebuilding*. London: RICS. Dec 2010, www.rics.org/ukhousebuilding.

Gordon, P., Kumar, A. and Richardson, H. (1989) Congestion, changing metropolitan structure and city size in the United States. *International Regional Science Review*, **12**(1), pp. 45–56.

Gordon, P. and Richardson, H.W. (1997) Are compact cities a desirable planning goal? *Journal of the American Planning Association*, **63**(1), pp. 95–106.

Green New Deal (2011) Freiburg 'Green City'. Available at: http://greennewdeal.eu/de/energie/best-practice/en/freiburg-green-city.html.

Groom, B. (2013*a*) UK green technology faltering, says EEF. *Financial Times*, 19 February. Available at: http://www.ft.com/cms/s/0/c705045e-79eb-11e2-b377-00144feabdc0. html#axzz2M29EMasd.

Groom, B. (2013*b*) Cable welcomes UK branch of Fraunhofer research group. *Financial Times*, 23 May. Available at: http://www.ft.com/cms/s/0/4bcd67be-c3b9-11e2-8c30-00144feab7de.html#axzz2UEYVXZQy.

Halifax (2010) *The UK Housing Market Over the Past 50 Years*. Available at: www.lloydsbankinggroup.com/.../2010/50_Years_of_Housing_UK.p.

Hall, P. (1987) Metropolitan settlement strategies, in Rodwin, L. (ed.) *Shelter, Settlement and Development*. London: Allen and Unwin, pp. 236–259.

Hall, P. (1988) *Cities of Tomorrow: An Intellectual History of Urban Planning and Design in the Twentieth Century*. Oxford: Basil Blackwell. Updated edition 1996.

Hall, P. (1998*a*) *Cities in Civilization: Culture, Technology and Urban Order*. London: Weidenfeld and Nicolson.

Hall, P. (1998*b*) Conclusions, in Banister, D. (ed.) *Transport Policy and the Environment*. London: E&FN Spon, pp. 333–336.

Hall, P. (1999) Planning for the mega-city: a new Eastern Asian urban form? in Brotchie, J., Newton, P., Hall, P. and Dickey, J. (eds.) *East West Perspectives on 21st Century Urban Development: Sustainable Eastern and Western Cities in the New Millennium*. Aldershot: Ashgate, pp. 3–36.

Hall, P. (2001) Global city-regions in the twenty-first century, in Scott, A.J. (ed.) *Global City-Regions: Trends, Theory, Policy*. Oxford: Oxford University Press, pp. 79–77.

Hall, P. (2006) The north's existential dilemma. *Town and Country Planning*, **75**, pp. 229–230.

Hall, P. (2012) Can we reverse the long downward slide? *Town and Country Planning*, **81**, pp. 252–253.

Hall, P. and Pain, K. (2006) *The Polycentric Metropolis: Learning from the Mega-City Regions in Europe*. London: Earthscan.

Hall, P., Thomas, R., Gracey, H. and Drewett, R. (1973) *The Containment of Urban England*. 2 volumes. London: George Allen and Unwin.

Hall, P. and Ward, C. (1998) *Sociable Cities: The Legacy of Ebenezer Howard*. Chichester: Wiley.

Hanson, S. (1982) The determinants of daily travel-activity patterns: relative location and sociodemographic factors. *Urban Geography*, **3**(3), pp. 179–202.

Harding, A. and Robson, B. (2006) *A Framework for City-Regions*. London: ODPM.

Harrison Church, R.J., Hall, P., Lawrence, G.R.P., Mead, W.R. and Mutton, A. (1967) *An Advanced Regional Geography of Northern and Western Europe*. London: Hulton.

Hauser, H. (2010) *The Current and Future Role of Technology and Innovation Centres in the UK: A Report by Dr. Hermann Hauser for Lord Mandelson, Secretary of State, Department for Business Innovation & Skills*. London: DBIS.

Headicar, P (1996) The local development effects of major new roads: M40 case study. *Transportation*, **23**, pp 55–69.

Headicar, P. and Curtis, C. (1998) The location of new residential development: its influence on car-based travel, in Banister, D. (ed.) *Transport Policy and the Environment*. London: E&FN Spon, pp. 223–242.

Heinker, H.H. (2004) *Boomtown Leipzig*. Leipzig: Faber und Faber.

Heseltine, M. (2012) *No Stone Unturned: In Pursuit of Growth*. London: Department of Business Innovation and Skills. Available at http://www.bis.gov.uk/assets/BISCore/corporate/docs/N/12-1213-no-stone-unturned-in-pursuit-of-growth.pdf.

Hesselmann, M. (2011) Berlin's gentrification needs. Radical ideas. *The Guardian*, 7 February.

Hickman, R. and Banister, D. (2002) Reducing Travel by Design: What happens over Time? Paper presented at the 5th Symposium of the International Urban Planning and Environment Association, Oxford.

Hilber, C.A.L. and Vermeulen, W. (2010) *The Impact of Restricting Housing Supply on House Prices and Affordability*, Final Report. London: DCLG. Available at: www.communities.gov.uk/documents/housing/pdf/1767142.pdf.

Holmans, A., Monk, S. and Whitehead, C. (2008) *Research Report: Homes for the Future: A New Analysis of Housing Need and Demand in England*. London: Shelter. Available at: http://england.shelter.org.uk/professional_resources/policy_and_practice/policy_library/policy_library_folder/homes_for_the_future_-_a_new_analysis_of_housing_need_and_demand_in_england.

Holmans, A. and Whitehead, C. (2008) *New and Higher Projections of Future Population in England*. Town and Country Planning Tomorrow Series, Paper 10. London: Town and Country Planning Association.

Holmans, A. and Whitehead, C. (2011) *New and Novel Household Projections for England with a 2008 Base*. London: TCPA. Available at http://www.tcpa.org.uk/pages/new-and-novel-household-projections-for-england-with-a-2008-base.html.

Holzapfel, H. (2012) The city that came out of the shadows. *Town and Country Planning*, **81**, pp. 135–138.

ICB (Independent Commission on Banking) (2011) *Final Report: Recommendations (Vickers Commission)*. September 2011. London: ICB. Available at: http://bankingcommission.independent.gov.uk/.

IW (Institut der deutschen Wirtschaft Köln) (2011) *Städteranking 2011: Die 50 größten deutschen Städte im Test*. Available at: www.insm-wiwo-staedteranking.de/.../endbericht_...

Jackson, A.A. (2006) *London's Metroland*. Harrow: Capital Transport Publishing.

Jacobs, J. (1969) *The Economy of Cities*. New York: Vintage.

Jenkins, S. (2012*a*) Elected mayors will destroy our shadowy civic mafias. *The Guardian*, 17 April.

Jenkins, S. (2012*b*) Sixty years of progress? *Prospect*, 25 May.

Jenks, M., Burton, E. and Williams, K. (1996) *The Compact City: A Sustainable Urban Form?* London: Spon.

Killian, J. and Pretty, D. (2008) *Planning Applications: A Faster and More Responsive System – Final Report* (Killian Pretty Report). London: DGCL. Available at: http://www.planningportal.gov.uk/planning/planningpolicyandlegislation/reform/killianpretty/finalreport.

Krätke, S. (2000) Berlin: the metropolis as a production space. *European Planning Studies*, **8**(1), pp. 7–27.

Krätke, S. (2003) Global media cities in a worldwide urban network. *European Planning Studies*, **11**(6), pp. 605–628.

Krätke, S. and Borst, R. (2000) *Berlin. Metropole Zwischen Boom und Crise*. Opladen: Leske+Budrich.

Krätke, S. and Taylor, P.J. (2004) A world geography of global media cities. *European Planning Studies*, **12**(4), pp. 459–477.

Krugman, P. (2012) *End this Depression Now!* New York: W.W. Norton.

Kunzmann, K.R. (2010) *Industrial Heritage: an Asset for Structural Change in Old Industrial Regions: The Ruhr in Germany 10 Years after the IBA Emscher Park*. Sesto San Giovanni: A History and a Future Industrial Heritage for the Whole World. International Symposium. Available at: http://www.sestosg.net/convegno_unesco/KUNZMANN_PDF.pdf.

Kunzmann, K.R. (2013) Strategic urban development by building exhibitions: a German success story. *Urban Flux*, forthcoming.

Kunzmann, K.R. and Tata, L. with Buchholz, T. (2003) *Dortmund: A Story of Change*. Dortmund: Universität Dortmund, Fakultät Raumplanung, Fachgebiet Europäische Raumplanung.

Lambert, R. (2013) UK's Energy policy restricts growth. *Financial Times*, 20 February. Available at: http://www.ft.com/cms/s/0/cf236024-7b51-11e2-8eb3-00144feabdc0.html#axzz2M29EMasd.

Lane, T. (2013) Green for growth: zero-carbon homes. *Building*, 25 February. Available at: http://www.building.co.uk/story.aspx?storyCode=5049330.

Lange, B. (2010) *SWOT Analysis on the status of Creative Industries in Leipzig* (EU Interreg IVB project 'Creative City Challenge'). Leipzig: Leibniz-Institute for Regional Geography Leipzig e.V.

Lansley, S. (2011) *The Cost of Inequality: Why Economic Equality is Essential for Recovery*. London: Gibson Square.

Larkin, K. (2009) *Public Sector Cities: Trouble Ahead*. London: Centre for Cities. Available at http://www.centreforcities.org/publicsectorcities.html.

Le Galès, P. and Mawson, J. (1995) Contracts versus competitive bidding: rationalising urban policy programmes in England and France. *Journal of European Policy*, **2**(2), pp. 205–241.

Lefèbvre, H. (2003 [1970]) *The Urban Revolution*. Minneapolis, MN: University of Minnesota Press.

Library House (2007) *An Analysis of UK University Technology and Knowledge Transfer Activities*. Cambridge: Library House.

Liefooghe, C. (2005) Services: the future of industry? From coalmining and textile industries to environmental services and distance selling in the Nord-Pas-de-Calais Region – France. Paper presented to the working group of the Regional Studies Association 'The Role of Industrial Knowledge in economic development of post-industrial regions'. Available at: http://www.staff.ncl.ac.uk/p.s.benneworth/oirs/liefooghe.pdf.

Lin, G.C.S. and Ma, L.J.C. (1994) The role of small towns in Chinese regional development. *International Regional Science Review*, **17**(1), pp. 75–97.

Local Data Company (2011) *'The Good, the Bad and the (Very) Ugly' Annual Survey*. London: Local Data Company.

Lock, D. (2012) Parties are plotting a new wave of reforms. *Planning*, No. 1937, 29 June, pp. 14–15.

McDowell, L. (2003) *Redundant Masculinities: Employment Change and White Working Class Youth*. Oxford: Blackwell.

McGee, T.G. (1995) Metrofitting the emerging mega-urban regions of ASEAN, in McGee, T.G. and Robinson, I (eds.) *The Mega-Urban Regions of Southeast Asia*. Vancouver: University of British Columbia Press.

McKay, D. (2008) *Sustainable Energy Without Hot Air*. Cambridge: UIT.

Maitland, R. (2007) Culture, city users and the creation of new tourism areas in cities, in Smith, M.K. (ed.) *Tourism, Culture and Regeneration*. Wallingford: CABI, pp. 25–35.

Maitland, R. and Newman, P. (eds.) (2009) *World Tourism Cities: Developing Tourism Off the Beaten Track*. London: Routledge.

Mallet, V. and Johnson, M. (2012) The bank that broke Spain. *Financial Times*, 21 June. Available at: http://www.ft.com/cms/s/0/d8411cf6-bb89-11e1-90e4-00144feabdc0.html#axzz20Q5il6cK.

Marshall, S. (2001) The challenge of sustainable transport, in Layard, A., Davoudi, S. and Batty, S. (eds.) *Planning for a Sustainable Future*. London: Spon, pp. 131–147.

Matthiessen, C.W. (1993) Copenhagen on the European scene, in City of Copenhagen, Lord Mayor's Department, *Copenhagen! Views and Visions*. Copenhagen: City of Copenhagen, pp. 40–43.

Matthiessen, C.W. (2000) Bridging the Öresund: potential regional dynamics: integration of Copenhagen (Denmark) and Malmö–Lund (Sweden). A cross-border project on the European metropolitan level. *Journal of Transport Geography*, **8**, pp. 171–180.

Matthiessen, C.W. (2004) The Öresund area: pre- and post-bridge cross-border functional integration: the bi-national regional question. *GeoJournal*, **61**, pp. 31–39.

Matthiessen, C.W., Schwarz, A.W. and Find, S. (2010) World cities of scientific knowledge: systems, networks and potential dynamics. An analysis based on bibliometric indicators. *Urban Studies*, **47**(9), 1879–1897.

Meadows, D.H., Meadows, D.I., Randers, J. and Behrens, W.W. III (1972) *Limits to Growth: A Report for the Club of Rome*. New York: Universe Books.

Meadows, D., Randers, J. and Meadows, D. (2004) *Limits to Growth, The 30-Year Update*. Available at: http://www.mnforsustain.org/meadows_limits_to_growth_30_year_update_2004.htm.

Menerault, P. (2008) *Gares ferroviaires et projets métropolitains: une ville en mutation: Métropole Lilloise (Extrait du thème 1: la stratégie métropolitaine)*. Lille: POPSU: Plate-forme d'Observation des Projets et Stratégies Urbaines.

Menzl, M. (2010) *Reurbanisierung? Zuzugsmotive und locale Bindungen der neuen*

Innenstadtbewohner – Das Beispiel der HafenCity Hamburg. Diskussions-papier zur HafenCity Nr. 2. Hamburg: HafenCity Hamburg GmbH. Available at: www.hafencity.com/.../DP_Menzl_Reurbanisierun...

Mignon, E. (1962) *Les Mots du Général de Gaulle*. Paris: Fayard.

Mills, G. (2001) New tramways in France: the case of Montpellier. *Transport Reviews*, **21**(3), pp. 337–352.

Milmo, D. (2012) In Orgreave, hope rises from the fields where miners fought and lost. *The Observer*, 8 July. Available at: http://www.guardian.co.uk/business/2012/jul/08/orgreave-hope-miners-fought-lost?INTCMP=SRCH.

Mowat, C.L. (1955) *Britain between the Wars 1918–1940*. London: Methuen.

NAO (National Audit Office) (2008) *Planning for Homes: Speeding Up Planning Applications for Major Housing Developments in England*. London: NAO.

Naess, P. and Sandberg, S.L. (1996) Workplace location, modal split and energy use for commuting trips. *Urban Studies,* **33**(3), pp. 557–580.

Naess, P., Roe, P.G. and Larsen, S. (1995) Travelling distances, modal split and transportation energy in thirty residential areas in Oslo. *Journal of Environmental Planning and Management*, **38**(3), pp. 349–370.

Netherlands, Ministry of Housing, Physical Planning and the Environment (1991) *Fourth Report (EXTRA) on Physical Planning in the Netherlands: Comprehensive Summary: On the Road to 2015*. The Hague: Ministry of Housing, Physical Planning and the Environment, Department for Information and International Relations.

Newman, P.W.G. and Kenworthy, J.R. (1989) Gasoline consumption and cities: a comparison of U.S. cities with a global survey. *Journal of the American Planning Association*, **55**, pp. 24-37.

Newman, P. and Kenworthy, J. (1999) *Sustainability and Cities: Overcoming Automobile Dependence*. Washington DC: Island Press.

Newman, P. and Kenworthy, J. (2000) The ten myths of automobile dependence. *World Transport Policy & Practice*, **6**(1), pp. 15–25.

Newman, P. and Thornley, A. (1996) *Urban Planning in Europe*. London: Routledge.

Nuissl, H. and Rink, D. (2003) *Urban Sprawl and Post-Socialist Transformation – the Case of Leipzig (Germany)*. UFZ Report 4/2003. Leipzig: UFZ Centre for Environmental Research.

ODPM (Office of the Deputy Prime Minister) (2003) *Sustainable Communities: Building for the Future*. London: ODPM. Available at: http://www.communities.gov.uk/publications/communities/sustainablecommunitiesbuilding.

OECD (Organization for Economic Cooperation and Development) (2008) *Territorial Reviews: Newcastle in the North East, The United Kingdom*. Paris: OECD.

Oxley, M., Brown, T., Nadin, V., Qu, L., Tummers, L. and Fernández-Maldonado, A.M. (2009) *Review of European Planning Systems*. Fareham: National Housing and Planning Advice Unit.

Owens, S.E. (1984) Spatial structure and energy demand, in Cope, D.R., Hills, P.R. and James, P. (eds.) *Energy Policy and Land Use Planning*. Oxford: Pergamon, pp. 215–240.

Owens, S. (1986) *Energy, Planning and Urban Form*. London: Pion.

Palmer, J. and Cooper, I. (2011) *Great Britain's Housing Energy Fact File*. London: DECC. Available at: www.eclipseresearch.co.uk/.../energy/...

Paris, D. and Baert, T. (2011) Lille 2004 and the role of culture in the regeneration of Lille métropole. *Town Planning Review*, **82**(1), pp. 29–43.

Paris, D. and Stevens, J.-F. (2000) *Lille et sa région urbaine: la bifurcation métropolitaine*. Paris: L'Harmattan.

Paris, D. and Baert, T. (2011) Lille 2004 and the role of culture in the regeneration of Lille métropole. *Town Planning Review*, **82**, pp. 29–43.

Parity Projects (2008) *Energy Options Appraisal for Domestic Buildings in the London Borough of Sutton*. Available at: https://www.sutton.gov.uk/CHttpHandler.ashx?id=5173&p=0.

Parkinson, M., Champion, T. *et al.* (2006) *The State of the English Cities*, Vols. 1 and 2. London: ODPM.

Parkinson, M., Hutchins, M., Simmie, J., Clark, G. and Verdonk, H. (2004) *Competitive European Cities: Where do the Core Cities Stand?* London: ODPM. Available at: http://www.ljmu.ac.uk/EIUA/67773.htm.

Plöger, J. (2010) Leipzig, in Power, A., Plöger, J. and Winkler, A. (2010) *Phoenix Cities: The Fall and Rise of Great Industrial Cities*. Bristol: Polity Press for Joseph Rowntree Foundation, pp. 107–129.

Power, A., Plöger, J. and Winkler, A. (2010) *Phoenix Cities: The Fall and Rise of Great Industrial Cities Across Europe*. Bristol: Policy Press.

Pradeilles, J.-C. with Chapoutot, J.-J. (1981) *Régulation politique et contradictions territoriales: Les politiques locales de transport des agglomérations lilloise et grenobloise, 1972–1978*. Grenoble: Ministère des Transports/Institut d'Urbanisme de Grenoble, Mission de la Recherche Université des Sciences Sociales.

Priemus, H. (2011) Synergy between transport infrastructures and cities – towards better places, in Chisholm, S. (ed.) *Investing in Better Places: International Perspectives*. London: The Smith Institute.

Reeds, J. (2011) *Smart Growth: From Sprawl to Sustainability*. Totness: Green Books.

Ries, R. (2011) Sustainable Mobility. Interview with Roland Ries, Senator and Mayor of Strasbourg, by sustainable-mobility.org. Available at: http://www.youtube.com/watch?v=IbuCrgpZ54s.

Rightmove (2011) House Price Index October 2011. Available at: http://www.rightmove.co.uk/news/house-price-index/october-2011.

Rudlin, D. and Falk, N. (2009) *Sustainable Urban Neighbourhood: Building the 21st Century Home*. Oxford: Architectural Press.

RuSource (Rural Information Network) (2006) *Food security and the UK* (Briefing 445). Available at: www.ifr.ac.uk/waste/Reports/RuSource_foodsecurity.pdf.

Savills (2012) *Residential Markets in Germany Current Developments, Prospects and Opportunities*. Available at: http://www.savills.de/pdf-de/savills-research-residential-market-report---executive-summary.pdf.

Schaer, C. (2010) The challenge of making HafenCity feel neighborly. Spiegelonline. 28 August 2010. Available at: http://www.spiegel.de/international/germany/hamburg-s-new-quarter-the-challenge-of-making-hafencity-feel-neighborly-a-714008-2.html.

Schelkes, R., Schuster, M. and Selle, K. (2005) *Baugruppenarchitektur in Freiburg: vom Experiment zur Rege*. Freiburg: Modo Verlag.

Science Communication Unit, the University of the West of England (2012) *In Depth Report: Soil Sealing*. Brussels: European Commission DG Environment. Available at: http://ec.europa.eu/environment/integration/research/newsalert/pdf/IR2.pdf.

Scott, A.J. (2001) *Global City-Regions: Trends, Theory, Policy*. Oxford: Oxford University Press.

Sear, C. (2012) *Tax Increment Financing*. Standard Note SN/PC/05797/ London: House of Commons Library, Parliament and Constitution Centre.

Seebohm, F. (1968) *Report of the Committee on Local Authority and Allied Personal Social Services*. London: HMSO.

Seltmann, G. (2007) *Renaissance of an Industrial Region: 'Internationale Bauausstellung Emscher*

Park' Achievements and Future Model for Others. Flechtingen: GseProjekte-Office for Regional Development. Available at: http://www.riss.osaka-.ac.jp/jp/events/point/P. Seltmann.pdf.

SenFin (Senatsverwaltung für Finanzen) (2007) *Haushalt und Finanzen Berlins. Ein Überblick*. Berlin: SenFin.

Sheppard, F.H.W. (1971) *London 1808–1870: The Infernal Wen*. London Secker and Warburg.

SINTROPHER (Sustainable Tram-Based Transport Options for Peripheral European Regions) (2011) *Evaluation of Transport Linkages between the Region of Kassel and the European Metropolises*. Findings Report WP2A1. Available at: http://sintropher.eu/index.php?id=reports.

Sit, F.S.V. and Yang, C. (1997) Foreign-investment-induced exo-urbanization in the Pearl River Delta, China. *Urban Studies*, **34**(4), pp. 647–677.

Skidelsky, R. (2010) *Keynes: The Return of the Master*. Harmondsworth: Penguin.

Skidelsky, R. and Skidelsky, E. (2012) *How Much is Enough? The Love of Money, and the Case for the Good Life*. London: Allen Lane.

Stadt Leipzig (2006a) *Monitoringbericht 2006 – kleinräumiges Monitoring des Stadtumbaus*. Leipzig: Department of Urban Development.

Stadt Freiburg (2006b) *Freiburg Solar Energy Guide*. Freiburg: City of Freiburg Environmental Protection Agency.

Stadt Freiburg (2012) *Green City Freiburg: Approaches to Sustainability*. Available at http://www.fwtm.freiburg.de/servlet/PB/show/1199617_l2/GreenCity.pdf.

Stadt Heidelberg (2012) *Internationale Bauausstellung (IBA) Heidelberg: 'Wissen-schafft-Stadt'*. Available at: http://www.heidelberg.de/servlet/PB/menu/1213166/index.html.

Stadt Leipzig (2005) *Monitoringbericht 2005 – kleinräumiges Monitoring des Stadtumbaus*. Leipzig: Department of Urban Development.

Stadt Leipzig (2007) *Abschlussbericht zum Forschungsprojekt Kleinräumiges Monitoring des Stadtumbaus in Leipzig*. Leipzig: Department of Urban Development.

Stern, N. (2007) *The Economics of Climate Change. The Stern Review*. Cambridge: Cambridge University Press.

Stiglitz, J.E. (2012) *The Price of Inequality*. London: Allen Lane.

TCPA (Town and Country Planning Association) (2010) *Making Planning Work: Briefing Paper 4, Incentives for Growth*. London: TCPA.

Thomson, J.M. (1977) *Great Cities and Their Traffic*. London: Gollancz.

Treanor, J. and Jowit, J. (2012) Cable laments destruction of building societies. *The Guardian*, 18 June. Available: http://www.guardian.co.uk/politics/2012/jun/18/cable-laments-destruction-building-societies.

Turner, C. (2011) Welcome to HafenCity – Germany's crazy ambitious urban redesign project. Mother Nature Network, 11 July. Available at: http://www.mnn.com/green-tech/research-innovations/blogs/welcome-to-hafencity-germanys-crazy-ambitious-urban-redesign-p.

UK Technology Strategy Board (2012) *Catapult Update: Shaping the Network of Centres*. March 2012. London: UK Technology Strategy Board. Available at: http://www.innovateuk.org/_assets/0511/Catapultupdate_final.pdf.

UN-Habitat (2004) *The State of the World's Cities 2004/2005: Globalization and Urban Culture*. London: Earthscan.

Urban Task Force (1999) *Towards an Urban Renaissance*. London: Routledge.

Urbed (2002) *Towns and Cities: Partners in Urban Renaissance*. London: ODPM.

Urbed (2004) *Selby District Renaissance*. Available at http://www.urbed.coop/projects/selby-district-renaissance.

Veltz, P. (1996) *Mondialisation, villes et territoires: l'économie d'archipel*. Paris: Presses Universitaires de France.

von Petz, U. (2010) News from the field: city planning exhibitions in Germany, 1910–2010. *Planning Perspectives*, **25**, pp. 375–382.

Wacknernagel, M. and Rees, W. (1996) *Our Ecological Footprint*. London: New Society Publishers.

Wapshott, N. (2011) *Keynes Hayek: The Clash That Defined Modern Economics*. New York and London: W.W. Norton.

Ward, C. (1978) *The Child in the City*. London: Architectural Press.

Watson, H. (2006) Berlin's empty heart. *Architectural Design*, **76**(3), pp. 100–103.

Webber, C. (2008) *Innovation, Science and the City*. London: Centre for Cities.

Wellings, F. (2006) *Private Housebuilding Annual 2006*. London: Troubadour Publishing.

Wilkinson, R.J. and Pickett, K. (2009) *The Spirit Level: Why More Equal Societies Almost Always Do Better*. Harmondsworth: Allen Lane.

Wo-Lap, L.L. (2002) Race to become China's economic powerhouse. CNN, 11 June.

Wooldridge, A. (2013) *Northern Lights: Special Report, The Nordic Countries. The Economist*, 2 February.

Wright, O. and Cooper, C. (2012) George Osborne slammed by his own climate change advisors over 'dash for gas'. *The Independent*, 13 September. Available at: http://www.independent.co.uk/news/uk/politics/george-osborne-slammed-by-his-own-climate-change-advisors-over-dash-for-gas-8135035.html.

Index